# The Vygotsky Reader

*Edited by*

## René van der Veer
*and*
## Jaan Valsiner

BLACKWELL
Oxford UK & Cambridge USA

Copyright © Basil Blackwell Ltd 1994

First published 1994

Blackwell Publishers
108 Cowley Road
Oxford OX4 1JF
UK

238 Main Street
Cambridge, Massachusetts 02142
USA

*British Library Cataloguing in Publication Data*

A CIP catalogue record for this book is available from the British Library.

*Library of Congress Cataloging-in-Publication Data*

Vygotskiĭ, L. S. (Lev Semenovich), 1896–1934.
   [Essays. Selections. English]
   The Vygotsky reader / edited by René van der Veer and Jaan Valsiner.
     p.  cm.
   Translated by Theresa Prout and René van der Veer.
   Includes bibliographical references and index.
   ISBN 0-631-18896-7 (alk. paper). – ISBN 0-631-18897-5 (pbk.: alk. paper)
   I. Veer, René van der, 1952–.  II. Valsiner, Jaan.  III. Title.
  BF109.V95A2513  1994
  150 – dc20

93-37353
CIP

Typeset in 10 on 12 pt, Garamond 3
by Best-set Typesetter Ltd, Hong Kong
Printed in Great Britain by T.J. Press Ltd, Padstow, Cornwall

This book is printed on acid-free paper

# Contents

# Preface

Editing an annotated reader of a sample of Vygotsky's writings is a time-consuming and complicated endeavour and we now well understand why it had not been tried before. The basic problem we had to solve was that Vygotsky virtually never referred to authors in the way that has now become common usage in academic circles: by giving the exact source, date of publication, page number, etc. As a consequence, we spent our time in many libraries reading countless potentially relevant books written by Vygotsky's predecessors and contemporaries and looking for the passages his cryptic references might refer to. Each reference successfully located in this way should be seen against the background of many initial failures. However, the publications we were forced to read were often extremely valuable in their own right and we have often wondered how far psychology would develop if we stopped all new and experimental research for several years and instead reflected upon and elaborated the treasures found in psychological archives. Naturally, we have not been able to locate all of Vygotsky's references. In such cases we have admitted our defeat in the notes and we would be grateful to readers for any information that might help us fill in these annoying gaps. The references which we did find and the strictly explanatory notes which we added should enable the reader to understand Vygotsky's texts in themselves – as fascinating attempts to deal with the major psychologies and psychological questions of his time which have their relevance even today – and to see the embeddedness of his thinking in the work of his contemporaries and predecessors in accordance with the motto of this reader. All information in the text given in square brackets was supplied by the editors. All translations from the original Russian were made by Theresa Prout with the exception of chapter 3 which was translated by René van der Veer. All quotes from languages other than Russian were checked against the original sources. No attempts were made to modernize the texts to fit contemporary standards. The editors express their gratitude to Ellen Bakker who managed to unriddle some puzzling references and who compiled the subject index. For a detailed account of Vygotsky's life and work and an elaborate analysis of his basic ideas the reader is referred to the companion volume *Understanding Vygotsky* (Van der Veer and Valsiner, 1991).

René van der Veer
Jaan Valsiner
Leiden and Chapel Hill

'One must look at science in a very mechanical and unhistorical manner not to understand the role of continuity and tradition at all, even during a revolution.'

Lev Vygotsky, *Istoricheskij smysl psikhologicheskogo krizisa*

# Introduction

# Reading Vygotsky: from fascination to construction

Reading Vygotsky is a fascinating enterprise. With the present reader, the availability of his works in English begins to resemble a representative sample. It can be said that over the last decade the international scholarly world has largely conquered the bastion of access to the work of that lonely socialite poet of European psychology (see Van der Veer and Valsiner, 1991).

Vygotsky was an integrative thinker whose personal style matched his interests. In order to think through complicated issues, he needed to talk. And he could talk well – a literary scholar turned psychologist could captivate his listeners. That vigour of the oral speech style can be seen in his writings, many of which had Vygotsky's oral presentations (stenographed) as their origin. One can encounter long philosophical speculations which turn suddenly into recitations of poetry, or an allusion to a literary symbol. Vygotsky was not afraid of being emotional in his scientific argument, as science, after all, is a form of art.

It is perhaps exactly Vygotsky's personal speech style which has maintained his popularity within an otherwise empiricist international psychology. In contrast with the rule-following rationality (bordering upon unimaginativeness) of most modern psychology, it may be Vygotsky's flowery escapades into literature, his sharp and often arrogant looking criticism of his contemporaries, and his ability to synthesize knowledge from different sources, which keep us fascinated with his writings.

Yet it is better not to lose track of other reasons in contemporary psychology that may have made Vygotsky into a popular figure. The socio-political discourse of the international social sciences during the last decades may have been right for his sanctification in the science of child and educational psychology. In other words, can we partly explain the interest in Vygotsky on topics that were often almost directly borrowed from his contemporary psychologists?

## Social construction of importance: a means of communication

It is interesting to apply Vygotsky's own idea of semiotic mediation to the process of construction of his status as a 'classic' of developmental psychology. In the course of communication about scientists in and around science, different kinds of narrative strategies are purposefully put into practice (Valsiner, 1994). A given discipline of a certain historical period gains from creating hero myths around its scientists for their own work, as well as for the public image of the discipline. Beyond that, other social institutions (which have no connections with actual interests of any science – here considered as a social institution) may elect to create myths about scientists for consumption of the mass communication system (for example, Albert Einstein in Missner, 1985).

Vygotsky's fate in the realm of socially constructed importance was as ambiguous as all of his life. Entering into the enthusiastic social construction effort of 'new psychology' in the Soviet Union in the early 1920s, he soon became dissatisfied with the dominance of highly vocal 'Marxist psychologists' who tried to solve complex psychological problems by endless referencing of Marx, Engels or Plekhanov (who was later dropped to be replaced by Lenin, Stalin and other similar great philosophers). As we described in our analysis of Vygotsky's entrance into psychology (Van der Veer and Valsiner, 1991, chs 6 and 7), his standing was from the very beginning that of a somewhat distant yet devoted and very intelligent outsider. He went along with Kornilov's 'Marxist reactology' (even attempting some – unsuccessful – empirical research!) as long as it satisfied his intellectual quest. Of course, Vygotsky's satiation with Marxist psychology in its public and naively fascinating version was soon reached, and he located for himself work in the areas of defectology and paedology, domains where he could develop his version of innovative psychology (he was no less emphatic in understanding the value of his own quest than were his Marxist contemporaries of their declarative innovations).

However, in both defectology and paedology, Vygotsky remained somewhat distant from the core of activities in 'Soviet science'. True, he was well known, respected (especially as his speeches captivated large audiences) and active in the organization of research and its application – yet he would never be considered as important as his more socio-politically active colleagues. His small research group (see Van der Veer and Valsiner, 1991) was a truly functioning collective – yet it consisted mostly of devoted students and a few co-workers. In contrast, one is reminded of the administrative activities of Konstantin Kornilov in his role as the director of the Institute of Experimental Psychology in Moscow to lead the 'construction of Marxist psychology'. And, of course, the most extraordinary contrast to Vygotsky's social standing was the never tiring energy of Vladimir Bekhterev, who since 1907 to his death in 1927 was establishing (and re-establishing) different kinds of research institute in St Petersburg (and later Leningrad), continuing through wars and revolutions with immense organizational power (and the social importance that came and went with it). Even the hypermarxist Aron Zalkind was actively involved in the organization of psychoneurology onto 'new rails' – without much substance, yet with a revolutionary fervour.

In contrast to these activists, Vygotsky's importance was decidedly content-bound and limited to those areas of his activities that were dear to his personal goals. Thus, he was always interested in improving the practical conditions for children's education – in the case of normality or pathology. Of course, his activities were hampered by recurrent episodes of tuberculosis (and corresponding uncertainties of cure and death), and after 1930 (see Van der Veer and Valsiner, 1991, ch. 16) by the uncertainties about the ideological purges against 'cosmopolitanism' (of which indeed he was a good example and without any ways to hide his international connections).

All in all, Vygotsky's social importance in Soviet psychology during his lifetime was largely limited – he was known, but was not really playing a 'leadership' role. He was both Marxist (honouring some of Marx's and Engels' productive ideas) and non-Marxist (citing formalist poets and not bothering to take his contemporary Marxists seriously); he was part of the contruction of 'new society' but at the same time did not embrace the proletarian revolutionary ferment.

After his death and until his name became mentionable again in the context of the Soviet Union (in 1956), Vygotsky's importance vanished (along with his main promoters A. Luria and V. Kolbanovsky, who hid from the mainstreams of Soviet psychology). Its reappearance was linked completely with transformations in Soviet society after 1956 and the active promotion of Vygotsky's name and ideas both in the Soviet Union and internationally.

It is here that a special tribute should be paid to the role of Alexander Luria in maintaining and propagating Vygotsky's ideas. In his interactive cosmopolitan way, he had made Vygotsky internationally known already at the end of the 1920s. When international connectedness for Soviet psychologists became available again after 1956 (although it was never encouraged), Luria resumed this role. In fact, it is thanks to his efforts that one of the original translations published for the first time in the present reader has become available ('Tool and Symbol'). In the early 1970s Luria, with Michael Cole's help, tried to get this published internationally, but without success. It is thanks to Michael Cole's collaboration with our present project that the work is now published in the form overseen by Luria.

However, the international community of psychologists had its own socio-political reasons for paying attention to Vygotsky. Extra-psychological factors – the Cold War and Soviet technological surprises (e.g. the 'sputnik effect', or Nikita Khrushchev's innovative use of a shoe as a diplomatic tool) – had channelled Western attention toward the mysterious Soviet 'giant' which made threatening noises and primacy claims in everything from the steam engine to the first manned space flight, and to the establishment of a free society where everybody was blissfully happy in their personal ways. The old truth of propaganda – of telling big lies as often as possible – had definitely worked in favour of the Soviet system. Even if the Western audience was sceptical about many of the Soviet claims, the latter's self-assured nature would leave a trace of doubt (well, maybe there was something in those claims). So persisting interest was maintained, and had Vygotsky been linked with some less visible country interest in him (and in Soviet psychology at large) might never have advanced so far.

There were also a number of personal factors that contributed to Vygotsky's selection as an object of international interest. First, he died young and brilliant (and was of Jewish origin – a fact that Soviet sources persistently overlooked until it was given due attention by Levitin, 1982), which is always an asset for poets and scientists. Secondly, he was Marxist in a time when this was still considered fashionable – but not too Marxist for the Western taste. Thirdly, he was a literary scholar who turned into a psychologist, and a theoretician at a time when theory-building in international psychology had declined in favour and he thus provided a welcome alternative to existing practices. And, of course, the few glimpses the international audience received of his work were teasing modern psychology's overquantified ego.

Of course, the irony of history reveals that part of Vygotsky's ideas was not unavailable internationally even during his lifetime (see chapters 4, 5 and 11 of the present reader). But at the time international psychologists attributed no special status to a special context called 'Soviet psychology'. Psychology in the Soviet Union was justifiably viewed as internationally meaningful psychology which just happened to be done in a particular country. Similarly, Vygotsky and his more thoughtful colleagues were never building a segregated Soviet or Marxist psychology. Instead, their work was very closely intertwined with the current psychological research in Europe and North America, and special pride was given to the feeling of working at the level of the best in the world.

The recent history of international referencing of Vygotsky is provided elsewhere (see Valsiner, 1988, pp. 156–62). It reveals the prominence of the two book-format publications (*Thought and Language*, 1962; and the cocktail-type mixing of various of his ideas to fit the American audience, published as *Mind in Society* in 1978). Although the more sophisticated scholars were citing Vygotsky's journal articles alongside the two books, still the majority of references to Vygotsky in the 1970s and early 1980s is to those two books. Vygotsky became more of a name than a real scholar, he was attacked by Westerners who did not (or could not) understand him (e.g. Fodor, 1972) or, alternatively, glorified (Toulmin, 1978).

Furthermore, Vygotsky seemed to have something to say to educationalists in different Western countries. In the United States, the fashion for partial borrowing of Piaget's ideas was about to decline in the 1970s, and a new identity figure was to be created. Vygotsky's message – of the role of the 'social other' in child development (even if not original to him, nor very unusual among other sociogenetic thinkers) – fitted into American education contexts where Piaget-ascribed individual learning freedom of pupils was threatening the authority and control functions of the teachers. Remnants of the one-sided borrowing from Vygotsky of the importance of the social other can still be seen today, where educationalists continue to address issues of teacher–child cooperation in learning, and try to prove that learning with the help of 'more experienced others' is necessarily more productive than a similar activity alone. Applications of (would-be) Vygotskian ideas in US educational contexts begin to resemble some of the practices of the famous American educator John Dewey (whose role in Vygotsky's development of ideas was undoubtedly relevant), yet the Russian Jewish thinker seems to be given credit for them.

Along similar lines, countries of Western Europe took interest in Vygotsky in their own way. There as well, he was mostly seen as an educational theorist whose 'optimistic' ideas about pupils' learning potential formed the needed contrast with the 'pessimistic' ideas ventured by Piaget. These and other ideas were discovered and propagated by small groups of 'progressive' young Marxists who saw his work as providing, among other things, a foundation for a criticism of the prevailing tendency to attribute individual failure and success to genetic endowment (see Van IJzendoorn and Van der Veer, 1984). In this connection Vygotsky was seen as one of the founding fathers of a critical or dialectical psychology together with such other 'anti-establishment' psychologists as Riegel (in the US), Leont'ev (in the USSR) and Holzkamp (in Germany). It is fascinating to see how part of mainstream psychology gradually absorbed the former leftist hero and made him a common name in psychology textbooks.

All in all, by the 1980s an international fascination with Vygotsky's ideas was widespread and yet most of his texts were only appearing in Russian in first (and still incomplete) versions, not to speak of new translations into English or other international languages. Also, Vygotsky's importance was enhanced by the movement for activity theory (e.g. Wertsch, 1981). Here the interest in Leont'ev's activity theory spilt over to Vygotsky (as Leont'ev himself claimed direct heritage from Vygotsky's and Luria's cultural–historical theory – a claim much disputed and proven questionable in Van der Veer and Valsiner, 1991).

Thus, Vygotsky arrived at an internationally prominent status and yet the bases for such ascent are embedded in the history of the development of (developmental) psychology and education in different countries. Fame is a socially constructed entity which functions for the purposes of the constructors, rather than for the designated bearers of that role themselves. A fitting proof of the societal construction of Vygotsky's stature is the list of ideas that the fascinated public has been persistently overlooking in the discourse about Vygotsky.

## 'Blind spots' in socially constructed importance

As we have shown elsewhere (Van der Veer and Valsiner, 1991, 1992), the 'blind spots' in the understanding of Vygotsky have been rather prominent. The existence of such myopia leads one to look for the semiotic mediation used in the discourse. Fully in line with Vygotsky himself, we can claim that societal meanings are not only vehicles for remembering scientific ideas, but also (and equally effective) the means to purposefully forget some.

A number of blind spots can be detected in contemporary uses of Vygotsky's ideas. First (and foremost), it is the contemporary overlooking of Vygotsky's *intellectual interdependency with his European and American contemporaries and predecessors*. Much of our analysis of Vygotsky's ideas has been devoted to filling in this gap (see Van der Veer and Valsiner, 1991). We have attempted to show that modern European and American researchers in their justified fascination with Vygotskian ideas are often dealing with extended and assimilated versions of theories that originated in their own research traditions and whose original co-founders have gone undeservedly into oblivion.

Secondly, *the focus on the individual developing person* which Vygotsky clearly had (as did most European psychologists of the time) has been persistently overlooked. Thus, Vygotsky has been presented as an irreconcilable opponent to Piaget, with whom he differed in the evaluation of egocentric speech, but not in the focus on the developing personal–cognitive (and affective) structures. The actual closeness of the basic personalistic standpoints of both, as well as to William Stern's general ideas (see Kreppner, 1992) has gone without attention. Our contemporary child and educational psychology seems to be in its socially orientated mode, within which the simple primacy of the individual's personal experiencing is yet to find its prominent place (again).

Thirdly, in the educational applications of Vygotsky a very curious oversight can be observed – the *role of the 'social other'* (teacher, more capable peer, parent, etc.) *is presented as always helpful*, concerned about the future advancement of the child, etc. The (very real) possibility that under some circumstances educational interference ahead of the present developmental possibilities (i.e. within the zone of proximal development) might be purposefully harmful, promote ignorance and be potentially detrimental in other ways, is not considered. The real world is more complex than an educational utopia, and borrowing from Vygotsky has concentrated on the latter rather than on the former. The favourite topics of investigators – mother–child 'dialogue', or teacher–students' 'collective problem solving', or any other linkage of the social context and individual performers' relations within it – are investigated in their positively hedonistic and educationally progressive flavour. It is interesting to note that nowadays countless investigators of mother–child dialogues and joint problem solving (with their emphasis on the steering role of the more experienced other in an intimate setting) feel obliged to refer to Vygotsky, although in fact Vygotsky never discussed these situations and instead focused more upon culture as providing tools for thinking.

It is clear, then, that the reception of Vygotsky's ideas in the West has been selective. In a sense this is inevitable and may even be productive: we all create our own Freud, Piaget or Vygotsky and extend their ideas according to our own insights. The case of Vygotsky is slightly different, however, as his works have not been generally available in English and (consequently) a sober appraisal of his work does not yet seem to have been made. It is here that publications like the present reader may perform a beneficial role.

## The present reader: from reading to novelty construction

Our goal in putting together the present reader was to provide the interested reader with systematic access to Vygotsky's ideas in their own development. Obviously we had to make a selection and some facets of Vygotsky's creativity are not as well represented as others. For example, his literary criticism – a very important source for his psychological ideas – is not represented here. The avid reader is encouraged to dive into *The Psychology of Art* (in English: Vygotsky, 1971) for further in-depth understanding. Also, Vygotsky's defectological work has not received much prominence, as there seemed no need to replicate a major translation of exactly that side of Vygotsky's texts (Vygotsky, 1993).

These under-represented aspects of Vygotsky's creativity aside, the present reader fills in a number of prominent gaps in our knowledge. Chapter 1 gives us an insight into Vygotsky's and Luria's early evaluation of Freud's ideas which was on the whole more positive than one perhaps would expect. In chapter 5 of *Understanding Vygotsky* (Van der Veer and Valsiner, 1991) we have discussed Luria's prominent role in the psychoanalytic movement and the gradual change of both Vygotsky's and Luria's attitude towards Freudian theory both on internal and external grounds. In chapter 2 of this book we see the only concrete evidence of Vygotsky's first and last trip abroad: the lecture he delivered in London about the social education of deaf and dumb children. It formed the result of his organizational activities in what was called the field of 'defectology' at the time and it is fascinating to see the fervour with which Vygotsky defends the view that most important in physical 'defects' are the social results they cause for the child, results which might not be felt in another, better society. In chapter 3 we present one of Vygotsky's major theoretical papers in which he combines a sharp attack against reflexology with a plea for an objective study of consciousness. The content of this paper as well as the way it was presented during a conference in Moscow played its part in Vygotsky's entrance into academic psychology (see Van der Veer and Valsiner, 1991, pp. 39–47). Chapters 4, 5 and 11 present an overview of the key ideas and research methods of the cultural–historical theory as developed by Vygotsky and his associates in the late 1920s. They were published in the *Journal of Genetic Psychology* thanks to Luria's efforts and subsequently ignored by their contemporaries. In chapters 6, 9, 12 and 15 the reader may learn about the major role that Vygotsky attached to the formation of academic or scientific concepts in human cognitive development. It is a feature of Vygotsky's thinking which is known in the West, but has received rather less attention lately than such topics as the zone of proximal development. In our opinion, this is unfortunate as Vygotsky himself clearly (and perhaps incorrectly) attributed a key role to concept formation (see Van der Veer, 1992). The critical evaluation of Vygotsky's thinking, therefore, cannot do without a thorough study and critical examination of this aspect of his work. In chapter 7 we publish Vygotsky's and Luria's major paper, 'Tool and symbol in child development'. This book-length paper comprised their provisional formulation of the main tenets of the cultural–historical theory and an overview of some of its applications to major psychological problems. In chapters 8 and 13 we get a glimpse of Vygotsky's involvement in matters of politics and ideology. We can see how he takes a clear leftist stand – sometimes fiercely attacking his opponents – without for one moment loosing sight of the standards of scientific reasoning (which was quite remarkable in the Soviet Union of his time). Chapter 10 deals with an aspect of Vygotsky's thinking which has so far been generally ignored: his analysis of children's imagination and creativity. It is little known that Vygotsky wrote a book on the subject and took an avid interest in the development of children's drawings, etc. Finally, chapter 14 provides us with a fine analysis of the role of the environment in child development. It is interesting to see how Vygotsky in a very informal manner avoids some of the pitfalls that many later researchers would still fall into.

All in all, the present reader presents the interested student of education and psychology with some 250 pages of material which was never (re)published in English. Combined with the new and authoritative translations of known material and the notes provided by the editors they should allow the reader to gain a fair impression of the scientific work of Lev Vygotsky and his associates.

## References

Fodor, J. 1972: Some reflections on L. S. Vygotsky's 'Thought and Language'. *Cognition*, 1, 83–95.

Kreppner, K. 1992: William L. Stern, 1871–1938: A neglected founder of developmental psychology. *Developmental Psychology*, 28, 4, 539–47.

Levitin, K. 1982: *One is not born a personality*. Moscow: Progress Publishers.

Missner, M. 1985: Why Einstein became famous in America? *Social Studies of Science*, 15, 267–91.

Toulmin, S. 1978: Mozart in psychology. *New York Review of Books*, 25, 14, 51–7.

Valsiner, J. 1988: *Developmental psychology in the Soviet Union*. Brighton: Harvester Press.

Valsiner, J. 1994: Narratives in the making of history of psychology. In A. Rosa and J. Valsiner (eds), *Historical and theoretical discourse in socio-cultural studies*. Madrid: Infancia y Aprendizaje.

Van der Veer, R. 1992: The concept of development and the development of concepts. Paper presented at the workshop 'Apprentissage et développement, zone proximale de développement'. Bordeaux: 11–12, December 1992.

Van der Veer, R. and Valsiner, J. 1991: *Understanding Vygotsky: a quest for synthesis*. Oxford: Blackwell Publishers.

Van der Veer, R. and Valsiner, J. 1992: Voices at play: Understanding Van der Veer and Valsiner. *Comenius*, 12, 4 (whole No. 48), 423–9.

Van IJzendoorn, M. H. and Van der Veer, R. 1984: *Main currents of critical psychology: Vygotsky, Holzkamp, Riegel*. New York: Irvington Publishers.

Vygotsky, L. S. 1926/1982: Istoricheskij smysl psikhologicheskogo krizisa. Metodologicheskoe issledovanie. In L. S. Vygotsky, *Sobranie Sochinenij. Vol. 1: Voprosy teorii i istorii psikhologii* (pp. 291–436). Moscow: Pedagogika.

Vygotsky, L. S. 1971: *The Psychology of Art*. Cambridge, MA: The MIT Press.

Vygotsky, L. S. 1993: *The Collected Works of L. S. Vygotsky. Vol. 2: The fundamentals of defectology*. New York: Plenum Press.

Wertsch, J. V. 1981: *The Concept of Activity in Soviet Psychology*. New York: Sharpe.

# 1

# Introduction to the Russian translation of Freud's *Beyond the pleasure principle*

## Lev Vygotsky and Alexander Luria

### I

Among the great minds of our times, Freud's was probably one of the most intrepid. A quality such as this was always considered to be a virtue more suited to a practical man than to a scholar and thinker. Courage is needed for a man of action, but it seems that an infinitely greater amount of daring is required for thinking. At every turn, scholarship is populated by so many indeterminate minds, timid thoughts and spineless hypotheses that it almost seems as if wariness and following in other people's footsteps have become obligatory attributes of official academic work.

Freud made his debut as a revolutionary. The degree of opposition which psycho-analysis elicited in official academic circles, bears incontestable witness to the fact that it was guilty of having severely infringed age old traditions of bourgeois morality and scholarship and had overstepped the limits of what is acceptable. This new scientific idea and its creators were forced to spend many years in dismal isolation. The most virulent hostility and open resistance rose up against the new science at all levels of society. Freud himself says, that he 'was one of those who have "disturbed the sleep of the world", as Hebbel says'.[1] And this is exactly what did happen.

The uproar surrounding the new sciences gradually subsided. Nowadays, any new work in the field of psychoanalysis no longer elicits such a hostile reception. If not entirely, then at least partially, the former harassment has been replaced by general acceptance of the new discipline in an atmosphere of intense interest, profound regard and strong curiosity which even its principal opponents cannot deny it. Psychoanaly-sis has long ceased to be just a technique used in psychotherapy – it has grown to include a number of general basic problems in general psychology, biology, history of culture and all so-called 'Geisteswissenschaften'.

Particularly here in Russia, Freudian psychology is very popular, not only in learned circles, but also among the general reading public. During the past few years almost all of Freud's works have been translated into Russian and published. In front of our eyes, a new and original trend in psychoanalysis is beginning to form in Russia, which, with the help of the theory of the conditional reflexes, attempts to synthesize Freudian psychology and Marxism and to develop a system of 'reflexological Freudian psychology' in the spirit of dialectical materialism. Such a translation of Freud into Pavlov's language is an objective attempt to decode the dark 'depth psychology', and is a living proof of the great vitality of this theory and its inexhaustible research potential.

But for Freud, with the recognition of his work, the 'heroic age' did not merely become a thing of the past, but it required infinitely greater courage and even greater heroism than before. Whereas earlier he had been consigned to his own 'splendid isolation' and had arranged his life 'like Robinson Crusoe on a desert island', now he was faced with new and serious threats such as misrepresentations of the basic tenets of the new theory and the need for the scientific truth to conform to the exigencies and tastes of the bourgeois world view. In a word, earlier the threat came from the enemy side, now it came from the allies. And indeed, many of the leading lights, who 'have found their stay in the underworld of psycho-analysis too uncomfortable for their taste', abandoned it.[2]

This internal struggle required a much greater effort than confrontation with enemies. Freud's fundamental idiosyncrasy lies in the fact that he is bold enough to take every idea to its logical and final conclusion. He did not always manage to take others along with him on this difficult and frightening journey and many abandoned him immediately after the starting point and turned off the road. This maximalist thinking process resulted in Freud remaining essentially isolated as a scholar even at the very peak in the rise of scientific interest in psychoanalysis.

The present translation of the book *Jenseits des Lustprinzips* (1920) which is being offered to the reader, belongs to a number of just such lonely works by Freud. Even orthodox psychoanalysts sometimes pass over this work in silence; as far as a wider circle of readers is concerned, both abroad and in Russia, one keeps coming up against definite prejudice which must be clarified and dispelled.

This book reaches such astounding and unexpected conclusions that, at first glance, they appear to contradict sharply everything which we all have become accustomed to consider to be irrefutable scientific truth. And what is more, it contradicts some fundamental claims which had been put forward by Freud himself in earlier times. Here, Freud challenges not only general opinion, but calls his own assertion underlying all psychoanalytic revelations in question. The intrepidity of his thinking reaches its zenith in this book.

We have become accustomed to consider the principle of self preservation of a living organism and the principle of its adaptation to the conditions of the environment in which it has to live as basic explanatory principles for all biological sciences. The instinct to preserve life and the life of the species, as well as the drive to adapt to the environment in the best and most painless way, appear to be the main forces driving all organic development. In complete agreement with these premises of traditional biology, Freud had earlier formulated a theory about two principles of psychic activity. He named the higher tendency to which psychic processes are subordinate, the pleasure principle. However, the pursuit of pleasure and the avoidance of pain do not completely hold sway and are not exclusively the forces which direct psychic processes. The necessity of having to adapt creates the need for a careful awareness of the external world; at this stage a new principle of psychic activity is introduced, namely, the reality principle which at times dictates a denial of pleasure for the sake of 'something more dependable even if postponed'.[3] All this is extremely elementary, a truism that to all appearance belongs to the realm of irrefutable, self evident truths.

However, the facts which are obtained by psychoanalytical research, propel the mind beyond the narrow confines of this self evident truth. *It is this attempt of the mind to reach farther than this truth — beyond the pleasure principle — which was the creative force behind this book.*

But according to Freud, even more elementary than this principle, and however paradoxical it may sound, is the principle of the death instinct, which is a basic primordial and universal principle common to all living matter. One has to differentiate between two sorts of instincts. The one which is more accessible to observation and has been studied for a long time is Eros in its wider sense, the Libido, which includes not only the sexual drive and its various manifestations, but the whole instinct of self preservation — these make up the life instinct. The other type of instinct, a typical example of which one can consider to be sadism, can be designated as the death instinct. As Freud says in another book, the purpose of this kind of impulse is 'to lead organic life back into the inanimate state', i.e. its goal is 'to re-establish a state of things that was disturbed by the emergence of life', for all life to regress to the inorganic existence of matter.[4] At the same time, all positive life protecting tendencies such as the striving for self preservation etc. are regarded as component instincts, whose function is to assure that the organism shall follow its individual journey towards death and to ward off all extraneous probabilities of its returning to inorganic existence. At the same time, all life represents a drive to restore the disturbed life energy equilibrium, like circuitous paths (Umwege) towards death; this amounts to a perpetual struggle and compromise between two irreconcilable and opposite instincts.

A construction such as this produces natural resistance against itself for two reasons. Firstly, Freud [1920, p. 59] himself points out that this work stands in contrast to some of his other arguments. These had been nothing but direct and accurate translations of factual observations into the language of theory. But in this case, reflection frequently supplants observation — speculative thinking replaces the meagre factual material. Therefore, one may easily get the impression that in this case we are dealing with metaphysical speculation rather than scientifically reliable propositions. So it is not difficult to place an equals sign between what Freud himself calls the metapsychological point of view and a metaphysical one.

Secondly, on this point, anyone may find that another objection against the very essence of these ideas inevitably comes to mind. The suspicion arises that perhaps these concepts are permeated with the psychology of hopeless pessimism and that the author may be attempting to smuggle in the decadent philosophy of Nirvana and death under the guise of biological principles. Does not the very suggestion that the only purpose of life is death, amount to nothing short of trying to dynamite the very foundations of scientific biology, the science of life?

Both objections should prompt anyone to approach the present work extremely cautiously and some may even find that there is no room for it within the system of scientific psychoanalysis and that it can be dismissed within the construction of any structured reflexological Freudian psychology. However, any careful reader will not find it difficult to persuade himself that both of these objections are unfounded and will not stand up to even the lightest touch of critical thinking.

Freud [1920, p. 57] himself points out the endless complexity and obscurity of the problems under investigation. He calls this field of study an equation with two unknown quantities or mysteries, where not so much as a ray of a hypothesis has penetrated. The scientific methods he uses completely put out of court any accusations as to the metaphysical nature of his speculations. It is, indeed, speculation, but a scientific one. It is metapsychology, not metaphysics. This work is a step beyond the boundaries of empirical knowledge, but not into the realm of the transcendental and supersensory, only into the domain of the hitherto insufficiently explored and illuminated. What is discussed throughout is the yet undiscovered, not the unknowable. Freud himself [1920, pp. 37, 60] insists that his only objective is sober results. He would be only too happy to exchange the metaphorical language of psychology for physiological and chemical terminology if this did not entail a renunciation of all attempts to describe the phenomena he was studying. Biology is a land of unlimited possibilities, and the author is prepared to concede that his positions may well end up being overturned.

Does this then mean that the author's own doubts about his suppositions deprive them of any scientific value or significance? Not on any account. The author [Freud, 1920, p. 59] says that he himself is equally unconvinced of the truth of his assumptions and he does not want to incline others to accept them either. He is not sure how far he believes in them himself. He thinks that at this stage one should completely do away with 'the emotional factor of conviction', that is the whole point. This demonstrates the true nature and scientific value of the ideas expressed in this work. Science does not consist exclusively of ready made judgements, found answers, viable theses and reliable facts and rules. In equal measure it includes the quest for truth, the processes of discovery, suppositions, experience and risks. Scientific thought differs from religious thought, in that it does not demand a belief in itself as a prerequisite. 'It is surely possible to throw oneself into a line of thought', says Freud [1920, p. 59], 'and to follow it wherever it leads out of simple scientific curiosity.' Freud himself says 'that psychoanalysis tried very hard not to become a system'.[5] And if giddy thoughts await us on this journey, then we must exhibit courage to follow this endeavour fearlessly like a walk along Alpine mountain tracks, risking a fall down a precipice at any moment. 'Nur für Schwindelfreie', 'only for those free of vertigo', according to Lev Shestov's wonderful phrase, do these Alpine routes open up in philosophy and science.[6]

In a situation such as this, when the author himself is ready to turn off his road at any moment and is the first to have doubts about the truth of his ideas, there obviously cannot be any talk about this book supposedly being saturated with the philosophy of death. There is no philosophy of any kind to be found in it; its origins are in exact science and it is directed toward exact science, but what it does do is to take a gigantic, vertiginous leap from the most extreme point of firmly established scientific facts into the undiscovered sphere beyond the obvious. But one must not forget that, in general, psychoanalysis has as its objective to battle its way through beyond what is apparent, and in some sense, the role of all scientific knowledge is not just to verify the obvious, but to uncover facts which are more credible and real than what is self evident; in the same way as Galilei's discoveries take us away beyond the obvious, so must the discoveries of psychoanalysis.

Misunderstandings are bound to occur, if only because some of the psychoanalytical terminology used by the author tends to be a bit ambiguous when it is applied to biological and chemical concepts. The death instinct and the striving towards death which is ascribed to all living organic matter may indeed, at first glance, easily appear to be a throw-back to pessimist philosophy. But the reason for this is the fact that until now, psychology was always in the habit of borrowing from biology its basic concepts, explanatory principles and hypotheses, and applying them and what had hitherto been accepted as valid for simpler living organisms to the realm of psychology. It seems that for the first time ever, in this instance, biology owes a debt to psychology and scientific thinking has simply been put into reverse gear, drawing its conclusions from the analysis of human psychology and applying them to universal laws of organic life. In this case biology borrows from psychology. Because of this, it is hardly necessary to point out that terms such as instinct, drive, etc., *lose their original character of psychological powers, and come to signify only general tendencies to be found in a living cell, without dependence on any philosophical evaluation of life and death within the framework of the human mind.* Without exception, Freud attributes such instincts to chemical and physiological processes within the living cell and only uses them to designate the direction of the restoration of the energy equilibrium.

The value and merit of any scientific hypothesis is measured by its practical advantage, that is, its contribution to progress and its use as a working explanatory principle. In this sense, the best evidence of the full scientific value of the hypothesis of a primary Todestrieb, is the subsequent development of the same ideas in Freud's book *Das Ich und das Es* (*The Ego and the Id*),[7] where the psychological theory about the complex structure of personality, about ambiguity and the destructive instinct, etc., are directly linked with the ideas which are developed in the present book.

But Freud's bold hypothesis for general biological conclusions shows even more promise. Once and for all it completely breaks with any teleological concepts in the spheres of psychology and biology. Every instinct is causally dependent on its previous condition which it strives to reinstate. Every instinct has a conservative character and it is impelled backwards and not forwards. And this is how a bridge (a hypothetical one) is thrown across from the science of the origins and development of organic life to that dealing with inorganic matter. For the first time in this hypothesis, the organic whole is so decisively integrated into the general context of the world.

Freud is willing to concede that 'in every particle of living substance,' in every cell, both sorts of instincts coexist in mixed, unequal portions. And only as a result of the combination of the most primitive unicellular organisms to form multicellular forms of life 'the death instinct of the single cell can successfully be neutralized and the destructive impulses be diverted on to the external world'.[8] Such ideas open up enormous possibilities for the study of social sublimation of these death instincts. 'The multicellular' social organism creates grandiose, countless possibilities for neutralizing and sublimating this death instinct by transforming it into creative impulses of the social human being.[9]

In view of all these reasons, we think that Freud's new book, because of its extraordinary courage and originality of thought, will be received both in learned circles and by the general reader with the attention and interest which it deserves. This interest should not, in any way, depend on whether or not the hypothesis put forward meets with approval or receives factual confirmation in the course of subsequent research and critical scrutiny. The very discovery of a new America – a country beyond the pleasure principle – like Columbus, provides a great service, even if it does not produce an exact geographical map of the new continent or colonize it. After all, the quest for truth is more fascinating, more enlightening, more fruitful and worthwhile than the already discovered, ready-made truth.

## II

Even before the appearance of the Russian translation of this book, a lively discussion of the problems raised in it began in Russian scholarly circles. Among the opinions being expressed were claims that Freud had abandoned his initial position and that in this book he had entered upon a road which diverged widely from contemporary materialist thinking.

We think that a more fruitful approach to this book does not justify these suspicions. In *Jenseits des Lustprinzips* Freud develops ideas which he had presented in greater depth and breadth as the foundation stones of psychoanalysis, but now he invites us into his thinking laboratory. Essentially, everything in this book stems logically from Freud's earlier ideas, but still how new, and at times how shocking and original do these pages seem to us.

Nowhere does the author claim that his proposals are absolutely correct; he himself is not certain about their validity and by giving vent to his ideas, he only wishes to draw general biological conclusions based on data from aspects of psychic life which he had previously investigated. Where does this lead? What tendencies which may have general methodological applications are hidden beneath these sometimes incomprehensible conjectures?

At the root of all the proposals in this book lies one single tendency, namely an attempt to produce a general biological scheme for psychic life. Freud is not entirely happy with psychic principles such as, for example, 'the pleasure principle,' which according to psychoanalysis regulate all human behaviour; he is searching for a deeper, more generally meaningful biological conformity with the laws of nature and he finds it in the general principle of the preservation of equilibrium – a general tendency observed in the inorganic world to maintain an evenly distributed level of energy tension. Stability and regression to inorganic existence, these are the basic tendencies of pure biology, whose echoes we find in the depths of the human psyche ('the compulsion to repeat former states').[10] However, these strange processes found in psychic life are not special attributes of 'the spirit'; they only tell us something about the existence of more far-ranging laws which include both psychic activity and more fundamental biological processes. In this work, psychology is incorporated within the orbit of general biological phenomena and the same tendency which plays its part in the inorganic world is reflected in this psychology. For us, such a strange sounding concept as 'the death instinct' (Todestrieb) should mean nothing more than an ascertainment of an echo of some more profound laws of biological nature, an attempt to get away from a purely psychological concept of 'instinct' and to discover its true biological meaning.

From a purely psychological approach to the principles of psychic life and instincts to a biological approach – this is the route Freud takes in order to expand his earlier hypotheses.

However, if the biological conservative tendency to preserve the inorganic equilibrium is concealed in the deeper layers of psychic life, how can humanity's development from lower to higher forms be explained? Where are we to look for the root of the stormy progression of the historical process? Freud provides us with a highly interesting and deeply materialistic answer, i.e. if in the deep recesses of the human psyche there still remain conservative tendencies of primordial biology and if, in the final analysis, even Eros is consigned to it, then the only forces which make it possible for us to escape from this state of biological conservatism and which may propel us toward progress and activity, are external forces, in our terms, the external conditions of the material environment in which the individual exists. It is they that represent the true basis of progress, it is they that create the real personality and make it adapt and work out new forms of psychic life; finally they are the ones that suppress and transfer the vestiges of the old conservative biology. In this respect Freud's psychology is thoroughly sociological and it is up to other materialistic psychologists who find themselves in better circumstances than Freud to reveal and validate the subject of the materialistic foundations of this theory.

So, according to Freud, the history of the human psyche embodies two tendencies, the conservative–biological and the progressive–sociological. It is from these factors that the whole *dialectic of the organism* is composed and they are responsible for the distinctive 'spiral' development of a human being. This book represents a step forwards and not backwards along the path to the construction of a whole, monistic system, and after having read this book a dialectician cannot fail to perceive its enormous potential for a monistic understanding of the world.

It is quite unnecessary to agree with every one of Freud's many postulates, and it is not necessary to share all his hypotheses, but what is important is to be able to discover one general tendency within the singular (perhaps not all of them of equal value) notions, and to manage to make use of it for a materialistic explanation of the world.

But one thing has definitely been accomplished in this work, and that is that psychology has lost its mystical specificity. Freud revealed that the same general biological laws which govern the rest of the world apply to it as well and that it has finally been totally debunked as a bearer of some 'higher' import [1920, p. 60]: 'The deficiencies in our description would probably vanish if we were already in a position to replace our psychological terms by physiological or chemical ones'.

Bourgeois science is giving birth to materialism; such labour is often difficult and prolonged, but we only have to find where in its bowels materialistic buds are showing, to find them, to rescue them and to make good use of them.

## Notes

First published in Freud, S. 1925: *Po tu storonu principa udovol'stvija {Beyond the Pleasure Principle}* (pp. 3–16). Moscow: Sovremennye Problemy. Quotations and page numbers refer to the Standard Edition of Freud's complete works edited by J. Strachey and published by The Hogarth Press.

1   Refers to Freud's words in his 'On the history of the psycho-analytic movement' (1914, p. 21). See vol. 14 of the Standard Edition.

2   This whole account is based on Freud's own romantic description in his 'On the history of the psycho-analytic movement'. The terms 'splendid isolation', 'heroic age', the comparison to 'Robinson Crusoe on a desert island', and the phrase about 'the underworld of psycho-analysis' were all used by Freud himself to picture the alleged general resistance against his ideas. See pp. 22, 66 of vol. 14 of the Standard Edition.

3   Paraphrase of a passage in *Beyond the Pleasure Principle* (1920). See p. 10 of vol. 18 of the Standard Edition.

4   Quoted from Freud's text in *The Ego and the Id* (1923, p. 40). See vol. 19 of the Standard Edition.

5   Possibly a paraphrase of a passage in one of Freud's (1923) encyclopedia articles. See pp. 253–4 of vol. 18 of the Standard Edition.

6   Quotation from Shestov, L. *Apofeoz bespochvennosti* (1905/1991, p. 180). Leningrad: Izdatel'stvo Leningradskogo Universiteta. One of Shestov's (1905/1991, pp. 110; 178–80) major themes and the motto of part 2 of his book was that really interesting, metaphysical thinking requires the banishment of the dogmas of logic and science and is only feasible for those who do not fear the Alpine mountain tracks of speculation.

7   Available in Russian translation. Academia Publishers, Leningrad, 1924 [original footnote].

8   This quote and the one that follows it are taken from 'The Ego and the Id' (1923, p. 41). See vol. 19 of the Standard Edition.

9   The term 'multicellular' is used by Freud in *Beyond the Pleasure Principle*. See p. 50 of vol. 18 of the Standard Edition.

10   Paraphrase of Freud's argumentation in *Beyond the Pleasure Principle*. See pp. 36–7 of vol. 18 of the Standard Edition.

# 2

# Principles of social education for deaf and dumb children in Russia

## *Lev Vygotsky*

The system of social education of deaf and dumb children, based upon principles of which I shall be chiefly speaking today, is not only a theoretical construction but also real, living facts taken from daily life in various fields of pedagogical observation, facts which have been developing before us in the Union of Socialist Soviet Republics, and particularly in the Russian Socialist Federative Soviet Republic. Of course, it should be understood that the theoretical and the practical work of this system has not yet been completed, and therefore I should be right in saying that I am here today for the purpose of sharing with you the experiments of the first steps in this direction, the first attempts of scientific thought and pedagogical conquests leading to the creation of a system of social education of the deaf and dumb. However, the chief principles of this system can already be formulated with such exactitude and clearness that I am hoping for some success in my endeavour to acquaint you with the principles of the new movement we are putting into operation.

Before proceeding to the actual principles of social education of deaf and dumb children, I should like to mention certain scientific principles on which the new system is based. These principles refer to the psycho-physiological peculiarities of a deaf and dumb child, and to the process of its upbringing. Every physical defect, be it blindness or deafness, alters the child's attitude towards the universe and, primarily, towards its fellow beings. Let us take, for instance, the geometrical place of a human being in the social sphere, his part and his fate as partaker of life and all functions of social existence, and we shall come to the conclusion that everything is to be entirely altered in the case of a human being with any defect. A physical defect provokes a social sprain, with unavoidable consequences, just in the same way as a sprained ankle or injured arm interferes with our movements and makes us suffer from pains and inflammation. It means that an organ is out of order and regular functioning of the body is interfered with.

The problem of children's defectiveness dealt with psychologically and pedagogically should be made an important social problem. Up to the present this question has been considered of secondary importance; it is now necessary to change this attitude in giving this question a distinct social significance.

If a psycho-physical defect means a social sprain, then to bring up such a child properly means to place him safely in life, in the same way as a sprained organ is put back to its right place. It goes without saying that blindness and deafness are biological facts and not at all of a social nature, but the teacher has to deal not so much with these facts as with the social consequences of these facts. When we have a blind child as an object of education before us, we are compelled to deal not so much with blindness in itself, as with the conflicts which arise therefrom within the child when it enters life. It is obvious that its contact with surroundings does not proceed in the usual way as compared with a normal child. Blindness or deafness, as a psychological fact, is not at all a misfortune, but, as a social fact, it becomes such.

I am now approaching the starting point, the very first stage of the system of social education of deaf and dumb children, namely, their pre-school education, the importance of which, as far as I know, has not yet been sufficiently appreciated, either in theory or in practice, in quite a number of countries. The foundation of all future educational work, particularly the teaching of speech, is being laid at the children's home during pre-school education. It is exactly this very point, the central one of the system, that I shall discuss in order to let you see the fundamental importance of pre-school education which occupies the most prominent position in the whole system. It is in the children's home that the little ones first learn to speak; the teaching is based upon natural impulses, such as prattling and mimicry. Speech is considered as part of the child's general social life. Under the old traditional methods of teaching the deaf and dumb, these natural impulses of speech were neglected, and used to gradually disappear under unfavourable conditions; this stage was usually followed by a period of speechless development, and thus the child's speech and consciousness went quite different ways so far as development was concerned, and only towards the beginning of school days was the child taught to speak by sounds; by that time the general development of the child was so advanced that it could not possibly take an interest in the slow teaching of speech, and considered the task as a very unpleasant one without any practical advantages. On the other hand, the habit of mimicry became so strong that it was very difficult for the verbal speech to fight it, especially when the child's interest in the verbal speech had been absolutely killed. The only way out of this position was to make use of artificial measures, exceptional severity and cruelty, and appealing to the consciousness of the pupil, and thus the child was successfully taught to speak; but we all know that methods based only on conscious efforts of the pupil, against his fundamental interests and habits, are not reliable.

At the Pre-School Children's Home, children are taught to speak from the age of two years. Synthetic reading of words, phrases, names, commands from the lips and reflexive, unconscious imitation of verbal speech are the two fundamental methods. The habit of expressing wishes and thoughts verbally is being developed here from early childhood. Speech is taught straight away in a most practical and social manner. When the child is playing and working daily, it learns unconsciously to speak and understand the spoken word; it also learns to concentrate on speech, organize its life and the conduct of it; these achievements would be inaccessible to a dumb child. At the early stage, from two to five years, there are no sounds to be dealt with. The exercises consist of children's first prattlings which are preparatory to each new word and reading from the lips; simultaneously with it, the organs of speech – voice, breathing – are also working and developing in quite a natural way. These exercises are being practised before the child actually acquires correct speech. The child's speech is being organically developed directly from its chatter and is from the beginning intelligent and adapted to its function. If we were to wait until the child learned to pronounce each sound correctly, and then were to compose the sounds into syllables, the syllables into words – if we were to proceed from the elements of speech to synthesis – we would never hear a natural and real speech from the child. The natural method is just vice versa: from the complex to the simple elements of speech and their combining. If you look into the history of the development of human speech and that of a single child, you will find that the phrase precedes the word, the word the syllable and the syllable the sound. Even a single phrase is practically an abstraction. The speech is being made up of more than one sentence, and therefore children are much quicker at learning an intelligent, useful, socially necessary speech – by that I mean a logical speech and not an articulation. 'The consecutiveness in the development of speech of a deaf and dumb', says Natalia Rau, founder of the first Children's Garden for the Deaf and Dumb in Russia, 'must be copied from that of a normal child: the stages of development of speech must be the same, the difference is only so far as means and time are concerned – a deaf and dumb child will be able to say at the age of three to four what a normal child will say at the age of one year.'

The foundation of future speech is being laid here during the pre-school education. Speech does not only serve as a means of intercourse between children, but also as an instrument of thought. 'Synthetic reading from the lips', says Natalia Rau,

is already the beginning of thinking through the verbal word. When reading from the lips and observing the picture of the mouth and the movements of the speech organs, the child is intimately associating this picture with the idea, the idea with the movement of the mouth and tongue. Let us assume, for instance, that the child is already familiar with the sentence 'Come here', when it has to go itself or call somebody else – it sees mentally the uttering of the sentence in itself, and the muscles of the speech organs which are instrumental in the producing of this sentence become involuntarily strained. Gradually, in proportion as the frequent reading from the lips is being practised, the child's ideas and inner mental uttering are also becoming strengthened, and though not able to pronounce verbally, the child already speaks mentally; the result thereof is that the most precious thing in our work with the pre-school child is being formed, viz. the habit of understanding, thinking and expressing its thoughts verbally.

Thus real speech stands out in all its variety of functions; it becomes organically part of the child's life and begins to shape its life and conduct around the centre of its social experience, of which the chief organ is speech. Therefore, Natalia Rau is quite right in her summing up: 'Experience proves that the pre-school education of the deaf and dumb serves as a strong basis for the natural verbal speech, and is the only means of intercourse between a deaf and dumb person and a normal one. *Through pre-school education to the natural verbal word, through the verbal word into the midst of hearing beings*'.[1]

The further teaching of verbal speech at school is proceeded with on the same principles as in the Children's Garden. The fundamental principle, which is combating the analytical, artificial, dead method of sounds, remains; it is the fight for a whole word, an intelligent sentence, a logical, natural speech.

I shall speak to you only of two new, original methods which are based upon this principle and are being put into practice at our schools. The first one, that of Mr I. Golosov, Instructor of the Moscow Institute for the Deaf and Dumb, is considered to be the first and original attempt to build the teaching of verbal speech on the method of whole words. The fundamental idea of the author is to attempt to teach the deaf and dumb in the same way as our little children are taught. The preliminary working out of this method started in 1910; its practical work commenced at Warsaw in 1913, and only during the revolution were the theory and practice of this method completed in Moscow. The essential feature of this method is that children deal with a word and not with a part of it. 'The word', says Mr I. Golosov, 'arouses their interest in speech and makes them feel confident that they will learn to speak.' During the study of words and sentences, sounds are dealt with simultaneously. The results of this method were exceptionally good: thus, for instance, in the 1923–1924 semester, October to June, in the first group, children were taught by this method and mastered 22 sounds.

The essential part of this method is the reading from the face, whereas the analytical method deals with the technique of uttering. Reading from the face is connected with the reading of the same material written and printed. The sound is not dealt with separately, but is worked out in whole words, starting with short words (one syllable), and in whole sentences and even in short stories. I should like to mention that this method coincides in its essential features with that of Mr Malisch, though it came into existence in an independent and original way. This coincidence is likely to suggest that we are moving in the right direction.

Mr Malisch holds a similar view with regard to natural speech; its teaching must begin straight away with logical speech. 'Children should be taught', says Mr Malisch, 'only those things that are now, or may be later, directly useful in life'. Reading from the face, reading from letters, writing and articulation – all those four aspects of teaching are intimately connected here, but reading from the face is given the most prominence. 'Satisfactory pronunciation is being attained', says Mr Malisch, 'in a purely automatic manner', whereas in the analytical method it is based upon a conscious uttering of each sound and corresponding sensation connected with it.[2] However, we cannot be satisfied with a technical reform and partial improvement. Our principles are urging us towards entire revision of the whole system. We must have courage to go to the end without stopping half way. This attempt is being made by Mr Sokoliansky through his method.[3] This method leads to the mastering of speech chiefly through reading from the lips. Speech sensations, which are very indistinct, are *not* chosen here as a basis for thinking, but what is more prominent and familiar to the deaf and dumb, viz. sight sensations, such as images of words on the lips of the speaker, words written on a blackboard, and motor sensations of the hand when writing. An intelligent, logical whole sentence is given to the deaf and dumb under these three aspects. The problem is, so to speak, to 'throw' the deaf and dumb into our speech, with the result that the child gets mechanically into logical speech without special effort. The chief characteristic of this method is its mechanical and reflexive nature. At first, sentences are given only in the imperative, and always with the corresponding action. Conditional reflexes are being developed. According to the accepted order, the sentence is first read from the lips accompanied by a direct instruction, i.e. a natural gesture: 'Children, get up!' – and the teacher shows with the hand what they should do. This is repeated two, three times; this is followed by the reading of the sentence from the lips without a gesture, it means with a conditional instruction: this is repeated seven, eight times, and the children master the sentence. When the children get hold of a considerable number of sentences in the imperative, the same material is used for the descriptive form in the present and past tenses. But the most remarkable feature of this method is that children learn not only one phrase but, in about 12 minutes, they learn a number of signs, phrases and a whole chain of sentences. These are, for instance: 'Children, get up!' 'Children, come here!' 'Children, lift up your hands!' 'Children, put down your hands!' 'Children, go to your seats!' 'Children, sit down!'

When the children master the chain of sentences by reading from the lips, they are given the same sentences to read separately in order to ascertain whether they really know what they have learned in the whole chain; the results are always very satisfactory. The same chain of sentences is given in writing: it is either written on a blackboard or on a wall poster. This exercise must be repeated from three to four times. The children take about 12 minutes to get hold of the chain of sentences by reading from the lips, and from six to seven minutes by reading from the poster. The subsequent chains are composed on the basis of the preceding.

The most striking feature of this method is that the children learn very quickly to write. The technical working out of the pronunciation is dealt with separately at special lessons, but it is always subordinated to the fundamental lessons in speech, viz. reading from the lips, which is practised two hours daily. It is difficult to say when the child will be able to speak as quickly as it reads from the lips, but we must not forget that even the normal child is passing through a period when it understands more than it can say.

Though these methods are subject to revision and correction, there is no doubt as to the direction which the education of the deaf and dumb will take, and that is that the principle of logically connected speech will be in future the dominant feature of the education of deaf and dumb children. I shall even go so far as to say that there is no one method which, by itself, can completely solve the problem of teaching the deaf and dumb to speak. There is no solution of this problem outside of the general system of education; here methods can be blamed or approved of. Thus, for instance, the verbal method was killing in the old system; it may become beneficial in the new one. It is necessary to organize the child's life in such a way as to make speech necessary and interesting. The teaching must appeal to the children and should not be directed against them. We must make the children's interests our allies and not our enemies. Desire for speech should be created, and the child is more likely to learn to speak when it is urged by necessity; this very motive is being completely destroyed by the traditional school which separates the deaf and dumb child from normal surroundings and places it in a special environment, where everything is adapted to its infirmities; thus, the circle of its interests becomes very narrow and this encourages unsociable instincts.

The only way out of this difficult position is a fundamental change in education as a whole; and this idea has been put into practice in the Russian Socialist Federative Soviet Republic, and the problem of the education of the deaf and dumb has been solved on the basis of a general new school of labour education for normal children. The chief principle upon which our schools are based is that education is considered as a part of social life; school is an organization where children participate in the life which surrounds them. 'The bringing up and education of children must proceed within society, through society and for society.' This is the basis for social education as defined by one of the theorists of the new school of labour education.[4] The education of the deaf and dumb is based on the same principle.

Just as it is impossible to become a swimmer by standing and looking from the shore, so it is quite impossible for the deaf and dumb to learn to speak outside of the general social life. Work, Society and Nature are the three leading subjects upon which the training and educational work is based. Such a practical education is the best and safest way into life, because the child becomes accustomed to take an active part in life from early childhood. The deaf and dumb being brought up and educated in these surroundings, enjoy company and speech, take an active interest in life and are quite prepared for an independent future.

'Through the study, from a practical, working point of view', says Krupskaja, 'of connections and relationships between man and nature, individual and society, economics, politics and civilization past and present, the teaching of subjects acquires a general educational and polytechnical nature.'[5] Upon such a technical working education is the professional training based; through the latter the pupil receives a finishing touch, so far as a certain aspect of labour is concerned, so that he may be fitted to take up his work in society. The organization of Children's Social Bodies is based on the same principle, and perhaps I shall not be wrong in saying that the world's first experiment of self-governing among deaf and dumb children has been made in our schools. The children organize their own life; they have their own school governing body, with sanitary, cultural and other committees, and all these interests go to make up their whole life. As a result, social habits, conscious instincts, initiative, organizing abilities, collective responsibility are developing and strengthening through this system.

Then comes the deaf and dumb Children's Communist movement, participation of children in detachments of young pioneers. The pioneer movement is, from a pedagogical point of view, an experiment of building and organizing children's games in an international and universal spirit. Through these games, children are put in direct touch with the life of the working class; they learn to understand the experiences and hardships of the grown-ups. The pulse of universal life is beating in the pioneer movement, and the child learns to realize that it takes part in universal life. There is one more new feature of these children's games: it concentrates the child's interest on the present and future, whereas the usual games were based on the historical past. It is obvious that, in this manner, the deaf and dumb child enjoys life just as fully as the normal one. This very system of social education contains the newest and most significant reforms gained through the revolution on behalf of the education of the deaf and dumb.

In the Union of Socialist Soviet Republics, the education of the deaf and dumb is a state business directed by the organizers of the People's Education. Of course, we are still poor in means and forces, and therefore unable to do as much for the deaf and dumb as we should like to. We went through very hard times during the war, blockade and hunger and, naturally, together with everybody else, the deaf and dumb suffered. When things became generally better, more care and attention was also extended to the deaf and dumb. Moreover, if we compare the number of schools for the deaf and dumb and the number of pupils in them in the territory of the Union before and after the revolution, we shall find that both the number of schools and pupils have increased since the revolution. Thus we had 51 schools on the present territory of the Socialist Soviet Republics before the revolution, and towards 1 June, 1925 we had 63 schools. There were 2,377 deaf and dumb pupils before the revolution; by 1 June, 1925 we had 3,250. In Moscow we had six institutes for the deaf and dumb; three school institutes with 260 pupils, and three pre-school institutes with 60 pupils before the war; by 1 June, 1925 we had eight institutes (612 pupils): four for children of school age (466 pupils) and four for children of pre-school age (147 pupils).

I should like to emphasize once more that we are very far from thinking that we have reached something final in this matter. On the contrary, we think that we are only starting, but we consider that the path chosen by us is the right one, and that the future belongs to the social education of the deaf and dumb.[6]

## Notes

First published as Vygotsky, L. S. 1925: Principles of social education for deaf and dumb children in Russia. In *International conference on the education of the deaf* (pp. 227–37). London: William H. Taylor & Sons. Vygotsky was indicated as Dr Leo Vygotsky (or Vigotsky), Director of Education of children with defects, under the People's Commissariat of Education, Russian Socialist Federative Soviet Republic, and Lecturer of the Second Moscow State University. The presentation at the conference in London took place in June 1925 as part of the only trip abroad Vygotsky ever undertook. It seems he travelled by train and boat and paid visits to research centres in Germany, Holland and France. No details of this trip have so far been unearthed and one can only guess that he visited Gestalt colleagues in Berlin and defectologists/educationalists in Amsterdam and Paris.

A slightly longer Russian version of the same paper has been published in vol. 5 of Vygotsky's Collected Works. See Vygotsky, L. S. 1983: Principy social'nogo vospitanija glukhonemykh detej. In L. S. Vygotsky *Sobranie Sochinenij. Tom 5. Osnovy defektologii* (pp. 101–14). Moscow: Pedagogika. Some of the biographical and bibliographical information provided in notes 1 to 4 is based on the notes to this edition.

1   Rau, Natalia Aleksandrovna (1870–1947), Russian expert in the education of the deaf. Vygotsky refers to p. 59 of Rau, N. A. 1926: Doshkol'noe vospitanie glukhonemykh [Preschool education of deaf and dumb children]. In S. S. Tizanova and P. P. Pochapina (eds), *Puti vospitanija fizicheski defektivnogo rebenka* [*Ways of Educating the Physically Defective Child*]. Moscow. Apparently, Vygotsky saw some unpublished version of this book as his talk was held one year before its publication.

2   Malisch, Konstantin (1860–1925), Austrian specialist in the education of deaf children. Vygotsky's quotes are taken from p. 81 of Külpe, G. I. 1926: Metod celykh slov i fraz Malisha [Malisch's method of whole words and phrases]. In S. S. Tizanova and P. P. Pochapina (eds), *Puti vospitanija fizicheski defektivnogo rebenka*. Moscow.

3   Sokoliansky, Ivan Afanas'evich (1889–1960), Russian expert in the education of deaf and blind children. Started his first educational experiments with a group of pupils in Kharkov in 1923. Was soon generally regarded as the founder of a new system of education for deaf, dumb and blind children. His most successful pupil Ol'ga Ivanovna Skorodokhodova was as well known in the Soviet Union as Helen Keller in the Western world. His work was continued by his student A. I. Meshcherjakov. Vygotsky's description of Sokoliansky's method is based on pp. 74–5 of Kotel'nikov, M. N. 1926: Na novom puti: (chtenie s gub kak osnova obuchenija glukhonemykh ustnoj rechi) [On a new path: (lip reading as the basis of teaching deaf and dumb vocal speech)]. In S. S. Tizanova and P. P. Pochapina (eds), *Puti vospitanija fizicheski defektivnogo rebenka*. Moscow.

4   This may have been the German school reformer Georg Kerschensteiner (1854–1932), whose ideas were very well known by the Soviet theorists of the labour school – such as P. P. Blonsky – and greatly inspired them, but whose name was not very popular as he was considered to hold bourgeois and authoritarian views.

5   Krupskaja, N. K. (1869–1939), wife of Lenin. Took great interest in educational matters and was active in the People's Commissariat of Education. Published papers and pamphlets discussing school reform and boy scouts. See, for instance, Krupskaja, N. K. 1925: *Vospitanie molodozhi v Leninskom dukhe* [*Education of the Youth in Lenin's Spirit*]. Moscow: Molodaja Gvardia. The present quote can be found on p. 214 of Krupskaja, N. K. 1978: Sistema narodnogo obrazovanija v RSFSR. In N. K. Krupskaja, *Pedagogicheskie Sochinenija. Tom 2*. Moscow.

6   Vygotsky's paper was followed by four tables which gave an overview of the number of deaf and dumb people in Russia and the Ukraine, the institutes taking care of them, the trades the children were taught, etc.

# 3

# The methods of reflexological and psychological investigation

## *Lev Vygotsky*

The methods of the reflexological investigation of man have now reached a turning point in their development. The necessity (and inevitability) of a turnaround results from the discordance between, on the one hand, the enormous tasks which reflexology sets itself – that of studying the whole of man's behaviour – and, on the other hand, those modest and poor means for their solution which the classic experiment of creating a conditional (secretory or motor) reflex provides. This discordance becomes more and more clear as reflexology turns from the study of the most elementary links between man and his environment (correlative activity in its most primitive forms and occurrences) to the investigation of the most complex and diverse interrelations necessary for the detection of the fundamental laws of human behaviour.[1]

Here, outside the domain of the elementary and primitive, reflexology was left only with its general bare claim – equally well applicable to all forms of behaviour – that they constitute systems of conditional reflexes. But neither the specific details of each system, nor the laws of the combination of conditional reflexes into behavioural systems, nor the very complex interactions and the reflections of some systems on others, were clarified by this general, far too general statement and it did not even prepare the way for the scientific solution of these questions. Hence the declarative, schematic character of reflexological works when they state and solve problems of human behaviour that are somewhat more complex.

Classical reflexology sticks to its elaboration of the universal scientific principle, the law of Darwinian significance, and reduces everything to a common denominator. And precisely because this principle is too all-embracing and universal it does not yield a direct scientific means for the study of its particular and individual forms. After all, it is for a concrete science of human behaviour as impossible to confine itself to it as it is for concrete physics to confine itself to the principle of gravity. We need scales, we need our instruments and methods in order to appreciate the concrete, material, limited terrestrial world on the basis of this general principle. It is the same in reflexology (everything incites the science of behaviour to transcend the boundaries of the classic experiment and to search for other cognitive means).

And now the tendency to broaden the reflexological methods has not only clearly revealed itself, but the line this broadening will follow has taken shape as well. This line is directed towards the increasing approximation of and eventual definitive merging with the methods of investigation that were established in experimental psychology a long time ago. Although this sounds paradoxical with regard to such hostile disciplines, and although in this respect within the milieu of reflexologists themselves there is no complete unanimity and they assess experimental psychology completely differently – despite all this we may speak of this merging, of the creation of unified methods for the investigation of human behaviour, and therefore also of its unified scientific discipline, as if it were a fact that is realized before our eyes.

The short history of this approximation is as follows. Initially an electro-cutaneous stimulus was applied on the sole, which evoked a defensive reflex of the foot or the whole leg. After that Professor Protopopov[2] introduced a very essential change in the procedure – he changed the leg for the hand, reasoning that it is much more profitable to select the arm as a criterion for the reaction as it is the most perfect response apparatus, more finely tuned to the orienting reactions to the environment than the leg (cf. Prof. Protopopov, V. P., 1923, The methods of the reflexological investigation of man, *Zhurnal Psikhologii, Nevrologii i Psikhiatrii*, 3. Moscow–Petrograd: Gosudarstvennoe Izdatel'stvo). He argues extremely convincingly the importance of a suitable choice of responding apparatus for the reaction. Indeed, it is clear that if we choose the speech apparatus as the responding apparatus in the case of a stutterer or a mute, or with a dog the extremity of which the corresponding cortical motor centre has been removed, or, in general, an apparatus that is little or not suitable for the corresponding type of reaction (the leg of a person for grasping movements) – that in all these cases we will establish very little about the speed, accuracy and perfection of the animal's orientation, although the analysing and synthesizing functions of the nervous system are completely preserved. 'And indeed, the experiment proved', says Professor Protopopov, 'that the formation of conditional reflexes in the hand is reached much faster, the differentiation is also reached faster and is more stable' (ibid. [p. 22]). Moreover, the change in methods of the reflexological experiment makes it very much like the psychological ones. The hand of the subject is placed freely on a table and his fingers touch a plate through which runs an electric current.

Thus, if in the study of human reflexes we wish to go further than the establishment of a general principle and set ourselves the goal of studying the different types of reactions that determine behaviour, the choice of the reacting organ is a factor of vital importance. 'Man and animal have many responding apparatuses at their disposal, but undoubtedly they respond to the various environmental stimuli with those that are for them the most developed and most suitable for the given case', says Professor Protopopov.

Man runs away from danger with his legs, defends himself with his arms, etc. Of course, it is also possible to create a defensive synthesizing reflex in the foot, but if it is necessary to investigate not only the synthesizing function of the cerebral hemispheres as such

(= the general principle, LV), but also the degree of rapidity, accuracy and perfection of the orientation, then for this type of investigation it turns out not to be indifferent which type of responding apparatus to choose for observation. (ibid. [p. 18])

But in for a penny, in for a pound. Professor Protopopov has to confess that the reform cannot stop here.

Man has at his disposal an effector apparatus in that same motor area that is much more developed (than the arm), with the help of which he can establish a much broader link with the surrounding world – here I have in mind the speech apparatus . . . I think it already possible and useful to turn in reflexological investigations to the use of the object's speech, considering this latter as a specific case of those conditional links that determine the interrelation between man and his environment through his motor area (ibid. [p. 22]).

That speech has to be considered a system of conditional reflexes hardly needs any discussion: it is for reflexology almost a truism. The benefits that the use of speech can bring to reflexology by broadening and deepening the circle of the phenomena studied are also evident to everyone.

Thus, with respect to the reacting apparatus, there is no longer a disagreement and difference of opinion with psychology. Academician Pavlov pointed to the suitability of the salivary reflex in the dog as being the least voluntary, conscious. That was indeed extremely important as long as it regarded the solution of the principle as such of the conditional reflexes, the 'mental saliva' at the sight of food. But new tasks require new means, the advance forward requires a changed road map.

The second and more important circumstance is that the methods of reflexology stumbled upon 'certain facts' that are well known to every child. The process of stimulus discrimination is not quickly established in man. Much time is required for the established reflex to turn from generalized into differentiated, that is, for man to learn to react only to the main stimulus, and to inhibit his reactions to irrelevant ones. And here 'it turned out (my emphasis, LV) that by influencing the object with corresponding suitable speech it was possible to create both inhibition and excitation of the conditional reflexes' (ibid. [p. 16]). When we explain to a person that only one specific sound will be combined with the electric current and no others, discrimination is realized immediately. Through speech we can also evoke the inhibition of the conditional reflexes to the *main* stimulus and even of the unconditional reflex to an electric current – we only have to tell the subject not to withdraw his hand.

Thus, 'corresponding suitable speech' is included in the methods of the experiment in order to establish discrimination. But the same means can not only be used to evoke inhibition but also to stimulate the reflex activity. 'If we verbally suggest to the object to withdraw his hand after any signal', then the result will be nothing worse than in the case of a withdrawal of the hand after the electric current passed through the plate. 'We will always elicit the desired reaction' (ibid.). It is clear that from the point of view of reflexology the withdrawal of the hand after a verbal instruction is a conditional reflex too. And the whole difference between this conditional reflex and the one established with a reflex to an electric current is that here we have a *secondary* conditional reflex and there a *primary* one. But also Professor Protopopov acknowledges that this circumstance is rather to the credit of such methods. 'Undoubtedly', he says, 'in the future the reflexological investigation of man will primarily have to be carried out with secondary conditional reflexes' (ibid. [p. 22]). And, indeed, is it not evident that in analysing human behaviour the most essential aspect – both quantitatively and qualitatively – is precisely the *superreflexes*, and that precisely they explain behaviour in its statics and dynamics?

But with these two assumptions, (1) the stimulation and limitation (differentiation) of reactions with the help of verbal instruction; (2) the use of all sorts of reactions including verbal, speech ones, we enter fully the area of the methods of experimental psychology.

Twice in the quoted historical article Professor Protopopov raises this issue. He says: 'The set-up of the experiments in the given case . . . is fully identical to the one used for a long time in experimental psychology in the investigation of the so-called simple psychological reactions'. He further includes 'various modifications in the set-up of the experiments. It is, for example, possible to use the so-called associative experiment of Jung for reflexological goals and, with the help of it, to take account of not only the present object, but to detect the traces of earlier stimuli, including inhibited ones as well' (ibid.).

Turning with such resolution from the classical experiment of reflexology to the very rich variety of psychological experimentation – so far forbidden for physiologists – outlining with great courage new roads and methods for reflexology, Professor Protopopov, for all his high assessment of the psychological experiment, leaves *two extremely essential points* unsaid. The present article is devoted to the foundation and defence of these points.

The first point concerns the techniques and methods of investigation, the second one the principles and goals of the two (?) sciences. Both are intimately connected with each other and both are connected with an essential misunderstanding that obscures the problem. The acknowledgement of both of these remaining points is dictated both by the logically inevitable conclusions from the tenets already accepted by reflexology and by the next step that is already implied by the whole line of development of these methods and which will be taken in the very near future.

What is left that prevents the final and complete coincidence and merging of the methods of the psychological and reflexological experiment? In Professor Protopopov's understanding of the problem *only one thing*: the interrogation of the subject, his verbal account of the course of some aspects of the processes and reactions that cannot be perceived by the experimenters in another way, the utterance, the testimony of the object of the experiment himself. It would seem that the root of the difference of opinion is to be found here. Reflexologists are not against making this difference of opinion a principal and decisive one.

Thereby they connect it with the second question, that of the different goals of the two sciences. Professor Protopopov not once mentions the interrogation of the subject.

Academician Bekhterev frequently says that 'from the standpoint of reflexology subjective investigation is permissible only on oneself' (V. M. Bekhterev, 1923: *General Foundations of the Reflexology of Man*, Gosudarstvennoe Izdatel'stvo; chapter XVIII; [1932, pp. 61–2; p. 220]).[3] Meanwhile, *precisely from the point of view of the completeness of the reflexological investigation* it is necessary to introduce the interrogation of the subject. Indeed, the person's behaviour and the creation of new conditional reactions is not only determined by the exposed (manifest), complete, fully disclosed reactions, but also by reflexes that are not demonstrated in their external part, that are half-inhibited, interrupted. Following Sechenov academician Bekhterev demonstrates that a thought is only an inhibited reflex, a reflex that is non-manifest, interrupted after two-thirds; verbal thinking, in particular, is the most frequent case of a non-manifest speech reflex.[4]

One may ask why it is allowed to study complete speech reflexes and even to put great hopes on this area, and why it is forbidden to take account of these same reflexes when they are inhibited, not exposed in their external part, but nevertheless undoubtedly exist objectively. When I pronounce aloud, audible for the experimenter, the word 'evening', then this word that comes to my mind by association is taken into account as a verbal reaction = a conditional reflex. But when I pronounce it inaudibly, for myself, when *I think it*, does it really stop being a reflex and change its nature? And where is the *boundary* between the pronounced and the unpronounced word? When the lips started moving, when I whispered, but inaudibly for the experimenter, what then? Can he ask me to repeat this word aloud, or will that be a subjective method, self-observation and other forbidden things? When he can (and with this, probably, almost everybody will agree), then why can't he ask one to pronounce aloud a word that was pronounced *in thought*, that is, without the movement of the lips and the whispering – for it still was and remains a motor reaction, a conditional reaction, without which there would be no thought. And this is already an interrogation, an utterance of the subject, his verbal testimony and declaration about reactions that *undoubtedly objectively existed* but were not manifest, not perceived by the experimenter's ear (here we have the sole difference between thoughts and speech, only this!). We can convince ourselves in many ways that they existed, existed objectively with all the signs of material being. And what is most important, they themselves will take care to convince us of their existence. They will *express themselves* with such a force and vividness that they *force* the experimenter to take them into account, or to refrain fully from the study of such streams of reactions in which they pop up. And are there many of those processes of reactions, of those courses of conditional reflexes in which non-manifest reflexes (= thoughts) would not pop up? Thus, either we refrain from the study of human behaviour in its most essential forms, or we introduce the obligatory registration of these non-manifest reflexes into our experiment. Reflexology has to study both thought and the whole mind if it wishes to understand behaviour. The mind is only inhibited movement, and what is objective is not only what can be felt and seen by everyone. That which is only visible through the microscope or telescope or with x-rays is objective too. Inhibited reflexes are equally objective.

Academician Bekhterev [1932, p. 411] himself points out that the results of the Würzburg school in the area of 'pure thought', in the highest spheres of the mind, essentially coincide with what we know about conditional reflexes. And Professor Krol' ('Thinking and speech', official talk at the State Institute in Minsk – 'Trudy BGU', vol. 2) openly says that the new phenomena detected by the Würzburg investigations in the area of imageless and non-verbal thinking are nothing other than Pavlovian conditional reflexes.[5] And much sophisticated work in the study of reports and verbal testimonies of subjects was required in order to establish that the act of thought itself cannot be perceived through self-observation, that it is found ready-made, that one cannot account for it, i.e. that it is a pure reflex.

But it is evident that the role of these verbal reports, of this interrogation, and its meaning for both reflexological and psychological investigations does not fully coincide with the ones attributed to them at times by subjective psychologists. How do psychologists–objectivists have to look at them and what is their place and meaning in the system of scientifically verified and rigorous experimentation?

Reflexes do not exist separately, do not act helter-skelter, but club together in complexes, in systems, in complex groups and formations that determine human behaviour. The laws of composition of reflexes into complexes, the types of these formations, the sorts and forms of interaction within them and the interaction between whole systems – all these questions have paramount meaning for the most acute problems of the scientific psychology of behaviour. The theory of reflexes is only in its beginning, and all these areas still remain to be investigated. But already now we may speak, as if it were a fact, about the undeniable interaction of different systems of reflexes, about the *reflection* [interpenetration] of some systems on others, and we can even in general and rough traits provide a preliminary clarification of the mechanism of this reflection. *The response part of each reflex (movement, secretion) becomes itself a stimulus for a new reflex from the same system or another system.*

Although I never came across such a formulation in any of the works of the reflexologists, its truth is so evident that it is evidently only omitted because it is tacitly implied and accepted by everybody. The dog reacts to hydrochloric acid by salivating (a reflex), but the saliva itself is a new stimulus for the reflex of swallowing or rejecting it. In free association I pronounce 'nasturtium' to the word stimulus 'rose' – this is a reflex, but it also constitutes a stimulus for the next word 'buttercup'. (This is all within one system or between related, interacting systems.) The howling of a wolf elicits, as a stimulus, the somatic and mimic reflexes of fear in me; my changed respiration, my palpitation, my trembling, my dry throat (the reflexes) force me to say: I am afraid. Thus, a reflex can play the role of stimulus with regard to another reflex of the same or another system and elicit it in the same way as an extraneous stimulus. And in this respect the association of reflexes is evidently fully determined by all the laws governing the formation of conditional reflexes. A reflex is linked to another reflex according to the law of conditional reflexes, and will under certain circumstances become its conditional stimulus. This is the obvious and fundamental first law of the association of reflexes.

This mechanism also leads us to a very rough and global understanding of the (objective) meaning that verbal reports of the subject may have for scientific investigation. Non-manifest reflexes (mute/silent speech), internal reflexes which are not accessible to direct observation by the observer can often be exposed indirectly, in a mediated way, via the reflexes that are accessible to observation and for which they form the stimuli. Through the presence of a full reflex (a word) we judge about the presence of a corresponding stimulus, which in this case plays a *double* role: of stimulus for the full reflex and of reflex to a preceding stimulus. Taking into account the gigantic, colossal role that precisely the mind (that is, the non-manifest group of reflexes) plays in the system of behaviour, it would be suicidal to refrain from exposing it through the indirect path of its reflection [bearing] on other systems of reflexes. (Recall academician Bekhterev's theory about the internal, external–internal etc. reflexes. All the more as we often have internal stimuli hidden from us, hiding in somatic processes, but which can nevertheless be exposed via the reflexes they elicit. The logic is the same here, as is the line of thought and the proof.)

In this understanding the report of the subject is not at all an act of self-observation that as it were puts a spoke in the wheels of scientifically objective investigation. *No self-observation whatsoever*. The subject is not put in the position of an observer, does not help the experimenter to observe reflexes hidden to him. The subject *fully* remains – also in his own account – the *object* of the experiment, but in the experiment itself some changes, a transformation, are introduced through this interrogation. A new stimulus (the new interrogation), a new reflex is introduced that allows us to judge the unclarified parts of the foregoing. In this respect the whole experiment is as it were filtered through a double objective.

Indeed awareness itself, or the possibility of becoming conscious of our acts and mental states, must evidently be understood, first of all, as a system of transmission mechanisms from some reflexes to others, which functions properly in each conscious moment. The more correctly each internal reflex, as a stimulus, elicits a whole series of other reflexes from other systems, is transmitted to other systems, the better we are capable of *accounting* for ourselves and others for the experienced, the more consciously it is experienced (felt, fixed in words, etc.). 'To account for' means to translate some reflexes into others. The psychological unconscious stands for reflexes that are not transmitted to other systems. Endlessly varied degrees of awareness, that is, interactions of systems included in the system of the acting reflex, are possible. The consciousness of one's experiences does not stand for anything other than their being changed into an object (a stimulus) for other experiences. Consciousness is the experience of experiences in precisely the same way as experience is simply the experience of objects. But precisely this, the capacity of the reflex (the experience of an object) to be a stimulus (the object of an experience) for a new reflex (a new experience) – this mechanism of awareness is the mechanism of the transmission of reflexes from one system to another.

It is approximately the same as what academician Bekhterev [1932, p. 44; pp. 421–2] calls the accountable and non-accountable reflexes. The results of the investigations of the Würzburg school speak, in particular, in favour of such an understanding of awareness. They established, among other things, the unobservability of the thought act itself – 'one cannot think a thought' – which escapes from perception, that is, cannot itself be the object of perception (the stimulus), because here we speak about phenomena of a different order and a different nature than the other mental processes, which can be observed and perceived (= can serve as stimuli for other systems). And the act of thought, the act of consciousness is in our opinion not a reflex, that is, it cannot also be a stimulus, but it is *the transmission mechanism between systems of reflexes.*

Of course, in such an understanding, which makes a *principled* and radical methodological distinction between the verbal report of the subject and his self-observation, the scientific nature of the instruction and interrogation also changes in a most radical way. The instruction does not suggest the subject do part of the observation himself, to split his attention and direct it to his own experiences. *Nothing of the sort.* The instruction, as a system of conditional reflexes, as a preliminary, elicits the reflexes of the set necessary for the experiment, which determine the further course of the reactions, and the set reflexes of the transmission mechanisms, precisely those which have to be used in the course of the experiment. Here the instruction regarding the secondary, reflected reflexes in principle differs not at all from the instruction regarding primary reflexes. In the first case: say the word which you just pronounced for yourself. In the second: withdraw your hand.

Further: the interrogation itself is not any more the *questioning* of the subject about his experiences. The case changes principally and radically. The subject is not any more a witness testifying about a crime, which he witnessed as an eyewitness (his role earlier), but the criminal himself and – what is most important – at the very moment of the crime. Not interrogation *after* the experiment, when the experiment is finished but interrogation as the continuation of the experiment, as its organic inherent part, as the experiment itself. Interrogation is absolutely inseparable from the first part and merely utilizes the experimental data in the process of the experiment itself.

The interrogation is no superstructure on the experiment but the experiment itself which has not yet been finished and still continues. The interrogation has to be composed, therefore, not like conversation, speech, an interrogation by the experimenter, but as a *system of stimuli* with an accurate registration of each sound, with the strictest choice of only those reflected systems of reflexes, which in the given experiment can have an absolutely trustworthy, scientific and objective meaning. This is why each system of modifications of the interrogation ( to take the subject unawares, a partial method, etc.) has great meaning. A strictly objective system and methods of interrogation have to be created as parts of the stimuli introduced in the experiment. And, of course, non-organized self-observation, as most of its testimony, can have no objective meaning. One has to know about what one can ask. In the case of the vagueness of words, definitions, terms and concepts we cannot in an objectively trustworthy way connect the testimony of the subject about 'a slight feeling of difficulty' with the objective reflex-stimulus that elicited that testimony. But the testimony of the subject – 'at the sound "thunder" I thought "lightning"' – can have a perfectly objective meaning which can indirectly establish that to the word 'thunder' the subject reacted with the non-manifest reflex 'lightning'. Thus, a radical reform of the methods of the interrogation and instruction is needed which will take into account the testimony of the subject. I claim that in each particular case such perfectly objective methods are possible, which will turn the interrogation of the subject into a perfectly accurate scientific experiment.

Here I wish to raise two points: one restricting what was said before, the other extending its meaning.

The restricted sense of these claims is clear of itself: this modification of the experiment is applicable to the adult, normal person, who can understand and speak our language. Neither with the newly born infant, nor with the mental patient, nor with the criminal, who hides something, can we conduct an interrogation. We will not do it precisely because with them the interlacing of the systems of reflexes (consciousness), the transmission of reflexes to the speech system, is either not developed, disturbed by a disease or inhibited and suppressed by other, more powerful set reflexes. But for the adult, normal person who has of his own free will agreed to the experiment this experiment is indispensable.

Indeed, in man a group of reflexes that we should correctly call the system of reflexes of social contact (A. Zalkind) easily stands out.[6] These are reflexes to stimuli that in their turn can be created by man. The word that is heard is a stimulus, the pronounced word a reflex that creates the same stimulus. These reversible reflexes, that create the basis for consciousness (the interlacing of the reflexes), also serve as the basis of social interaction and the collective co-ordination of behaviour, which, by the way, points to the social origin of consciousness. From the whole mass of stimuli one group clearly stands out for me, the group of social stimuli, coming from people; it stands out because I myself can reconstruct these stimuli, because they very soon become reversible for me, and thus determine my behaviour *in another way* from all others. They make me comparable, identical with myself. The source of social behaviour and consciousness also lies in speech in the broad sense of the word. Speech is on the one hand a system of reflexes of social contact and on the other hand primarily a system of reflexes of consciousness, that is, for the reflection of the influence of other systems.

That is why the key to the solution of the problem of the external Ego, of the cognition of another person's mind, lies here. The mechanism of consciousness of the self (self-consciousness) and the cognition of others is the same; we are conscious of ourselves because we are conscious of others, and with the same method as we are conscious of others, because we are the same *vis-à-vis* ourselves as others *vis-à-vis* us. We are conscious of ourselves only to the extent that we are another to ourselves, that is, to the extent that we can again perceive our own reflexes as stimuli. There is in principle no difference in mechanism whatsoever between the fact that I can repeat aloud a word spoken silently and the fact that I can repeat a word spoken by another: both are reversible reflex-stimuli. That is why in the social contact between the experimenter and the subject, when this contact proceeds normally (with persons who are adult etc.), the system of speech reflexes has all the trustworthiness of a scientific fact for the experimenter provided that all conditions have been observed, and something absolutely correct has been selected, something absolutely needed and of which the connection with the reflexes under study has been taken into account by us beforehand.

The second, extended sense of what was said above can be most easily expressed as follows. The interrogation of the subject with the goal of a perfectly objective study and account of non-manifest reflexes is *an essential part of each* experimental investigation of a normal person in the waking state. I do not have in mind here the testimony of the self-observation of subjective experiences that academician Bekhterev rightly considers to have but supplementary, secondary, subsidiary meaning, but the objective part of the experiment that cannot be missed by *hardly any* experiment and that itself serves as a verifying instance which provides the sanction of trustworthiness to the results of the preceding part of the experiment. Indeed, compared to the complete reflexes mind in general plays a larger and larger role in higher organisms and man, and to not study it is to refrain from the study (precisely the objective study and not its one-sided, subjective carricature) of human behaviour. In experiments with intelligent persons *there is not one case* where the factor of inhibited reflexes does not in one or the other way determine the behaviour of the subject and could be completely eliminated from the phenomena under study and ignored. There is no experimental study of behaviour where the manifest reflexes are unaccompanied by reflexes that are not accessible to the eye or the ear. Therefore, there can be no case where we could refrain from this, albeit purely verificatory, part of the experiment. And in essence it, this element, is introduced by experimenters (it cannot be not introduced) but precisely as speech, as a conversation, which is not taken into account on the same scientific level as the other elements of the experiment.

When your subject tells you that he did not understand the instruction, do you really not take into account this speech reflex later as a clear testimony of the fact that your stimulus did not elicit the set reflexes you needed? And when you yourself ask the subject whether he understood the instruction, is not this natural precaution really an appeal to a complete reflecting reflex of the word 'yes' or 'no', as to a testimony about a series of inhibited reflexes? And the declaration of the subject 'I recalled something unpleasant' after a very delayed reaction, is it really not taken into account by the experimenter? Etc., etc. We could give thousands of examples of the *unscientific* use of this method, for the method cannot be avoided. And when a reaction is delayed unexpectedly and not in line with the other series of tests, would it really not be useful to turn to the subject ourselves with the question 'Were you thinking of something else during the experiment?' and to receive the answer 'Yes, I was all the time calculating whether in all places I received enough change today'? And not only in these cases, in these *accidents*, is it useful and essential to ask for a testimony from the subject. In order to determine the reflexes of his set, to take into account the essential hidden reflexes elicited by us, to check whether there were no extraneous reflexes – yes, for a thousand other reasons – it is necessary to introduce scientifically elaborated methods of interrogation instead of the talk, the conversation that inevitably pops up in the experiment. But, of course, these methods are in need of complex modifications in each particular case.

Curiously enough, to finish this topic and switch to another one intimately connected with it, the reflexologists who have fully and entirely accepted the methods of experimental psychology omit precisely this point, evidently because they think it superfluous and in principle without anything to do with objective methods, etc. In this respect volume four of *New Ideas in Medicine* (Petrograd: Obrazovanie, 1923) is very interesting. In a number of articles a new line of development in methods is outlined that goes in the same direction as that of Professor Protopopov, and with the same peculiarity – the exclusion of the interrogation.

Matters stand the same in practice. When it turned to experiments with humans the Pavlovian school reproduced all methods of psychology with the exception of interrogation. Would not this partially explain the meagreness of the conclusions, the poverty of the results of the investigations which we witnessed in this congress during the presentations about these experiments? What can they establish other than the general principle that has been established a long time ago and more eloquently, and the fact that in man reflexes can be created faster than in dogs? This is clear without any experiments. To ascert the obvious and to repeat the ABC remains the inevitable fate of all experimenters who do not wish to alter radically the methods of their investigation.

Here I have set myself the goal of creating a plan for the construction of a *unified* scientific–objective system of methods for the investigation of and experiment with human behaviour and to defend this attempt theoretically.

But this technical problem is intimately connected, as I have said already, with another difference of opinion of a theoretical nature which the reflexologists emphasize even when they acknowledge the methods of investigation shared with psychology. Professor Protopopov expresses himself as follows:

> The inclusion into these methods (of reflexology) of methods of investigation applied already a long time ago in experimental psychology . . . formed the result of the natural development of reflexology and does not at all imply the transformation of reflexology into psychology. The gradual perfection of the reflexological methods *by accident* (my emphasis, LV) led to forms of investigation that *only seen from the outside look like* the ones applied in psychology. The foundations of principle, the subject, and the goals of these two disciplines remain completely different. While psychology studies mental processes as spiritual experiences from their objective side . . .' (ibid.)

etc., etc. – the rest is well known to anyone who reads the booklets on reflexology.

It seems to me that it is not difficult to show that this rapprochement is *not accidental* and that the similarity in forms is *not only external*. To the extent that reflexology aspires to explain the *whole* behaviour of man it will inevitably have to deal with the same material as psychology. The question is as follows: can reflexology dismiss and fully ignore the mind as a system of non-manifest reflexes and interlacings of different systems? Is a scientific explanation of human behaviour possible without the mind? Does the psychology without a soul, the psychology without any metaphysics, have to be transformed into a psychology without a mind – into reflexology? Biologically speaking it would be absurd to suggest that the mind is completely unnecessary in the behavioural system. We would either have to accept that clear absurdity or deny the existence of the mind. But for this not even the most extreme physiologists are prepared – neither academician Pavlov, nor academician Bekhterev.

Academician Pavlov [1928/1963, p. 219] openly says that our subjective 'states are for us a reality of the first order, they give direction to our daily life, they determine the progress of human society. But it is one thing to live according to the subjective states and quite another to analyse their mechanism in a purely scientific way' (*Twenty Years of Experience with the Objective Study of Higher Nervous Activity*, Petrograd, 1923).[7] Thus, there is a reality of the first order that gives direction to our daily life – this is the most important – and yet the objective study of higher nervous activity (behaviour) can ignore this reality that gives direction to our behaviour, this mind.

'Only one thing in life', says academician Pavlov, 'is of actual interest for us – our psychical experience . . . What interests man most of all is his consciousness, the torments of consciousness' (ibid. [1928/1963, p. 80]). And academician Pavlov himself acknowledges that 'we cannot ignore them (the mental phenomena), because they are intimately connected with the physiological phenomena that determine the integral functioning of the organ' (ibid.). After this can we refrain from the study of the mind? Academician Pavlov himself very correctly defines the role of each science when he says that reflexology builds the foundation of nervous activity and psychology the higher superstructure:

> And as the simple and elementary is understandable without the complex, whereas the complex cannot be explained without the elementary, it follows that our position is better, for our investigations, our success, do not in any way depend on their investigations. On the contrary, it seems to me that our investigations should have great significance for psychologists, as they eventually will have to lay the main foundation of the psychological building (ibid. [1928/1963, p. 113]).

Any psychologist will subscribe to that: reflexology is the general principle, the foundation. *Until now*, while the building of the foundation common to animals and man was in process, while we were talking of the simple and elementary, there was no need to take the mind into account. But this is a temporary phenomenon: when the 20 years of experience will have become 30 years the situation will change. That is what I said in the beginning, that the crisis of methods in reflexology begins precisely when they turn from the foundation, from the elementary and simple, to the superstructure, to the complex and subtle.

Academician Bekhterev expresses himself even more decidedly and openly and, therefore, takes a view that is still more intrinsically inconsistent and contradictory. 'It would be big mistake', he says, 'to regard subjective processes as completely superfluous or subsidiary phenomena in nature (epiphenomena), for we know that everything superfluous in nature becomes atrophied and obliterated, whereas our own experience tells us that the subjective phenomena reach their highest development in the most complex processes of correlative activity' (*General Foundations of the Reflexology of Man*, Gosudarstvennoe Izdatel'stvo, 1923; [1932; p. 103]).

Is it possible, one may ask, to exclude the study of those phenomena that reach their highest development in the most complex processes of correlative activity in that science that has *precisely* this correlative activity as its subject of study? But academician Bekhterev does not exclude subjective psychology and draws a boundary line between it and reflexology. For it is clear to everyone, that here only one of two things is possible: (1) a complete explanation of the correlative activity without a mind – this is accepted by academician Bekhterev – and then the mind is made into a superfluous, unnecessary phenomenon – which Bekhterev denies; (2) or such an explanation is impossible – is it possible then to accept a subjective psychology and mark it off from a science of behaviour, etc? Accepting neither of the two alternatives academician Bekhterev talks about the relation between the two sciences, about the possible rapprochement in the future, 'but as for this the time has not yet come. We can for the time being defend the point of view of the close interaction of one and the other discipline' (ibid., first edition).

Further, academician Bekhterev speaks about 'the possible and even inevitable future construction of a reflexology with particular consideration for subjective phenomena' (ibid., second edition [1932, p. 380]). But if the mind is inseparable from correlative activity and reaches its highest development precisely in its highest forms – how can we then study them separately? That is only possible when we assume that both sides of the matter are heterogeneous and essentially different, which for a long time has been defended by psychology. But academician Bekhterev dismisses the theory of psychological parallelism and interaction and claims precisely the unity of mental and nervous processes.

Academician Bekhterev often speaks about the relation between subjective (mind) and objective phenomena but all the time clearly defends a dualistic point of view. And in essence, *dualism* is the real name of academician Pavlov's and Bekhterev's point of view. For Bekhterev, experimental psychology is unacceptable precisely because it studies the internal world of the mind with the method of self-observation. Academician Bekhterev wishes to consider its results irrespective of the processes of consciousness. And about the methods he openly says that reflexology 'uses its own strictly objective methods' (ibid. [1932, p. 220]). With regard to methods, however, we have seen that reflexology itself acknowledges their complete coincidence with the psychological methods.

Thus, two sciences with *the same* subject of investigation – the behaviour of man – and that use *the same methods*, nevertheless, despite everything, remain different sciences.[8] What prevents them from merging? 'Subjective or mental phenomena' the reflexologists repeat in a thousand ways. But is the mind equivalent to subjective phenomena? In their views on this question – the decisive question – the reflexologists defend purely idealistic points of view and a dualism which might more correctly be called an idealism turned upside down. For academicians Pavlov and Bekhterev they are non-spatial and non-causal phenomena – they have no objective existence *whatsoever* as they can only be studied on oneself. But both Bekhterev and Pavlov know that they rule our life. Nevertheless they consider these phenomena, the mind, to be something different from the reflexes, something which has to be studied separately, and independently of which we have to study the reflexes. This is of course materialism of the purest order – to ignore the mind, but it is materialism only in its own area; outside of it is idealism of the purest order – to single out the mind and its study from the general system of human behaviour.

*Mind without behaviour is as impossible as behaviour without mind,* if only because they are the same. Subjective states, mental phenomena exist, according to academician Bekhterev, in the case of an electric potential, in the case of reflexes (NB!) of concentration connected with the inhibition of a nervous current, in the case where new connections are set going – what kind of mysterious phenomena are they? Is it not clear now that they can be completely and fully reduced to reactions of the organism, to reactions that are reflected by other systems of reflexes – by speech, by feelings (mimic–somatic reflexes), etc. Psychology has to state and solve the problem of consciousness by saying that it is the interaction, the reflection, the mutual stimulation of various systems of reflexes. It is what is transmitted in the form of a stimulus to other systems and elicits a response in them. Consciousness is a response apparatus.

That is why subjective experiences are only accessible to me – only I perceive my own reflexes as stimuli. In this sense James, who showed in a brilliant analysis that nothing forces us to accept the fact of the existence of consciousness as something distinguished from the world, is profoundly right although he denied neither our experiences, nor the awareness of them ('Does consciousness exist?').[9] The whole difference between consciousness and the world (between the reflex to a reflex and a reflex to stimuli) is only in the context of the phenomena. In the context of stimuli it is the world, in the context of my reflexes it is consciousness. This window is an object (the stimulus of my reflexes), the same window with the same qualities is my sensation (a reflex transmitted to other systems). Consciousness is only the reflex of reflexes.

To claim that consciousness too has to be understood as a reaction of the organism to its own reactions, one has to be a bigger reflexologist than Pavlov himself. So be it, if one wishes to be consistent one sometimes has to raise objections to half-heartedness and be a bigger papist than the pope, a bigger royalist than the king. Kings are not always royalists.

When reflexology excludes mental phenomena from the circle of its investigations because they do not fall under its jurisdiction, it acts just like idealistic psychologists who study the mind as having nothing whatsoever to do with anything else, as an isolated world. By the way, psychology hardly ever excluded from its jurisdiction on principle the objective side of mental processes and did not isolate the circle of internal life [viewed] as a desert island of the spirit. Subjective states in themselves – out of space and causality – do not exist. Therefore a science studying them cannot exist either. But to study the behaviour of man without mind as reflexology wishes to do is as impossible as to study mind without behaviour. There is no place, consequently, for two different sciences. And it does not require great perspicacity to see that the mind is the same correlative activity, that consciousness is correlative activity within the organism itself, within the nervous system, correlative activity of the human body with itself.

The contemporary state of both branches of knowledge urgently raises the question of the necessity and fruitfulness of a complete merging of both sciences. Psychology experiences a most serious crisis both in the West and in the USSR. 'A heap of raw material', it was called by James. The contemporary state of the psychologist is compared by a Russian author to that of Priam on the ruins of Troy. Everything collapsed – that is the result of a crisis that was not confined to Russia (cf. N. Lange, 'Psychology', in *The Results of Science*).[10] But reflexology, having built the foundation, reached a dead end too. The two sciences cannot manage without each other. It is imperative and vital to elaborate common scientifically objective methods, a common formulation of the most important problems that each science treats separately and that can no more be posed, let alone solved. And isn't it clear that the superstructure cannot be built except on the foundation, but that the builders of the foundation too, having finished it, cannot lay another stone without checking it against the principles and the character of the building to be erected?

We have to speak openly. The enigmas of consciousness, the enigmas of the mind cannot be avoided with any methodological tricks or subterfuges of principle. You cannot cheat them. James asked whether consciousness exists and answered that breathing exists, of this he was convinced, but about consciousness he was in doubt. But that is an epistemological statement of the problem. Psychologically speaking consciousness is an indisputable fact, a primary reality, a fact of the greatest significance, and not a secondary or accidental one. About this there is no dispute. Thus, we should have and might have *put aside* the problem, but not have *removed* it. As long as in the new psychology one does not make both ends meet, the problem of consciousness will not be stated clearly and fearlessly and it will not be solved in an experimentally objective way. On which level do conscious indications of reflexes evolve, what is their nervous mechanism, the details of their course, their biological sense? These questions we have to pose, and we have to prepare to work on them, to solve them in an empirical way. The only thing is to state the problem correctly and timely, and then the solution will sooner or later be found. Academician Bekhterev in his 'energetic' enthusiasm talks to the point of panpsychism, stating that plants and animals are animated beings. In another place he cannot bring himself to repudiate the hypothesis about a soul.[11] And in such primitive ignorance with respect to the mind reflexology will remain as long as it steers clear of the mind and isolates itself in the narrow circle of *physiological materialism*. To be a materialist in physiology is not difficult – try to be it in psychology and if you cannot, you will remain an idealist.

Quite recently the issue of self-observation and its role in psychological investigation sharpened acutely under the influence of two facts. On the one hand objective psychology, which apparently initially was inclined to sweep aside introspection completely and thoroughly, begins lately to try to find the *objective* meaning of what is called introspection. Watson, Weiss[12] and others spoke about 'verbalized behaviour' and they link introspection with the functioning of this verbal side of our behaviour; others talk about 'introspective behaviour', about 'symptomatic speech' behaviour, etc. On the other hand the new current in German psychology, the so-called *Gestalt-psychologie* (Köhler, Koffka, Wertheimer and others), which acquired tremendous influence in the last three to four years, raised sharp criticisms on both fronts, accusing both empirical psychology and behaviourism of the same sin – not to be able to study the real, daily behaviour of man with a *single* accepted method (objective or subjective).

Both of these facts add new complications to the question of the value of self-observation and therefore compel us to carry out a *systematic* examination of those essentially different forms of self-observation that are used by the three sides in the debate. The following lines present an attempt to systematize this question. But as a preliminary we make some general remarks.

It is first of all remarkable that in this new complication of the problem attempts to solve it take place during a more and more explicit crisis within empirical psychology itself. Nothing could be more false than the attempt to picture the crisis that breaks up Russian science into two camps as a local Russian crisis. The crisis in psychology now takes place on a worldwide scale. The rise of the psychological school of *Gestalt-theorie*, which came from the depths of empirical psychology, clearly testifies to this. Of what do these psychologists accuse introspection? Essentially, that in using this method of investigation the mental phenomena inevitably *become* subjective because introspection, which requires analytical attention, always isolates contents from their own connections and inserts them into a new connection – 'the connection of the subject, the Ego' [Koffka, 1924, p. 151].[13] Using this method the experience inevitably *becomes* subjective. Koffka compares introspection which can only study *clear* experience with a pair of glasses and a magnifying glass, which we utilize when we cannot read a letter. But whereas a magnifying glass does not alter the object but helps to observe it more clearly, introspection *changes* the very object of observation. When we compare weights, Koffka [1924, p. 151] says, the real psychological description in this view should not be 'this weight is heavier than that', but 'my sensation of tension is now stronger than before'. In this way such a method of study *transforms* that which is objective in itself into something subjective.

The new psychologists acknowledge the heroic bankruptcy of the Würzburg school and the impotence of empirical (experimental) psychology as a whole. It is true, these psychologists also acknowledge the futility of the purely objective method. These psychologists put forward a functional and integrative point of view. For them the conscious processes 'are only part-processes of larger wholes' [Koffka, 1924, p. 160], and therefore we may subject our ideas to a functional verification by the objective facts by following 'the conscious part of a larger process-whole beyond its conscious limits' [Koffka, 1924, p. 160]. A psychology, which accepts that self-observation is not the main, most important method of psychology, speaks only about real, about reliable self-observation, which is tested by the consequences that functionally follow from it and is confirmed by the facts.

Thus we see that while on the one hand Russian reflexology and American behaviourism attempt to find 'objective self-observation' the best representatives of empirical psychology seek for 'real, reliable self-observation' as well.

In order to answer the question of what it involves it is necessary to systematize all forms of self-observation and to consider each one separately. We can distinguish five main forms.

1   The instruction to the subject. This is, of course, partially introspection for it presupposes the internal conscious organization of the subject's behaviour. He who attempts to avoid it in experiments with man is in error, for he changes the manifest and accountable instruction for the self-instruction of the subject, an instruction which is suggested by the circumstances of the experiment, etc. Hardly anyone will now dispute the necessity of instruction.

2   The utterances of the subject concerning the external object. Two circles are shown: 'this one is blue, that one is white'. Such a form of introspection, in particular when it is verified by the functional change of a series of stimuli and a series of utterances (not one blue circle, but a series of blue circles that become gradually darker or lighter), can also be reliable.

3   The utterances of the subject concerning his own internal reactions: I have pain, I like it, etc. This is a less reliable form of introspection; however, it can be objectively verified and can be accepted.

4   The disclosure of a hidden reaction. The subject mentions a number he has thought of; tells how his tongue lies in his mouth; repeats a word he has thought of, etc. This is that form of indirect disclosure of a reaction which we defended in this article.

5   Finally, the detailed descriptions of his internal states by the subject (the Würzburg method). This is the type of introspection that is most unreliable and most difficult to verify. Here the subject is put in the position of an observer; he is the observer ('observer' as the English psychologists say), the subject, and not

the object of the experiment; the experimenter only observes and records what happens. Here, instead of facts we get ready-made theories.

It seems to me that the question of the scientific reliability of self-observation can only be solved in a way similar to the practical value of the testimonies given by the victim and the culprit in an inquest. Both are partial, we know that *a priori*, and therefore they include elements of deception, maybe they are completely false. Therefore it would be madness to rely on them. But does this mean that in a lawsuit we do not have to listen to them at all and only have to interrogate the witnesses? This would be madness as well. We listen to the accused and the victim, verify, compare, turn to the material evidence, documents, traces, testimonies of the witnesses (here too we may have false evidence) – and that is how we establish a fact.

We should not forget that there are whole sciences that cannot study their subject through direct observation.[14] The historian and the geologist reconstruct the facts (which already do not exist) indirectly, and nevertheless in the end *they study the facts that have been*, not the traces or documents that remained and were preserved. Similarly, the psychologist is often in the position of the historian and the geologist. Then he acts like a detective who brings to light a crime he never witnessed.

## Notes

The paper is based on a talk presented at the combined session of the psychological and reflexological sections of the 2nd All-Russian congress on psychoneurology in Leningrad, 6 January, 1924 [original footnote]. The paper was first published as Vygotsky, L. S. 1926: Metodika refleksologicheskogo i psikhologicheskogo issledovanija. In K. N. Kornilov (ed.), *Problemy sovremennoj psikhologii* (pp. 26–46). Leningrad: Gosudarstvennoe Izdatel'stvo. The background of this paper can be found on pp. 39–43 of Van der Veer, R. and Valsiner, J. 1991: *Understanding Vygotsky: a quest for synthesis*. Oxford: Blackwell Publishers.

1  'Correlative activity' ('sootnositel'naja dejatel'nost') was a term introduced by Bekhterev to designate any activities bound up with the establishment of the relation of an organism to its environment and which replaced such 'subjective' terms as 'psychical' or 'neuro-psychical' functions. See Bekhterev's explanation of the term in Bekhterev, V. M. 1932: *General Principles of Human Reflexology*. New York: International Publishers; p. 17.

2  Protopopov, V. P. (1880–1957). Soviet psychiatrist.

3  Bekhterev, V. M. (1867–1927). Russian physiologist, neurologist and psychologist. Founder of reflexology. The fourth edition of the book was translated into English as Bekhterev, V. M. 1932: *General Principles of Human Reflexology*. New York: International Publishers. The page numbers refer to this edition.

4  Sechenov, I. M. (1829–1905). Russian physiologist and psychologist. See Sechenov, I. 1866/1965: *Reflexes of the Brain*, p. 86. Cambridge, MA: MIT Press.

5  Krol', M. B. (1869–1939), Soviet neurologist.

6  Zalkind, A. B. (1888–1936). Soviet pedagogue and psychologist.

7   Here and in the following page numbers refer to Pavlov, I. P. 1928/1963: *Lectures on Conditioned Reflexes*. New York: International Publishers.

8   In the report about the conference, published in the volume *Recent Developments in Reflexology* (Gosudarstvennoe Izdatel'stvo, 1925), in the commentary to my talk it is said with respect to this idea that the author 'again attempted to erase the border between the reflexological and psychological approach, even making some remarks concerning reflexology which has fallen into intrinsic contradictions' (p. 359). Instead of refuting this idea the reviewer refers to the fact that 'the speaker is a psychologist who, apart from that, also attempts to assimilate the reflexological approach. The results speak for themselves'. A very eloquent passing over in silence! Although an accurate statement of my error would have been more appropriate, and needed [original footnote].

9   'Does consciousness exist?' See Burkhardt, F. H. (ed.) 1976: *The Works of William James: essays in radical empiricism* (pp. 3–19). Cambridge, MA: Harvard University Press. In contradistinction to Vygotsky, James did not refer to the reflex concept in his analysis.

10  Lange, N. N. (1858–1921), Russian psychologist.

11  Bekhterev was inclined to equate consciousness with the subjective states that accompany the inculcation of an association reflex. It followed that wherever the formation of association reflexes proved possible (e.g. in protozoa) one had to accept the existence of subjective processes. He also said that the irritability of tissue in general is associated with subjective processes, which led to the same result, that is, the hypothesis that unicellular organisms manifest a subjective aspect (cf. Bekhterev, V. M. 1932: *General Principles of Human Reflexology*. New York: International Publishers; pp. 70–5).

12  Weiss, A. (1879–1931), American psychologist.

13  Koffka, K. 1924: Introspection and the method of psychology. *The British Journal of Psychology*, 15, [149–161] [original footnote].

14  Cf. V. Ivanovsky, 'Methodological introduction into science and philosophy', 1923, pp. 199–200. The author points out that some psychologists objected to the introduction of the unconscious into psychology on the grounds that it cannot be directly observed. The psychologist–objectivist studies the phenomena of consciousness as indirectly as the previous psychologists studied the unconscious, by its traces, its manifestations, influences, etc. [original footnote]. Ivanovsky, V. N. (1867–1931), Russian philosopher and psychologist.

# 4

# The problem of the cultural behaviour of the child

## *Alexander Luria*

Man differs from animals in that he can make and use tools. This fact, recognized long ago, acquires a new meaning enormous in its bearing if we make it a starting point in working out the methods of child study from a psychological standpoint.

As a matter of fact, the tools used by man not only radically change his conditions of existence, they even react on him in that they effect a change in him and in his psychic condition. In the complicated inter-relations with his surroundings his organization is being differentiated and refined; his hand and his brain assume definite shapes, a series of complicated methods of conduct are being evolved, with the aid of which man adapts himself more perfectly to the surrounding world.

No development – that of the child included – in the condition of modern civilized society can be reduced merely to the development of natural inborn processes and the morphological changes conditioned by the same; it includes, moreover, that social change of civilized forms and methods which help the child in adapting itself to the conditions of the surrounding civilized community.

It is natural that these forms of cultural adaptations on the part of the child are far more dependent on the conditions of the environment in which the child was placed than on constitutional factors.

These methods and forms of conduct are instilled in him, first of all, owing to the demands made on him by his environment; these demands and conditions are precisely the factors which may either check or stimulate his development. In urging the child to work out new forms of adaptation, they may create sudden starts in his development. In fine, we obtain undoubtedly 'cultural formations' which play a most important part in the evolution of the child.

Modern psychology has, therefore, an important task to perform – to investigate the laws which govern the evolution of these cultural forms of adaptation, to establish that consecutiveness in which the predominance of certain manners and forms of cultural behaviour of the child is supplanted by others. In a word, we have to consider the *psychogenesis of the cultural forms of the child's behaviour*. No doubt psychology faces in this task a series of specific problems, the solution to which is hardly possible for a simple physiological investigation which limits its scope to the development of the natural forms of conduct. It is precisely in the investigation of the change of separate cultural habits that psychology can successfully reveal its biosocial character.

In realizing these tasks we inevitably take another road to that of the classical school psychology. Psychology in approaching the study of a child was mainly interested in the changes of individual functions in the process of natural growth and maturation of the child. Classical works were devoted to the study of the evolution of children's associations, their quickening and widening, to the child's memory, development of attention and of ideas. The authors strove everywhere to study first of all the quantitative increase in these functions in the process of a child's growth. We are interested mainly in other matters. We consider that the development of the child's conduct can be reduced to a series of transformations, that these transformations are due to the growing influence of cultural environment, the constant appearance of new cultural inventions and habits, and that each invention of a new 'artificial' habit involves a change of structure of the child's conduct. Compare the conduct of a pupil in his first year at school with that of a pre-school pupil. Compare the course of mental processes of these two, and you will note two structures essentially different in principle. Compare a village boy with another boy of the same age who lives in a town, and you will be struck by a huge difference in the mentality of both, the difference being not so much in the development of natural psychical functions (absolute memory, the quickness of reactions, etc.) *as in the subject matter of their cultural experience and those methods which are used by those two children in realizing their natural abilities.*

This example enables us to show exactly the bearing of the investigations undertaken by the psychologists of the new formation on the work of school psychology. School psychologists based themselves on the accurate measurements of memory in the artificial conditions of a laboratory, and in consequence arrived at the conclusion that memory develops very slowly during the course of the child's growth, and that sometimes we witness even the deterioration of natural memory. It looks as if there is no perceptible progress in this most important psychic function, and we are at a loss to understand that enormous widening of the intellectual life of the child (the practical memory of the child) which we cannot ignore. The aspect will radically change if we look at the *methods* by which the child uses its natural memory. We shall see that it is precisely these methods, manifold and various, complicated and organized, that draw the line between a schoolboy and a pre-school child, a civilized man and a savage, an intelligent person and one who is mentally undeveloped. By teaching the child such cultural methods, by encouraging his peculiar inventive capacities, we can in a short time achieve an extraordinary development of the given function, and this development can be explained only by the fact that the child has mastered his natural psychic abilities, that he has mobilized those functions which he hitherto did not know how to use.

The transition to civilized habits of conduct is thus reduced to the alteration in the main scheme of behaviour: instead of applying directly its natural function to the solution of a definite task, the child *puts in between that function and the task a certain auxiliary means*, a certain manner, by the medium of which the child manages to perform the task. If he wishes to remember a difficult series, he invents a conventional sign, and this sign, being wedged between *the task and memory*, assists in the better mastering of that task. The direct, natural use of the function is replaced by a complicated, cultural form. The simple reactive form of psychics is replaced by a complex 'instrumental' form.

This fact is the most important from our standpoint; it determines the technique we should apply in investigating the evolution of cultural forms of a child's behaviour.

If we desire to study that evolution by experiment, we can choose one of two methods. We can place a child in difficult situations, give him a task so difficult that he cannot solve it without the application of some special technical means. We are urging him to search for such means, to enter the field of inventions. In offering the child the corresponding material which he could utilize as such means, we are making such research visible and render it capable of being observed.

However, we know that at various stages of development a child can master different forms of methods. If our task is to find out which category of cultural methods and 'instruments of behaviour' can be mastered by a given child, we must substantially change our technique. We must place before that child a series of ready methods and watch to what extent these methods are up to him.

In both instances the process of using artificial methods is carried outwards; but in the first instance we set a problem and watch the child inventing a means of solving it, in the second case we set a ready method and watch how the child applies it. Both methods differ from school psychological experiments in that the forms are being investigated with the help of which the child masters his conduct and, furthermore, these methods are constructed on the principle of wedging between the task and its fulfillment an intermediate function – 'the executive instrument' on the principle of 'double stimulation'. It is precisely in view of this latter feature that we think it right to call this method 'the method of instrumentally psychological research'.

Along with the purely external methods which help the child in solving different problems, we must recognize the existence of a huge number of internal methods and habits evolved in school and which are due to character and surroundings; we place under this head all the child's habits connected with speech, thought, logic; in short, using the expression of Claparède, the whole of his 'inner technique'.

Our experimental task consists in demonstrating these forms of adaptation, in giving the child under examination not only the fundamental series of stimuli which copes with the problem set to him, but also a second series which plays a functionally different part and which serves him as an instrument in solving this problem. The problem of 'double stimulation' ('I shall tell you certain words by means of these signs – paper, pictures, etc.; you must remember them') serves to cause a new form of behaviour on the part of the examinee which is complicated by the functional use of the stimuli. In observing the various degrees of such methods we come nearest to the description of those phases of cultural development through which a child has to pass.

Our experiments are largely based on the classical investigations carried out by Köhler. That author has demonstrated that even animals (apes) are capable of instrumental use of the objects of the outer environment. Having studied the manifestations of the intellect at this primitive stage of development, he elucidated its dependence on the structure of the field of observation; the use of instruments and the success of mental operations of the ape depended on the relative situation of its aim and its instruments.

We observed in children the same dependence of primary intellectual operations on the outer form of the object, and we can suppose that it is precisely the conception of form which predetermines the success of the intellectual activity at the primary stages of development.

If we throw building blocks before a child haphazardly and make him count them, it will transpire that the task will not be so easy for the child. It will be different if we place these blocks in a definite form, let us say a cross, a square, etc.; then the child will be able to count the blocks quickly and without mistake as elements of a single system. Experience has taught us that the right system will enable a child of seven or eight to count. Let us place the blocks in the shape of two intersecting lines, in the shape of a cross; let us make the child count them and the following rule will always be observed: the child counts the block as many times as there are systems of which the block is part. Therefore that block at the crossing of a cross or at the intersection of two squares (see figure 4.1) will be counted twice, a block in a star forming part of three lines will be counted three times, etc. A child's counting system at that age entirely depends on the natural laws governing his field of observation; at that stage counting is a function of form. Only considerably later is the cultural process of counting emancipated from the field of observation, and the child counts correctly elements independently of their situation.

Sometimes the conception of form does not determine a child's counting; it simply takes the place of counting. Make a rectangle of four blocks (see figure 4.2) and ask

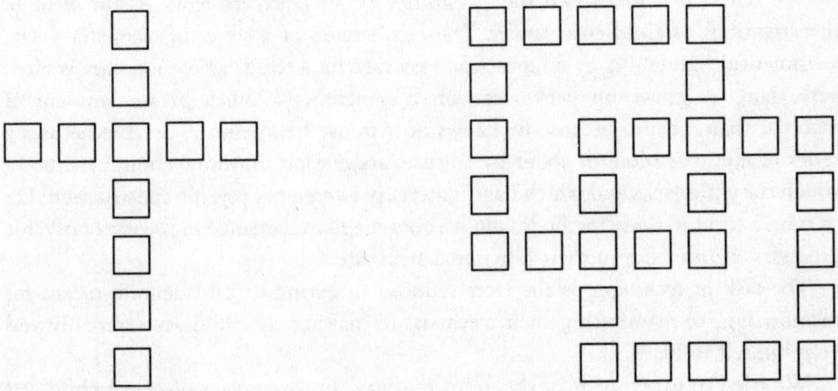

**Figure 4.1**

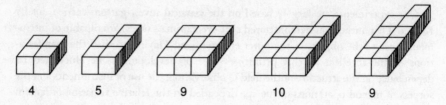

Figure 4.2

the child whether the number of blocks is odd or even. The child says at once that it is even. If there is an incomplete rectangle of five blocks, the child will also say at once that the number of blocks is odd. We observe the rapidity with which the child can answer these questions and arrive at the conclusion that it is due not to counting nor drawing any complicated conclusion, but to a simple conception of a regular (complete) or irregular (incomplete) form. To prove this let us offer a child of seven or eight nine blocks forming a regular square; he will say at once that the number is even; if we add a tenth block or change the form to make it irregular, the child will say that the number is odd. This is by no means merely a defective notion of odd and even, it is precisely that stage of development when cultural methods of counting are subservient to the natural laws of form.

How are we to examine methodically the origin of these children's cultural forms of adaptation? How can we make manifest their hidden mechanism? How can we evoke them in the process of experiment in order to master completely these processes? We are facing here a problem of great pedagogical importance. We must create in the process of experiment a model of cultural behaviour.

It is obvious that first we must put before a child a problem which he is incapable of solving and afterwards induce him to solve it by means of some methods which are brought to the surface and registered in detail.

We tried to demonstrate the possibility of such experiments in the field of investigations of children's *memory*. The recollection of a series of elements – say, arithmetical figures – is by no means an easy task for a child, whose memory is often very short. A grown-up person can often remember a much greater amount of material than a child, because he knows how to use his memory, because he uses a series of methods brought about by culture, association, mnemotechnical methods, which the child lacks and which have materially altered his psychic construction. Let us train a child in those methods, and we obtain a radical change in the use of psychic processes, a difference in their functional structure.

The task of technique is therefore reduced to giving a child definite means for memorizing, to manifesting such methods, to making the child act externally and help himself in his work.

We tried to experiment in the following way. In the process of play a child was given a series of ten figures to memorize, coupled with the task of repeating them in a given order. A series was given orally, and the child usually found that he could not memorize it. Then we gave him some material and asked him to use it for the purpose of memorizing these ten figures. A child was obviously in need of that material as a means of memorizing, making by that means certain signs and notes which stimulated him in the course of recollection. It was then a question of the necessity of somehow utilizing that object functionally, to invent in the process of experiment some cultural sign, some system of writing.

A child was given different materials: paper, strings, counters, blocks, pins, hailshot; the whole process of manipulation was taken outwards, the experiment was based on the principle of the functional use of stimuli, and we had an opportunity to observe how separate conditions, such as age, development of the child, the material offered, etc., influence the process of invention and the functional use of material offered.

These experiments of ours brought us face to face with the following fact; if the child passed from a simple, natural memory to artificial means of memorizing, the task of memorizing ten or even 15 figures in a definite order became easy and the whole structure of the process was reconstructed. Simple, natural memory was replaced by a system of signs and their subsequent reading, and the maximum work was usually shifted from recollection to a recognition of series.

However, this process was not equal for all ages in facility or structure; the older children were not only capable of *better* adapting themselves to our experiment, not only did their memory work better, but their remembrance was of a *substantially different kind*; in observing them we found that the development of the child not only affects his growth, but his *refitment* with new psychological habits.

Let us put the above-mentioned problem to a pre-school child of six or seven who cannot write or count in writing. We usually observe the following course: at first, the child does not retain in memory the series offered to him in the usual way and refuses to memorize it with the aid of a piece of paper or of a string. The functional application of the material offered is not clear to him; a piece of paper or a piece of string has nothing to do with the task given. The younger and backward children stop at that, and we find that the clearest indication of mental (cultural) backwardness is the *inability to use functionally the means at disposal*; backward children are incapable of grasping the conception of functional relations.

On the other hand, pre-school children, who have attained a higher stage of development, go farther; after some time (some require more, others less) the child guesses the possibility of utilizing paper for the purpose of memorizing and straightaway begins to use a method invented by himself. This is usually some system of *quantitative marks*: a child makes marks on the paper corresponding in number to the figure stated (six times for the figure six, twice for two), or else he tears off the corresponding number of bits or makes a corresponding number of knots on a bit of string.

This is a process which reproduces in an experimental fashion the string letter or the scoring sticks, etc., which were used in the early days of human culture, the only exception being that here the task of functional utilization of the material was set by us, whereas in the historical instance it was evolved under the influence of economic life and growing culture.

It is noteworthy that the invention does not take place at once, but, so to say, passes through two phases. At first the child guesses that he must make marks, but he does not guess how to make them distinguishable. He tears off bits of paper or counts hailshots and puts them in a heap; he makes knots, but leaves no intervals between them to denote figures. Obviously when he tries to reproduce them he finds himself helpless; his work was lost labour. Then, after some fruitless efforts, the child usually guesses that his notes must assume a different shape; he *differentiates* his marks in little heaps, in groups. Once the child has made that discovery, he outlines his work without difficulties, and can reproduce it after the lapse of several days; he has mastered the functional use of means and now can perform his task with the aid of any material put before him. Using objective methods the child increases enormously the productivity of his psychic activity.

We can easily discern in these experiments processes very much like those which Köhler observed among the apes (sudden decisions and 'Aha-Erlebnis', functional use of outside objects, the perpetuality of acquired habits, the changes of their structure).

In one or two sittings we have shown the child the way to use new methods and thereby have materially altered the course of his psychological processes and achieved a great increase in his productivity. We have really carried out a pedagogical experiment which enables us to study more closely the ways in which the transformation of natural psychological functions into cultural ones takes place.

By varying the material (starting from the simplest 'leading' question to a preschool child concerning hailshots, grains, etc., and ending with the most difficult one), by varying the problems (including in the series of figures zero or double figures), we are enabled to observe in detail the application of cultural methods on the part of the child to the simplest mnemonic operations. One thing proves really interesting in these series: the experiment proves that the difference between the intellectual operations of a pre-school child and a schoolboy is not of a purely quantitative kind, that the schoolboy is armed differently from a pre-school child in terms of quality, that the structure of his processes is essentially different.

To prove this let us set the same problem to a schoolboy of the first or the second year of study, and we shall witness something very different. It is quite natural that a child who has mastered the writing of letters and figures will not attempt to invent a new system of signs, but will rather apply the ready-made system of writing, as evolved in the history of culture. This system he will apply in spite of any difficulties. In fact, a child who is given a strip of paper for the purpose of memorizing will first of all attempt to make on it the signs of figures; by tearing out of that strip pieces which roughly represent figures he simply inscribes the series set to him, only instead of using a pencil he does it in a different way.

In the course of the experiment this representation of figures becomes more schematic. In the end they lose the delineation of figures and acquire the form of some code; in the process materials of various types may be used simultaneously, such as matches, pens, blocks, paper, etc. However, everywhere the signs represented will have the common feature of integral signs, and not be a mere quantitative inscription representing the number.

It is extraordinary how children always represent figures in that way. The same tendency is exhibited by children when they are given material such as strings, counters and pins, out of which they attempt to form figures although it would be easier in that case to adopt the system of knots and scoring-stick marks; it is interesting to note that if you forbid them to represent figures you will make them quite helpless to cope with the task, and we have hardly ever seen among children of these school groups any instances of reversion to the method of quantitative counting so characteristic of pre-school children. For that very reason the material easiest to handle for pre-school children, namely hailshots, grains, etc., often becomes the stumbling block for schoolboys. A pre-school child inscribes by laying aside in heaps the corresponding number of hailshot; a schoolboy, on the other hand, tries to lay them in the shape of a figure. The former invents scoring-stickes; the latter uses the time-honoured system of recording, of figures representing numbers. We are here witnessing by way of experiment the process of evolution of cultural methods of writing which resuscitates before our eyes the most ancient primitive forms of writing; we see how our schoolboy refits himself with new weapons and how the whole of his psychic condition is being reconstructed under the influence of such refitment.

The cultural–historical development of psychology goes along the path of complication of cultural methods and habits; the history of culture starts with a primitive outward technique and ends with a complicated psychological technique. It inevitably develops in man the functional utilization of his own conduct. It is this latter process of changing one's own attitude to psychological processes functionally used in their new qualitative forms which we observe in experimenting. We can demonstrate this, for example, in our experiments with memory, in the course of which a child learns how to use the most important internal mechanism – *the structural connection*.

A child who can hardly memorize five or six words of the series read out to him is asked to commit them to memory with the aid of pictures laid out on the table (e.g. lotto). Not one of the pictures actually reproduces the word in question, and the task can be performed only if the child connects in one structure the word in question with one of the pictures. It is obvious that for such an experiment it is essential somehow to evidence one's power of association in order to direct associative ideas every time in a definitely fixed direction. We note that such mastering of the ideas of association can be acquired, but by no means by all the children.

It is an obviously impossible task for a child of five or six or a backward child during his first years at school to establish a connection between the word 'village' and the picture of a house, between the word 'tail' and the picture of a dog, and, what is most important, to appreciate truly that connection and use it so as to memorize the material offered to him; on the other hand, a well developed child will perform that task without great difficulties. We had occasion to observe how a child in establishing and utilizing such connections could, by looking at the cards, reproduce 25–30 and more words after one reading, while his natural memory could fix five or six at the most. Moreover, the connecting links were established with extraordinary subtlety. Thus, in order to remember the word 'spade' the child chose a picture of chickens picking up grains 'because they picked it just as the spade digs the earth'; for the word 'theatre' the child chose the picture of a crab on the seashore 'because the crab looks at the pebbles in the sea, and they are just as pretty as a theatre', etc.

The experiment with memory can be transferred from the plane of natural processes, 'stimulus-reaction', to the plane of instrumentality by wedging between the words and their repetition the stimulus of the second kind, with which the given word is artificially connected, a stimulus that serves as a means, as an instrument of memorizing. In so doing we reconstruct the whole structure of the process and reach the maximum heightening of productivity. We are attempting to reach here that which could hardly attain with an animal: the functional instrumental use of one's own psychic processes for the problem set in the experiment.

By operating with auxiliary means, by artificially connecting with them the stimuli in question, the object of our experiment learns how to use his natural capacities to the utmost by replacing their direct application by a complicated cultural application.

Experiments carried out by us in accordance with that method gave the following interesting results. The use of pictures and the 'cultural' memorizing when applied to schoolboys of ten to 12 gives a 60 per cent increase in the productivity of their memory as compared to the ordinary memory of a 'natural' kind; the same method on mentally defective schoolboys produced no effect whatsoever in improving their memory, and when applied to weak minded children it even caused 20–30 per cent deterioration of their 'natural' memory. It is clear that the difference in efficacy of this method is due to the fact that a weak child is not able to grasp the mnemonic method which is thoroughly mastered by a normal child of nine or ten. It is this difference in ability to use functionally cultural methods, which we are inclined to regard as a test which determines whether the child is intellectually normal or backward.[1]

In the course of investigation of the child's behaviour we came to the conclusion that it passes through several stages, each of them differing in quality. We can mention roughly the following stages:

1    The child is not in a state to perform the task by the complicated auxiliary means. He is incapable of connoting the objects offered as the auxiliary means and fails to remember a series of words 'with the aid' of cards; such is the *pre-instrumental* stage of development.

2    The child begins to attempt to use the objects offered as the means for attaining the object, but does it clumsily, without attempting to establish a rational connection between the task and the auxiliary means, looking at the latter as a sort of magic. For example, in wishing to memorize a series of words he puts

before himself a series of equal nails, in no way differing from each other, and no longer troubles to remember the set words; each of these nails must, so to say, be a reminder of a definite word. It is obvious that such 'method' proves inadequate and the result is disappointing to the child. This phase is characterized by a purely formal attitude to the method adopted, a blind faith in its efficacy though it is thoroughly inadequate. This phase (which we have observed in children of five to seven though it may appear in later years) we can call the magical or the *pseudo-instrumental* phase.

3 Finally, much later, we observe the *real instrumental* stage in the development of the child, the main features of which are the complicated structure of acts of behaviour, the ability to adapt one's self to difficult tasks by using adequate means and the outer auxiliary stimuli. It is precisely this part of behaviour which develops most in a schoolboy and the modern civilized man, and is of utmost significance.

It is obvious that the above classification of phases is arbitrary; it emphasizes only one, perhaps not the most important though in any case essential, feature in the evolution of man's conduct. Their dynamics, characteristic features and limits will be the subject of my other article.[2]

Let us sum up the method applied by us and once more indicate its main features.

We believe that the principles of investigation submitted by us open up new and important prospects in the science of psychology. This method investigates the cultural forms of adaptability of man and thus raises questions of great pedagogical importance. The development of a child at school is after all reduced to his refitment with new cultural arms and the forging of new psychological weapons. It is by studying the cultural forms of behaviour that we acquire the faculty of mastering and of regulating them. The scientific analysis of laws which underlie the cultural behaviour of the child can help us in framing a series of concrete pedagogical and didactical measures. A further working out of this method can bring us to the framing of a series of tests which, instead of evaluating the natural qualities of the child, will be devoted to the analysis of their degree of cultural utilization. The precise measurements of these features, hitherto consistently ignored, will now certainly have the greatest pedagogical and pedological importance.

Finally, we are inclined to regard in the instrumental–psychological investigation great progress in objective technique. In connecting the performing of tasks with a series of external operations we are carrying outward whole systems of psychological processes and acquire the possibility of observing objectively how their structure is changed under the influence of inoculating new instruments, and new cultural methods. And, what is most important, we obtain by this method a key to the problem of how the child's behaviour is transformed into the behaviour of a cultured adult living in complicated industrial–cultural conditions and armed with a complicated social–cultural outfit.

## Notes

Originally published as Luria, A. R. 1928: The problem of the cultural behavior of the child. *Pedagogical Seminary and Journal of Genetic Psychology*, 35, 493–506. The article formed the first in a series of three presenting the cultural–historical ideas of Vygotsky and his associates to the foreign reader. As always, it was Luria – who joined the editorial board of the *Journal of Genetic Psychology* – who was instrumental in making foreign publication outlets available to Vygotsky and his colleagues. Meanwhile, amidst the countless publications on rat learning scores the articles seem not to have made much impression. The present editors, at least, know of no Western article or book from the 1920s or 1930s that refers to them.

1   The results of this work will be presented in detail in another article [original footnote].
2   This article was never published but Vygotsky's and Leont'ev's subsequent articles in the same journal provided additional information to the English readership.

# 5

# The problem of the cultural development of the child

## *Lev Vygotsky*

### The problem

In the process of development the child not only masters the items of cultural experience but the habits and forms of cultural behaviour, the cultural methods of reasoning. We must, therefore, distinguish the main lines in the development of the child's behaviour. First, there is the line of natural development of behaviour which is closely bound up with the processes of general organic growth and the maturation of the child. Second, there is the line of cultural improvement of the psychological functions, the working out of new methods of reasoning, the mastering of the cultural methods of behaviour.

Thus, of two children of different ages the elder can remember better and more than the younger. This is true for two entirely different reasons. The processes of memorizing of the older child have undergone, during his additional period of growth, a certain evolution – they have attained a higher level – but only by means of psychological analysis may we reveal whether that evolution proceeded on the first or on the second line.

Maybe the child remembers better because his nervous and mental constitutions which underlie the processes of memory were developed and perfected, because the organic base of these processes was developed; in short, because of the mneme or mnemic functions of the child. However, the development might follow quite a different path. The organic base of memory, mneme, might remain substantially unaltered during the period of growth, but the methods of memorizing might have changed. The child might have learned how to use his memory in a more efficient way. He could have mastered the mnemotechnical methods of memorizing; in particular, he may have developed the method of memorizing by means of signs.

In fact both lines of development can always be revealed, for the older child not only remembers more facts than the younger one, but he remembers them in a different way. In the process of development we can trace that qualitative change in the form of behaviour and the transformation of some such forms into others. The child who remembers by means of a geographical map or by means of a plan, a scheme or a summary, may serve as an example of such cultural development of memory.

We have many reasons to assume that the cultural development consists in mastering methods of behaviour which are based on the use of signs as a means of accomplishing any particular psychological operation. This is not only proved by the study of the psychological development of primitive man, but also by the direct and immediate observation of children.

In order to understand the problem of the cultural development of the child, it is very important to apply the conception of children's primitiveness which has recently been advanced. The primitive child is a child who has not undergone a cultural development, or one who has attained a relatively low level of that development. If we regard children's primitiveness in an isolated state as a special kind of under-development, we shall thereby contribute to the proper understanding of the cultural development of behaviour. Children's primitiveness, i.e. their delay in cultural development, is primarily due to the fact that for some external or internal cause they have not mastered the cultural means of behaviour, especially language.

However, the primitive child is a healthy child. Under certain conditions the primitive child undergoes a normal cultural development, reaching the intellectual level of a cultural man. This distinguishes primitiveness from weakmindedness. True, child's primitiveness may be combined with all the levels of natural capacities. Primitiveness, as a delay of cultural development, nearly always retards the development of a defective child. It is often combined with mental retardation.

But even in this mixed form, primitiveness and weakmindedness remain two phenomena essentially different in kind, the origins of which are totally different. One is the retardation of the organic or natural development which originates in defects of the brain. The other is a retardation in the cultural development of behaviour caused by insufficient mastery of the methods of cultural reasoning.

Take the following instance. A girl of nine years, quite normal, is primitive. She is asked, 'in a certain school some children can write well and some can draw well. Do all children in this school write and draw well?' She answers, 'How do I know; what I *have not seen with my own eyes*, I am unable to explain. If I had seen it with my eyes . . .'.

Another example: a primitive boy is asked, 'What is the difference between a tree and a log?' He answers, 'I have not seen a tree, nor do I know of any tree, upon my word'. Yet there is a lime tree growing just opposite his window. When you ask him, 'And what is this?' he will answer, 'This is a lime tree'.

The retardation in the development of logical reasoning and in the formation of concepts is due here entirely to the fact that children have not sufficiently mastered the language, the principal weapon of logical reasoning and the formation of concepts. Petrova [1925, p. 85], the author of the work containing the above examples, states: 'Our numerous observations prove that the replacing of one *imperfect* language by another equally imperfect always prejudices psychic development. This substitution of *one form* of reasoning *by another lowers especially the psychic activity wherever the latter is in any case weak*'.[1] In our first example, the girl has changed her imperfect Tartar language for the Russian, and has not fully mastered the use of words as means of reasoning. She displays her total inability to think in words, although she speaks, i.e. can use the words as means of communication. She does not understand how one can draw conclusions from words instead of relying on one's own eyes. The primitive boy has not as yet worked out a general abstract concept of 'tree', although he knows individual kinds of trees. That reminds us that in the language of many primitive races there is no such word as 'tree'; they have only separate words for each kind of tree.

## The analysis

Usually the two lines of psychological development (the natural and the cultural) merge into each other in such a way that it is difficult to distinguish them and follow the course of each of them separately. In case of sudden retardation of any one of these two lines, they become more or less obviously disconnected as, for example, in the case of different primitiveness.

The same cases show that cultural development does not create anything over and above that which potentially exists in the natural development in the child's behaviour. Culture, generally speaking, does not produce anything new apart from that which is given by nature. But it transforms nature to suit the ends of man. This same transformation occurs in the cultural development of behaviour. It also consists of inner changes in that which was given by nature in the course of the natural development of behaviour.

As has already been shown by Höffding, the higher forms of behaviour have no more means and data at their disposal than those which were shown by the lower forms of that same activity. In the words of the author:

> The fact that the association of ideas, when we reason, becomes the object of special interest and conscious choice, does not, however, alter the laws of associations of ideas. The thought, properly speaking, can no more dispense with these laws than an artificial machine with the laws of physics. However, psychological laws as well as physical ones can be utilized in such a way as to serve our ends.[2]

When we purposely interfere with the course of the processes of behaviour, we can do so only in conformance with the same laws which govern these processes in their natural course, just as we can transform outward nature and make it serve our ends only in conformance with the laws of nature. Bacon's principle, 'Natura parendo vincitur', is equally applicable both to the mastering of behaviour and to the mastering of the forces of nature.[3]

This indicates the true relation between the cultural and primitive forms of behaviour. Every cultural method of behaviour, even the most complicated, can always be completely analysed into its component nervous and psychic processes, just as every machine, in the last resort, can be reduced to a definite system of natural forces and processes. Therefore, the first task of scientific investigation, when it deals with some cultural method of behaviour, must be the analysis of that method, i.e. its decomposition into component parts, which are natural psychological processes.

This analysis, if carried out consistently and to completion, will always give us the same result. This proves precisely that there can be no complicated or high method of cultural reasoning which did not in the last resort consist of some primary elementary psychological processes of behaviour. The methods and insignificance of such analysis can best be explained by means of some concrete examples.

In our experimental investigations we place the child in such a situation that he is faced by the problem of remembering a definite number of figures, words or some other data. If that task is not above the natural abilities of the child, he will master it by the natural or primitive method. He remembers by creating associative or conditional reflexive connections between the stimuli and reactions.

However, we rarely obtain such a situation in our experiments. The task set the child is usually above his natural capacities. It cannot be solved in such a primitive and natural method. We put before the child some object, quite irrelevant to the task set, such as paper, pins, string, small shot, etc. We thus obtain a situation very similar to the one which Köhler created for his apes. The problem occurs in the process of the natural activity of the child, but its solution requires some detour or the application of some means. If the child finds such a solution, he takes recourse to signs, the tying of knots on the string, the counting of small shots, the piercing or tearing of paper, etc.

Such memorization based on the use of signs is regarded by us as a typical instance of all cultural methods of behaviour. The child solves an inner problem by means of exterior objects. This is the most typical peculiarity of cultural behaviour. It also distinguishes the situation created in our experiments from the Köhler situation which that author, and afterwards other investigators, tried to apply to children. There the problems and their solutions were entirely in the plane of external activity, as opposed to ours which are in the plane of internal activity. There an irrelevant object obtained the 'functional importance'[4] of a weapon, here it acquires the functional importance of a sign.

Mankind moved along the latter path of development of memory based on signs. Such an essentially mnemotechnical operation is the specifically human feature of behaviour. It is impossible among animals.

Let us now compare the natural and cultural mnemonics of a child. The relation between the two forms can be graphically expressed by means of the schematic triangle in figure 5.1: in case of natural memorization a direct associative or conditional reflexive connection is set up between two points, $A$ and $B$. In case of mnemotechnical memorization, utilizing some sign, instead of one associative connection $AB$, the others are set up $AX$ and $BX$, which bring us to the same result, but

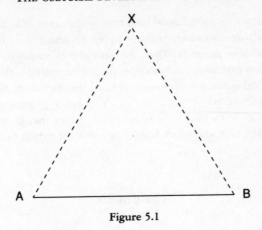

**Figure 5.1**

in a roundabout way. Each of these connections *AX* and *BX* is the same kind of conditional–reflexive process of connection as *AB*.

The mnemotechnical memorizing can thus be divided without remainder into the same conditional reflexes as natural memorizing. The only new features are the substitution of two connections for one, the construction or combination of nervous connections, and the direction given to the process of connection by means of a sign. Thus new features consist not in the elements but in the structure of the cultural methods of mnemonics.

### The structure

The second task of scientific investigation is to elucidate *the structure* of that method. Although each method of cultural behaviour consists, as it is shown by the analysis, of natural psychological processes, yet that method unites them not in a mechanical, but in a structural way. In other words, all processes forming part of that method form a complicated functional and structural unity. This unity is effected, first, by the task which must be solved by the given method, and secondly, by the means by which that method can be followed.

The same problem, if solved by different means, will have a different structure. If a child in the above mentioned situation turns to the aid of external memorizing means, the whole structure of his processes will be determined by the character of the means which he has selected. Memorizing on different systems of signs will be different in its structure. A sign or an auxiliary means of a cultural method thus forms a structural and functional centre, which determines the whole composition of the operation and the relative importance of each separate process.

The inclusion in any process of a sign remodels the whole structure of psychological operations, just as the inclusion of a tool remodels the whole structure of a labour operation. The structures thus formed have their specific laws. You find in them that some psychological operations are replaced by others which cause the same results, but by quite different methods. Thus, for example, in memorizing mnemotechnically, the various psychological functions, such as comparison, the renewal of old connections, logical operations, reasoning, etc., all become aids to memorizing. It is precisely the structure which combines all the separate processes, which are the component parts of the cultural habit of behaviour, which transforms this habit into a psychological function, and which fulfills its task with respect to the behaviour as a whole.

## The genesis

However, that structure does not remain unchanged. That is the most important point of all we know concerning the cultural development of the child. This structure is not an outward, ready-made creation. It originates in conformance with definite laws at a certain stage of the natural development of the child. It cannot be forced on the child from outside, it always originates inwardly, although it is modelled by the deciding influence of external problems with which the child is faced and the external signs with which it operates. After the structure comes into being, it does not remain unchanged, but is subject to a lengthy internal change which shows all the signs of development.

A new method of behaviour does not simply remain fixed as a certain external habit. It has its internal history. It is included in the general process of the development of a child's behaviour, and we therefore have a right to talk of a genetic relation between certain structures of cultural reasoning and behaviour, and of the development of the methods of behaviour. This development is certainly of a special kind, is radically different from the organic development and has its own definite laws. It is extremely difficult to grasp and express precisely the peculiarity of that type of development. In basing our position on critical explanations and on a series of schemes suggested by experimental investigations, we shall try to take certain steps toward the correct understanding of this development.

Binet, who in his investigations was faced by these two types of development, tried to solve the problem in the simplest fashion. He investigated the memory of eminent calculators, and in this connection had occasion to compare the memory of a man endowed with a truly remarkable memory with the memory of a man endowed with an average memory; the latter, however, was not inferior to the former in memorizing a huge number of figures. Mneme and mnemotechnics were thus for the first time contrasted in experimental investigation, and for the first time an attempt was made to find an objective difference between these two essentially different forms of memory.[5]

Binet [1894, pp. 155–86] applied to his investigation and the phenomenon under investigation the term 'simulation of memory'. He believes that most psychological operations can be simulated, i.e. replaced by others resembling them only in external appearance, but differing from them in their essence. Thus mnemotechnics, according to Binet, is a simulation of eminent memory, which he calls artificial memory as distinguished from natural memory. The mnemotechnician who was investigated by Binet memorized by means of a simple method. He substituted word memory for figure memory. Every figure was replaced by the corresponding letter, the letters joined on in words, and the latter in phrases. Instead of a disconnected series of figures, he only had to remember and reproduce a sort of short story of his own invention. This example clearly shows us to what extent mnemonical memorizing leads to the substitution of certain psychological operations for others.

It is precisely this fundamental fact which was obvious to the investigators. It caused them to refer to this particular case as a simulation of natural development. This definition can hardly be called a successful one. It points out correctly that even though the two operations were similar (both calculators memorized and reproduced an equal number of figures with equal precision), yet in its essence one of the operations simulated the other.

If this definition was calculated to express *only* the peculiarity of the second type of memory development, we could not object to it. But it is misleading in that it conveys the idea that we have to deal here with simulation in the sense of false appearance, or deceit. This is the practical standpoint suggested by the specific conditions of investigations of individuals who appear on the stage with various tricks, and who are, therefore, apt to deceive. This is rather the standpoint of the investigating magistrate than the psychologist.

After all, as is admitted by Binet [1894, p. 164], such a simulation is not simply deceit. Every one of us possesses some kind of power of mnemotechnics, and mnemotechnics itself, in the opinion of that very author, should be studied in schools, the same as mental counting. Surely the author did not mean to say that the art of simulation should be taught in schools.

The definition of that type of cultural development as a 'fictitious development', i.e. one leading only to fictitious organic development, appears to us equally unsatisfactory. Here again the negative aspect of that case is correctly expressed; namely, that with a cultural development, the raising of the function to a higher level or the raising of its activity is based not on the organic, but on the functional development, i.e. on the development of the method itself. However, this term also conceals the undoubted truth that in this case we have not a *fictitious*, but a *real* development of a special type, which possesses its own definite laws.

We should like to emphasize from the outset that this development is subject to the influence of the same two main factors which take part in the organic development of the child, namely the biological and the social. The law of convergence of the internal and external factors, as it was called by Stern, is entirely applicable to the cultural development of the child.[6] In this case as well, only at a certain level of the internal development of the organism does it become possible to master any of the cultural methods. Also an organism internally prepared absolutely requires the determining influence of the environment in order to enable it to accomplish that development. Thus, at a certain stage of its organic development the child masters speech. At another stage he masters the decimal system.

However, the relation of the two factors in the development of this kind is materially changed. The active part is here played by the organism which masters the means of cultural behaviour supplied by the environment. But the organic maturation plays the part of a *condition* rather than a motive power of the process of cultural development, since the structure of that process is defined by outward influences. All means of social behaviour are in their essence social. A child mastering Russian or English and a child mastering the language of some primitive tribe, masters, in connection with the environment in which he is developed, two totally different systems of thinking.

If the doctrine that in certain spheres the behaviour of the individual is a function of the behaviour of the social whole to which he belongs is valid at all, it is precisely to the sphere of the cultural development of the child that it must be applied. This development is conditioned by outward influences. It can be defined as outer rather than as inner growth. It is the function of the social–cultural experience of the child. At the same time it is not a simple accumulation of experience as was stated above. It contains a series of inner changes which fully correspond to the process of development in the proper sense of that word.

The third and last problem of investigation of the child's cultural development is the education of the *psychogenesis* of cultural forms of behaviour. We shall give here a short sketch of the scheme of this process of development, as it transpired in our experimental investigations. We shall try to show that the cultural development of the child passes – if we may trust the artificial surroundings of the experiment – through four main stages or phases which follow consecutively one after another.

Taken as a whole, these stages form a complete cycle of cultural development of any one psychological function. The data obtained by means other than experiments fully coincide with the scheme set by us, fully agree with it, and thus acquire a definite significance and hypothetical explanation. Let us follow briefly the description of the four stages of the child's cultural development according to their consecutive changes in the process of the simple experiment described above.

The first stage could be described as the stage of primitive behaviour or primitive psychology. The experiment reveals this in that the younger child tries to remember the data supplied to him by a primitive or natural means in accordance with the degree to which he is interested in them. The amount remembered is determined by the degree of his attention, by the amount of his individual memory and by the measure of his interest in the matter.

Usually only the difficulties which the child meets on this path bring him to the second stage. In our experiments it usually took place in the following way. Either the child himself, after more or less protracted search and trials, discovers some mnemotechnical method, or we lend him our assistance in case he is unable to master the task with the resources of his natural memory. For example, we place pictures in front of the child and choose words to be memorized in such a way that they should be in some way naturally connected with those pictures. When the child who has heard the words looks at the picture, he easily reproduces a whole series of words, since such pictures, irrespective of the child's consciousness, will remind him of the words which he has just heard.

The child usually grasps very quickly the method which we suggest to him, but does not usually know by what means the pictures help him to remember the words. He usually reacts in the following manner: when a new series of words is given to him, he will again – but now on his own initiative – place the pictures in front of him, and look at them every time a word is given to him. But since this time there is no direct connection between words and pictures, and the child does not know how to use the pictures as a means of memorizing a given word, he looks at the picture and reproduces not the word he was given, but another suggested by the picture.

This stage is conventionally called the stage of 'naive psychology', by analogy with what the German investigators (Köhler, Lipmann) call the 'naive physics' in the behaviour of apes and children when using tools. The use of the simplest tools by children presupposes a certain naive physical experience of the simplest physical properties of one's own body and those of objects and tools with which the child is familiar. Very often that experience proves insufficient and then the 'naive physics' of an ape or a child avails him nothing.[7]

We note something similar in our experiment when the child grasped the external connection between the use of pictures and the memorizing of words. However, the 'naive psychology', i.e. the naive experience gathered by him concerning his own processes of memorizing proved to be insignificant, so that the child could not use the picture adequately as a sign or a means of memorizing. Contrary to the magical thinking of a primitive man when the connection between ideas is mistaken for the connection between things, in this case the child takes the connection between things for the connection between ideas. In the former case the magical reasoning is due to insufficient knowledge of the laws of nature: in the latter, to insufficient knowledge of its own psychology.

This second stage is usually transitory in its importance. In the course of the experiment the child usually passes on very quickly to the third stage of the external cultural method. After a few attempts the child usually discovers, if his psychological experience is rich enough, how the trick works, and learns how to make proper use of the picture. Now he replaces the processes of memorizing by a rather complicated external activity. When he is given a word, he chooses out of a number of pictures in front of him the one which is most closely associated with the word given. At first he tries to use the natural association which exists between the picture and word, but soon afterwards passes on to the creation and formation of new associations.

However, in the experiment even this third stage lasts a comparatively short time and is replaced by the fourth stage, which originates in the third. The external activity of the child remembering by means of a sign passes on into internal activity. The external means, so to speak, becomes ingrown or internal.

The simplest way to observe this is the study of a situation in which a child must remember given words by using pictures placed in definite order. After a few times the child usually learns the pictures themselves. He has no further need to recur to them. He already associates words given with the titles of pictures, the order of which he already knows. Such 'complete ingrowing' is based on the fact that inner stimuli are substituted for the external ones. The mnemotechnical map which lies before the child becomes his internal scheme.

Along with this method of ingrowing we observe a few more types of transition from the third into the fourth stage; of these we shall mention only the two principal ones. The first may be termed 'seam-like ingrowing'. The seam connecting two parts of organic texture very rapidly leads to the formation of the connecting texture, so that the seam itself becomes unnecessary. We observe a similar process in the exclusion of the sign by means of which some psychological operation was at first carried out.

We can best observe it in a child's complicated reactions of choice when every one of the stimuli offered to him is associated with the corresponding movement by means of an auxiliary sign, e.g. the above mentioned picture. After a series of repetitions the sign becomes no longer necessary. The stimulus is the immediate cause for the corresponding action.

Our investigation in that sphere has entirely confirmed the fact already established by Lehmann,[8] namely that in a complicated reaction of choice, certain names or other associative intermediaries are interposed at first between the stimulus and the reaction – associations which serve as a connecting link between the two. After exercise, these intermediate links fall out and the reaction passes immediately into a simple sensory or motor form. The period of reaction, according to Lehmann, decreases correspondingly from $300\sigma$ to $240\sigma$ and $140\sigma$. Let us add that the same phenomenon, but in a less obvious form, was observed by investigators in the process of simple reaction which, as shown by Wundt, may dwindle away to a simple reflex under the influence of exercise.[9]

Finally, the third type of transition from the third stage to the fourth, the 'growing in' of the external method into the internal, is the following: the child, after mastering the structure of some external method, constructs the internal processes according to the same type. He starts at once to use the inner schemes, tries to use his remembrances as signs, the knowledge he formerly acquired, etc. In this connection the investigator is struck by the fact that a problem once solved leads to a correct solution in all analogous situations even when external conditions have changed radically. We are naturally reminded here of the similar transpositions which were observed by Köhler [1921] in the ape which once solved correctly the task set for it.

The four stages which we have described are only a first hypothetical scheme of the path along which the cultural development evolves. However, we wish to point out that the path indicated by that scheme coincides with certain data which are already at hand in the literature on the psychology of this question. We shall quote three instances which reveal coincidences with the main outline of our scheme.

The first example has to do with the development of a child's arithmetical ability. The first stage is formed by the natural arithmetical endowment of the child, i.e. his operation of quantities before he knows how to count. We include here the immediate conception of quantity, the comparison of greater and smaller groups, the recognition of some quantitative group, the distribution into single objects where it is necessary to divide, etc.

The next stage of the 'naive psychology' is observed in all children and is illustrated in a case where the child, knowing the external methods of counting, imitates adults and repeats 'one, two, three' when he wants to count, but does not know for what purpose or exactly how to count by means of figures. This stage of arithmetical development was reached by the girl described by Stern. He asked how many fingers he had and she answered that she could only count her own fingers.[10] The third stage is when counting is made by the aid of fingers, and the fourth stage when counting is effected in the mind and the fingers are dispensed with. Counting in the mind is an illustration of 'complete ingrowing'.

It is equally easy to locate in this scheme the development of memory at a given age for any child. The three types indicated by Meumann [1912], the mechanical, the mnemotechnical and the logical (pre-school age, school age and mature age), obviously coincide with the first, third and fourth stages of our scheme. Meumann [1911, pp. 394–473] himself attempts elsewhere to prove that these three types represent a genetic series in which one type passes into another. From that standpoint the logical memory of an adult is precisely the 'ingrown' mnemotechnical memory.[11]

If these hypotheses are in any way justified, we should obtain another proof of how important it is to use the historical standpoint in studying the highest functions of behaviour. In any case there is one very weighty bit of evidence which speaks in favour of this hypothesis. It is first of all the fact that verbal memory, which precedes the logical memory, i.e. the memorizing in words, is a mnemotechnical memory.

We are reminded that Compayré has formerly defined language as a mnemotechnical tool.[12] Meumann was right in showing that words have a two-fold function in regard to memory. They can either appear by themselves as memorizing material or as signs by the aid of which we memorize.[13] We should also remember that Bühler has established by experimentation that memorizing of meaning is independent of the memorizing of words and of the important part played by internal speech in the process of logical memorizing, so that the genetic kinship between the mnemotechnical and logical memory should clearly appear owing to their connecting link, verbal memory.[14] The second stage, which is absent in the scheme of Meumann, probably passes very quickly in the development of memory and therefore escapes observation.

Finally, we must point out that such a central problem in the history of the child's cultural development as the development of speech and reasoning is in accord with our scheme. This scheme, we believe, allows us to discover a correct solution of this most complicated and puzzling problem.

As we know, some authors consider speech and reasoning as entirely different processes, one of which serves as the expression and the outer clothing of the other. Others, on the contrary, identify reasoning and speech, and follow Müller in defining thought as speech minus the sound. What does the history of the child's cultural development teach us in that connection? It shows first of all that genetically reasoning and speech have entirely different roots. This by itself must serve as a warning against the hurried identification of those concepts which differ genetically. As is established by investigation, the development of speech and reasoning both in ontogenesis and phylogenesis goes up to a certain point by independent paths. The pre-intellectual roots of speech, such as the speech of birds and animals, were known long ago. Köhler [1921] was successful in establishing the pre-speech roots of intellect. Also the pre-intellectual roots of speech in the ontogenesis, such as the squeak and lisping of a child, were known long ago and were thoroughly investigated. Köhler, Bühler and others were successful in establishing the pre-speech roots of intellect in the development of the child. Bühler proposed to call this age of the first manifestations of intellectual reactions in a child preceding the formation of speech the chimpanzee age.[15] The most remarkable feature in the intellectual behaviour both of apes and of the human child of that age is the independence of intellect from speech. It is just that characteristic which led Bühler [1929, pp. 15–20] to the conclusion that the intellectual behaviour in the form of 'instrumental thinking'[16] preceded the formation of speech.

At a certain moment the two lines of development cross each other. This moment in the child's development was regarded by Stern as the greatest discovery in the life of a child. It is the child himself who discovers the 'instrumental function' of a word. He discovers that 'each thing has its name'.[17] This crisis in the development of a child is demonstrated when the child starts to widen his vocabulary *actively*, asking about everything 'What is it called?' Bühler, and later on, Koffka, pointed out that there is a complete psychological similarity between this discovery of the child and the inventions of apes. The child's discovery of the functional importance of a word as a sign is similar to the discovery of the functional importance of a stick as a tool. Koffka stated: 'the word enters the structure of the thing just as a stick does for the chimpanzee in the situation which consists in the desire to acquire fruits'.[18]

The most important stage in the development of reasoning and speech is the transition from external to internal speech. How and when does this important process in the development of internal speech take place? We believe that the answer to this question can be given on the strength of the investigations carried out by Piaget on the egocentrism of children's speech.[19] Piaget showed that speech becomes internal psychologically prior to its becoming internal physiologically. The egocentric speech of a child is internal speech according to its psychological function (it is speaking to oneself) and external in form. This is the transition from external to internal speech, and for this reason it has great importance in genetic investigations. The coefficient of egocentric speech falls sharply at the threshold of school age (from

0.50 to 0.25). This shows it is precisely at that period that the transition to internal speech takes place.

It is easy to observe that the three main stages in the development of reasoning and speech which we quoted above fully correspond to the three main stages of cultural development as they appear consecutively in the course of experiment. Pre-speech reasoning corresponds in this scheme to the first stage of the natural or primitive behaviour. 'The greatest discovery in the life of a child',[20] as shown by Bühler and Koffka, is entirely analogous to the invention of tools, and consequently corresponds to the third stage of our scheme. Finally, the transition of external speech into internal speech, the egocentrism of a child's speech, forms the connecting link between the third and fourth stage, which means the transformation of the external activity into an internal one.

## The method

The peculiarities of the child's cultural development demand the application of the corresponding method of investigation. This method could be conventionally called 'instrumental' as it is based on the discovery of the 'instrumental function' of cultural signs in behaviour and its development.

In the plan of experimental investigation this method is based on the 'functional method of double stimulation', the essence of which may be reduced to the organization of the child's behaviour by the aid of two series of stimuli, each of which has a distinct 'functional importance' in behaviour. At the same time the *conditio sine qua non* of the solution of the task set the child is the 'instrumental use' of one series of stimuli, i.e. its utilization as an auxiliary means for carrying out any given psychological operation.

We have reasons to assume that the invention and use of these signs, as an auxiliary means for the solution of any task set the child, present *from a psychological standpoint* an analogy with the invention and use of tools. Within the general inter-relation, stimulus *vs.* reaction, which is the basis of the usual methods of a psychological experiment, we must distinguish, in conformance with the ideas which we here stated, a *two-fold function* of the stimulus in regard to behaviour.

The stimulus in one case may play the part of object in regard to the act of solving any particular problem given to the child (to remember, compare, choose, estimate, weigh a certain thing). In another case it can play the part of a means, by the aid of which we direct and realize the psychological operations necessary to the solution of the problem (memorizing, comparison, choice, etc.). In both those cases the functional relation between the act of behaviour and the stimuli is essentially different. In both cases the stimulus determines, conditions and organizes our behaviour in quite different and specific ways. The peculiarity of the psychological situation created in our experiments consists in the simultaneous presence of the stimuli of both kinds, each playing a different part both quantitatively and functionally.

Expressing the idea in the most general form, the main promise lying at the root of this method is as follows: the child, in mastering himself (his behaviour), goes on the whole in the same way as he does in mastering external nature, e.g. by technical means. The man masters himself externally, as one of the forces of nature by means of a special cultural 'technic of signs'. Bacon's principle of the hand and the intellect could serve as a motto for all similar investigations: 'Nec manus nuda, nec intellectus sibi permissus multum valet: instrumentis et auxiliis res perficitur'.[21]

This method in its very essence is a historical–genetic method. It carries into investigation a historical point of view: 'behaviour can only be understood as the history of behaviour' (Blonsky). This idea is the cardinal principle of the whole method.

The application of this method becomes possible, (a) in the *analysis* of the composition of the cultural method of behaviour, (b) in the *structure* of this method as a whole and as a functional unity of all the component processes, and (c) in the psychogenesis of the cultural behaviour of the child. This method is not only a key to the understanding of the higher forms of a child's behaviour which originate in the process of cultural development, but also a means to the practical mastering of them in the matter of education and school instruction.

This method is based on natural science methods of studying behaviour, in particular on the method of conditional reflexes. Its peculiarity consists in the study of complex functional structures of behaviour and their specific laws. The objectiveness makes it akin to the natural science methods of studying behaviour. This method of investigation is connected with the use of objective means in psychological experimentation.

When we investigate the highest functions of behaviour which are composed of complicated internal processes, we find that this method tends in the course of the experiment to call into being the very process of formation of the highest forms of behaviour, instead of investigating the function already formed in its developed stage. In this connection, the most favourable stage for investigation is the third one, that is the external cultural method of behaviour.

When we connect the complicated internal activity with the external one, making the child choose and spread cards for the purpose of memorizing, and move about and distribute pieces, etc. for the purpose of creating concepts, we thereby create an objective series of reactions, functionally connected with the internal activity and serving as a starting point for objective investigation. In so doing we are acting in the same way as, for instance, one who wanted to investigate the path which the fish follows in the depths, from the point where it sinks into water until it comes up again to the surface. We envelop the fish with a string loop and try to reconstruct the curve of its path by watching the movement of that end of the string which we hold in our hands. In our experiments we shall at all times also hold the outer thread of the internal process in our hands.

As an example of this method we may cite the experimental investigations carried out by the author, or on his initiative, concerning memory, counting, the formation of concepts and other higher functions in children's behaviour. These investigations we hope to publish in a separate study.[22] Here we only wanted to describe in a most concise and sketchy form the problem of the child's cultural development.

## Notes

First published as Vygotski, L. S. 1929: The problem of the cultural development of the child II. *Journal of Genetic Psychology*, 36, 415–32. In a footnote it was said that A. R. Luria of the Editorial Board had received the paper for publication on 20 July 1928. The paper was essentially a translation of a paper that Vygotsky published somewhat earlier in *Pedologija* [*Pedology*], a journal which he co-founded. See Vygotsky, L. S. 1928: Problema kul'turnogo razvitija rebenka. *Pedologija*, 1, 58–77. The article formed the second in a series of three published in the *Journal of Genetic Psychology* on the problem of the cultural development of the child (see note 1 in the preceding chapter). The research on which it was based was carried out by Vygotsky, Luria, Leont'ev and their students at the Psychological Laboratories of the N. K. Krupskaja Academy of Communist Education in Moscow.

1 See Petrova, A. 1925: Deti-primitivy. Psikhologicheskij analiz [Child-primitives. A psychological analysis]. In M. Gurevich (ed.), *Voprosy pedologii i detskoj psikhonevrologii* [*Questions of Pedology and Psychoneurology*] (pp. 60–92). Moscow: Zhizn'i Znanie.

2 See Höffding, H. 1907: *Psychologie in Umrissen auf Grundlage der Erfahrung*, p. 240 Leipzig: Reisland.

3 Actually 'Natura non vincitur nisi parendo' ('Nature to be commanded must be obeyed') See Bacon, F. 1620/1960. *The New Organon and related writings*, p. 39 New York: Macmillan Publishing Company.

4 'Funktionswert'. See p. 26 of Köhler, W. 1921: *Intelligenzprüfungen an Menschenaffen*. Berlin: Julius Springer.

5 See Binet, A. 1894: *Psychologie des grands calculateurs et des joueurs d'échecs*. Paris: Librairie Hachette et Cie.

6 Stern's convergence theory said that in child development heriditary ('Vorwelt') and environmental ('Umwelt') factors merge or converge into a qualitatively new, meaningful whole – the personality. This led him to reject extreme views, such as nativism and empiricism, and to criticize quantative estimations of the contribution of either heridity or environment to specific mental abilities. See, for example, pp. 95–121 of Stern, W. 1919: *Die menschliche Persönlichkeit*. Leipzig: Johann Ambrosius Barth.

7 'Naive physics' See Lipmann, O. and Bogen, H. 1923: *Naive Physik*. Leipzig: Verlag von Johan Ambrosius Barth.

8 See Lehmann, A. 1905: *Die körperliche Ausserungen psychischer Zustande. Vol. 3: Elemente der Psychodynamik*. Leipzig: Reisland.

9 For a discussion of Wundt's reaction time research, see Boring, E. G. 1957: *A History of Experimental Psychology*. New York: Appleton-Century-Crofts.

10 Actually a boy of four years old. See p. 344 of Stern, W. 1927. *Psychologie der frühen Kindheit*. Leipzig: Quelle Meyer.

11 See Meumann, E. 1912: *Ökonomie und Technik des Gedächtnisses*. Leipzig: Klinkhardt; Meumann, E. 1911: *Vorlesungen zur Einführung in die experimentelle Pädagogik. Bd. I.* Leipzig: Engelmann.

12 Refers to Compayré, G. 1893: *L'évolution intellectuelle et morale de l'enfant*. Paris: Hachette.

13 Refers to pp. 412–13 of Meumann, E. 1911: *Vorlesungen zur Einführung in die experimentelle Pädagogik. Bd. 1*. Leipzig: Engelmann.

14 See pp. 205–7 of Bühler, K. 1918: *Die geistige Entwicklung des Kindes*. Jena: Verlag von Gustav Fischer.

15 'Schimpansenalter'. See Bühler, K. 1929: *Abriss der geistigen Entwicklung des Kindes*. Leipzig: Quelle & Meyer, p. 48.

16 'Werkzeugdenken'. See Bühler, ibid.

17 'Dass jedes Ding einen Name habe'. See pp. 135–6 of Stern, W. 1927: *Psychologie der frühen Kindheit*. Leipzig: Quelle & Meyer, or pp. 190–7 of Stern, C. and Stern, W. 1928/1981: *Die Kindersprache*. Darmstadt: Wissenschaftliche Buchgesellschaft.

18 See Koffka, K. 1925: *Die Grundlagen der psychischen Entwicklung. Eine Einführung in die Kinderpsychologie*. Osterwieck am Harz: Verlag von A. W. Zickfeldt, p. 243.

19 See pp. 34–49 of Piaget, J. 1923/1959: *The Language and Thought of the Child*. London: Routledge & Kegan Paul.

20 Words used by the Sterns to express the importance of the phenomenon discussed in note 17 – that children suddenly discover that all things have names. See p. 190 of Stern, C. and Stern, W. 1928/1982: *Die Kindersprache*. Darmstadt: Wissenschaftliche Buchgesellschaft.

21 'Neither the naked hand nor the understanding left to itself can effect much. It is by instruments and helps that the work is done.' See p. 39 of Bacon, F. 1620/1960: *The New Organon and related writings*. New York: Macmillan Publishing Company.

22 This may refer to 'Tool and symbol in child development' (see chapter 7), in which some of the experimental research into higher psychological functions is discussed. But the finer details can only be studied by reading the monographs, doctoral dissertations and graduate theses that Vygotsky's co-workers and students published over the years. The results of the memory research, for example, were published by Leont'ev, A. N. 1931: *Razvitie pamjati. Eksperimental'noe issledovanie vysshikh psikhologicheskikh funkcij* [*The Development of Memory. An experimental study of the higher psychological functions*]. Moscow-Leningrad: Uchpedgiz. Reports on the formation of concepts were published by Shif, Zh. I. 1935: *Razvitie nauchnykh ponjatij u shkol'nika* [*The Development of Scientific Concepts in the School-child*], Moscow-Leningrad: Uchpedgiz; and Zankov, L. V. 1935: *Ocherki psikhologii umstvenno-otstalogo rebenka* [*Outlines of the Psychology of the Mentally Retarded Child*]. Moscow: Uchpedgiz. See Van der Veer, R. and Valsiner, J. (1991) for a detailed discussion of part of the research.

# 6
# Methods for investigating concepts

## Leonid Sakharov

### Method of definition and its role in the study of children's concepts

One of the problems that has contributed to a refinement of the 'functional procedure of double stimulation' in experiments is the problem of concept formation in children. To form an idea of the significance of this experimental method for the study of children's concepts, it must be viewed against the background of other methods that have been used to deal with the same problem. The psychology of children's concepts not only is of tremendous theoretical interest but also undoubtedly has applied psychological importance since the accumulation of concepts, their nature and the way they are used are unquestionably correlated with a child's level of intellectual development and are, to some extent, indicators of that level. It is therefore not surprising that tests on concepts occupy an honoured place among existing systems of tests, and their diagnostic value has earned widespread recognition.

The *method of definition* is the best known of the various methods for studying children's concepts. It has also found its way into numerous different systems of tests for measuring intellectual aptitude. The following techniques for studying children's concepts are modifications of the method of definition: the experimenter enumerates attributes that are part of the content of a concept and asks the child to name the concept or concepts, or the child must produce a generic concept uniting them all. In both the first and the second case, the inductive method is chosen – from attributes to object, from species to genus. However, the deductive method is also used: a generic concept is given, and the child is required to name the species that are part of it; the child is offered a generic concept and an identifying attribute (*differentia specifica*) and asked to name the corresponding species; he is asked what differences exist among species of the same genus, or between the genus and the species. All these procedures complement the method of definition. Since they make fewer demands on the child, they are used with more success than direct definition in some cases – when, for example, a child has obvious difficulties in verbal expression.

The method of definition has been used not only as a test for measuring intellectual aptitude (Binet, Bobertag and other authors of versions of a metric scale, Gregor,
Roloff, etc.) but also in experimental studies devoted particularly to children's
concepts (Pelman, Eng). What place does the method of definition and all techniques
similar to it occupy among methods for studying children's concepts? They are, so to
speak, indirect methods for studying concepts (Moede).[1]

Indirect methods focus on the store of concepts a child already possesses. The
nature of this store is studied. The purpose of the investigation is not the process of
genesis of new concepts in the child, but the qualitative characteristics of already
existing concepts. But even these qualitative characteristics have by no means been
thoroughly studied – perhaps not even their most important aspect. The method of
definition cannot tell us how the child uses concepts in solving different life tasks.
Indeed, an index of the qualitative characteristics of a concept is, in the particular
case, not the child's practical use of this concept in his responses to objects in the
world around him, but the verbal description of the content or the scope of the
concept. We obtain this description under experimental or test conditions. However,
this index is not only incomplete: it is not even clear.

The same definition of a concept may have a fundamentally different meaning for
two different children. In the one case, it may be a mechanical reproduction of a
formula that has been imprinted, but not worked through. The child simply repeats
what he has heard from memory. In another case, the definition may be the result of
actual activity and persevering, logical work. This is why the German psychologists
speak about *Scheinbegriffe* and *echte Begriffe* (quasi concepts and genuine concepts).
Varied advice has been given on how to combat the ambiguity of the results of the
method of definition. Thus, it has been said that the questions asked should not
presume any special knowledge, for then we shall often find ourselves dealing with
rote repetition of what is written in books.

However, everyone knows how difficult it is to avoid this point. A special differ-
ential attribute of the active nature of definitional activity has further been pointed
out, namely the consternation and confusion of the child after he has received the
assignment. However, even if it were possible to find a relevant criterion that would
be sufficiently objective and practical, the difficulties would not end there. Further,
the results of logical work are communicated through language. The formula for
definition consists of a series of words that should stand for the particular concepts.
We also know that as a child learns a language, he absorbs a multitude of words, but
the content of those words he usually learns in extremely imperfect, rudimentary
form. The meaning of a word sometimes remains hidden for him, or at least somewhat
indeterminate. All this is, of course, capable merely of intensifying the ambiguity of
the experimental results. What does a child put into the words out of which he has
fashioned the definition of a concept? This question still remains open. For example,
Lindworsky considered it necessary for the experimenter to work individually with
each child and to determine by means of special questions how the child understands
the words he uses to define the concept. 'Mass tests are of little help', says Lindworsky,

'if the significance and the value of each individual case are not established'.[2] Need we mention that in the mass studies that have been carried out thus far using the method of definition, [Lindworsky's injunction] has, for the most part, not been complied with?

## Experimental study of processes of abstraction in children

Thus, the main flaws in the method of definition are that it fails completely to take into account the process of concept generation in children and works only with finished concepts; that even the latter are studied in terms of only one aspect, and not the most important one at that; and that the studies are carried out under conditions that cast doubt on the unequivocal nature of the results obtained. The reason for these shortcomings lies in the conditions of any experiment using a method of definition.

The stimuli eliciting behaviour from a child in an experiment are words that express corresponding concepts, i.e. they represent definite groups of attributes, common to different objects and abstracted from them. These objects themselves do not serve as stimuli in the experiment. The child's reaction is again limited to 'vocal representation' of the corresponding attributes. But the scope of the generalized response to stimuli in the surrounding world and, especially, the problem of the genesis of this response are at the centre of psychology's interest in the study of concepts, particularly children's concepts.[3] How do conditional responses to discrete situations result in the elaboration of a typical concept-like reaction to several situations similar to one another in terms of one attribute? What factors play a role; what psycho-physiological processes are taking place here? Finally, if a concept-like response by the child has already been elaborated, what are its characteristics in action? These are questions of cardinal importance that are almost never touched upon by the method of definition. Hence, the second group of methods is of much greater interest, i.e. direct methods of investigating concepts and studying directly processes that underlie concept formation.

In the first place, there are experimental methods of studying processes of abstraction in children. Since our report concerns only methods of investigation, we shall omit anything that has to do with the definition of abstractions, with existing theories on this question, etc. In experiments on abstraction, the subject is presented with a set of impressions, either simultaneously or successively. Some elements of this set are repeated. The subject selects from the total number of impressions those elements that are similar, either on instruction or without instructions, and positively abstracts them. The speed and accuracy in following the instructions serve as indicators of the level of development of processes of abstraction in the subject. Experiments that study processes of abstraction fall into two groups depending on what general recurrent impressions must be abstracted positively by the subject. In one case, they may be comparatively independent objects; in the other, independent attributes common to a number of objects, e.g. colour, shape. Examples of studies of this type are those by Koch, Habrich and von Kuenburg, with normal children, and by Heffler with deaf mutes. These four authors have introduced into child psychology a method of investigating abstraction that was first used with adults by Grünbaum.[4] In its general features, the method consists of the following. The child is presented with a group of meaningless figures separated by a line into two groups; either a projection light or a slide projector is used. In the easiest case, each sub-group contains two figures; there are also sub-groups of three, four, five or six figures each. One figure is repeated in both sub-groups; all the others are different. The time of presentation is 3 seconds. The child's task is to find the identical figure in the two sub-groups, point out, on an empty chart, the place that it occupied and then seek it on a control sheet among 20–25 figures. These experiments have shown that the child's capacity for abstraction increases with age, and is correlated with intelligence. Moreover, the more difficult the task, i.e. the larger the number of figures in a group, the greater is the influence of the superiority of gifted children.

Eliasberg, in a study of the psychology and pathology of abstraction, offers serious criticism of the Koch, Habrich and von Kuenburg method.[5] He points out that these experiments require of the children, in addition to processes of abstraction, completion of a number of operations of a secondary order, e.g. seeking two similar figures, remembering them, recognizing them in a series of many others, locating them in a specific place on a sheet of paper, etc. Successful or unsuccessful accomplishment of these operations has an essential influence on the outcome of the experiment, and so the results obtained are not sufficiently indicative of processes of abstraction. Heffler, on the other hand, proved that, in these experiments, children with a visual type of imagination had a considerable advantage and ultimately did better than more intelligent children who had another kind of imagination. From the standpoint of studying the process of concept formation in children, the most serious shortcoming of this method lies elsewhere. However, this shortcoming is also inherent in other methods of studying abstraction in children. Therefore, let us dwell briefly on them.

An example of experiments in which it is independent attributes of objects, colour, form, etc. that are abstracted instead of comparatively independent objects (e.g. individual figures) are those by Katz.[6] Katz showed pre-school children a simple geometric figure, e.g. a red triangle, and had them select from a group of figures lying on a table exactly the same figure as that in the model. The task could clearly not be accomplished since among the figures on the table there were some that were similar to the model in shape, but were different colours, while others were identical in colour, but different in shape. Katz set up his experiment to see whether pre-school children could abstract positively at all, i.e. to determine a stable positive response to any attribute existing in combination with other attributes. The instructions in Katz's experiments required the child to respond to total similarity. However, this response was impossible under the experimental conditions. What would a child do? Would he act completely at random, or would he display a constant response to one specific attribute? To which one, colour or shape? Thus, the principal characteristic of Katz's method was that the child himself was required to select the criterion of abstraction, if he was capable of abstraction at all. It was found that in most instances the children chose figures of the same colour as the model. For example, if the experimenter displayed a red triangle and there were three red circles and three white triangles on the table, the children would almost invariably choose the red circles. Katz therefore concluded that pre-school children had the capacity to single out a specific attribute common to a number of objects and to react to it (and that colour had a greater impact than shape on children between the ages of two years, nine months, and five years). In experiments in which competing colours were eliminated, the children positively abstracted shape.

Because Katz's experiments aroused some doubts, Tobie tested his method in 1924 in a mass study involving about a thousand children.[7] Tobie established three phases in a child's development. The first phase, up to three years, eight months, is characterized by the fact that an orientation toward colour or shape depends on the saliency (Aufdringlichkeit) of one or the other of these attributes in the particular situation, not on general conditions. This he calls the zone of suggestibility (*Zone der Suggestibilität*). Then follows a colour zone (from three years, nine months, to five years old), when the child is orientated toward colour by virtue of constitutional factors. In the last months of this zone, the child makes the transition to an orientation toward shape. At the age of five years, two months, a new zone begins in which orientation toward shape dominates; but later, the capacity to abstract positively in both directions appears.

We may mention one other type of method for studying processes of abstraction in children. This is the method of Eliasberg, who used it mainly in experiments with pre-school children. The experiments may be described as follows. Sheets of thin cardboard 4 × 10 cm in diameter and of different colours (green, red, blue and yellow) are prepared. These sheets are bent in an arc, and small paper sticks are attached on the inside half of the sheets of a particular colour. It is impossible to see which of the sheets the sticks are attached to merely by looking at them from the top from the outside; to see this they have to be turned over. Sheets of two colours are used in each experiment. The sheets of one colour have the sticks attached; those of the other colour do not. For example, five yellow sheets with sticks and five blue sheets without them are placed in random order on the table.

The experimenter gives the child two extra sheets, one yellow with a stick, the other blue without it, and asks him to turn both of them over. Then he takes them away from the child and hides them. Now the experimenter points to the sheets lying on the table and says: 'Now look there'. The child begins to play with the sheets, turning them over and rearranging them from place to place, uttering his thoughts and asking questions. Finally, he indicates that he has nothing else to do. If there are some children who from the very beginning do not know what they are to do and show no sign of activeness, the experimenter lets them know that they should put the sheets of paper with the sticks aside. Then the child is taken aside, and during this time, some of the paper sheets or all of them are replaced by others. For example, the blue sheets without the sticks are replaced with sheets of a new colour, also without the sticks. The positive colour remains the same (yellow), and the negative colour (blue) is replaced by a new one. In another case, the positive colour is changed. In still other cases, the positive and negative colours change places; and in a fourth case, one pair of colours is completely replaced by another pair, etc. One of the most interesting modifications is for one or two sheets of a positive colour to be replaced by one or two sheets of the same colour but without sticks. This is a disruptive experiment, as it is called, which violates the law linking two attributes (the colour and the presence of sticks). When one of the above modifications has been made, the child is again taken to the table and given the freedom to play with the sheets, and the experimenter records all of his actions and words as he does so. Then a pause is made again, a new modification made, etc. Thus we see that in Eliasberg's experiments the subject's behaviour has nothing to do with carrying out a specific task. Eliasberg studies natural, spontaneous processes of abstraction in children. The only instruction the child receives from the experimenter or from the entire situation is to seek out the sheets with the sticks. Eliasberg is interested in how fast and in what way the child arrives at an understanding of the connection between the colour of the sheets and the presence or absence of sticks under them. All the modifications made in the material during the experiment serve to develop in the child a purely abstract understanding of this connection, namely, 'that of two colours, only one has the given attribute (stick)'.

Eliasberg points out that, in all preceding studies of abstraction in children, abstraction proved to be too closely related to and limited by the sensory nature of the material. Abstraction did not go beyond the limits of the concrete. In the final analysis, Koch, Habrich, von Kuenburg and Katz required of the child that he perceive relations of similarity among concrete attributes of objects undifferentiated in terms of sensory context. Eliasberg's studies for the first time posed the question of whether processes of abstraction that lead to the development of common generalized reactions not only to known, mutually similar sensory stimuli but also to a wholly formal relation among any stimuli, regardless of their sensory nature, take place in the natural behaviour of pre-school children.

We have examined the basic methods for studying processes of abstraction in children. Anyone who approaches these methods from the standpoint of the problem of concept formation cannot help but notice one property common to them all: that processes of abstraction are studied in experimental situations that are essentially alien to the natural conditions in which these same processes lead to concept formation. In [natural] concept formation, abstraction is directed and guided by words. The products of abstraction therefore enter into a close relation with language, and a concept is born: the meaning of a word. But the procedures of Koch, Habrich, von Kuenburg, Katz and Eliasberg differ in that processes of abstraction are studied in a situation that precludes taking into account the functional role of words, the most important factor in concept formation. Actually, in all these experiments, the role of words, as a factor that organizes and guides the processes of abstraction, is reduced to a minimum. In Eliasberg's method, words do not even determine the ultimate objective toward which the child should strive, for in general there are no such objectives in these experiments. One of Katz's principal conclusions is that, regardless of whether the child is given the task of finding figures exactly like the models, or vice versa, i.e. completely different figures, he will behave in exactly the same way and choose figures similar in colour. Thus, because of the as yet insufficient development in the child of an understanding of speech, the instructions, so to speak, only set the process in motion, without determining either its direction or its individual stages. The child's behaviour is stimulated exclusively by a series of stimulus objects. Verbal stimuli are either completely absent or at least have no direct influence on the child's relations to the objective stimuli. In the experiments of Koch, Habrich and von Kuenburg, the direction of abstraction is determined by the instructions, namely to seek similar figures; but it is determined precisely as in any experiment in which the subject is set some task by means of instructions. Through words, the subject receives the actual task of abstracting from a given set of similar elements; but as soon as he begins to carry out this task, his actions are determined exclusively by the objective world with which he is dealing. Divergences from this logic serve as indicators of the defectiveness and unsuccessfulness of the psychological operations. Words do not guide the psychological operations; hence, the obtained product does not form a concept. We do not even mention the fact that Grünbaum's method, which these three authors used, is based on the abstraction of comparatively independent elements of a set, not interdependent attributes common to a number of objects. This also deprives it of any value for the study of processes of concept formation, since concepts also include interdependent attributes.

Thus, whereas the method of definition goes no farther than the words that participate in the process of concept formation, the method of investigating abstraction is limited exclusively to objects on the basis of which a concept is formed, without taking into account that a concept arises only if the child's psychological operations directed toward the objects are guided by words, i.e. if the child uses words as a means to guide the process of abstraction in one direction or another. 'Words without sensory material, or sensory material without words': that, in a nutshell, is the contrast between the method of definition and the method of studying abstractions.

It is all the more interesting that all the above-enumerated studies of processes of abstraction in children ran up against the fact that the level of development of processes of abstraction and the role of speech in the child's behaviour depend on the extent of his verbal resources. Data on the pace of development of processes of abstraction in relation to age for normal and deaf mute children are interesting in this respect (Habrich, Heffler). In normal children the process is especially intensive during the first half of the school period, and considerably slower in the second half. For deaf mutes, the contrary is the case: at first deaf mutes lag considerably behind normal children, but then they catch up considerably. According to Lindner's data, the backwardness of young deaf mutes in processes of abstraction is combined with a clear superiority over normal children in terms of recognizing people; and, with regard to remembering meaningless figures, they barely lag behind normal children at all. The same is true of their memory of *Schriftbilder*.[8] On the other hand, in every case in which the processing of data of sense experience, singling out what is essential, perceiving and utilizing relations, or abstracting is the task rather than simple remembering, the deaf mute child is quite a bit behind his normal peer. This seems clearly to be a question of retarded development of the corresponding functions because of deafness and lack of speech, as evidenced by the fact that by the third to fourth year of schooling, when deaf mute children learn to speak, their capacity for abstraction begins to increase sharply, and the gap between them and normal children narrows considerably. As Heffler says, an intellectual revolution takes place in a deaf child who at this time learns speech in a school for deaf mutes; this revolution is similar to what takes place in three-to-six-year-old children who can hear. In both cases, the discovery of the significance of language and of its function of naming is the source of a fundamental change in the child's behaviour. Spontaneous questions about the names of objects and about the purposes and the causes of things and processes are proof that, at this point, the young child who can hear and the deaf mute schoolchild begins to carry out differentiations and ordering in the infinite diversity surrounding them; they begin to recognize relations and systems of relations, and thus grow into the world of concepts of the adult human being. Interesting data about the role of language in the process of abstracting are provided by Descoeudres and Beckmann.[9] These authors observed that normal children between the ages of six and eight found it much easier to imagine a corresponding number of objects on the basis of a numeral given to them than to name the number of objects presented to them. This means that the speech abstraction of a symbol, used repeatedly and in many ways, furthers the process of abstraction from infinite sets of objects of counting to the concept of number. Language propels our thought along the path of abstraction, says Lindner. We encounter similar findings in Eliasberg. In his study, discussed above, Eliasberg demonstrated different results depending on which of three types the subject belonged to. The first group consisted of children with good general development and speech development. The second group was composed of children of normal development who were a bit retarded in speech. The third group of children consisted of those who were poorly and weakly developed in general and very retarded in speech. It was found that children of the second group, those who had developed normally, but were retarded in speech, had more difficulty than children of the first group in abstracting from sensory experience, and were more bound to concrete sensory situations.

Thus, the educationally stimulating role of words in processes of abstraction is beyond a doubt. Study of processes of abstraction as they take place under the direct guidance of words is therefore all the more interesting. The above analysed experimental methods, however, do not allow us to study them.

## Methods of experimental study of the process of concept formation in children

We have outlined in general contours the immediate environment in which the method of double stimulation was born and was gradually developed for use in studying children's concepts. A brief schematic history of it reduces roughly to the following. We have found the sources of it in old experimental psychology. In 1912, a study by the English subjectivist psychologist Aveling was published entitled *On the Consciousness of the Universal and the Individual*. The author himself called his work a 'contribution to the phenomenology of the thought processes'. And in fact, its purpose was to study, from a phenomenological perspective, processes of thought. 'What is discoverable in our consciousness when we think about the general or the individual, when we think "man"? Is it "this man" of "all men"?' asks the author.[10] The question was similarly posed in empirical psychology long before Aveling. One of the first was Ribot with his 'Inquiry into general ideas'.[11] Just before Aveling, psychologists of the Würzburg school, using the method of self-observation, attempted to give a phenomenological characterization of the processes of thought and, in particular, the processes of subjective experiencing of the meaning of words, judgements, inferences, etc. But Aveling made a substantial change in the experimental method. He proposed studying the subjective experience of concepts associated not with words of one's native language, but with artificial words created experimentally. Aveling showed his subjects a series of pictures. Each series contained five pictures portraying some objects that were similar to one another, e.g. five different fruits, five different flowers, five different musical instruments, five birds of different species, etc. A meaningless word was under each picture, the same for all pictures in each series. For example, all flowers had the inscription 'Kumic'; all birds, 'Tuben'; and all fruits, 'Digep'. Over a period of several days, the subjects learned by heart the meaning of the nonsense words and created associations between these words and the pictures corresponding to them. This was done as follows. The subjects were presented, in random order, with pictures from the different series. They had to read aloud the meaningless words and look at the corresponding picture attentively for 10–15 seconds. In the second half of each session, after a ten-minute pause, the experimenter would name the nonsense words the subjects had been studying and begin the rehearsal session. The subject had to listen attentively and answer with the word 'yes' as soon as the meaning of the experimental word he heard arose in his consciousness. Then the subject would give a detailed description of his experiences based on self-observation. After 20 sessions, after the associations between the nonsense words and the corresponding objects were more or less firmly entrenched, Aveling carried out some test involving the 'Completion of Part Judgements'. Aveling would say some incomplete sentences in which the experimental words were the subjects and the subject had to give a suitable adjective. The experimental words had now an individual and then a general meaning. For example, the experimenter would begin as follows: 'All Digep are . . .', and the subject would have to finish the sentence. Or 'No Kumic is . . .', 'The first Sorab is . . .'. After completing the sentence, the subjects would communicate what they had observed in self-observation. What was unique about Aveling's procedure? The old studies of the problem of the subjective experience of the meaning of words by psychologists of the empirical school used the same method. The experimenter would present the subject with a stimulus word, and the subject had to respond to it with some other word, or not respond to it at all, and then, at a given signal, describe experiences elicited by the stimulus word. Aveling remained wholly on the foundation of self-observation.

What made him decide not to use native language words as stimuli? Solely interests of self-observation. He hoped in this way to avoid the difficulties self-observation constantly encountered. These were difficulties in distinguishing the subjective experiences of the meaning of a word from the subjective experiences associated with the perception of the word itself as an auditory or visual stimulus. We are unable to hear any word of our native language without its meaning surging up into our heads, so closely are they related. Aveling wanted in some way to slow this process of transition from the subjective experience of the verbal form to experience of the meaning of the word, and so introduced new words that were not so tightly fused with the corresponding concepts. Hence, it is quite clear that Aveling did not study the process of concept formation, but only processes of the subjective experience of what had already been completed, of the concepts the subjects already possessed, e.g. the concepts of fruit, musical instruments, etc.

But the inclusion in the experiment, together with pictures of the objects, of words related to these objects and the use of special experimental words – this was the part of Aveling's procedure that had a future in the study of processes of concept formation – of course, with rejection of Aveling's purely phenomenological, subjective position. A study by Ach, the founder of the school of 'Determinationspsychologie', marked a decisive advance. His study was published in the book *Über die Begriffsbildung*, which came out in 1921.[12] Ach conducted experiments not only with adults but also with children. His method of studying concepts, the so-called search method [*Suchmethode*], was based on the following theoretical postulates, the formulation of which was doubtless one of Ach's merits.

1  One cannot be limited to the study of ready made concepts; the process of formation of new concepts is important.
2  The method of experimental investigation should be genetic–synthetic; during the course of the experiment, the subject must gradually arrive at the construction of a new concept – hence the need to create experimental concepts with an artificial grouping of attributes that belong to them.
3  It is necessary to study the process by which words acquire significance, the process of transformation of a word into a symbol and a representation of an object or of a group of similar objects – hence the necessity of using artificial experimen-

tal words that are initially nonsense to the subject, but acquire meaning for him during the course of the experiment.

4 Concepts cannot be regarded as closed, self-sufficient structures, and they cannot be abstracted from the function they serve in the sequence of mental processes. The processes of the objective conditions, i.e. a set of objects possessing common properties, is not sufficient for concept formation. A human being cannot be visualized as a passive photographic plate on which images of objects fall, reinforcing one another in their similar parts and forming a concept, like Galton's collective photograph. Concept formation also has subjective preconditions and requires the presence of a definite (psychological) need, which it is the function of the concept to satisfy. In thought and action, the development of a concept plays the role of an instrument for achieving certain ends. This functional aspect must be taken into account in an investigatory procedure; a concept must be studied in its functional context. We must pursue the path taken by Köhler, who in his study of the intelligence of anthropoids would put them in situations that could be resolved only by using certain tools, so that the functional use of those tools became an indicator of the level of the animal's intellectual behaviour.[13] Similarly, in an experiment, the subject must be confronted with tasks that can be accomplished only if the subject develops certain concepts. The development of those concepts will require the use of a series of nonsense verbal signs to solve the problem, and as a result those signs will acquire a specific sense for the subject.

These are the main postulates on which Ach based his search method.[14] Let us now go on to a concrete description of the procedure as it was used with children.

The experimental material was a collection of geometric figures made of cardboard, 48 in all: 12 red, 12 blue, 12 yellow and 12 green. The 12 figures of each colour were separated by size, weight and shape. Six figures of each colour were large, and six were small. The six large items were divided by shape into two cubes, two pyramids and two cylinders, the pairs being outwardly identical. One cube, pyramid and cylinder were filled, and were heavy, whereas its partner was light. The same division was made for the six small units of each colour: two cubes, two pyramids and two cylinders, one of each shape being heavy and the other light. The units of each colour thus consisted of three large heavy and three large light items and three small heavy and three small light items.

We see that the collection of figures was strictly symmetrical. The experiments were carried out in three phases. The first was a practice period (eine Übungsperiode); the second, a period of search (Suchperiode); and the third, a period of testing (Prüfungsperiode). Each session began with a period of teaching/learning and practising. The figures were arranged in front of the child. Pieces of paper were attached to them on which experimental words were written. To all the large heavy figures, labels with the word 'Gazun' were attached; the large light objects bore labels with the word 'Ras'; the small heavy objects, the word 'taro'; and the small light ones, the word 'fal'. At first the subject had to deal with only a small number of figures. Then, in each new session, the number of figures increased until it reached 48. On the first day of the experiments, the children began with only six large blue figures. They were arranged in a *standard order*. The heavy figures with the label 'Gazun' were placed closest to the subject in a first row. To the left was a cube, followed by a pyramid and, finally, a cylinder. The light figures with the inscription 'Ras' were added in a second row. These were arranged in the same order so that the light cube stood behind the heavy cube, etc. The figures in the second row appeared no different to the eye than the figures standing in front of them. To determine the differences, they had to be picked up. The experimenter gave the child the instruction to lift a figure slightly and to say aloud what was written on it. Initially he lifted the large heavy cube to the side of the subject, and then the light cube behind it, then the heavy pyramid, followed by the light pyramid, etc. This procedure was usually repeated three times. Then the child was turned around while the pairs of figures were rearranged: a heavy figure of any shape, together with its inscription, was shifted to the second row in the place of the light object, and the latter was placed in the first row where the heavy one had stood. As a result, the 'normal order' (normale Ordnung) was replaced by an 'exchanged order' (vertauschte Ordnung). The child again lifted the figures in the same sequence and read what was written on them.

After three rehearsals, the figures were again rearranged. Now they were without any spatial pattern, in complete disorder (the so-called bunte Ordnung). Three new exercises were performed, then there was a four minute pause, during which the experimenter removed the inscriptions from the figures, hid them and shifted the figures into a new order without any pattern at all, as before. The practice period, which consisted of a normal, an exchanged and a random order, ended, and a search period (Suchperiode) began. The child received the instructions: 'Find and put to the side all figures on which a piece of paper with the word "Gazun" was once written. You should pick them up'. When this task was completed, in whatever way, the child was asked why he thought that 'Gazun' had been written on the figures put aside. The time elapsed in completing the assignment, the order of placement of the figures and the explanation given by the child were recorded. If the task was performed incorrectly, the experimenter would say, 'You were wrong', without indicating what the mistake was.

The first task was followed by a second, third and fourth. The child had to tell what remained and what was written on the figures that remained. If he worked incorrectly or hesitantly, the practice period was repeated, after a five minute pause, with the same figures, and the child had to solve the same problems.

The child then moved on to practice and perform the tasks with the six small figures, 'taro' and 'fal'. Everything was done in the same order. At the end of this session, or in the next session on the following day, 12 blue figures arranged in normal order were immediately presented to the subject, the large ones to the left, and the small ones to the right. After three practice sessions, the figures were rearranged in altered order, and then in random order. In the search period the child had to perform not two, but four tasks, namely: to select figures on which the words 'Gazun', 'taro' and 'Ras' had been written and to say what remained. In the following sessions, the subject was presented with 24, 36 and 48 figures immediately after preliminary practice and had to perform the same tasks. The solution of each task required setting out six figures rather than three when there were figures of two colours, and their total number was 24, nine figures when there were figures of three colours, and 12 when figures of four colours were presented. In fact, when there were 48 figures on the table, there were 12 large, heavy 'Gazuns', three blue, three red, three green and three yellow.

After five to seven sessions, a normal child in most cases will have fully mastered the tasks required of him, will abstract from the colour, form and shape of the figures, and will begin to justify his choice of the same two attributes of the figures that were part of the concepts, namely heaviness and colour. The time spent in performing the task becomes considerably shorter, and in selecting the necessary figure the child ceases to act at random and does not make superfluous movements. To some degree or another, he begins to follow a certain order, based on, for example, the principle of colour or shape, etc., and seeks what is useful to him, first among figures of the same colour, then among figures of another colour, etc.; or else he begins with cubes, then selects from the pyramids and finally from among the cylinders. Counting is used to check on the thoroughness of completion of the task (whether everything has been selected). After becoming acquainted with the structure of the collection, the child is now able to solve the tasks by reasoning. Thus, for example, if the big light figures are 'Ras' and have already been selected, then when the child receives the task of selecting 'Gazun' figures, he may put aside all the remaining large figures without weighing them, since in the collection there are only two kinds of large figures, and if 'Ras' has already been selected, only 'Gazun' remain. Of course, not all children are equally able to develop such helping techniques for work with concepts. There are different levels of intelligence, and a broad range of age as well. Finally, the experiment enters its last phase, the testing phase. This period is necessary to establish whether the previous nonsense words 'Gazun', 'Ras', 'taro' and 'fal' have acquired some meaning for the child because of their functional utilization (Prüfungsperiode). The experimenter asks a number of questions: 'How do "Gazun" differ from "Ras"?' 'Are "Gazun" bigger than "taro"?' 'Are "taro" heavier or lighter than "fal"?'. 'What is "Ras"?' 'What is "taro"?' etc. The child answers the questions without looking at the figures, and his answers and the time required to answer are recorded. Then a Maselonovsky sentence formation experiment begins.[15] For example, a child is asked to compile a sentence in which the words 'Ras' and 'Gazun' appear. This ends the experiments.

Thus we see that during the testing period, Ach used a method of definition and techniques similar to it with regard to newly formed concepts. This requires either the definition of new concepts or indications of differences between them. If we now examine carefully the overall course of the experiments from beginning to end, it is not difficult to see that the experiments pass through two stages in terms of the number of attributes that must be positively abstracted and associated with the

experimental words. The first stage (Stufe der Grundeigenschaft) involves work with
only six blue figures – first, with large ones, and then with small ones. At this stage
the experimental word induces the subject to make a positive abstraction of only one
attribute, weight. To be able to select 'Gazun' or 'Ras' figures from among the large
figures the child must know that 'Gazun' is written on the heavy figures. To resolve
the same tasks with the small figures, the child must again take into account only the
fact that 'taro' is written on the labels on the heavy objects and 'fal', on the light ones.
When the child has 12 figures directly before him, the experiments enter the second
stage, the stage of primary differentiation. The combination of two pairs of signs,
'Gazun' and 'Ras', and 'taro' and 'fal' in one verbal series impels the subject to make
a positive abstraction of one more attribute, size. For completion of the task, the
subject now has to associate two attributes, weight and size, with each experimental
word: 'Gazun' are large and heavy, 'taro' are small and heavy, etc. This becomes the
final content of the experimental concepts. However, after the first series of experiments was ended, Ach usually did a second series using the same procedure, as a
continuation of the first. The only difference from the first was that the concept
included one more attribute, colour, and later, also a fourth attribute, shape. In place
of the four concepts 'Gazun', 'Ras', 'taro' and 'fal', there were now 16: 'bu-Gazun'
(large heavy blue), 'ge-Gazun' (large heavy yellow), 'ro-Gazun' (large heavy red) and
'nu-Gazun' (large heavy green); then 'bu-Ras' (large light blue), 'ge-Ras' (large light
yellow), etc. Following the same principle, instead of just 'taro', we now have 'bu-
taro', 'ge-taro', 'ro-taro' and 'nu-taro'; and in place of 'fal', we have 'bu-fal', 'ge-fal',
'ro-fal' and 'nu-fal'. Retaining the same series of objects, but enriching and differentiating the series of signs, Ach observed a new aspect of the abstraction process as well
as new concepts.

Ach calls this stage of the experiment the stage of secondary differentiation.
Primary differentiation took place in the first series, when the attribute of size was
added to the attribute of weight. The experiments were completed with a third stage
of differentiation when each of the 16 concepts elaborated in the preceding stage was
differentiated into three new concepts with respect to the attribute of shape. The
experimental words were now no longer 'bu-Gazun', 'ro-Gazun', etc., but 'bu-Gazun-
I' (which means large heavy blue cube), 'bu-Gazun-II' (large heavy blue pyramid),
'bu-Gazun-III' (large heavy blue cylinder), 'ro-Gazun-I', 'ro-Gazun-II', 'ro-Gazun-
III', etc. Each concept now contained the attribute of size, weight, colour and shape;
and since in Ach's collection of figures there were no two figures with the same
combination of these four attributes, the product of the third stage of differentiation
was 48 individual concepts. The content of a concept increased from stage to stage,
but the scope diminished steadily, until it reached unity.

Such was Ach's procedure. Ach [1921, p. 33] described it briefly as follows:

> The subject receives assignments he cannot complete without the help of some initially
> meaningless signs . . . These tasks can be correctly performed only on the basis of
> attentive prior observation of the words and of attributes (written on the labels) of

objects assigned to these words . . . The signs (words) are means by which the subject can achieve a specific end, namely, to solve the problems posed by the experimenter; and because they are given such use, they acquire an unequivocal meaning. They begin to be vehicles of concepts for the subject. The subject can use these signs, now full of meaning, to make statements about the state of things, and these statements will be understood by the experimenter.

Perhaps it should be stressed, in connection with this description, that the analogy that naturally suggests itself between Ach's experimental words and Ebbinghaus's nonsense words for the study of memory is correct in only one respect: in both cases the reason for using the nonsense syllables or words was the desire to achieve unequivocal results in experiments and to work with material that would be independent of the subject's past individual experience. However, everything else appears totally different. The nonsense syllables for studying memory continued to remain lifeless, meaningless syllables during the course of the experiments. But in Ach's experiments (owing to the influence Köhler's experiments had on his method), the meaninglessness of the words plays the role of something that must be eliminated; the entire design of the experiment, and all the efforts of the subject, are directed against it, and the process of the experiment is at the same time one of transforming a meaningless sign into a meaningful word.

Ach set up his experiments almost exclusively for adults. To test the applicability of his Suchmethode to children, he also included four children aged five, six, seven and eight. The five-year-old and six-year-old were unable to read, and so they would pick up their figures and repeat the corresponding words after the experimenter. The procedure was found to be fully applicable to children. They formed concepts only after considerably more exercises and searches compared with adults. But whereas the seven-year-old and eight-year-old not only finally learned correctly to choose figures but also began to present two essential attributes forming a concept to justify their choice, the younger children did not yet have the ability to provide an adequate justification for what they did. They continued even in the stage of primary differentiation to give explanations suitable only for the first stage (Stufe der Grundeigenschaft), i.e. they would point out a specific attribute of the figures, e.g. weight.

The systematic nature of the actions and the use of inferences and conclusions were at a much lower level in the children than in the adults, as was to be expected. Ach observed considerable qualitative differences among his four subjects in this respect; in addition to a total absence of a definite form of behaviour, the children were unable to carry it out to completion, or to use it rationally.

Ach's method was later put to a much broader use by Rimat and Bacher with, however, certain modifications.[16]

Rimat used Ach's method to study intelligence. It was his view that intelligence could not be reduced to purely passive discernment (Einsicht) of objective relations in the surrounding world; a factor of no less importance for characterizing intelligence was the voluntary factor, i.e. the strength of determining tendencies. This factor is important first and foremost because it will serve different ends for the person. The character and level of intelligence are expressed most distinctly in the process of creating and using the different means necessary to solve problems and achieve life objectives. For example, in tests and experiments we encounter such problems as drawing a conclusion from two premises. But life perhaps never confronts us with premises in such an open and pristine form, nor requires us to draw conclusions from them. It usually presents us with veiled, masked problems; and it is our task to create and use this or that means to resolve them. Hence, even in intelligence tests, a child should not be directly required to accomplish specific psychological operations: he must be given tasks to which such psychological operations serve as a means of access. The problem is then to determine whether the child is able to carry out these psychological operations and use them as means for solving problems. According to Rimat it is wrong, and moreover essentially futile, to attempt to study specific functions in isolation and to combine the results of discrete analytic tests in order to obtain a general picture of the subject's intelligence. Such mosaics leave out of account the unity: 'die Einheit der Leistung'. When we are required to accomplish something in some life situation, we always not only activate some isolated mental function but use every way and means suitable to achieve our end, and the failure of one function may be compensated for by increased utilization of other functions.

Since, according to Rimat, intelligence is primarily a capacity to use one's own intellectual processes as means to achieve different goals, the symptomatic value of a test for rating intelligence will be greater the richer and more diversified the psychological operations that must be called upon for doing the test. It is just this property that distinguishes Ach's search method. What is more, in most existing intelligence tests, it is impossible to eliminate the role of knowledge acquired in school and the influence of the environment. Often test performance depends on reproduction, not on new creations. Thus, for example, tests of concept definition depend largely on school knowledge, not on intelligence. A precondition for the usability of tests of concept definition, as well as of intelligence tests, is that all the children must have had the same experience, which happens very rarely. Differences in the performance of many tests depend also on differences in the degree of mastery of a language. According to Rimat, Ach's method has none of these flaws when it is used as a test: the child is given a task, and he is forced to employ a range of means and techniques to accomplish it. The final result will then depend largely on the extent to which the child's behaviour is determined by the task, whether it links together the child's actions into a single integral process. Ach's method enables us to determine whether a child is capable of using his own psychological operations of abstraction, concept formation, judgement and inference to solve a problem, linking all these operations together in a single sequence directed toward the contemplated end. Differences in school knowledge and in the richness of children's experience cannot reflect on the solution of the task because the only aspect of experience relevant to solving Ach's test is that created during the experiments themselves.

Then, as Ach himself pointed out, we are able in such a case to meet the requirement of parallel tests set by Karstädt,[17] for it permits the most varied modifications of the test in terms of selecting objects, varying the test words, varying the relations between the objects and the series of words (by new combinations of the attributes making up the experimental concepts, e.g. substituting shape + size for size + weight, colour + weight for shape + weight, etc.). It also permits broad possibilities for introducing different gradations of difficulty into the tasks. For example, the number of attributes making up the concepts can be increased, or the normal and modified order can be eliminated from the training period so that the practice sessions use exclusively figures arranged in random order. This, of course, makes the work considerably more difficult since the subject is no longer able to obtain help from complex perception, which facilitates concept formation.

Finally, there is one more advantage in using the Suchmethode as a test: we obtain an indication of not only theoretical but also practical intelligence. In the search periods (Suchperiode), problem solving requires a certain practical activity, which may take place in the most varied ways. On the other hand, the processes of abstraction and concept formation that underlie this practical activity, and then the children's justification for their actions, their answers to questions about what remained and to questions during the testing period (Prüfungsperiode), characterize theoretical intelligence.

In the light of these considerations, Rimat did some investigatory work necessary for transforming the search method into a system of tests. He created a number of intermediate experimental set-ups in which he varied in the most diverse ways both the nature of the problems and the conditions of their presentation and tested the practical value of each variant. After finding that for children between the ages of 10 and 11 experiments done with a straightforward Ach-procedure were too easy and provided no means of distinguishing the more intelligent children from among those of average intelligence, Rimat made the problem solving more difficult: the tests began immediately with 12 figures instead of six, and training was done in hodgepodge order; the normal and the altered order were totally discarded. Then, to obtain a uniform assessment and grading of the solution of all the tests, Rimat introduced some substantial changes in the search period. For example, the experimenter gave the child the problem of pulling out figures with the inscription 'Gazun'. The child would do so. However, before assigning the next task, the experimenter returned the withdrawn figures so that in his new searches the child had to work with the same number of figures as before.

Then, to facilitate the processing of results, the experimenter evaluated not the solutions of the entire task, as Ach did, but the withdrawal of each individual figure: if the subject mistakenly withdrew some figure, the experimenter immediately called attention to the mistake. This enabled Rimat to distinguish five groups on the basis of their task performance: the first group – tasks accomplished by the subjects correctly without any help; second group – slight help (e.g. at first, not all the figures were set out, it was necessary to remember, etc.); the third group – the task was performed with one mistake; fourth group – the task was performed with several mistakes; and the fifth group – unsuccessful accomplishment of the task. By substituting the numbers of these groups in place of the tasks, Rimat obtained a numerical series characterizing the process of variation in the performance level of problem solving, beginning with the first and ending with the last.

As for the reasons the children gave for their actions, Rimat only ascertained in which task a child would begin to include the two attributes that characterized the content of the experimental concepts in his reasons explaining his action, i.e. at what point it was possible to say with absolute certainty that concept formation had set in. A comparison of these data with data on problem solving is interesting from the standpoint of the relationships between theoretical and practical intelligence. Rimat arranged the children in a rank order on the basis of the average number of mistakes made on a task, i.e. on the basis of the relation of the total number of erroneously withdrawn figures to the total number of tasks. Rimat totally discarded the testing period in view of the difficulties of describing it quantitatively.

On the other hand, preliminary exercises were introduced before the beginning of the experiments with each child, since it was found that the comparability of the test results was endangered because of the influence of differences in the speed at which the children became accustomed to the experiment, and also because of differences in the children's disposition at the beginning of the experiments, when they would pick up the figures and read what was written on them without understanding why this was done. This risk was eliminated if, before the beginning of the experiments, the child went through a series of preliminary trials, i.e. a number of practice exercises and problem solving sessions with the same figures, but with other experimental words and other concepts.

If, for example, a child had the words 'vushir', 'gak', 'zubi' and 'dipu' in the main experiments and attributes of shape and colour were included in the content of the concepts that they designated, in the preliminary exercises the child would meet 'Gazun', 'Ras', 'taro' and 'fal' and also another combination of attributes making up the content of the concepts, i.e. weight and size. In special experiments Rimat also showed that preliminary trials made it possible to compare results obtained from children who were being acquainted with the search method for the first time and children who had worked with it earlier.

It was found that during the preliminary experiments, children familiar with the search method had better results than beginners; but in the main experiments, this advantage disappeared and the principal factor determining test performance was the child's intelligence.

By placing his subjects in a rank order on the basis of the average number of mistakes made on a problem, Rimat obtained a high correlation with school ratings of the children's intelligence.

Because Rimat's individual test requires three days of work (one and a half hours each day) with each child, it is very difficult to use it to study patient groups. Hence, Rimat also devised a weighted test. In a mass test, Rimat had to discard the search period, which he replaced with a testing period that in the individual test played no role at all. The test was done as follows: the children were seated in a specific way, and individual figures were given to them with notes attached. Each child would read the inscription to himself, look attentively at the figure and then pass it on to his neighbour, and would himself receive a new figure from his other neighbour. The figures were presented in random order. After a series of repetitions, the number of which depended on the child's age and the nature of the problem, the learning period ended and the check began. Each child received a sheet of paper and wrote on it his answers to questions written on the blackboard: 'How do you recognize all the figures on which the word "Gazun" or "Ras" is written?' etc. Then more exercises followed; the errors made by the subjects in answering the questions, their lack of confidence and even their inability to answer the questions led, in the new exercises, to a fundamental reorganization of attention, which was now directed toward the connection between the words and the objects. Thus, the role of the search period, which was completely left out, was taken over by the questions in the testing period. Throughout the test, which lasted three days (an hour every day), six groups of concepts with four concepts in each group were developed. The first preliminary experiments and the two groups of concepts formed on that day (heaviness + size, size + shape) were not taken into account in the evaluation and in determining the children's rank position. The subjects' responses to the questions divided them into five groups. The first group contained children with completely correct answers; they were given a score of four; the third group gave answers in which only one correct attribute in the composition of the concept was indicated, and scored two. The fifth group gave completely wrong answers or no answers: score zero. The rank position of the subject was established by adding together all the points of each subject.

In doing his mass test with several groups of school children between the ages of 11 and 14, Rimat found that the lower limit of applicability of the test was about age 12. After the age of 12 years, a considerable advance is noted in children's capacity for independent formation of new concepts. But concept formation and thought freed of sensory ingredients make demands that, as a rule, exceed the capacity of children under the age of 12. This was Rimat's basic conclusion.

## The functional method of double stimulation and study of concept formation in children

Now let us characterize the last stage in the development of the procedure for the experimental study of concept formation in children, the stage in which the method of double stimulation acquired a new use under the influence of Vygotsky's idea of the development of higher forms of behaviour. Aveling, a psychologist of the era when the Würzburg school was in the ascendancy, used double stimulation not as a method for creating the principal conditions of the process of concept formation in order to analyse that process, but as a technical means for phenomenological description of the inner experience of the meaning of fully formed concepts. For psychologists of the school of Determinationspsychologie, i.e. Ach, Bacher[18] and Rimat, double stimulation plays the role of an environment outside of which it is impossible to study the process of concept formation. But it must be said that the problem of double stimulation, the problem of forms of behaviour and thought with regard to which external stimuli fall into two series, each with a different functional significance, is a problem the proponents of Determinationspsychologie had not yet posed. Ach understood that for concept formation it was necessary to have a number of objects under whose influence concepts could form, and a number of words requisite for their formation; but his attention was not centred on the question of the specific role of each of these nor, in particular, on the question of the fundamental role of the verbal series. In accordance with the basic idea of Determinationspsychologie, Ach thought it important to show that, in processes of concept formation and in other thought processes, we are dealing with phenomena that are not so much regulated by the laws of association and reproduction of ideas as by 'determining tendencies'. As Ach himself pointed out, the essential feature of this concept is 'regulation of mental processes in accordance with the meaning (sense) of goal conception (Zielvorstellung)'.

These special influences, which are directed toward the Bezugvorstellung and derive from goal conception, determine the course of mental processes in accordance with the image of the goal; Ach therefore called them 'determining tendencies deriving from goal perception'. A number of specific characteristics of Ach's procedure for studying concepts are derived from this theoretical proposition (which we cannot undertake to criticize here). The principal task is to show that the presence of a series of objects and words and the mechanical accumulations of associations between them is insufficient for the formation of a concept. The preconditions for concept formation are present only when the subject has a goal conception, a task. Under the influence of a task and the determining tendencies deriving from it, mental processes undergo an abrupt change.

A re-ordering of the entire plane of consciousness takes place: what had earlier been in the forefront now recedes into the background, and vice versa. Attention, which has previously been centred on the correctness of the arrangement of objects, is now directed toward the connection between signs and objects: some sets are replaced by others, and signs begin to be used as means of orientation in the series of objects. A specific order of completely repetitive psychological operations, the operations of setting out the objects, etc., occurs. But all these processes are linked together in a single organic whole directed toward solving the problem.

It is only if the task is able to consolidate itself in the subject with sufficient force, if the determining influences coming from it are sufficiently powerful to steer psychological operations in a new direction and to use them as means for accomplishing the task, that concept formation is possible. An idea of the level of a child's intelligence may be gathered from how the process of concept formation takes place. This points up a number of distinctive characteristics of Ach's method. The experiments begin with a mechanical association of individual objects with individual signs. The subject does not know why he is doing this, he does not have a 'task'. The grouping of the figures, by virtue of its symmetry, diverts his attention from the conditional connections forming between the objects and the verbal signs, leading to the formation of new connections, namely, connections among the objects themselves. As a result, the mechanism of association (even when the first exercise period is deliberately prolonged to several dozen repetitions) becomes impotent: a concept is not formed. Though having received a task, the subject is unable to resolve it. However, now a decisive turning point occurs: a task and a goal conception have appeared; all processes are gradually re-ordered, the mechanism of association acquires a new use and, after one or several attempts, the task of selecting a group of figures is resolved on the basis of a concept formed with the aid of words. That is the substance of Ach's method.

We approached the process of concept formation from another angle; hence, a criticism and an objective psychological interpretation of Ach's results are totally superfluous here. We were interested not in the determining role of the task, but in the special functional significance of the verbal signs that, in the particular case, organize the subject's reactions that are directed toward objective stimuli, the material. In our laboratory we term verbal stimuli that play this role 'instrumental' stimuli, to refer to their use in the subject's behaviour. On the request of the laboratory, I made an attempt to develop a new method in which principal attention would be directed toward the role of words in concept formation in children. In the summer and autumn of 1927, I conducted an experimental study using Ach's procedure and involving ten normal children and five mentally retarded children between the ages of six and 17. I shall focus here only on the procedural aspect and the results of this study. We found that the distinctive features that were justified under Ach's conditions were in our case not only superfluous but also directly harmful. The main flaw in the procedure was that the psychological operations in which we were interested were not sufficiently brought to the surface in the child, they were not outwardly manifested. During the practice period, the child's behaviour seemed outwardly to be confined to the framework of a stereotyped operation, namely picking up the figures in a specific order and reading the inscriptions on them. This outward, monotonous behaviour concealed the active internal processes of the subjects' responses to double stimulation. Although the internal processes were in a state of continuous development during the exercise period for the five to ten days of the experiments, this was in no way outwardly expressed.

Hence, Ach's description of the stages traversed by the process of concept formation is based mainly on self-observation of his adult subjects, which of course is totally inapplicable to an objective psychological procedure. The period in which the subject undergoes double stimulation is the exercise period.

While this was going on, it was very important to bring out the subject's free reaction in order to assess the role verbal and object stimuli play in its genesis. Ach's procedure imposes upon the subject (in the interests of solving the problem: association and the determining tendency) a specific, stereotyped reaction, whose symptomatic value is equal to zero. The dynamics of development of an experimental concept in a child and the stages it undergoes may be clarified only by observing it during the search period – not to mention the fact that certain intermediate stages are beyond the investigator's purview, and that the nature of the response to double stimulation, i.e. the nature of the child's use of language, is totally beyond it. The fundamental flaw in Ach's method from the standpoint of the objectives we were pursuing was the way it organized the series of objects. We are dealing with an artificially, symmetrically constructed microworld that enables us to discover quite efficiently phenomena that are very important from the standpoint of Determinationspsychologie, i.e. the succession of complexes under the influence of determining tendencies, the emergence of a certain number of principles of ordering (Ordnungsprinzipien), the use of interferences, counting (Hilfskriterien). All these phenomena are specially organized by Ach's experimental design to show that not only the process of concept formation but also the use of fully formed concepts are under the influence of goal conceptions, as a result of which a set of auxiliary techniques to economize effort is developed with their assistance. By contrast, in natural processes of concept formation, objects are never grouped into such a smooth symmetrical system. However, the flaw of the procedure is not simply its artificiality, but the fact that this artificiality contributes to obscuring the interaction that takes place between reactions to verbal stimuli and reactions to object stimuli, with which our experiments are most concerned. To determine the contribution made by words to a child's reaction to the objective world, it is most expedient to present this objective world as a motley, unorganized diversity, so that it can be mastered only by using words. But the relationship between the series of objects and the series of words should be such that any reaction of the child will typify the extent and the originality of this [word] use. On the basis of these considerations, a procedure was developed under Vygotsky's leadership, the main principles of which I shall now present to conclude this essay.[19]

On a game board divided up into fields, about 20–30 wooden figures resembling draughtsmen are placed in one field. These figures are differentiated as follows: (1) by colour (yellow, red, green, black, white), (2) by shape (triangle, pyramid, rectangle, parallelepiped, cylinder), (3) by height (short and tall), (4) by planar dimensions (small and large). A test word is written on the bottom of each figure. There are four different test words: 'bat' written on all the figures small and short, regardless of their colour and shape; 'dek', small and tall; 'rots', large and short; 'mup', large and tall. The figures are arranged in random order. The number of figures of each colour, shape and of each of the other attributes varies. The experimenter turns over one figure – a red, small, short parallelepiped – and asks the child to read the word 'bat' written on its exposed underside. Then the figure is placed in a special field on the board. The experimenter tells the child that he has before him toys that belong to children from some foreign country. Some toys are called 'bat' in the language of this people, for example, the upturned figure; others have a different name. There are other toys on the board that are also called 'bat'. If the child guesses after thinking carefully where there are other toys called 'bat' and picks them up and places them on a special field of the board, he receives the prize lying on this field. The prize may be a sweet, a pencil, etc. The toys cannot be turned upside down to read what is written on them. The child must work without hurrying, as well as possible, so as not to pick up any toy that has another name and so as not to leave any toy in place that should be taken away. The child rehearses the conditions of the game and removes a group of figures. The time and the order in which the child removes the figures are recorded. The most varied types of responses are observed: test reactions without any reasons, choice on the basis of a set (e.g. forming a collection), choices on the basis of maximum similarity, on the basis of similarity with regard to one attribute, etc. The experimenter asks why the child picks up these toys and what toys were called 'bat' in the language of the foreign people. Then he has the child turn over one of the figures not removed and finds that 'bat' is written on it. 'Here, you see, you made a mistake; the prize isn't yours yet'. For example, if the child picks up all the parallelepipeds regardless of their colour and size on the basis of the fact that the model is a parallelepiped, the experimenter has him expose the unremoved small short red circle 'bat' similar to the model in colour. The overturned figure is placed with the inscription up alongside the recumbent model, the figures removed by the child are taken back, and he is asked again to try to win the prize by picking all the 'bat' toys on the basis of the two toys known to him. One child will remove all red figures; another, all parallelepipeds and cylinders; a third will select a collection of figures of different shapes; still others will repeat their preceding response; a fifth will make a completely arbitrary choice of figures, etc. The game continues until the child picks up all the figures correctly and gives a correct definition of the concept 'bat'. Thus, the basic principle of our procedure is that the series of objects is given in complete form at the very beginning of the game, but the verbal series is gradually augmented; all the new items of this series gradually enter into the game one by one. After each change in the verbal series, i.e. after each change in the nature of the double stimulation, the child gives us his free reaction, on the basis of which we can evaluate the degree of functional utilization of the items in the verbal series and the child's psychological reactions to the series of objects.

We did a preliminary study of the process of concept formation in adults using a similar method, and at present are completing an analogous study of children.

The basic features of the procedure we developed amount to the following. There is a collection of figures of different shapes, colours, height and planar dimensions. Unlike Ach's set of figures, this collection is a motley, unorganized whole: it is irregular and unsymmetric. Different attributes occur an unequal number of times. The collection is based on four experimental concepts associated with test words, which are written on the bottoms of the figures, not visible to the child. Each concept contains two attributes, e.g. height and planar dimensions. One concept embraces all tall and large figures; the other, all tall and small; the third, all short and small; and the fourth, all short and large. The experiment is done as a game. The figures are arranged on a game board at random, without any pattern. These are toys of a foreign nation. One of them is turned upside down, and its name in the language of this people is read aloud. According to the rules of the game, the child must remove all the toys that have the same name as the up-ended model and place them in a special field on the board without turning them over and looking at the inscription. He obtains in exchange for these toys a sweet, a pencil or something else of the sort from the experimenter as a prize. The entire game consists of the child's attempts to place correctly all the figures with the same inscription as the model. After each such attempt, the experimenter turns over the new figure, revealing the child's mistake, which is either that among the removed figures there is one figure with a different name from that which is on the model, or that among the figures not removed there is one with the same name as the model and hence belongs to the field. Since after each placement of the figures the child discovers the name of a new figure (which the experimenter has up-ended), every new attempt of the child to solve the problem is done on the basis of a larger number of models.

Thus, the principle of the experiment is that the series of objects is given to the child immediately as a whole but the series of words is given gradually, and the nature of the double stimulation continually varies. After each such change we obtain the child's free response, which enables us to assess the changes that have taken place in the child's psychological operations as a consequence of the fact that the series of objects now contains a new element from the verbal series. This enables us to assess the degree to which a child makes use of words. Of course, the task can be accomplished correctly only if the experimental concepts that underlie the test words have been formed. In a similar procedure, we carried out a study of concept formation in adults and ascertained its productiveness. We are now completing a study of concept formation in schoolchildren and are beginning to work with pre-school children, for whom verbal signs are replaced by arbitrary colour tokens. We are also in the process of developing and testing a new test.[20]

An illustration of the nature of the data that can be obtained on the basis of this procedure can be seen in the fact that a word in our experiments passes through three stages that are present in outline in the ontogeny of children's concepts. Initially, it is an individual sign with its own name; then it becomes a family sign with its own name associated with a series of concrete objects (complex concept); finally, it becomes a general abstraction. Some children pass through all these three stages; others remain at the middle stage. Thus, we have an experimentally organized picture of the ontogeny of concepts and are able to carry out analytical studies of the functional role of words in all stages of this ontogeny.

## Notes

First published as Sakharov, L. S. 1930: O metodakh issledovanija [On the methods of investigating concepts]. *Psikhologija*, 3, 3–32. The present translation by Michel Vale was first published in the July/August issue of *Soviet Psychology*, 1990, 28, 35–66. The article was based on a talk which Sakharov presented at the Pedological Congress in Moscow on 1 January 1928. Shortly thereafter – on 10 May 1928 – Sakharov died under unknown circumstances. Leonid

Solomonovich Sakharov (1900–1928) worked with Vygotsky at the Experimental Institute of Psychology (headed by Kornilov) and soon started co-operating with Vygotsky. His only other publication that we know of also concerned (German) methods of investigating concept formation. See Sakharov, L. S. 1928: Obrazovanie ponjatij u umstvenno-otstalykh detej (Referat) [The formation of concepts in mentally retarded children (A synopsis). *Voprosy Defektologii*, 2, 24–33.

1 This paragraph refers to the following publications: Binet, A. 1903: *L'étude expérimentale de l'intelligence*. Paris: Schleicher; Bobertag, O. 1911: Über Intelligenzprüfungen (nach der Methode von Binet und Simon). *Zeitschrift für angewandte Psychologie*, 5, 105–203; Eng, H. 1914: Abstrakte Begriffe im Sprechen und Denken des Kindes. *Zeitschrift für angewandte Psychologie*. Beiheft 8; Gregor, A. 1915: Untersuchungen über die Entwicklung einfacher logischer Leistungen. *Zeitschrift für angewandte Psychologie*, 10, 339–451. The reference to Pelman is inaccurate. It may refer to John R. Pelsma who asked his four-year-old daughter to define the words she knew. She Pelsma, J. R. 1910: A child's vocabulary and its development. *The Pedagogical Seminary*, 17, 328–69. Another possibility is that Sakharov intended to refer to the work of Hans Pohlman. In that case a plausible source is Pohlman, H. 1912: Beitrag zur Psychologie des Schulkindes. *Pädagogische Monographien*. Vol. 13 Leipzig: Otto Nemnich Verlag. Pohlmann investigated the development of children's understanding of word meanings; Roloff, H. P. 1922: *Vergleichend-psychologische Untersuchungen über kindlichen Definitionsleistungen*. Leipzig: Barth; Moede, W. 1916: Die Methoden der Begriffsuntersuchung. *Zeitschrift für pädagogische Psychologie und experimentelle Pädagogik*, 17, 149–66.

2 Lindworsky, J. 1916: *Das schlussfolgernde Denken. Experimentelle psychologische Untersuchungen*. Freiburg: Herder.

3 In the present talk we use the word 'concept' in the traditional sense it has in experimental psychology, which inherited the definition of this term from formal logic. A concept in this sense (a general idea, the meaning of a word) is not a concept for dialectical logic; however, it is synthetically related to the latter as a specific stage in its development [original footnote].

4 Refers to the following publications: Grünbaum, A. A. 1908: Über die Abstraktion der Gleichheit. *Archiv für die Gesamte Psychologie*, 12, 340–478; Habrich, J. 1914: Über die Entwicklung der Abstraktionsfähigkeit von Schülerinnen. *Zeitschrift für angewandte Psychologie*, 9, 189–244; Koch, A. 1913: Experimentelle Untersuchungen über die Abstraktionsfähigkeit von Volkschulkinderen. *Zeitschrift für angewandte Psychologie*, 7, 332–91; Kuenburg, M. von 1920: Über Abstraktionsfähigkeit und die Entstehung von Relationen beim vorschulpflichtigen Kinde. *Zeitschrift für angewandte Psychologie*, 17, 270–312. We have not been able to locate Heffler's paper and do not know whether Heffler is the correct spelling of the author's name (it may have been Alois Höfler, for instance).

5 Eliasberg, W. 1925: Psychologie und Pathologie der Abstraktion. *Zeitschrift für angewandte Psychologie*. Beiheft 35. Leipzig: Barth.

6 Katz, D. 1913: Über gewisse Abstraktionsprozesse bei vorschulpflichtigen Kindern. *Wissenschaftliche Beiträge zur Pädagogik und Psychologie*, 4. Leipzig: Quelle & Meyer.

7 Tobie, H. 1926: Die Entwicklung der teilinhaltlichen Beachtung von Farbe und Form im vorschulpflichtigen Alter. *Zeitschrift für angewandte Psychologie*. Beiheft 38.

8 There are several plausible sources here, e.g. Lindner, G. 1882: Beobachtungen und Bemerkungen über die Entwicklung der Sprache des Kindes. *Kosmos*, 6, 321–42; 430–41; Lindner, G. 1885: Zum Studium der Kindersprache. *Kosmos*, 9, 161–73; 241–59; or Lindner, G. 1906: Neuere Forschungen und Anschauungen über die Sprache des Kindes.

*Zeitschrift für pädagogische Psychologie, Pathologie, und Hygiene*, 7, 337–92. 'Schriftbilder' (German) are mental images or representations of a written text.

9 Refers to Descoeudres, A. 1921: *Le développement de l'enfant de deux à sept ans*. Neuchatel: Delachaux et Niestlé; and Beckmann, H. 1923: Die Entwicklung der Zahlleistung bei 2– 6 jährigen Kindern. *Zeitschrift für angewandte Psychologie*, 22, 1–72. (The original Russian text had Beckinann instead of Beckmann.)

10 See p. 75 of Aveling, F. 1912: *On the Consciousness of the Universal and the Individual*. London: Macmillan.

11 Refers to Ribot's 1891: 'Enquête sur les idées générales' in *Revue Philosophique*, 32, 376–88; and Ribot, Th. 1897: *L'évolution des idées générales*. Paris: Alcan.

12 Ach, N. 1921: *Über die Begriffsbildung. Eine experimentelle Untersuchung*. Bamberg: C. C. Büchners Verlag.

13 Köhler, W. 1921: *Intelligenzprüfungen an Menschenaffen*. Berlin: Julius Springer.

14 Ach used, in addition to this method, another method of studying concepts, the so-called 'Verständigungsmethode' (the method of communication), which is based on the development of a concept using a new functional aspect: a word, which serves as a means of mutual clarification and communication, acquires a meaning, and becomes a bearer of a concept [original footnote].

15 A puzzling reference. It is clear that the children were required to construct sentences with the newly acquired concepts, but who Maselonovsky was (if that is how his name was spelled) is unknown to the editors.

16 Refers to Rimat, F. 1925: Intelligenzuntersuchungen anschliessend an die Ach'se Suchmethode. *Untersuchungen zur Psychologie, Philosophie und Pädagogik*, 5, 3/4, 1–116; and Bacher, G. 1925: Die Ach'sche Suchmethode in ihrer Verwendung zur Intelligenzprüfung. Ein Beitrag zur Psychologie des Schwachsinns. *Untersuchungen zur Psychologie, Philosophie und Pädagogik*, 4, 3/4, 209–89.

17 Karstädt, O. 1918: Zur Schaffung von Paralleltests. *Zeitschrift für angewandte Psychologie*, 13, 305–53.

18 On Bacher's investigation and procedure, see: L. S. Sakharov 1928 [Concept formation in mentally retarded children], *Voprosy defektologii*, No. 2 [original footnote].

19 In the present article, only that variant developed in studies of concept formation in children is considered. I have presented the methodological and theoretical justification for this procedure elsewhere with respect to the basic variant of study of concept formation in adults [original footnote].

20 At present, the study, begun and for the most part carried out by L. S. Sakharov at the State Insitute for Experimental Psychology (Moscow), and completed by L. S. Vygotsky, Yu. V. Kotelova and E. I. Pashkovskaya, is being prepared for the press in the form of a monograph. The principal results of this investigation were presented by Vygotsky at the First Congress on the Study of Human Behaviour, in Leningrad in January 1930 (Section on Psychology, Reflexology and Physiology of the Nervous System). See Vygotsky, L. S. 1930: Eksperimental'noe issledovanie vysshikh processov povedenija [The experimental study of higher behavioural processes]. In A. B. Zalkind (ed.) Psikhonevrologicheskie nauki v SSSR [*Psychoneurological sciences in the USSR: Materials of the 1st All-Union Congress on the Study of Human Behaviour*] (pp. 70–1). Moscow: Gosmedizdat [original footnote].

# 7

# Tool and symbol in child development

## Lev Vygotsky and Alexander Luria

## 1  The problem of the practical intelligence in animal and child

From the moment when child psychology began to develop as a special branch of psychological investigation, Stumpf[1] attempted to outline the character of this new scientific field through a comparison with botany. 'Linnaeus,' said he,

> as is well known, qualified botany as 'scientia amabilis' or 'pleasant science'. This scarcely applies to contemporary botany . . . If, indeed, any science deserves to be called pleasant, it is the psychology of childhood, the science of what we most cherish, love and take pleasure in, the thing we care most for in the world and which we therefore must study and learn to understand.

Behind this pretty comparison, however, there lies more than meets the eye, more than the mere introduction of Linnaeus' attitude toward the botany of his time into child psychology. For this comparison actually shielded an entire philosophy of child psychology, a specific concept of child development which, without saying so much in words, based all its experiments on the premise proclaimed by Stumpf. This concept stressed the botanic, vegetable character of child development, while psychological development of the child was understood, chiefly, as a growth phenomenon.

In a certain sense contemporary child psychology is not yet completely free from these botanical tendencies, which act as blinkers and hinder the light of true perception from being shed on the highly specific character of psychological development in the child as compared with growth in plants. Therefore Gesell is absolutely right when he points to the fact that our approach toward, and notions of, child development still teem with botanical comparisons. We speak of the development (growth) of the child, we qualify kindergarten as a system of early-age upbringing. It was only during the process of long investigations, lasting entire decades, that psychology overcame the first concept which saw the processes of psychological development as following and proceeding along the lines of botanic patterns.

Nowadays psychology has begun to realize that growth processes alone do not account for the whole complexity of child development; what is more, when it comes to the most complex and specific forms of human behaviour, growth, in the literal sense of the word, while remaining an element of the process of development, is but a subordinate factor. The processes of development display such complicated qualitative transformations of one form into another, as Hegel would say, such a transition of quantity into quality, and vice versa, that the notion of growth cannot be applied.

If, however, modern psychology has as a whole indeed parted company with the botanic model of child development, now, as it were, ascending the ladder of science, it abounds with ideas that centre around the concept of child development essentially being merely a more complicated and developed type of the origins and evolution of those forms of behaviour which are observed in the animal kingdom. Once the captive of botany, child psychology is now mesmerized by zoology, and many of the leading trends in modern psychology seek to receive a direct answer concerning the psychology of child development through experiments conducted on animals. These experiments, with slight modifications, are transferred from the laboratory of animal psychology into the nursery. Thus one of the most authoritative investigators in this field was obliged to acknowledge that the most important methodological achievements in child investigations are due to animal zoopsychology.

Such convergence of child and animal psychology has contributed significantly in creating a biological basis to psychological research. It has certainly led to the establishment of many highly important points which link child and animal behaviour where lower and elementary psychological processes are concerned. But recently we have been witnessing a most paradoxical stage in the development of child psychology: the chapter even now being written and dealing with the development of the higher intellectual processes native to man as a human being, evolves[2] as the direct continuation of the corresponding chapter of animal psychology.

Nowhere does this paradoxical attempt to solve the mystery of the specifically human in child psychology, and its development through analogous forms of behaviour observed in higher animals, display itself with such evidence as in the teaching of practical intelligence of the child, the most important function of which is the use of tools.

### Experiments on the practical intelligence of the child

The beginning of this new and fruitful series of investigations was marked by the well known works of Köhler conducted on apes. Köhler, as we know, from time to time compared child response in his experiments to those of a chimpanzee in similar conditions. This was fatal to all following investigators. The direct comparison of practical intelligence in the child with analogous actions of apes became the guiding principle of all further experimental work in this field.

Thus one is at first tempted to qualify all these experiments, originating from Köhler's work, as the direct continuation of the ideas which are evolved in his classic study. But this applies only to one's first impression. An attentive approach quickly shows that, all exterior and interior similarities notwithstanding, the new works actually represent a tendency basically opposed to, and opposite to, those which guided Köhler.

One of Köhler's fundamental ideas, as was correctly shown by Lipmann, is the similarity of behaviour of anthropoids and man in the field of practical intelligence. Köhler's chief concern throughout his entire work was to show the human-like behaviour of anthropoids. At the same time, the point of departure of Köhler's work is based on the tacit assumption that the corresponding behaviour of man is evident to all from everyday experience. Contrary to this, new investigators[3] who tried to transfer to the child[4] the laws of practical intelligence discovered by Köhler, were guided by the opposite tendency which found an exact reflection in the interpretation of Bühler's experiments as given by the author himself.

This investigator relates his experiments concerning the earliest manifestations of practical thought in the child. 'These manifestations were absolutely similar to those of the chimpanzee, and therefore this phase of a child's life might quite justly be called. "The chimpanzee-like age" . . . In the given chimpanzee-like age the child makes its first little inventions, of course, most primitively, but from the psychological point of view of a most important nature.'[5]

The application of Köhler's methods to such a child naturally calls for many changes. But the principle of investigation and its fundamental psychological contents remain unchanged. The child play of grasping objects was used by the author to investigate the child's capacity to apply roundabout ways to achieve a goal and to use primitive tools. In that sense some of these experiments may be regarded as a direct transfer of Köhler's experiments (for instance, the experiment where a ring must be removed from a stick, or the series with the piece of toast attached to a string).

Bühler's experiments led him to the important discovery that the first manifestations of practical intelligence in the child, as well as the actions of the chimpanzee, are entirely independent of speech (this was later re-affirmed in the works of Ch. Bühler, with the first manifestations of practical intelligence in the child being placed at an even earlier date between the sixth and seventh months).

Bühler establishes the genetically extremely important fact that 'prior to speech exists instrumental thought' ('Werkzeugdenken'), i.e. the 'grasping of mechanical concatenations and finding of mechanical means for mechanical ends'.[6] Actually, active practical thinking does precede the first beginnings of intelligent speech in the child, thus evidently comprising genetically the most initial phase in the development of its intellect.

However, even in these investigations Bühler's basic idea comes out with great clarity. Where Köhler was concerned with uncovering the human-like in the actions of anthropoids, Bühler aims to show the chimpanzee-like in the actions of the child.

This tendency, with a few exceptions, remains unchanged in the work of all following investigators. It is here that the danger of what might be called the 'animalization' of child psychology, mentioned earlier, finds its clearest expression as the prevalent feature of investigation in this field (see earlier reference).

However, this danger is at its smallest in Bühler's experiments. Bühler deals with the pre-speech period of the child, which makes it possible to fulfil the basic conditions necessary to justify the psychological parallel between chimpanzee and child. It is true that Bühler underestimates the importance of the similarities of these basic conditions when he states: 'The chimpanzee's activities are totally independent of speech, and in man's later period of life technical, instrumental thinking is much less connected to speech and concepts than other forms of thought'.[7]

Bühler, thus, proceeds from the assumption that the relation between practical thought and speech characteristic of the ten-months-old-child – the independence of intelligent action from speech thought – remains intact throughout man's life, which in turn means that the development of speech does not cause fundamental changes in the structure of the practically reasoned activities of the child. As we shall see later, this assumption finds no factual confirmation throughout experimental investigation, conducted with the aim of discovering the connection between speech thinking in ideas [rechevoe myshlenie v ponjatiakh – more adequately rendered as 'thinking with the use of concepts' – eds], and practical, instrumental thinking. As will be demonstrated further, our experiments show that the independence of practical activity from speech, typical of apes, has no place in the development of the child's practical intelligence – in fact, the latter proceeds chiefly in the opposite direction, i.e. close integration of speech and practical thinking.

Nevertheless, as we already said, Bühler's premise is shared by the majority of investigators, including those whose experiments deal with more mature children of speaking age. In this article it is impossible for us to give a complete and detailed review of all the important investigations which concern this problem. We shall dwell only very briefly on their fundamental conclusions which are of essential importance to our topic: the connection between practical action and symbolic forms of thinking in child development.

While carrying out a superb and highly systematic series of experiments, Lipmann and Bogen reached conclusions which differ little from Bühler's thesis.[8] They applied a more complex method of investigation which made it possible to include in their experiments the practical intelligence of the grade school age child, yet they saw the experiments as basically only the confirmation of the dogma concerning the chimpan-zee-likeness of the child's practical activity, i.e. the fundamental identity of the psychological nature of the use of tools by animals and man, the fundamental similarity of the road leading to the development of practical intelligence in ape and child, which in both cases proceeds[9] due to the growing complexity of the interior factors determining the operation of our interest, but not due to any basic or radical alteration in its structure.

Bühler correctly remarked that a child is psychologically much less stable, biologi-cally less formed, physically less powerful than a four-year-old or seven-year-old (that is, almost adult) chimpanzee. This approach is apparent in the work of other investi-gators who advance a wealth of distinctions between child and chimpanzee activity; however, these distinctions basically follow along the lines proposed by Bühler.

Lipmann and Bogen see the domination of the physical structure in child behaviour as the main distinction, as compared to the optic structure of ape behaviour. If ape behaviour in an experimental situation which requires the use of tools is, according to Köhler, determined chiefly by the structure of its optic field, the determining factor in the child is 'naive Physik' (naive physics) i.e. primitive experience concerning the physical nature of its environment and of its body.

'Without dwelling on details,' says Bogen,

> we could briefly sum up the results of our comparison of activity in children and anthropoids as follows: as long as physical action depends chiefly on the visual structural components of the situation, the only difference between child and ape is quantitative. If, however, the situation requires in addition the realization of the physical structural properties of things, then we must acknowledge that the actions of the ape differ from those of the child. As long as we have no new explanations concerning the ape's behaviour we may define this distinction by saying, along with Köhler, that the ape's actions are determined chiefly by visual, and those of the child chiefly by physical, relations.[10]

Thus we see that the distinction in the development of practical intellect between child and ape boils down to physical structures taking the place of optical structures, i.e. is chiefly determined by purely biological factors rooted in the biological distinction between man and chimpanzee. It is also interesting to note that although the author does not refute the possibility of a change in this thesis as a result of new investigations of the ape's actions, he hardly expected that child activity, when attentively studied, would furnish the grounds for the revision of his views.

Therefore there is nothing surprising in the fact that, having concluded their experiments, these authors are forced to acknowledge that in Köhler's descriptions of the chimpanzee, much is highly pertinent in what concerns child behaviour. They object to some extent to Köhler's statement qualifying the description of practical activity in man as *terra incognita*. Therefore it cannot be supposed *a priori* that the comparison of child and ape activity will give us something fundamentally new. The authors see the importance of the investigation only in that it allows for great clarity in the similarities and differences traced by Köhler. Hence, one should not be surprised when the authors conclude their investigation with the confession that, had children served as the subject of their experiments, the results would [not – eds] have led to a fundamentally different picture of the teaching of intelligent activity, than the one so beautifully and convincingly drawn by Köhler on the basis of his experiments with apes. 'Therefore we must arrive at the conclusion,' they say, 'that, as far as our experiments show, no qualitative distinction between the behaviour of child and ape may be defined during the process of teaching.'[11]

Further investigations in the same field differ little in principle from those of Bühler and Bogen. Analogous experiments on mentally handicapped or ungifted children closely follow Köhler's methods; as, for instance, those included in Schlüter's book.[12] The same may be said of the application of these experiments to psychotechnical selection, as carried out by some investigators; their application to deaf and dumb children, their use as non-verbal tests and, finally, their systematic use for the comparative study of children of different ages: none of these studies contributed toward principally new findings in our particular field of interst.

As an example, let us cite one of the latest investigations which was published in 1930, and was also conducted in careful comparison with Köhler's experiments. Undertaken by Paul Brainard,[13] these experiments were an exact, step by step reproduction of Köhler's experiments; they led the author to the conclusion that all the children tested were identical in general attitudes, skills and methods of solution. The older children solve problems more adroitly but by the same processes. A three-year-old child shows the same difficulties in solving the problems as did Köhler's apes. Where the child has the advantage of speech and understanding of instructions, the apes have the advantage of longer arms and greater experience in handling objects.

Thus we see that the response of a three-year-old child in principle is equated to an ape's response, while speech which, by the way, is noted by all these authors as present in the process of solution of a practical problem, is treated as a secondary factor and is equated to the arm length of the ape. What most investigators do not acknowledge is that with speech the child acquires a fundamentally different attitude toward the entire situation in which the solution of practical problems is carried out, and that the child's practical actions represent, from a psychological point of view, a completely different structure.

Summing up the results of his experiments, the author openly says: 'The results show that the response of a three-year-old child is almost identical to that of a grown-up ape'.[14]

The first attempt to uncover not only similarities but also the distinctions between the practical intellect of child and ape was carried out in the laboratory of M. Y. Basov.[15] In the introduction to their series of experiments, Shapiro and Guerke[16] note that social experience plays a dominant role in man. 'Drawing a parallel between chimpanzee and child, we shall do so always keeping the aforementioned fact in view,' they wrote. The authors see the effect of social experience in the fact that the child through imitation and the application of tools or objects, following a given pattern, develops not only ready-made stereotype modes of action, but learns to master the very principle involved in the given activity. As the authors say,

> All these repeated actions pile up, one upon the other, as in a multi-exposure photograph, with common traits acquiring clarity and differences becoming blurred. The final result is a crystallized scheme, a defined principle of activity. As it becomes more experienced, the child acquires a greater number of models of what it understands. These models represent, as it were, a refined cumulative design of all similar-type previous actions; at the same time, they are also a rough blueprint for possible types of action in the future.[17]

We shall not speak in detail of the fact that the appearance of such blueprints, somewhat remindful of Galton's collective photography, revives in the theory of practical intellect the theory of the formation of ideas or generic ideas corresponding to word meaning – a theory long abandoned in psychology. We shall also not touch on the problem as to what extent the factor understood as a function of adaptation to new circumstances (and thus differing in principle from the intellect) is introduced along with the blueprints for solution of problems, formed in a purely mechanical way as the result of repetition. We shall only point to the fact that the significance of social experience in this case is understood exclusively from the point of view of the presence of suitable patterns which the child finds in its environment. Thus social experience without changing anything in the interior structure of the child's intellectual operations simply gives these operations another content, forming a series of clichés, a series of stereotyped motor-forms, a series of motor-schemes which the child applies for the solution of a problem.

True, the authors, just as almost all other investigators, while describing their experiments are forced to point to the 'specific role fulfilled by speech' in the practical effective adaptation of the child. However, its role is indeed of a strange nature for, as the authors would have it, 'speech replaces and compensates for real adaptation, it does not serve as a bridge leading to past experience and to a purely social type of adaptation which is achieved via the experimenter'.[18] Thus speech does not create a principally new structure of the practical activity of the child, and the old statement concerning the prevalence of ready-made schemes in the child's behaviour, and of resorting to clichés extracted from the archives of old experience holds true. The new element here is that speech is regarded as a substitute which replaces an unsuccessful action by a word or the action of another.

At this point we could discontinue our brief review of the most important experimental research pertaining to our particular subject of interest. But before making a general conclusion, we would like to call the reader's interest to a very recently published work (1930), for it puts into bold relief the general defect common to all the above-mentioned works and helps define the starting point for an independent solution of our particular problem. We have in mind Guillaume and Meyerson's study, to which we shall have occasion to revert in the course of our article.[19] These authors devoted their research to the use of tools by apes. Children were not involved in their experiments. But when comparing the general results of their work with the corresponding activity of man, the authors conclude that ape behaviour finds its analogy in the behaviour of a man suffering from aphasia, i.e. in the behaviour of a person deprived of speech.

We see this indication as extremely telling and pertaining directly to the heart of our problem. In essence we come around full circle to the opening words of our review. If, as Bühler's experiments confirm, the practical activity of the child, prior to speech development, is identical to that of the ape, then, as Guillaume and Meyerson's investigations confirm, the activity of a man struck by aphasia, through a pathological process, begins again to resemble in principle something analogous to the activity of the ape. But can it be said that the varied forms of man's practical activity situated between these two extreme cases, can it be said that all the practical activity of the speaking child is also analogous in structure and in psychological nature to the activity of speechless animals? This is the cardinal question to be answered. Here we must turn to our own experimental investigations carried out by ourselves and our staff and based on principally different premises from those which served for almost all the above-mentioned works.

Our research had as its first aim to bring to light the specifically human traits in child behaviour and how these traits are historically established. In the problem of practical intellect our primary interest was the history of origin of those forms of practical activity which could be qualified as specifically human.

We felt that many previous investigations, the fundamental methodological premise of which was animal psychology, lacked this most important aspect. Those works are, of course, extremely important, for they show the ties between the development of human forms of activity and their biological beginnings in the animal world. Yet they record nothing in child behaviour than what it has already inherited from former animal forms of thought. The new type of attitude toward environment, typical of man, the new forms of activity which led to development of labour as the determining form of man's relation with nature, the connection between use of tools and speech – all that remains beyond the range of previous investigators, due to the fundamentally different starting points. We mean to analyse this problem in the light of new experimental investigations aimed at uncovering the specifically human forms of practical intellect in the child and their main lines of development.[20]

### The function of speech in tool use: the problem of practical and verbal intelligence

This article deals with two processes of vital psychological importance: the use of tools and of symbols; until now they were treated in psychology as isolated and independent of each other.

For many long years scientific opinion held that practical intelligent action connected to the use of tools had no basic relation to the development of sign or symbolic operations, such as, for instance, speech. Psychological literature almost ignored the question of the structural and genetic relations of these two functions.

All the information that could be obtained by modern science led rather to the treatment of these two psychological processes as two quite independent lines of development which, although they might come into contact, basically had nothing in common.

In the classic work on the use of tools by apes, Köhler obtained what one might call the pure culture of practical intellect, developed to a fairly high degree, but having no ties with the application of symbols. Having described brilliantly examples of the use of tools by anthropoids, he went on to demonstrate how futile it was to attempt to develop even the most elementary sign and symbolic operations in animals. The practical intellectual behaviour of the ape proved to be absolutely independent from symbolic activity. Further attempts to cultivate speech in the ape (see works by Yerkes and Learned)[21] also gave negative results, thus showing once more that the practical 'ideational' behaviour of the animal is completely autonomous and isolated from speech-symbol activity, and that, notwithstanding the similarity of both man's and the ape's vocal apparatus, speech remains beyond the ape's grasp.

The acceptance of the fact that the beginning of practical intellect may be observed to almost its full extent in the pre-human and pre-speech period, led psychologists to the assumption that the use of tools, which originates as a natural operation, remained the same in the child. A number of authors, engaged in the study of practical operations of children of different ages, attempted to define as exactly as possible the age period during which child behaviour resembles in all respects that of the chimpanzee. The addition of speech in the child's case was regarded by those authors as exogenous, secondary and independent of practical operations. Speech, at the most, was looked on as an element accompanying operations just as harmony assists the main melody. The tendency to ignore speech while studying the laws of practical intellect was a normal development; the analysis of the child's practical action boiled down to the simple mechanical subtraction of speech from the integral system of child activity.

The isolated examination of the use of tools and of symbolic activity was a common tendency in the research work of authors who studied the natural history of practical intellect: psychologists, studying the development of symbolic processes in the child, followed the same principle.

The origin and development of speech, and of all other symbolic action, was treated as a factor having no ties with the organization of the child's practical activity, the child being regarded as purely *res cogitans*. Such an approach could not but lead to the proclamation of pure intellectualism; psychologists, preferring to study the development of symbolic activity as the spiritual, as opposed to the natural, history of the child, often attributed this activity to the spontaneous discovery by the child of the relationship between signs and their meaning. This happy moment, according to the well known expression of W. Stern, constitutes 'the greatest discovery in the child's life'.[22] A number of authors fix this moment at the borderline between the child's first and second year, and regard it as the result of the child's conscientious activity. The problems of the *development* of speech and other forms of symbolic activity was thus erased, being supplanted by a purely logical process projected into early childhood, and containing in complete form all the stages of future development.

From the examination of symbolic speech activities on the one hand and practical intellect on the other, as isolated phenomena, it followed that not only the genetic analysis of these functions led to their being regarded as having completely different origins, but also to their participation in a common operation being considered as accidental and of no basic psychological importance. Even in cases when speech and the use of tools were closely linked in one operation, they were still studied as separate processes belonging to two completely different classes of independent phenomena. At the most, the reason for their mutual appearance was defined as exterior.

If authors, studying practical intellect in its natural history, concluded that its natural forms were not in the slightest degree connected to symbolic activity, child psychologists who studied speech made the similar assumption, albeit from the opposite side. Observing psychological development of the child, they established the fact that, during the whole period of development, symbolic activity, accompanying the general activity of the child, discloses its egocentric nature but, being in essence separated from action, does not co-act but merely runs parallel to it. In his description of the egocentric speech of the child Piaget held this viewpoint. He did not attribute any important role to speech in organizing the child; nor did he admit its communicative functions, although he was obliged to admit its practical importance.

A series of observations lead us to assume that such an isolated examination of practical intellect and symbolic activity is absolutely wrong. If the one could exist without the other in the case of higher animals, then one must logically conclude that the unity of these two systems is the very thing to be regarded as specific to the complex behaviour of man. For this results in symbolic activity's beginning to play a specific organizing part, penetrating into the process of tool use and giving birth to principally new forms of behaviour.

We arrived at this conclusion after the most careful study of child behaviour and new research which helped to establish the functional features strictly pertaining to the child as opposed to animals, while simutaneously defining the child's specific behaviour as a human being.

Further research convinced us that nothing can be more false than the two viewpoints discussed earlier and which, while continuing to dominate the scene, regard practical intellect and speech thought as two independent and isolated lines of development. The first of these, as we have seen, expresses the extreme form of the zoological tendency which, once having found the natural root of human behaviour in anthropoids, attempts to examine the higher forms of human labour and thought as the direct prolongation of these roots, thus ignoring man's leap forward, made in his transition to social existence.

The second viewpoint, which proclaims the independent origin of the higher forms of speech-thought and qualifies it as the 'greatest discovery in the child's life', made on the threshold of the second year and consisting of the discovery of the relation between sign and meaning, this viewpoint expresses, first and foremost, an extreme form of spiritualism typical of those modern psychologists who regard thought as a purely spiritual act.

### Speech and action in child behaviour

Our research leads us not only to the conviction of the fallacy of this approach, but also to the positive conclusion that *the great genetic moment of all intellectual development, from which grew the purely human forms of practical and gnostic intellect, is realized in the unification of these two previously completely independent lines of development.*

The child's use of tools is comparable to that of an ape's only during the former's pre-speech period. As soon as speech and the use of symbolic signs are included in this operation, it transforms itself along entirely new lines, overcoming the former natural laws and for the first time giving birth to authentically human use of implements.[23]

From the moment the child begins to *master the situation with the help of speech, after mastering his own behaviour*, a radically new organization of behaviour appears, as well as new relations with the environment. We are witnessing the birth of those specifically human forms of behaviour that, breaking away from animal forms of behaviour, later create intellect and go on to become the base of labour: the specifically human form of the use of tools.

This unification appears with the greatest clarity in our experimental genetic research.

The very first observations of a child in an experimental situation similar to that in which Köhler observed the practical use of tools by apes, show that the child not only acts endeavouring to achieve its goal, but at the same time also *speaks*. This speech as a rule arises spontaneously in the child and continues almost without interruption throughout the experiment. It increases and is of a more persistent character every time the situation becomes more difficult and the goal more difficult to attain. Attempts to block it (as the experiments of our collaborator, R. E. Levina,[24] have shown) are either futile or lead to the termination of all action, 'freezing' as it were the child's behaviour, something quite apparent and easily observed in the experiment.

In this situation, it thus seems both natural and necessary for the child to speak while it acts, and experimenters are under the impression that speech does not simply follow in the wake of practical activity, but plays some kind of specific role of no little importance. The impressions we are left with as the result of similar experiments place the observer face to face with the following two facts, both of capital importance:

1  A child's speech is an inalienable and internally necessary part of the operation, its role being as important as that of action in the attaining of a goal. The experimenter's impression is, that the child not only speaks about what he is doing, but that for him speech and action are in this case *one and the same complex psychological function*, directed toward the solution of the given problem.
2  The more complex the action demanded by the situation and the less direct its solution, the greater the importance played by speech in the operation as a whole. Sometimes speech becomes of such vital importance that without it the child proves to be positively unable to accomplish the given task.

These observations lead us to the conclusion that *the child solves a practical task with the help of not only eyes and hands, but also speech*. This newly born unity of perception, speech and action, which leads to the inculcation[25] of the laws of the visual field, constitutes the real and vital object of analysis aimed at studying the origin of specifically human forms of behaviour.

Investigating experimentally the egocentric speech of the child engaged in one activity or another, we were able to establish yet another fact of great importance for the explanation of psychological function and the genetic description of this stage in the development of speech in the child. This fact is that the coefficient of egocentric speech, calculated according to Piaget, quite obviously increases along with the introduction of difficulties and obstacles into the child's activity.

As our experiments have shown, for a given group[26] of children this coefficient almost doubles during moments of difficulty as compared with other moments[27] of the same situation.

This one fact forced us to assume that egocentric speech in the child at a very early age begins to fulfil the function of primitive speech-thinking:[28] thinking aloud. The further analysis of the character of this speech and of its connection with difficulties fully support this assumption.

On the basis of these experiments we developed a hypothesis that egocentric speech in the child should be regarded as the transitional form between external and internal speech. According to this hypothesis, egocentric speech, if we take into consideration its function, is psychologically inner speech, but in its form of expression it is external speech.

From this point of view, we are inclined to assign to egocentric speech the function performed by inner speech in the developed behaviour of an adult, i.e. the intellectual function. From the genetic point of view, we are inclined to regard the general sequence of fundamental stages in speech development as formulated, for instance, by Watson:[29] external speech – whispering – inner speech; or in other words: external speech – egocentric speech – inner speech.

What is it that really distinguishes the actions of the speaking child from the solution of practical problems by an ape?

The first thing that strikes the experimentalist is the incomparably greater *freedom* in children's operations, their incomparably greater independence from the structure of the given visual or actual situation, as compared to that of the animal. The child constructs with words much greater possibilities than the ape can realize through action.

The child is much more easily able to ignore the vector that focuses attention on the goal itself, and to execute a number of complex preliminary acts, using for this purpose a comparatively long chain of auxiliary instrumental methods. The child proves able to include independently, in the process of solution of the task, objects which lie neither within the near nor the peripheral visual field. By creating through words a certain intention, the child achieves a much broader range of activity, applying as tools not only those objects that lie near at hand, but searching for and preparing such articles as can be useful in the solution of its task and planning its future actions.

Two facts seem remarkable in the transformation undergone by practical operations through the inclusion in them of speech. First of all, the practical operations of a child that can speak become much less impulsive and spontaneous than those of the ape that makes a series of uncontrolled attempts to solve the given problem. Due to speech, the child's activity is divided into two consecutive parts: the first consists of the solution of the problem in the field of speech, achieved through speech-planning, while the second is the simple motor realization of the prepared solution. Direct manipulation is replaced by a complex psychological process, where inner motivation and the creation of intentions, postponed in time duration, stimulate their own development and realization. These entirely new psychological structures are absent in apes in even moderately complex forms.

On the other hand – and this is of decisive importance – among the different objects open to the child's transformation, speech introduces *the child's own behaviour*.

Words directed toward the solution of the problem pertain not only to objects belonging to the external world, but also to the child's own behaviour, to its actions and intentions. With the aid of speech the child for the first time proves able to the mastering of its own behaviour, relating to itself as to another being, regarding itself as an object. Speech helps the child to master this object through the preliminary organization and planning of its own acts of behaviour. Those objects which were beyond the limits of accessible operations, now, thanks to speech, become accessible to the activities of the child.

The fact described here cannot be regarded as a secondary issue in the development of behaviour. Here we see cardinal changes in the very attitude of the individual toward the outside world. On closer examination these changes prove to be exceptionally important. The behaviour of an ape, described by Köhler, is limited to the animal's manipulation in a given field of vision, whereas the solution of a practical problem by a speaking child becomes, to a great extent, removed from this natural field. Thanks to the planning function of speech, geared to the child's activity, the child creates, parallel to the stimuli of his environment, a second series of auxiliary stimuli standing between him and his environment and directing his behaviour. And it is due to this very secondary series of stimuli, created with the aid of speech, that the behaviour of the child reaches a higher level, acquiring a relative freedom from the situation that directly attracts it, and impulsive attempts are transformed into a planned, organized behaviour.

These auxiliary stimuli (in the given instance, speech) which carry out the specific function of organizing behaviour, prove to be no other than those very symbolic signs that we have been studying here. They serve the child, first and foremost, as a means of social contacts with the surrounding people, and are also applied as a means of self-influence, a means of auto-stimulation, creating thus a new and superior form of activity in the child.

An interesting parallel to the facts cited above, pertaining to the role played by speech in the inception of specifically human forms of behaviour, may be found in the exceptionally interesting experiments of *Guillaume et Meyerson* involving the analysis of the use of tools by apes. Our attention centred chiefly on the conclusions of this work, which compares the intellectual operations of an ape with the process of solving concrete problems as exhibited by people suffering from aphasia (studied clinically and experimentally by Head).[30] The authors find that the methods used by the aphasic and the ape to accomplish a given task are similar in principle and coincide in certain essential points. This fact thus reaffirms our statement that speech plays an essential role the organization of higher psychological functions.

If, in the genetic plane,[31] we witnessed the unification of practical and speech operations and the birth of a new form of behaviour, a transition from lower forms of behaviour to higher, then, in the case of the disintegration of the entity of speech and action, we witness a diametrically opposed movement, namely man's transition from higher forms to the lower. The intellectual processes of a man with impaired symbolic functions, that is, an aphasic, does not result in a simple lowering of the functions of practical intellect or in difficulties concerning their realization, but reflects rather a picture of another, more primitive level of behaviour, that of the ape.

What is lacking in the actions of the aphasic and what, consequently, owes its origin to speech? It suffices to analyse the behaviour of a person suffering from aphasia in a practical situation new to him, to see how greatly that behaviour differs from that of a normal, speaking person in an analogous situation. The first thing that strikes the eye when we observe an aphasic in a similar experiment is his *extraordinary confusion*. As a rule, there is not even a trace of the slightest form of a complex plan for the solution of the problem. The creation of a preliminary intention with its consequent systematic realization proves to be absolutely beyond the capacity of our patient. Each stimulus arising from the situation and attracting his attention creates an impulsive attempt to respond directly; hence the corresponding reaction, without taking account of the situation and its solution as a whole. The complex chain of reactions, presupposing the creation of intention and its systematic, consecutive realization proves here unattainable and becomes a hodgepodge of disrupted and disorganized groups of attempts.

Sometimes these activities are retarded and assume a rudimentary form, sometimes they become a complex and unorganized mass of apractical actions.[32] If the situation proves sufficiently complex and can be solved only through a consecutive system of previously planned acts, the aphasic becomes bewildered and appears to be quite helpless. In simpler cases he solves the problem with the aid of simple simultaneous combinations within the limits of the visual field, and the methods of solution are fundamentally quite similar to what Köhler observed in his experiments with apes.

Unable to speak (speech would have freed him from being tied to the visually evident situation and rendered possible the planned consecutiveness of successive actions), he becomes the slave of the situation – one hundred-fold more than the speaking child.

## The development of the child's higher forms of practical activity

What has just been stated leads us to conclude that, in what concerns the behaviour of both child and adult, the practical use of tools and the symbolic forms of activity connected with speech do not represent two parallel links [tsep' – better 'chains' – eds] of reaction. They form a complex psychological entity in which symbolic activity is directed toward organizing practical operations by means of the creation of secondary order stimuli and the planning of the subject's own behaviour. Contrary to the higher animals, in man there occurs a complex functional connection between speech, the use of tools and the natural visual field, and without the analysis of this link, the psychology of man's practical activities would remain forever incomprehensible.

It would, however, be absolutely wrong to believe (as some behaviourists do) that this unity is simply the result of training and habit, and represents a line of natural development, beginning in animals, which only accidentally acquired an intellectual character. It would be just as erroneous to conceive the role of speech as the result of a sudden discovery on the child's part, as is presumed by a number of child psychologists.

The forming of the complex human unity of speech and practical operations is the product of a deeply rooted process of development in which the subject's individual history is closely linked to his social history.

Due to the lack of space, we have been obliged to simplify the actual problem as far as possible and to study the phenomena of interest to us in their extreme genetic forms, comparing for brevity's sake only the beginning and end of the examined process of development. The process of development itself, with its variegated phases and emergence of new factors, must remain here beyond our field of investigation. We consciously take the phenomenon in its most developed form, passing over transitional stages.

This makes it possible to present the final result of this development with the maximum clarity and, consequently, to evaluate the basic trend of the entire process of development. This merging of the logical and historical approaches to research which voluntarily ignores a number of stages of the examined process, has inherent dangers that have wrecked more than one seemingly faultless theory. The experimenter must avoid these dangers and bear in mind that this is only a way of studying a given phenomenon with its particular historic background, something he must inevitably turn to the analysis of.

We cannot dwell here on all the consecutive changes of the process we examined. Within the limits of this article we can only single out the central link, the examination of which will be sufficient to render a clear understanding of the general character and discretion of the entire process of development.

We must, therefore, once again turn to experimental data.

We observed a child's activity in a number of experiments, analogous in structure, but drawn out in time and representing a series of situations, each following one more difficult than the preceding. We established one most important point ignored by psychologists, which permits us to characterize with certainty the difference between the behaviour of an ape and that of a child in the genetic plane, while former observations allowed us to do the same with regard to the structure of activity. The fact is that over the course of a series of experiments, the examined activity of the child changes, not only perfecting itself as is the case in the process of teaching [russian *obuchenie* – better rendered as 'complex of teaching/learning' – eds], but undergoing such great qualitative changes as can only be regarded in their totality as development in the literal meaning of the word.

As soon as we moved on to the study of activity from the viewpoint of the process of its 'Werden'[33] (in a series of experiments drawn out in time), we immediately found ourselves faced with a cardinal fact: that, actually, we were not studying one and the same activity each time in its new concrete expressions, but that, over a series of experiments, the object of research itself changed. Thus, in the process of development, we acquired forms of activity that were completely different in structure. This represented an unpleasant complication for all psychologists who at any cost endeavour to preserve the invariability of the examined activity; but for us it as once became central, and we concentrated all our attention on its study. This study led us to the conclusion that the activity of the child differs in organization, structure and methods from the ape's behaviour, does not appear in a ready-made form, but arises out of the *consecutive changes of genetically inter-related psychological structures* and, thus, forms an *integral historical process of development of the higher psychological functions.*

This process is the key to the understanding of the organization, structure and methods of activity in child development. In it we are inclined to see from a new angle the basic difference distinguishing the complex behaviour of the child from that of the ape. Actually, the use of tools by apes essentially remains unaltered over the entire course of experiments, at least if we ignore secondary changes, probably due more to gradual perfection of these functions as a result of exercise than to changes in their organization. Neither Köhler nor any other investigator of the complex behaviour of higher animals ever observed in their experiments the appearance of qualitatively new operations, formed in a genetic series that were drawn out in time. The constancy of the operations observed and their invariability in various situations constituted one of these studies' most remarkable features.

The situation was, however, completely different in the case of the child. Having combined in experiments a whole series of evolutions [*preobrazovania* or 'transformations' – eds] and creating thus a model of development of sorts, we never observed (except in extreme cases of mentally handicapped children) this constancy, this invariability of activity. The actual transformation of the process was obvious to us at each new stage of the experiment.

We shall describe this process of transformation, first from the negative side.

The first thing that attracts our attention and might seem paradoxical is that the process of the forming of higher intellectual activity least of all resembles a developed process of logical transformations. This means that the subject forms, connects and separates the operations following a different law of connection than that which would inter-relate them through logical thought. Very frequently the psychological process of development of a child's thought is presented as being similar to the process of the discovery of logical thought. It is alleged that the child first encompasses the basic principle of thought, and later the individual, variegated concrete forms are deducted, resulting from the child's fundamental discovery as a logical, and not genetic, consequence. The process of development is here misunderstood: actually, Köhler's statement to the effect that intellectualism is nowhere so false as in the theory (and, we must add, in the history) of intellect, is here justified.

This is the first and basic conclusion which our experiments lead us to make. The child does not invent new forms of behaviour nor does he deduce them logically, but forms them in the same way as walking supplants creeping and speaking baby talk, and not because the child becomes convinced of the advantage of the one over the other.

Another accepted point of view that we must refute on the strength of our observations, is that the higher intellectual functions develop during the process of the perfection of complex habits, during the process of the child's training, and that all the qualitatively differing forms of behaviour represent changes of the same type as that of the memorizing of a text through repetition. This kind of possibility was excluded from the very beginning because each experiment created a different situation requiring the child to adapt adequately to new conditions and a new method of solving the problem. What is more, the problems presented to the child posed new and qualitatively different demands, following development. The complexity of the structure of the solution of the problems increased in accordance with these requirements, so that even the strongest and most 'trained' could only be inadequate in view of the new demands and became more of an obstacle than a helpful factor for the solution of a new problem.

In the light of the data characterizing the process of development under discussion, it becomes clear that, not only from the point of view of fact, but also from that of theory, the two assumptions we refuted initially are indeed false. According to one of them, the essence of the process is regarded as the *causa efficiens* of intelligent actions; according to the other, it is viewed as the product of the automatic process of the perfectioning of habit, appearing as a *deus ex machina* at the very end of the process. Both these theories to an equal extent ignore the presence here of development and both prove to be clearly unsatisfactory when faced by facts.

## Development in the light of facts

The actual process of development, as demonstrated by our experiments, is quite different in form.

Our records show that from the very earliest stages of the child's development, the factor moving his activities from one level to another is neither repetition nor discovery. The source of development of these activities is to be found in the social environment of the child and is manifest in concrete form in those specific relations with the experimentalist which transcend the entire situation requiring the practical use of tools and introduce into it a social aspect. In order to express in one formula the essence of those forms of infant behaviour, characteristic of the earliest stage of development, it must be noted that the child enters into relations with the situation not directly, but through the medium of another person. Thus we arrive at the conclusion that the role of speech, singled out by us as a separate point in the organization of the child's practical behaviour, proves decisive not only for the comprehension of the latter's structure, but also for its genesis – speech lies at the very beginning of the child's development and becomes its most decisive factor. The child who speaks as he solves a practical task calling for the use of tools and who combines speech and action into one structure, in this way introduces a social element into his action and thereby determines that action's fate and the future path of development of his behaviour. In this way, the child's behaviour is transferred for the first time to an absolutely new plane, is guided by new factors and leads to the appearance of social structures in the child's psychical life. His behaviour becomes socialized: this is the main determining factor of the entire further development of its practical intellect. The situation as a whole acquires for him a social meaning, where people act, just as do objects. The child views the situation as a problem posed by the experimentalist, and he senses that, present or not, a human being stands behind that problem. The child's activities acquire a meaning of its own in the system of social behaviour and, being directed towards a definite purpose, are refracted through the prism of his social thought.

The entire history of the child's psychological development shows us that, from the very first days of development, its adaptation to the environment is achieved by social means, through the people surrounding him. The road from object to child and from child to object lies through another person.

The transition from the biological to the social way of development constitutes the central link in this process of development, the cardinal turning point in the history of child behaviour.

This road – passing through another person – proves to be the central highway of development of practical intellect, as demonstrated by our experiments. Speech here plays a role of primary importance.

The following picture appears before the experimentalist's eyes: the behaviour of very small children in the process of solving a given task presents a very specific fusion of two forms of adaptation: to objects and people, to environment and the social situation, which are differentiated only in the case of adults. Reactions to objects and people represent in child behaviour an elementary undifferentiated entity which, later, gives birth to both actions directed at the external world and to social forms of behaviour. At that moment, the child's behaviour presents a strange mixture of the one and the other – a chaotic (from the adult's viewpoint) hodgepodge of contacts with people and reactions to objects. This union in one activity of different subjects of behaviour, explained by the child's entire preceding history of development beginning from the first days of his existence, is apparent in each experiment. The child, left to himself and stimulated to action by the situation, begins to act according to the very principles according to which its relations with environment were organized previously. That means that action and speech, psychological and physical influences are syncretically fused. We call this central peculiarity of child behaviour 'syncretism of action', by way of analogy to the syncretism of perception and verbal syncretism, so thoroughly studied in modern psychology in the works of Claparède and Piaget.

The records of the experiments carried out with children give a clear picture of syncretism of action in their behaviour.

The small child, placed in a situation where the direct attainment of his purpose seems impossible, displays a very complex activity which can only be described as a jumbled mixture of direct attempts to obtain the desired end, emotional speech, sometimes expressing the child's desire and at other times substituting actual and unattainable satisfaction by verbal 'Ersatz', by attempts to achieve the end through verbal formulations of means, by appeals to the experimentalist for help and so on. These manifestations present an imbroglio of actions, and the experimentalist is at first bewildered by this rich and often grotesque mixture of mutually contradictory forms of activity.

Further observations draw our attention to a series of actions that, at first, seem not to belong to the general scheme of the child's activities. The child, after having completed a number of intelligent and inter-related actions which should help him successfully solve the given problem, suddenly, upon meeting a difficulty in the realization of his plan, cuts short all attempts and turns for help to the experimentalist, asking him to move the object nearer and thus give him the possibility to accomplish his task. The obstacle in the child's way thus interrupts his activity, and his verbal appeal to another person represents an effort to fill this hiatus. The conditions that psychologically play the decisive role consist in the child appealing for help at the critical moment of his operation, thus showing that he knows what to do in order to attain his purpose, but cannot attain it by himself and that the plan of the solution is, in the main, ready although beyond the limits of his own action. That is why the child, first separating verbal description of the action from the action itself, crosses the border of co-operation, socializing his practical thinking by sharing his action with another person. It is due to this that the child's activity enters into new relations with speech. The child, consciously introducing another person's action into his attempts to solve a problem, thus begins not only to mentally plan his activity, but also to organize the behaviour of another person in accordance with the requirements of the given problem. Thanks to this, the socializing of practical intellect leads to the necessity of socializing not only objects, but also actions with the help of social means, creating thus reliable conditions for the problem's realization. The control of another person's behaviour becomes, in the given instance, a necessary part of the child's entire practical activity.

This new form of activity, aimed at controlling another person's behaviour, is not yet differentiated from the general syncretic whole. We have more than once observed that, over the whole course of fulfilling the task, the child flagrantly confuses the logic of his own activity with the logic of the solution of the task by co-operation, introducing into his own activity the actions of an outsider, absolutely foreign to him. The child seems to unite two approaches to his own activity, combining them into one syncretic whole.

Sometimes this syncretism of action manifests itself on the background of primitive child thought, and in a number of experiments we observed how the child, having realized the hopelessness of his attempts, appealed directly to the object of attraction, asking it to draw closer or lower, depending on the concrete conditions. In this case we see the same type of confusion of speech and action, as when the child, producing some kind of action, talks to the object, addressing it equally with both words and stick.[34] In these latter cases we witness the experimental demonstration of how fundamentally and inseparably speech and action are tied together in the child's activity and how great the difference of this tie is compared to that usually observed in the adult.

The behaviour of a small child in the situation just described presents, consequently, a complex skein; it consists of a mixture: direct attempts to attain the goal, the use of tools, speech either directed at the person conducting the experiment or simply accompanying the action, as if strengthening the child's efforts, and, finally, a paradoxical-sounding direct appeal to the object of attention.

This strange alloy of speech and action becomes meaningless if considered separately from dynamics. If, however, we analyse it genetically following each stage of the child's development or in a condensed form, in a number of consecutive experiments, this strange alloy of two forms of activity displays both a most definite function in the history of the child's development, and an inner logic of its own development.

We shall dwell here on two points in the dynamics of this complex process, two points which play, however, a decisive role in the appearance in the child of higher forms of controlling his own behaviour.

## The function of socialized and egocentric speech

The first of the processes we study here is connected with the formation of 'speech for oneself', which, as we noted earlier, regulates the child's actions and permits him to achieve a given task in an organized way, through preliminary control of himself and his activity.

If we study carefully the records of our experiments with small children, we find that, along with the appeals to the experimentalist for help, there is a wealth of manifestations of egocentric speech by the child.

We already know that difficult situations evoke excessive egocentric speech and that, under conditions of hyper-difficulties, the coefficient of egocentric speech is almost doubled in comparison to uncomplicated situations. In another case, hoping to achieve a deeper study of the connection between egocentric speech and difficulties, we created extra experimental difficulties in the child's activities; we were confident that a situation requiring the use of tools, the focal point of which was the impossibility of direct action, would create the best conditions for the appearance of egocentric speech. The facts confirmed our expectations. Both of the psychological factors related to difficulties — the emotional reaction and the de-automatization of action, requiring the intervention of intellect – determine in the main the nature of the egocentric speech and of the situation of interest. For a correct understanding of the nature of egocentric speech and for the clarification of its genetic functions in the process of the socialization of the child's practical intellect, it is important to remember that egocentric speech is linked to the child's social speech by thousands of transitional stages, a fact both experimentally proven and emphasized by us. Very frequently these transitional forms were not clear enough for us to determine to what form of speech one or another of the child's expressions could be related. This resemblance and mutual relation of both forms of speech is reflected in the close ties of those of the child's functions which are carried out by both forms of the child's verbal activity. It would be a mistake to think that his social speech consists solely of appeals to the experimentalist for help: it always consists of emotional and expressive elements, communications as to what he intends to do, and so on. It sufficed to obstruct his social speech during the experiment (for instance, by the experimentalist leaving the room, or by not answering the child's questions, etc.) for egocentric speech to increase immediately.

If at the earliest stages of a child's development egocentric speech does not yet indicate the method of solution [of a given problem faced by the child – eds], this is first expressed by speech addressed to the adult. The child, hopeless of attaining his end directly, turns to the adult and describes verbally the method, which he himself is unable to use in a direct way. The greatest change in child development occurs when this socialized speech, previously addressed to the adult, *is turned to himself*, when, instead of appealing to the experimentalist with a plan for the solution of the problem, the child appeals to himself. In this latter case the speech, participating in the solution, *from an inter-psychological category, now becomes an intra-psychological function*.

The child applies to itself the method of behaviour that it previously applied to another, thus *organizing its own behaviour according to a social type*. The source of intelligent action and control over his own behaviour in the solution of a complex practical problem is, consequently, not an invention of some purely logical act, but the application of *a social attitude to itself*, the transfer of a social form of behaviour into its own psychological organization.

A series of observations permits us to trace this complex path, followed by the child in his transition to the interiorization of social speech. The cases we described in which the experimenter, to whom the child formerly appealed for help, left the scene of the experiment, throw this climax into bold relief [demonstrates this decisive moment most clearly – eds].[35] It is in such a case when the child is deprived of the possibility of appealing to an adult that this socially organized function switches over to egocentric speech, and suggestions as to the ways of solving the problem gradually lead to their independent realization.

The series of consecutive experiments drawn out in time gives us the possibility of singling out a number of stages of this process, while the formation of a new system of behaviour of a social type becomes considerably clearer. The history of this process is, therefore, the history of the socialization of the child's practical intellect and, at the same time, the social history of its symbolic functions.

## The change of the function of speech in practical operation

We would like to emphasize the second, and no less important, transformation which the child's speech undergoes in the series of experiments described. Tracing the child's speech–action relation in time and studying that dynamic structure, displayed in time and arising from that relation, we were able to establish the following fact: this structure does not remain permanent over the entire course of the experiments; speech and action change in relation to each other, forming a mobile system of functions with a changing character of inter-relations. Ignoring certain complex changes, that are of interest only in a different area, we must single out the basic functional change in this system, bearing a decisive influence on its fate and bringing out its inner reconstruction. This change consists in the fact that the *child's speech, which previously accompanied its activity and reflected its chief vicissitudes* in a disrupted and chaotic form, *moves more and more to the turning and starting points of the process, beginning thus to precede action and throw light on the conceived of but as yet unrealized action.* In the development of practical intellect we observed a process analogous to that occurring in another mobile system of functions – speech-drawing [*risovanie s uchastiem rechi*]. Just as the child first draws and, only *post factum* seeing the results of its work, recognizes and states the drawing's theme in words, so in the practical operation the child begins by verbally describing the operation's result or its individual elements. At best, the child does not state the result but conveys the preceding moment of action. In our experiments the 'scheme of action' begins to be verbally described by the child directly prior to its beginning (just like in the development of drawing the naming of the theme of the drawing moves closer to the beginning of the process), thus anticipating its further development.

This displacement signifies not only the temporary transfer of speech as related to action, but also the transfer of the entire system's functional centre. In the first stage speech, following action, reflecting it and strengthening its results, remains structurally subject to action and provoked by it, while at the second stage speech, transferred towards the starting point of the process, begins to dominate over action, guides it and determines its subject and development. Therefore the second stage gives birth to speech's real function of planning, and thus speech begins to fix the direction of future operations.

This planning function has usually been studied separately from the reflective function of speech and was even seen as opposing it. The genetic analysis, however, shows that such an opposition is based on the purely logical construction of both functions. In experiments we noted, on the contrary, that there exist different forms of inner connection between both functions, and this fact leads us to the conclusion that the transition from one function to another, the emergence of the planning function of speech from the reflective, comprises that very vital genetic point that links the higher functions of speech with the lower and explains their true origin.

The child's speech – *due to the fact* that it is first a verbal mould of operation or its parts – reflects action and strengthens its results, starts at a later stage to move towards the action's beginning, to predict and direct the action, *forming it according to that mould of former operation, that was previously fixed by speech.*

This process of development has nothing in common with the process of logical 'deduction' of logical conclusions made by the child's discovery of the principle of speech's practical application. Studies furnish countless facts that force us to believe that this recapitulative speech, forming a mould of past experience, plays an important role in the formation of a process because of which the child acquires the possibility of not only accompanying his action by speech, but aided by it, of searching for and finding a problem's correct solution.

As speech becomes an intra-psychological function, it begins to prepare a preliminary verbal solution to a problem which, in the course of further experiments, perfects itself and, from a speech-mould recapitulating past experience, becomes the preliminary verbal planning of future action.

This reflecting function of speech helps us to trace the process of the formation of its complex, planning function and to understand its actual genetic roots. We are capable of following the origins of the higher stage of the intellectual activity in all its complexity and with all the wealth of its consecutive change of stages. What was formerly considered to be a process of sudden 'discovery' by the child, actually proves to be the result of a lengthy and complicated development where the emotional and communicative functions of primary speech, the reflecting and mould-creating[36] functions, each take their place at a given rung of the genetic ladder, the bottom rung corresponding to the child's primitive optical reactions, the top rung to complex operations planned in time.

This history of speech, which occurs over the course of practical activity, is tied in to a basic reconstruction of the child's entire behaviour. But there is more to this than the mere fact that speech, formerly an inter-psychological process, now becomes an intra-psychological function, or that, at first leading away from the solution of a problem, speech at the top genetic ladder begins to play an intellectual role, becoming the instrument of the problem's organized solution. The reconstruction of behaviour, mentioned above, is of an incomparably deeper nature. If, at the bottom of the genetic ladder, the child operated in a spontaneous situation, aiming his activity directly toward the object of attraction, now the situation becomes more complex. Between the object (attracting the child as its aim) and behaviour, there appear *stimuli of the second order*, now directed not immediately at the object but at the organization and personal *planning of the child's behaviour*. These self-directed speech stimuli, changing in the process of evolution from a means of stimulation of another person into *auto-stimuli*, radically reconstruct the child's entire behaviour.

The child proves to be able to adapt itself to the given situation by *indirect means*, through preliminary self-control and the preliminary organization of its behaviour, and this in principle differs from the behaviour of animals; it includes as a mandatory factor of its make-up a social attitude toward itself and its actions, and this attitude becomes social activity transferred ['to the realm' – eds] within the subject. The child acquires this as a result of the lengthy development it undergoes, thus acquiring that freedom of behaviour in respect to the situation, that independence from the concrete surrounding objects of which the ape is deprived, the latter being, according to Köhler's classic expression, 'the slave of its optic field'. What is more, the child ceases to act in the immediately given and evident *space*. Planning its behaviour, mobilizing and summarizing its past experience for the organization of its future action, the child passes over to active operations *drawn out in time*.

At the moment when, thanks to the planning assistance of speech, a view of the future is included as an active agent, the child's whole operational psychological field changes radically and its behaviour is fundamentally reconstructed. The child's perception begins to develop according to new laws that differ from those of the natural optic field. The fusion of sensory and motor fields is overcome, and the spontaneous impulsive actions with which it responded to each stimulus appearing in the optic field and attracting it, is now restrained. The child's attention begins to function in a new way, while its memory from a passive 'registrator' becomes a function of active selection and of active and intellectual recollection.

With the appearance of the complex indirect level of higher psychological functions, a new base is provided for a radical reconstruction of behaviour. Having examined the genetic progress achieved as a result of the inclusion of symbolic forms of activity in the development of the use of tools, we must now turn to the analysis of those reconstructions brought about by this progress in the development of the main psychological functions.

## 2   The function of signs in the development of higher psychological processes

After examining a period in the child's complex behaviour, we came to the conclusion that, in cases involving the use of tools, the small child's behaviour differs radically from that of the ape. It might be said, in fact, that in many respects it is diametrically opposed in structure to the latter: instead of the operation's total dependence on the structure of the visual field, we observe the child's considerable degree of emancipation from it. Thanks to the participation of speech in the operation, the child acquires an incomparably greater degree of freedom than that observed in the instrumental behaviour of apes. The child was thus given the possibility to solve practical problems of tool use outside its direct sensory field. The child mastered the external situation by first mastering itself and organizing its own behaviour. In all these operations the structure of the psychological process underwent an essential alteration; operations aimed directly at the field of action were supplanted by complex indirect acts, and speech, entering into the operation, proved to be that system of psychological signs which acquired an absolutely special functional importance, and led to the complete reorganization of behaviour.

A series of observations leads us to conclude that such a cultural *reorganization* is characteristic of not only that complex form of behaviour connected with the use of tools such as has been described by us. In fact, even separate psychological processes, of a more elementary nature and included as part of the complex act of 'practical intellect', appear in the case of the child to be profoundly altered as compared to their process in the higher animals.

Even these functions, usually regarded as the most elementary, are, in the case of the child, subject to completely different laws than those that rule at phylogenetically earlier stages of development and are characterized by the same indirect psychological structure as described in connection with the complex act of using tools. A detailed analysis of the structure of separate psychological processes participating in the described act of child behaviour furnishes us with the proof of this fact and shows that even the doctrine concerning the structure of separate 'elementary' processes of child behavior stands in need of a basic revision.

## The development of higher forms of perception

We will begin with *perception*, an act which always appeared to be entirely subordinate to the elementary natural laws, and we shall try to demonstrate that, over the course of the child's development, even this most dependent of all processes on the actual situation is reconstructed on an absolutely new basis. Preserving the external 'phenotypical' resemblance to this function in animals, it belongs, by reason of its internal composition, structure and mode of action, its entire psychological nature, to the higher functions, formed in the process of historical development and having their own particular history in ontogenesis. Here, in this higher function of perception, we shall meet with laws entirely different from those discovered through the application of psychological analysis to its primitive or natural forms. Obviously, the laws governing the psycho-physiology of natural perception are not nullified in the transition to the higher forms treated by us at the moment but, as it were, sink into the background, continuing to exist within these new laws in a shrunken and subordinate form. In the history of development of the child's perception, we observe a process analogous in its essentials to the one which has been well studied in the history of the formation of the nervous system, where the lower, and genetically more ancient systems, with their more primitive functions, become incorporated in the newer and higher 'storeys', continuing their existence as subordinated units within the new whole.

Köhler's work threw new light on the vital importance of the structure of the visual field in the process of the ape's practical operation; the entire process of the solution of a given task, from its very beginning to its conclusive moment, is essentially the function of perception. In this respect Köhler had ample grounds to state that these animals are the slaves of their sensory field to a much greater degree than adult humans, that they are incapable of following the given sensory structure by means of voluntary effort.[37] It is precisely in this subjection to the optic field that Köhler sees what links the ape with other animals, including such remote relatives in organization as the crow (M. Herz's experiments); indeed, it would probably not be very wrong to see this slave-like dependence on the structure of the sensory field as being a general law, governing perception in all the variations of its natural forms.

This is a common characteristic present in *all perception*, since it does not go beyond the limits of its natural psycho-physiological forms or organization.

A child's perception, since it becomes *human* perception, develops not as a direct continuation and further perfection of the forms seen in animals, including even those that stand nearest to man, but leaps from the zoological to the historical form of psychological evolution.

A special series of experiments conducted by us to clarify this problem enables us to discover the basic laws characterizing these higher forms of perception. We cannot, of course, discuss this problem here in all its magnitude and complexity, and we shall confine ourselves to an analysis of only one – yet central – fact of importance. The most convenient way to do this is by turning to tests on the development of perception of pictures at various stages of infant development.

The tests that made it possible for us to describe specific peculiarities of infant perception and its dependence on the inclusion of the higher psychological mechanism, were carried out earlier in their fundamental essentials by Binet, and analysed in detail by W. Stern.[38] As they studied the process of the description of pictures by small children, both these authors established the fact that this process differs at different stages of the child's development. If a two-year old usually limits it to indicating separate objects of a different kind when describing a picture, it later begins to describe actions, in order to complete the description at a still later stage by indicating the complex relation between the picture's several separate objects. All these facts led W. Stern to establish a certain path of development of infant perception and to describe the stages of perception of separate objects, actions and relations as stages that perception goes through during childhood.

These data alone, accepted by modern psychology as firmly established, force us to harbour the most serious doubts: indeed, it suffices to reflect on this material to see that it contradicts everything we know concerning the development of infant behaviour and its basic psycho-physiological mechanisms. What is more, a number of indisputable facts show that the development of psycho-physiological processes in the child has its origin in diffused, integral forms and only later becomes more differentiated.

A considerable number of physiological observations demonstrate this for motor reactions; tests carried out by Volkelt, Werner and others clearly indicate that this is the path followed also by the visual perception of the child. Stern's claim that the stage of perception of separate objects precedes that of perception of the whole situation stands in direct contradiction to all these data.

What is more, if we follow this to its logical conclusion, we are forced to suppose that at even earlier phases of development the child's perception bears an even more splintered and particular character, and that the perception of separate objects is preceded by a stage when the child is apparently able to perceive merely their separate parts or qualities and only later combines the latter into whole objects, and finally unites objects into effective situations.

We obtain a picture of the development of infant perception permeated with rationalism and contradictory to all that has been made known by the latest researches.

The contradiction observed between the main line of development of psycho-physiological processes in the child, and the facts described by Stern, can be explained only if we presume that the process of perception and description of pictures is considerably more complicated than a simple, natural psycho-physiological act, and that it includes new factors radically reconstructing the process of perception.

Our first task was to show that the process of describing pictures studied by Stern was not adequate to that direct perception of the child, the stages of which Stern endeavoured to disclose in his experiments. A very simple experiment made it possible for us to establish this. It sufficed to ask a two year old to describe for us the contents of a picture without using speech; we suggested that the description be made *in pantomime*: this was enough to become convinced that a child, still at the 'object' stage of development according to Stern, both perceived the actual situation in the picture and reproduced it with the greatest ease.[39]

Behind the phase of 'object perception' actually lay a living and integral perception, quite adequate to the picture while destroying the supposition of the 'elementary' character attributed to perception at this phase. What was usually regarded as a property of the child's natural perception, proved to be really a peculiarity of its *speech* or, in other words, a peculiarity of its *verbalized perception*.

A series of observations relating to very small children showed us that the primary function of speech as used by the infant is, in fact, limited to *indication*, to the singling out of a given object from the entire situation perceived by the child. The fact that the child's first words are accompanied by very expressive gestures, as well as a number of control observations, convinces us of this.

From the first steps of the child's development, the word intrudes into the child's perception, singling out separate elements overcoming the natural structure of the sensory field and, as it were, forming new (artificially introduced and mobile) structural centres. Speech does not merely accompany the child's perception, from the very first it begins to take an active part in it: the child begins to perceive the world not only through its eyes, but also through its speech, and it is in this process that we find an essential point in the development of the child's perception.

It is this very complex, indirect structure of perception that makes itself felt in the type descriptions obtained from children by W. Stern in his experiments with pictures. When the child renders an account of the pictures shown to it, it is not merely verbalizing its natural perception of them, expressing them in imperfect speech; speech articulates its perception, singles out in the entire complex salient points of support, introduces an analytical factor into perception, and thus supplants the natural structure of apperception by a complex and psychologically indirect one.

Later, when the intellectual mechanisms related to speech change, when the singling-out function of speech attains a new synthesizing function, then verbalized perception undergoes further change overcoming its primary articulative character and achieving a more complex form of perception [poznajushchee vosprijatie]. The natural laws of perception, most clearly observed in the receptive processes of the higher animals, undergo basic changes due to the inclusion of speech in human perception, and human perception thus acquires an entirely new character.

The fact that the inclusion of speech really does exercise a certain reconstructive influence on the laws of natural perception is especially evident in those cases when speech, interfering with the process of reception, complicates adequate reception and constructs it according to laws that differ in principle from the natural laws of reflection of a perceived situation.

This verbal reconstruction of perception in the child is best seen in a special series of tests designed for this purpose.[40]

For a more detailed study of the structure and development of the function of perception we used Kohs' non-verbal tests as experimental material, which usually are used for testing combinatory activity. In these tests the child must combine blocks with different coloured sides, so as to produce a copy of the more or less complex coloured figure offered as a model. In this experiment we have the possibility of studying how the child perceives both model and material, how it renders form and colour in various combinations, how it compares their structure with the model, and many other moments which characterize the activity of the child's perception. This research included over 200 subjects and was carried out in a comparative genetic aspect. Besides normal children (aged four to 12), adults were also studied (normal, of various cultural levels, and psychopathical: hysteria, aphasia, schizophrenia) and also handicapped children: deaf, dumb and olygophrenic (Dr L. S. Gueshelina).[41]

This experiment showed (if we dwell on the connection which interests us, only on the most fundamental and general of its results) that the commonly accepted viewpoint concerning the independence of the processes of perception from speech, and the possibility by means of non-verbal tests to study adequately the nature of the function of perception at all stages of its development, and quite independently of speech, is not supported by factual data.

Facts point to the contrary. Just as in our experiments concerning the description of pictures by verbal and by play action, where we discovered deep alterations introduced by speech into the process of perception, here, in this special study, we were able to follow how speech-thinking, becoming ever more an integral part of the process of perception, transforms the very laws of perception. This becomes apparent when we compare the solution of a given problem by a deaf-and-dumb and normal child, or by an aphasic and a normal subject; their respective stage of development notwithstanding. This is especially easy to observe because at the early stages both laws manifest diametrically opposed tendencies: perception is integral, speech analytical in character.

In processes of so-called 'immediate perception' and the transmission of perceived forms uninfluenced by speech, the child grasps and fixes an impression of the whole (spots of colour, the basic features of the form, etc.). Yet no matter how correctly and skilfully the child does it, at the very first stages of speech its perception ceases to be bound by the immediate impression of the whole; in its field of vision there arise new centres, fixed by words, and ties appear between these centres and the different parts of the situation being perceived; perception ceases to be the 'slave' of the field of vision and, independently of the degree of correctness and perfection of solution, the child transmits impressions transformed by words.

Very important conclusions may be drawn regarding non-verbal tests: should the solution of a problem occur without a sound being uttered, this certainly should not be conceived as meaning that speech did not participate – as shown in our experiments. 'The capacity of human thought, but without words, is given only by word.' This thesis of psychological linguistics (A. Potebnya) finds its full support and justification in the data of genetic psychology and particularly in the data of our investigation.

### The separation of the primary unity of the sensori-motor functions

The transition to qualitatively new forms of behaviour observed in the child is not, however, confined to the changes we described and which take place within the sphere of perception; what is much more important is the change in its relation to other functions participating in the integral intellectual operation, its place and part in that dynamic system of behaviour which is tied to the use of tools.

Even in the behaviour of the higher animals perception never acts in an independent and isolated way, but always forms part of a more complex whole, and it is only in connection with this whole that the laws of this perception can be understood. The ape does not perceive the visible situation passively, its entire behaviour is directed toward acquiring the object which attracts it. The complex structure, consisting of the real interweaving of instinctive, affective, motor and intellectual factors, is the only actual object of psychological research, from which, by means of abstraction and analysis only, it is possible to isolate perception as a comparatively independent self-contained system. Experimental–genetic research in perception shows that the whole dynamic system of connections and relations between separate functions changes no less radically in the process of the child's development than separate factors in the system of perception itself.

Among all these changes that play a decisive role in the psychological development of the child, the leading place, objectively speaking, must be given to the basic relation: perception–movement.

It has long been established in psychology that all perception has its dynamic continuation in movement; but only recent research, and particularly Gestalt-psychologie, has overcome the concept of past psychology according to which perception and movement, as separate independent elements, may enter into associative relations with each other in the same way as two meaningless syllables in memory tests. Modern psychology is moving ever closer to the concept that the primary unity of sensory and motor processes is a hypothesis that corresponds much more to facts than the concept of their separateness. As early as in primary reflexes and the most elementary reactions we observe such a fusion of perception and movement as to demonstrate beyond the shadow of a doubt that both the parts are indivisible features of one dynamic whole, of one psycho-physical process. The specific adaptability of the structure of the motor response to the nature of the stimulus (an unsolvable riddle to those holding old views) can be explained only if we admit the primary units and integrity of sensori-motor structures.

The same relation between the structure of sensory and motor processes, explained by the dynamic nature of perception, is to be found not only in the elementary forms of reactive processes but also in the higher stages of behaviour, in experiments concerning intellectual operations and the use of tools by apes. The self-observations made by the experimenter (Köhler) indicate that objects, as it were, appear to acquire 'vectors' and move within the visual field toward the goal, during the examination of a situation to be solved by an ape. The lack of self-observations on the monkey's part is perfectly made up for here by an excellent description of its movements which constitute an immediate dynamic continuation of its perception. A successful experimental commentary (which we had the opportunity of verifying in our laboratories) is given by E. R. Jaensch in his experiments with eidetics;[42] they solved the problem by purely sensory means, and the movements of the ape were replaced here by a shifting of the object in the field of vision. Thus, the unity of sensory and motor processes in intellectual operations appears here in a pure form; movement proves to be included already in the sensory field, and the internal mechanisms, accounting for the correspondence between the sensory and motoric parts of the intellectual operation of the ape, become absolutely clear. In experiments concerning the study of motorics[43] tied into affective processes, we[44] showed that the motor reaction is so fused to and inseparably part of the affective process that it can serve as a 'reflecting' mirror in which one can literally 'read' the structure of the affective process, hidden from direct observation. This fact, of intrinsic importance, makes it possible to use the involuntary correlated motor reflection as an excellent symptomatological medium that permits us to establish objectively both the patient's secret experiences (experiments concerning the diagnostic tracing of crime) and the repressed complexes hidden from the subject (as, for instance, post-hypnotic suggestion, subconscious affective traces and so on).

As is shown by experimental–genetic researches, this primary natural relation between perception and movement, their inclusion in a common psycho-physical system, disintegrates in the process of cultural development, and is replaced by relations of a quite different structure, beginning from the moment when words or some other sign is introduced between the initial and concluding stages of the reactive process, and the entire operation assumes an indirect character.

It is due only to such a psychological structure and to the disappearance of the primary relations between perception and movement which occurs because of the inclusion of functionally speaking new stimuli – signs – into this sphere, that the overcoming of primitive forms and possibilities of behaviour becomes possible, this in turn being a mandatory condition for the development of all specifically human higher psychological functions.

Experimental–genetic studies here, too, followed this complex and tortuous path of development in a special series of experiments, one of which it will be instructive to examine here.

Studying the movements of the child during the complex reactions of choice in experimental conditions, we were able to establish that these movements did not remain absolutely the same at all the stages but, on the contrary, underwent a complex evolution, the central and crucial moment of which consisted in a fundamental change in the relations between the sensory and motor parts of the reactive process.

Up to this turning point, the movement of the child is directly linked to the perception of the situation, blindly follows each move in the field, and also directly reflects the structure of perception in the dynamic of movement, as in Köhler's well known example where the hen near the garden fence repeats in movement the structure of the field perceived.

A concrete experimental situation gives us the opportunity to follow this. We pose before a small child, aged four or five, a problem, i.e. to press one of five keys of a keyboard when identifying a given stimulus. The task exceeds the natural capabilities of the child and, therefore, causes intensive difficulties and still more intensive efforts aimed at solving the problem. What we have here is the actual process of selection *in vivo* as differing from the analysis of memorized reaction of selection '*post mortem*', which always substituted the process of genuine selection by multiple-habit stereotyped functioning. But the most remarkable thing is that the entire process of selection by the child is not separate from the motor system, but is externally placed and concentrated in the motoric sphere: the child selects, directly achieving whatever moments the given situation, i.e. choice, calls for. The structure of the child's decision does not in the least resemble an adult's decision, for the latter begins by taking a preliminary decision, subsequently carried out in the form of one fulfilling movement. The child's choice resembles rather a somewhat delayed selection of its own movements, vacillations in the structure of perception find here their direct reflection in the structure of movement, and the mass of diffused gropings and trials delayed in the very motoric process, interrupting and succeeding one another, are in reality the child's process of selection itself: it suffices to glance at the cyclographic curve, recorded by us, to become convinced of the motor nature of the reactive process both in child and adult, as well as to grasp the basic difference between this act as standing at the source of all the complex forms of human behaviour and representing them in their completed aspects.

We cannot better express the main point of this difference in the process of selection in a child and in an adult than by saying that, in the former, a series of trial movements are substituted for selection. The child does not choose the *stimulus* (the necessary key) as the starting point for the consequent movement, but selects the *movement*, checking its result by the instructions. Thus, the child solves its problem of selection not in perception, but in movement, hesitating between two stimuli, its fingers hovering above and moving from one key to another, going halfway and then coming back; when the child transfers its attention to a new point, creating a new centre in the dynamic structure of perception, which is also *shaken by selection*, the child's hand obediently moves towards this new centre, forming one whole with the eye. In short, its movement is not separated from its perception: the dynamic curve of both processes coincides almost exactly in both one and the other case.

And yet this primitive diffusive structure of the reactive process undergoes a fundamental change as soon as a complex psychological function enters the process of direct selection, transforming the natural process, fully apparent in animals, into a higher psychological operation characteristic of man.

Directly upon having observed in the child a diffusive impulsive process, organically fused with perception of selection of movement, we attempted to simplify the task of selection by marking each key with a corresponding sign, which would serve as an additional stimulus, directing and organizing the process of selection. As early as age five or six, the child fulfils this task with the greatest ease,[45] marking the key that it must press, upon the appearance of a certain stimulus, with that stimulus's corresponding sign. The use of this auxiliary sign does not, however, remain a secondary and additional fact only slightly complicating the nature of the operation of choice; the structure of the psychological process is radically changed under the influence of the new ingredient applied to it, and the primitive natural operation is replaced here by a new and cultured one. When the child turns to the auxiliary sign in order to find the key corresponding to the given stimulus, it no longer has those motor impulses, arising directly from perception, those uncertain groping movements in the air, which we observed in the primitive reaction of choice. The use of auxiliary signs destroys the fusion of the sensory field with the motor system, it places a sort of 'functional barrier' between the primary and final moments of reactions replacing the direct switching over of the reaction to the motor sphere of preliminary circuits, achieved with the aid of the higher psychological systems. The child that formerly solved the problem impulsively, now solves it through the internal re-establishment of the connection between the stimulus and the corresponding auxiliary sign, while the movement which previously made the choice, now serves only as a system fulfilling the prepared operation. The system of symbols reconstructs the whole psychological process, and the speaking child masters its movement on a totally new foundation.

The inclusion of a 'functional barrier' transfers the complex reactive processes of the child to another plane. It excludes blind impulsive attempts, in the main affective and distinguishing the primitive behaviour of animals from the intellectual behaviour of man based on preliminary symbolic combinations. Movement detaches itself from direct perception and submits to symbolic functions included in the reactive act, thus breaking with the natural history of behaviour and turning a new page: that of the higher intellectual activity of man.

Pathological material affords us a particularly fine opportunity for becoming convinced that the inclusion in behaviour of speech and of the higher symbolic functions connected with it, reconstructs the motorics, transferring it to a new and higher level. We have observed that during aphasia – with loss of speech – the 'functional barrier', described by us, was also affected, and movement once again became impulsive, fusing with perception. We observed, in an experimental situation analogous to that described, a number of cases of aphasia: invariably, we met in all cases with diffused and premature motor impulses, attempted groping movement, by way of which selection was accomplished, and which showed that the movements ceased to be guided by that preliminary planning at the symbolic stages which transformed the movements of the cultured adult into intellectual behaviour.[46]

We have discussed the genesis and the fate of two fundamental functions in the behaviour of the child. We saw that, in the complex operation of the use of tools and practical intellectual activity, these functions, which indeed play a decisive role, do not remain one and the same over the course of the child's history, but in the process of its development undergo a complex transformation, not only changing their inner structure, but also entering into new functional relations with other processes. Hence, the use of instruments, as we have observed in the behaviour of the child, is not in its psychological content a simple repetition or direct continuation of what comparative psychology has observed before in apes. Psychological analysis finds in this act essential and qualitatively new features. The inclusion of higher, historically created symbolic functions (among which we have just discussed speech and the use of signs), reconstructs the primitive process of solving problems on an entirely new basis.

True, there is a certain external resemblance between the use of tools by apes and the child, and this has led certain scholars to consider these two cases as being akin in principle. This resemblance is due only to the fact that in both cases functions with ultimately analogous purposes are called into play. Research shows, however, that these externally similar functions differ from each other to no less degree than the various layers of the Earth's crust, each belonging to different geological periods. If, in the first case, functions of biological formation solve the problem set before the animal, in the second case analogical functions of historical formation come to the fore, and they begin to take a leading part in the solution of the problem. These functions which, from the point of view of phylogenesis, are not products of the biological evolution of behaviour but of the historical development of the human personality, possess also, from the point of view of ontogenesis, their own particular history of development, closely connected with its biological formation but not coinciding with it and forming along with it a second line of the child's psychological development. We call these functions *higher functions*, meaning by this, first and foremost, their place in the plan of development, while we are inclined to call the history of their formation, as distinguished from the biogenesis of the lower functions, *sociogenesis of the higher psychological functions*, having in mind above all the social nature of their inception.

The appearance in the process of child development of new historical formations, along with the comparatively primitive strata of behaviour, proves, hence, to be the key, without which the use of tools and all the higher forms of behaviour remain locked away from the research worker.

### The reorganization of the functions of memory and attention

The condensed character of these notes does not allow for any kind of detailed analysis of all the fundamental psychological functions that take part in the operations here studied. We will confine ourselves, therefore, to touching only in a very general way on the fate of the major functions without which the psychological structure of the use of tools would remain unclear to us.

According to the extent of its role in this operation, *attention* should be given first place among these functions. All scholars, beginning with Köhler, have noted that the corresponding direction of attention, or its distraction, is an essential factor in the success or failure of a practical operation. This fact, noted by Köhler, preserves its importance in the behaviour of the child. The essential point in the development of this process, however, is that the child, unlike the animal, proves to be capable of transferring its attention actively and independently, reconstructing its perception and thus freeing itself, to a tremendous extent, from submission to the structure of the given field. Linking the use of tools with speech at a certain stage of development (which enters into the operation at first syncretically and later synthetically), the child in this way transfers the activity of its attention to a new plane. With the help of the indicative function of words, noted above, the child begins to master its attention, creating new structural centres of the perceived situation. By this means, as Koffka[47] so aptly put it, the child evaluates not the degree of clarity of one or the other part of the perceived field, but its 'centre of gravity' (Schwerpunkt), the importance of its separate elements, singling out ever new 'figures' from its background, and thus limitlessly widening the possibilities for mastering its activities.

All this frees the child's attention from the power of the actual situation that immediately effects it. Creating along with the space field for its action, with the help of speech, *a time field* just as visible and real as the optic situation (although, perhaps, more vague), the speaking child obtains the possibility of dynamically directing its attention, acting in the present from the viewpoint of the future field, and often reacting towards the changes actively created in the present situation from the point of view of past activities. Owing to the part of speech and the transition to such a free distribution of attention, the future field of action is transformed from an old and abstract verbal formula to an actual optic situation; in it, standing out sharply as the basic configuration, are all the elements that make up the plan of this future activity, distinguishable thus from the general background of possible activity. The specific difference between the operation of the child and that of the higher animals lies in the fact that this field of attention, which does not coincide with the field of perception, with the assistance of speech singles out from the latter the elements of the actual 'future field'. In the case of the child, the field of perception is organized by the verbalized function of attention; if, in the case of the ape, the absence of direct optic contact between the object and the aim is sufficient to render the task unsolvable, in the instance of the child this is easily overcome by verbal interference; the child simply reorganizes its sensory field.

Owing to this circumstance, it becomes possible to combine in one field of attention the 'figure' of the future situation consisting of elements of the past and present sensory fields; thus the field of attention embraces not one perception, but a whole series of potential perceptions that form successive dynamic structural entity in time. The transition from the simultaneous structure of the optic field to the successive structure of the dynamic field of attention is achieved as a result of the reconstruction, on the basis of the inclusion of speech, of all the major connections between the separate functions that take part in the operation: the field of attention that has detached itself from the field of perception and unfolded itself in time, including the given actual situation, as one of the moments of a dynamic series.

The ape, perceiving a stick one moment in one optic field, ceases to pay attention to it the next moment, after its optic field has changed and when an aim appears in its centre. The ape must first see the stick in order to pay attention to it; the child may pay attention in order to see.

The possibility of combining in one field of attention elements of the past and present optic fields (for instance, tool and aim) leads, in turn, to a basic reconstruction of another vitally important function taking part in the operation: that of *memory*. Similar to the way in which the action of attention, as Koffka correctly noted, is apparent not in the increase in clarity of one or another part of the sensory field, but in the displacement of the centre of gravity, in its structure, in the dynamic alteration of this structure, in the alteration of figure and background, so the role of memory in the child's operation manifests itself *not simply* in the widening of that fragment of the past which actually fuses in a united whole with the present, but in the *new method of uniting the elements of past experience with present*; this method is based on the inclusion of *speech formulas* of past situations and past activities into a single point of attention. As we have seen, speech shapes the operation according to laws other than those of direct action. Similarly, it also fuses, unites and synthesizes the past and present in a different way, freeing the action of the child from the power and influence of direct recollection.

## The voluntary structure of the higher psychological functions

After subjecting to further analysis the psychological operation of practical intellect related to the use of tools, we see that the time field created for action with the help of speech extends not only backwards but also forwards. The anticipation of the following points of action in symbolic form allows for the inclusion in the present operation of special stimuli, which should represent in the operation these points of future activity and should actually achieve their influence in the organization of behaviour at the present moment.

Here, as in the case of the operations of memory and attention, the inclusion of symbolic functions does not lead to a simple lengthening of the operation in time, but creates conditions for an entirely new kind of connection between the elements of the present and the future: the actually perceived elements of the present situation are included in one structural system with symbolically represented elements of the future. An absolutely new psychological field for action is created, leading to the appearance of the function of *formation of intention* and previously planned *purposeful action*.

This change in the structure of the child's behaviour is related to alterations of a much more basic type. Lindner, comparing the way deaf and dumb children solved tasks with Köhler's experiments, called attention to the fact that *motives* pushing the ape and the child to the mastering of a given aim cannot be regarded as one and the same.[48] The instinctive disturbance predominating in the animal become secondary in the child's case, giving way to new motives of a social nature. These have no natural analogy but, nevertheless, attain in the child a considerable degree of intensity. These motives, also of decisive importance in the mechanism of a developed voluntary act, were called by Lewin 'Quasibedürfnisse',[49] who noted that their inclusion leads to a new reconstruction of the whole affective and voluntary system in the behaviour of the child and in particular, changes its attitudes to the organization of future action. The peculiarity of this new 'motor' strata of human behaviour consists in two main points: the mechanism of the fulfilment of intention is, in the first place, separated from the motorics at the moment of its arising; in the second place, it contains in itself the impulse to act, this being realized in the future field. Both these points are absent in action organized by natural needs in which motorics are inseparable from direct perception, and all the action is concentrated in the present psychological field.

The way in which this action, related to the future, arises has remained up to this time insufficiently accounted for. Now it can be explained from the viewpoint of study of symbolic functions and their participation in behaviour. The 'functional barrier' between perception and motorics, mentioned above, and which owes its origin to the intrusion of word or some other symbol between the initial and final points of action, explains this separation of impulse from the immediate realization of the act which, in turn, constitutes the mechanism preparing postponed future action. It is the inclusion of symbolic operations which makes possible the formation of an absolutely new psychological field in composition, a field that does not lean on the existing present, but rather sketches an outline of the future situation of action and thus creates free action, independent of the immediately effective situation.

By studying the mechanisms of the symbolic situations, with the help of which action is, as it were, torn away from those natural primary ties that are given by the biological organization of behaviour, and is transferred to an entirely new psychological system of functions, we achieve an understanding of by what means man arrives at the possibility of forming 'a free intention'. This is a fact on which too little attention has yet been focused and which, according to Lewin, distinguishes the civilized adult from the child and primitive man.

If we try to sum up the results of an analysis as to how separate psychological functions and their structural relations change under the influence of the inclusion of symbols, and if we compare the wordless operations of an ape with the verbalized operations of a child, we will find that one relates to the other as *a voluntary action to an involuntary*.

The traditional approach has been to qualify as voluntary action everything that is not primarily or secondarily automatic (instinct or habit). However, actions of a third order exist which are neither automatic, nor voluntary. These include, as Koffka has shown, the 'Intelligenzhandlungen' of apes which cannot be reduced to pure automatism, but are also not of a 'voluntary' character. Research upon which we base our views furnishes an explanation as to what is lacking in the ape's action which does not allow it to be qualified as 'voluntary': 'voluntary' action is manifest there, where we find *the mastering of one's own behaviour with the assistance of symbolic stimuli*.

Upon achieving this stage of development of behaviour, the child 'leaps' from the 'intelligent' action of the ape to the intelligent and free action of man.

## 3   Sign operations and the organization of the psychological processes

### Problems of signs in the formation of the higher psychological functions

The facts described in the previous pages bring us to psychological conclusions the significance of which leads us far beyond the limits of analysis of the specific, concrete group of phenomena that has, until now, been the principal subject of our research. The functional, structural and genetic laws that manifest themselves in the study of these facts prove on closer inspection to be laws of a more general order and force us to revise the question of the structure and genesis of all the higher psychological functions as conceived of today.

Two roads lead us to this revision and generalization: on the one hand, a broader study of other forms of the symbolic activity of the child shows that not only speech, but all operations related to the use of signs, their differing concrete forms notwithstanding, are governed by the same laws of development, structure and functioning, as ['is characteristic of' – eds] speech in the role discussed above. Their psychological nature proves to be the same as the speech activity examined by us, where we found, in a complete form, the properties common to all the higher psychological processes. We should, consequently, examine in the light of what we have learned concerning the functions of speech, other psychological systems akin to it, no matter whether we shall be dealing with second order symbolic processes (such as writing, reading, etc.) or with such basic forms of behaviour as speech.

On the other hand, not only operations related to practical intellect, but all no-less primary and, frequently, even more elementary functions belonging to biologically shaped forms of activity, manifest laws in the process of development that we discovered when analysing practical intellect. Hence, the route followed by the practical intellect of the child, discussed above, constitutes the common path of development of all the basic psychological functions; these, in turn, have one thing in common with practical intellect: they all have their 'man-like' forms in the animal world. This route is analogous to the one described on the previous pages in that, beginning with the natural forms of development, it soon outgrows them and causes radical reconstruction of these functions on the basis of the use of signs as a means of organizing behaviour. Thus, however strange it may seem from the point of view of traditional doctrine, the higher functions of perception, memory, attention, move-ment and so on, prove to be internally connected with the development of the sign using activity of the child, and their comprehension is possible only on the basis of an analysis of their genetic roots and of that reconstruction which they underwent in the course of their cultural history.

We stand, at this juncture, before a conclusion of great theoretic importance: we perceive the unity of the higher psychological functions as based on the essential sameness of their origins and mechanism of development. Such functions as voluntary attention, logical memory, the higher forms of perception and movement which, until the present time, were examined separately and were regarded as individual psychological facts, in the light of our experiments now appear as phenomena of essentially one psychological order, as the product of a fundamentally integral histori-cal development of behaviour. Through this, all the given functions are introduced into a broad field of genetic research, and instead of being treated as lower and higher varieties of several permanently co-existing and neighbouring functions, they are admitted as being what they actually are: different stages of the integral process of the personality's cultural formation. From this standpoint, we have as much reason to speak of logical memory or of voluntary attention, as we do of voluntary memory, of logical attention, of voluntary or logical forms of perception, which sharply differ from the natural forms of calculation by laws peculiar to another genetic stage.

The logical consequence of the recognition of the primary importance of the use of signs in the history of development of the higher psychological functions, is the inclusion of external symbolic forms of activity (speech, reading, writing, counting and drawing) into the system of psychological categories. They were usually regarded as foreign and additional in relation to the inner psychological processes, but from the new point of view we defend they are included into the system of higher psychological functions on an equal footing with all other higher psychological processes. We are inclined to regard them, first of all, as particular forms of behaviour, shaping themselves in the course of the social–cultural development of the child and forming an external line in the development of symbolic activity along with the inner line, represented by the cultural development of such functions as practical intellect, perception, memory, etc.

Thus, in the light of our historical theory of the higher psychological functions, the usual, customary borderlines dividing and uniting separate processes (as conceived by modern psychology) are shifted; what was formerly considered to belong to different compartments, now proves actually to belong to one and the same, and on the other hand, what seemed to belong to one class of phenomena, is actually located at absolutely different levels of the genetic ladder and proves subject to completely different laws.

Thus the higher functions form a psychological system, integral in its genetic character, although manifold in composition, built on foundations entirely different from those of the elementary psychological functions. The factors uniting the whole system, determining whether one or another individual psychological process should be attributed to it or not, is the common origin of their structure and function. *Genetically* they differ in that in their phylogenesis they are the *product not of biological evolution, but of the historical development of behaviour*, while in ontogenesis they have also a special social history. With regard to structure, their peculiarity consists in that, unlike the direct reactive structure of elementary processes, they are constructed on the basis of the use of stimuli-means (signs) and, depending on this, reflect an indirect character. Finally, they are characterized functionally speaking by the fact that behaviour-wise they fulfil a new and essentially different role as compared to the elementary functions, a role that brings about an organized adaptation to the situation, preceded by a preliminary mastering of one's own behaviour.

## *The social genesis of the higher psychological functions*

If, then, sign organization proves to be the most important distinguishing feature of all the higher psychological functions, it is natural that the first question the theory of higher functions must decide upon is that of the origin of this type of organization.

While traditional psychology sought for the origin of symbolic activity either in the series of 'discoveries' or other intellectual operations of the child, or in the processes of the formation of ordinary conditional ties [usually translated as 'conditioned associations' – eds], seeing them only as the product of invention or a complicated form of habit, our researches lead us to the necessity of singling out an independent history of sign processes as forming a special line in the general history of the child's psychological development.

In this history we find, occupying their subordinate place, both various forms of habit connected with the complete functioning of one or another system of signs, and the complex processes of thought so necessary for their intelligent application. But both of these can not only not furnish an exhaustive explanation as to the origin of higher functions, but can themselves be explained only in the broader context of their relation to those processes of which they constitute an auxiliary part; the process of origin of operations, related to the use of signs, can not only not be deduced from the formation of habits or inventions, but is, in general, a category not to be deduced at all as long as we remain within the confines of individual psychology. By its very nature *it is a part of the history of the social formation of the child's personality*, and only in the content of this whole can the laws governing it be disclosed. The behaviour of man is the product of development of a broader system of social ties and relations, collective forms of behaviour and social co-operation.

This social nature of all the higher psychological functions has until now escaped the attention of scholars, to whom it never occurred to regard the development of logical memory or voluntary activity as part of the child's social formation, for in its biological beginning and at the end of its psychological development it appears as an individual function. Only genetic analysis uncovers the path that connects the starting and final points. This analysis shows that every higher psychological function was formerly a peculiar form of psychological co-operation, and only later became an individual way of behaviour, transplanting inside the child's psychological system a structure that, in the course of such transfer, preserves all the main features of its symbolic structure, altering only its situation.[50]

Thus, the sign primarily appears in the child's behaviour *as a means of social relations, as an inter-psychological function*. Becoming afterward a means by which the child controls its behaviour, *the sign simply transfers the social attitude toward the subject within the personality*. The most important and basic of genetic laws, to which the study of the higher psychological functions leads us, reads that every symbolic activity of the child was once a social form of co-operation and preserves throughout its development, to its highest point, the social method of its functioning. The history of the higher psychological functions is disclosed here *as the history of the transformation of means of social behaviour into means of individual psychological organization*.

## The main rules of development of the higher psychological functions

These general propositions, lying at the basis of our historical theory of the higher psychological functions, lead to certain conclusions related to the main rules governing the process of development under discussion. We shall deal with these only in the form of the shortest indications that generalize what has been said and, hence, render a detailed discussion unnecessary.

1   *The history of the development of each of the higher psychological functions, contrary to being simply the direct continuation and further perfecting of the corresponding elementary function, presumes a radical change of the very direction of development and the further movement of this process along entirely new lines; each higher psychological function comprises, therefore, a specific new form.*

This viewpoint is easily observed in phylogenesis, since the biological and historical formation of all function are so sharply divided and so obviously belong to
different types of evolution that both processes are evident in a pure and isolated
form. In ontogenesis, however, both lines of development appear as an interwoven
complex combination, and this has frequently misled the research worker who,
perceiving these two lines as one integral entity, came to consider the higher processes
as the simple continuation and development of the lower.

We shall limit ourselves to only one factual consideration that confirms our
approach on the basis of data obtained concerning the most complex psychological
operations; let us examine the development of *counting and arithmetical processes.*

In a large number of psychological researches we meet a viewpoint according to
which the child's arithmetical operations are from the very beginning an example of
complex symbolic activity and that they proceed from elementary forms of operations
with quantities by way of uninterrupted development.

Experiments conducted in our laboratories (by Kuchurin and Menchinskaya)
convincingly show that there can be no question here of a direct and gradual
perfecting of elementary processes and that the change of form in counting operations
is of a profound qualitative nature, a change of the psychological processes participating in the operation. Observations have shown that, if at the beginning of development, quantitative operations are limited to *the immediate perception of given pluralities
and number groups,* and that *the child does not really count but perceives quantities,* further
development is characterized by *the breakdown of this immediate form* and its replacement by other processes. In these latter a number of *indirect auxiliary signs* take part,
in particular, articulative speech, the use of fingers and other aids that lead the child
to the *process of counting.* The further development of the counting operation is again
connected with the radical reconstruction of the participating psychological functions; calculation with the help of complex counting systems again presents a qualitatively new and specific psychological formation.

We arrive at the conclusion that the development of counting may be reduced to
the process of the participation in this operation of the main psychological functions;
the transition from pre-school to school arithmetics is not a simple, uninterrupted
process, but rather a process of the overcoming of primary elementary laws and their
replacement by new and more complex ones.

A concrete example of this may be found in the simplest experiment. If the
counting process for the small child is entirely determined by form perception, at a
later stage this attitude is reversed and form perception itself is determined by the
articulative tasks of counting. In our experiments a cross made up of counters (figure
7.1, A) was presented to a small child to count up.[51] Invariably the child made a
mistake: it perceived the figure as an integral system of a cross (B), twice counting the
central piece common to both the crossing systems. It was only much later that the
child proceeded to another type or process. Perception becomes determined by the
problem of counting and is broken down into three separate groups of elements,
which were consecutively counted (C). In this process we cannot but see the supplant-
ing of one psychological method of behaviour by another, the emancipation from

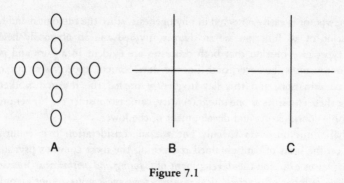

Figure 7.1

direct connection of the sensory and the motor field and the processing of perception by means of complex psychological attitudes.

All these researches show conclusively that evolutionism must give way, in the study of the development of child behaviour, to more adequate ideas that take into consideration the absolutely original and dialectic character of the process of formation of new psychological forms.

2   *The higher psychological functions are not superimposed as a second storey over the elementary processes, but represent new psychological systems which include a complex knot of elementary functions that, upon being included in the new system, begin to act according to new laws. Each higher psychological function thus presents a unity of a higher order, determined mainly by the particular combination of a series of more elementary functions into a new whole.*

This approach, of decisive importance concerning research on the formation and structure of the higher psychological functions, has been examined by us on the foregoing pages, where we dealt with experiments pertaining to the re-organization of perception due to the inclusion of speech and, in a broader sense, to the mutual and radical change of functions during the formation of the complex psychological system 'speech–practical intellectual operation'. In all these cases we actually observed the formation of complex psychological systems with new functional relations between separate parts of the systems and corresponding changes in the functions themselves. If perception, connected with speech, began to function not according to the laws of the sensory field, but to those of the organized system of attention; if the meeting of the symbolic operation with the use of tools resulted in new forms of indirect control of the object, with the preliminary organization of the child's own behaviour – then in this case we must speak of a certain general law of psychological development and formation of higher psychological functions.

After several series of psychological researches we became convinced that both the most primitive and the most complex of higher functions undergo such a reconstruction. Thus, experiments on the psychological study of imitation (carried out in our laboratories[52] by Bozhovich and Slavina) showed that primitive forms of reflective imitation form, upon entering the system of sign operations, a new entity built on entirely new laws and having another function. In other experiments pertaining to the psychological study of the process of concept formation (according to a method created by L. S. Sakharov), our collaborators Kotelova and Pashkovskaya demonstrate that at higher stages of psychological processes, too, the inclusion of complex speech functions is related to the creation of entirely new forms of categorial behaviour hitherto not observed.

3   *In cases of disintegration of the higher psychological functions due to pathological processes, the first link to be destroyed is that between the symbolic and natural functions; this results in the cutting off of a number of natural processes which then start functioning according to their primitive laws, i.e. as more or less independent psychological structures. If follows, then, that the disintegration of the higher psychological function represents a process which, quality-wise, is the reverse of their formation.*

It would be difficult to imagine a more clear cut example of such a general disintegration of the higher psychological functions, due to the disruption of speech, than in the phenomenon of aphasia. The breakdown of speech is accompanied here by the disappearance (or serious disruption) of sign operations. This disappearance, however, by no means takes place as an isolated monosymptom, but results in far reaching and general disruptions in the functioning of all the higher psychological systems. In a special series of studies we were able to establish the fact that the aphasic suffering from an affliction of higher sign operations becomes in his practical actions completely subject to the elementary laws of the optic field. In another series we experimentally established the sharp changes characteristic of the active operations of the aphasic as they return to the primitive indivisibility of the sensory and motor spheres. The most serious consequences of the affliction of the higher symbol systems manifest themselves in the following ways: the immediate motor manifestation of impulses coupled to an impossibility of delaying action and of forming an intention postponed in time; the inability of transforming a given image through transferred attention; the total incapability of abstracting judgement and action from intelligent and familiar structures; and, finally, the reversion to primitive forms of reflective imitation.

Studies of aphasia furnish an exceptionally convincing argument that the higher psychological functions do not exist simply next to, or on top of, the lower ones; in reality, they penetrate them and so radically reform them all, including even the deepest layers of behaviour, that their disintegration, related to the break off of lower processes in their elementary form, alters the whole structure of behaviour, throwing it back to the most primitive, 'paleopsychological' type of activity.

## 4   The analysis of sign operations in the child

We are now in a position to return to the subject mentioned at the beginning of this chapter, where we pointed out that the laws governing the development of the child's practical intellect are only a particular case of the laws pertaining to the construction of all the higher psychological functions. The conclusions we reached confirm this viewpoint and show that these higher functions arise as specific new forms, as a new structural entity, characterized by new functional relations established within it. We have already noted that these new functional relations are linked to the operation of sign use, this being the central and basic moment in the construction of all the higher psychological functions. This operation thus proves to be a symptom common to all the higher psychological functions (including the use of tools which remains our starting point), a symptom we must regard as a kind of common multiplier and, at the conclusion of our experiment, submit to special examination.

Several series of experiments, carried out during the last few years by my colleagues and myself,[53] dealt with this problem, and now, basing ourselves on the acquired data, we are able to describe in a schematic form the basic laws that characterize the structure and development of the child's sign operations.

It is only through experiments that we can hope to penetrate sufficiently deeply into the laws of these higher processes. Only experiment permits us to provoke in one artificially created process all those most complex changes that are so widely separated in time, often lying latent for years, changes that, in the child's normal genesis, are never accessible in all their real conjunctions, and cannot be taken in at one glance in their multiple co-relations. The research worker striving to comprehend the laws of a whole and who hopes to penetrate external manifestations so as to arrive at the causal and genetic links of these factors, must resort to a special form of experimentation. Its methodology will be touched on further. As for its essence, it consists in the creation of processes that, in the experiment, disclose the actual course of development of a given function.

This experimental genetic study gives us the opportunity to follow the problems interesting us in the three mutually inter-related aspects: we shall describe the structure, origin and further fate of sign operations in the child, these leading us to an understanding of the inner essence of the higher psychological processes.

## The structure of sign operation

We shall dwell here on the history of *child memory*, in the example of the development of which we shall try to show the general characteristics of sign operations along the lines mentioned above. Memory is an exceptionally advantageous subject for analysis for the comparative study of the structure and method of action of the elementary and higher functions.

The phylogenetic investigation of human memory shows that, even at the most primitive stages of psychological development, we can clearly see two, principally different types of memory functions. One, dominating in primitive man's behaviour, is characterized by the immediate impression of material by the simple after-effect of actual experiences, the retention of those mnemonic traces the mechanism of which was so brilliantly outlined by E. R. Jaensch in the phenomena of 'eidetic images'. This kind of memory is very near to perception, with which it has not yet broken off its immediate connection, and arises out of the direct influence of external impressions on man. From the point of view of structure the immediate character noted by us is the major point of the whole process, a point linking the memory of man with that of the animal. And that is what entitles us to call this form of memory 'natural memory'.

This form of memory functioning is not, however, the only one, even in the case of primitive man. On the contrary, even in his case other types of remembering may be seen alongside it, types that, upon closer analysis, prove to belong to a completely different genetic line and that lead us to an absolutely different formation of the human psyche. Even in such comparatively simple operations as the tying of a knot or marking something to remind oneself to remember, the psychological structure of the process changes completely.

Two essential factors distinguish this operation from simple elementary retaining in mind: the process here obviously goes far beyond the limits of elementary functions directly linked with memory and is supplanted by the most complicated operations that, *per se*, may have nothing in common with memory but carry out in the general structure of the new operation the function formerly fulfilled by direct retention. On the other hand, the operation here also goes beyond the limits of natural, intra-cortical processes, also adding to the psychological structure environmental elements that begin to be used as active agents governing the psychological process from without. As a result, both these factors produce an entirely new form of behaviour. After analysing its inner structure, we can call it *indirect* (*instrumental*); evaluating its difference from natural forms of behaviour, we can qualify that type of behaviour as 'cultural'.

An essential factor in this operation is the participation of certain *external signs*. Here the subject does not solve the problem by way of the direct mobilization of his natural capacities; he has recourse to certain external manipulations, organizing himself through the organization of objects, creating artificial stimuli which differ from others in that they have *reverse action*, being directed not at other people but at himself and allowing him to solve the problem of remembering with the aid of external signs.

Examples of such sign operations organizing the memory process are manifest at a very early period in the history of culture. The use of notched sticks and knots, the beginnings of writing and primitive *aides-mémoire* – all these serve to show that at the early stages of cultural development man already went beyond the limits of the psychological functions given to him by nature, and proceeded to a new, cultural organization of his behaviour.

Obviously, such a superior symbolic operation as the use of signs for remembering is the product of the most complex historical development; comparative analysis shows that such types of activity are absent in all species of animals, including the highest, and there is reason to believe that it is the product of specific conditions of *social* development; it is no less obvious that such auto-stimulation could appear only after similar stimuli had already been created for the stimulation of others, and that behind it lies a complicated process of social history. Sign operation, to all appearances, follows the same course as the one taken by speech in ontogenesis, speech having been formerly a means of stimulating another person and afterwards becoming an intra-psychological function.

With the transition to sign operations we not only proceed to psychological processes of the highest complexity, but in fact leave the field of the psyche's natural history and enter the domain of the historical formation of behaviour.

The transition to higher psychological functions by way of their becoming indirect (instrumented) and the construction of sign operation can be followed successfully in experiments on a child. With this aim in mind we can move from elementary direct reaction tests to tests in which the child solves problems with the aid of a number of auxiliary stimuli that organize the psychological operation. When the problem consists of remembering a certain number of words, we can give the child some objects or pictures that do not repeat any of the words to be remembered, but serve as conditional signs which might later help the child to reproduce the words. It follows that the process studied in this experiment must differ sharply from simple elementary memorizing. The task here must find its solution through an indirect operation, through the establishment of a definite relation between the stimulus and the sign. Instead of simple memorizing, we have here an integral process that presupposes a considerably more complicated method of organizing behaviour than that inherent in psychological functions. In fact, if every elementary form of behaviour basically presupposes a *direct* reaction to the task set before the organism, expressed by the simple formula S ——> R, the structure of sign operation proves to be much more complicated. Here an intermediate link appears between the stimulus and the reaction directly connected earlier, an intermediate link that plays a special role completely different from everything we observed in the elementary forms of behaviour. This *stimulus of a second order* must be drawn into the operation where it

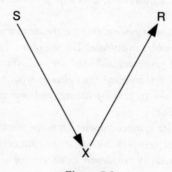

Figure 7.2

assumes the special function of serving its organization: it must be established by the individual, and must have reverse action, thus causing specific reactions. The formula of the simple reactive process is replaced, consequently, by that of the complex indirect act [figure 7.2],[54] where the direct impulse to react is held back, and the operation follows a roundabout way, establishing a certain auxiliary stimulus that fulfils the operation by indirect means.

Careful investigation demonstrates the fact that we see this structure in the higher psychological processes, although in much more sophisticated forms than that shown here. The intermediate link in this formula is not, as might have been supposed, simply a method of improving and perfecting the operation. By possessing the specific functions of reverse action, it transfers the psychological operation to higher and qualitatively new forms, permitting man, by the aid of outer stimuli, to *control his behaviour from without*; the use of signs, which are at the same time a means of auto-stimulation, leads man to a completely new and specific structure of behaviour, breaking away from the traditions of natural development and creating for the first time a new form of cultural psychological behaviour.

Memory tests with the use of external signs carried out in our laboratories[55] showed that this form of psychological operation is not only essentially new in comparison with direct memorizing, but that it helps the child *to overcome the limits set for memory by natural laws of mnema, and that, what is more, it is primarily this mechanism in memory which is subject to development.*

The presence of these higher or roundabout ways of memorizing is nothing new, no more than is the possibility of similar indirect operations. Their empiric description is the merit of experimental psychology. Classic studies, however, failed to see in them *new, specific and integral forms of behaviour, acquired in the process of historical development*. Such kinds of operations (as, for instance, mnemotechnical memorizing) were regarded as nothing more than simply an artificial combination of a number of elementary processes where, as a result of a lucky coincidence, a mnemotechnic effect occurred. This practical method, created *ad hoc*, was not conceived of in psychology as an essentially new form of memory, as a new method of activity.

Our tests lead to diametrically opposite conclusions. Examining the operation of memorizing with the help of external signs, and analysing its structure, we became convinced that, far from being a simple 'psychological trick', it presents all the features and properties of a *really new and integral function*: an entity of the highest order, the separate parts of which are united in relations *sui generis*. These cannot be reduced either to the laws of association or to those of structure, fundamentally studied in direct psychological operations. We define these specific functional relations as the *sign function of auxiliary stimuli*, on the basis of which a principally new correlation of psychological processes included in this operation takes place.

This integral and specific nature of the sign operation can be observed with particular clarity in experiments. The latter demonstrate that even if the links the child turns to, when striving to remember, by the sign, a given word, are indeed formed following the laws of association or structure (we do not in essence go into that question's solution here), the specific quality of the sign operation itself cannot be explained by these laws. Clearly, the simple associative or structural link is not reversible, and the sign linked to the word does not, on being produced, necessarily serve again as a reminder of the given word. We have a great number of cases when a process that proceeded according to the usual laws of structural or associative connections did not necessarily lead to the indirect operation, and the repeated demonstration of the picture evoked in the child new associations instead of bringing it back to particular word. What was needed was that the child realize the operation's purposeful character, that the child come into a specific *sign relation* with the auxiliary stimulus; only then will the structural or associative connection acquire its mandatory *reversive character* and the repeated demonstration of the sign will necessarily bring it back to the word, memorized earlier with the help of the sign.

At a later stage we shall dwell on the roots of these complex psychological processes; at this point, however, we should like only to remark that *associative or structural processes begin to play their auxiliary, indirect role, within the limits of this 'instrumental operation', and that what we witness here is not an accidental combination of psychological functions but a really new and special form of behaviour.*

The process described is characteristic only for the construction of the higher forms of memory. On the other hand, we would be wrong if we thought that such operations enhance only quantitative aspects of the activity of psychological functions. Special tests show that the described schema is a general principle of the construction of the higher psychological structures; due to them, new psychological structures are created which were formerly non-existent and, probably, impossible without such sign operations. We shall illustrate this with the example of a genetic study of the activity of the child's *voluntary attention*.

A child of seven or eight years was placed in conditions calling for a high degree of constant and concentrated attention (for instance, asking the child to name the colour of a number of objects without repeating the same colour or naming two 'forbidden' colours). A direct attempt to solve the task led to a total inability to achieve a correct solution. However, as soon as the child switches over to an indirect organization of the process by using certain auxiliary signs, the task becomes easy to solve.

In the experiments carried out in our laboratories[56] by Leont'ev, the child was given a number of coloured cards to be used for the simplification of the task. In cases when the child did not use them in its activities (as, for instance, putting 'forbidden' colours aside and removing them from the fixed field), the task proved to be unsolvable. It was easily carried out, however, when instead of naming the colours, the child used a complex structure of replies based on the auxiliary signs given him: placing the two 'forbidden' colours inside the fixed field and adding each newly named colour, the child thus formed an auxiliary control group, and the task was easily fulfilled. Replying each time *with the aid* of these auxiliary stimulus signs, the child organized its *active attention* from without, thus becoming adapted to a task that could not be solved by direct, elementary forms of behaviour.

## The genetic analysis of sign operation

We discussed the indirect nature of psychological operations as a specific feature of the structure of higher psychological functions. It would be a great mistake, however, to believe that this process appears in a purely logical way, that it is invented and discovered by the child in the form of a lightning-quick guess (a so-called 'aha' reaction), thanks to which the child once and for all comes to realize the relation between the sign and the method of using it, resulting in this entire operation's further development proceeding along purely deductive lines. It would be equally wrong to believe that the symbolic attitude to some stimuli is reached intuitively by the child, derived as it were from the depths of the child's own spirit, or that symbolization is the primary and further irreducible Kantian *facultas signatrix*, from the beginning a part of human consciousness capable of creating and comprehending symbols. Both these points of view – the intellectual and the intuitive – in essence metaphysically dispose of the question of the genesis of symbolic activity since, for one of them, the higher psychological functions are given previous to any experience, as if they were inherent to consciousness and only waiting for an opportunity to manifest themselves upon meeting with the empiric perception of things. This point of view leads inevitably to an *a priori* conception of higher psychological functions (see Cassirer).[57] For the other point of view, the question concerning the origin of the higher psychological functions poses no problems at all, since it postulates that signs are invented, and after that all corresponding forms of behaviour are deduced from them as conclusions from logical premises. Finally, we have touched on what we consider to be the failure of attempts to deduce complex symbolic activity from the simple interference and accumulation of habits.

Observations over a course of a series of experiments of various psychological functions, as well as a step-by-step study of development, led us to conclusions diametrically opposite those described above. Facts contributed to our realization of the tremendous importance of the process which we call the natural history of sign operations. We saw that sign operations appear as a result of the most complex and prolonged process that reflects all the typical features of real *development* and is subject to all the basic laws of psychological evolution. This means that they are not simply invented or passed down by adults, but rather arise from something that is originally not a sign operation and that becomes one only after a series of qualitative transformations, each of which conditions the next stage and is itself conditioned by the preceding one and thus links them like stages of an integral process, historical in nature. In this respect the higher psychological functions are no exception to the general rule and do not differ from other elementary processes. *They, too, are subject to the fundamental law of development which knows no exceptions*. They appear in the child's general process of psychological development not as something introduced from without or from within, but as the natural result of this same process.

True, if we include the history of the higher psychological functions in the general context of psychological development and attempt to arrive at an understanding of their source from its laws of development, we cannot but arrive at a new concept of the process itself and of its laws. *Within* this general process of development two qualitatively original main lines can already be distinguished: the line of biological formation of elementary processes and the line of the socio-cultural formation of the higher psychological functions; the real history of child behaviour is born from the interweaving of these two lines.

Accustomed as we were over the course of our observations to distinguish between these two lines, we nevertheless met with a stunning fact that threw light on the entire question of the origin of sign function in the child's ontogenesis: a series of studies established that a genetic link exists between both lines, i.e. that there exist a number of transitional forms between the elementary and higher psychological functions. We found that the earliest flowering of the most complex sign operation occurs as early as in the system of purely natural forms of behaviour, and thus that the higher functions have their 'pre-natal' period of development linking them with the natural foundation of the child's psyche. Objective observations showed that between the purely natural layer of the elementary functioning of psychological processes and the higher layer of indirect forms of behaviour, there lies a huge area of *transitional* psychological systems; in the history of behaviour, an area of primitive forms lies between the natural and the cultural. We qualify these two points, that is, the idea of the development of higher psychological functions and their genetic connection with the natural forms of behaviour, as '*the natural history of the sign*'.

The idea of development proves here to be the key to the comprehension of the unity of all psychological functions and, at the same time, of the inception of higher, qualitatively different forms. We arrive, therefore, at the conclusion that these *most complex psychological formations arise from the lower by way of development*.

Tests pertaining to the study of indirect memorizing provide the possibilities of studying this process of development in its entirety. A certain primitiveness of all psychological operations is found, to a considerable extent, to be characteristic of the first stage in the use of signs. Close study shows that the sign, applied here as a reminder of a certain stimulus, is not yet fully separated from the latter; along with the stimulus it forms a kind of *general syncretic structure embracing both the object and the sign* and as yet does not really serve as a *means of memorizing*.

The idea of purposefulness of the operation, linked to the use of signs, is still foreign to the child at this stage of development. Even if the child does turn to the auxiliary picture so as to memorize a given word, this does not necessarily mean that the reverse operation – reproducing the word upon being shown the sign – is as easy for him. Tests along such lines show that the child at this phase does not usually recall the primary stimulus when being shown the sign, but further produces a whole syncretic situation, as a result of this sign's influence, which, along with other elements, may also include the main stimulus that was to have been completed according to the given sign. In this case, instead of the usual scheme typical of indirect memorizing (figure 7.3) (where the word's auxiliary sign turns the subject back to the given word) we get a different scheme (figure 7.4), where the sign arouses

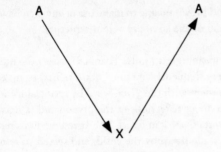

Figure 7.3

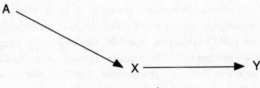

Figure 7.4

in the subject a new associative (or better, syncretic) series, and the entire operation does not as yet bear a definitely expressed, indirect, 'cultural' character.[58] During the further unwinding of the process this *y* may lead to a whole series of new associations, among which the subject may arrive at the starting point *A*. But the process here is still bereft of its purposeful 'instrumental' character, and correct reproduction can at best be the result of the interplay of complex associative or image laws. The period when the auxiliary sign does not act as a specific stimulus that always brings the child back to the starting point, but is always merely an impulse to the further development of the whole syncretic structure of which it is a part, is undoubtedly typical of the first, primitive phase in the history of the development of sign operations.

Certain facts certify that, at this stage of development, the sign acts as part of the general syncretic situation:

1   By no means does any sign prove to be useful in the child's operation, and not every sign can be linked to any meaning. The limitation of the use of a sign is related to its belonging mandatorily to a definite ready complex, which includes both the main meaning and the sign related to it. This tendency was especially apparent in the case of small children (aged four to six). Among the different signs offered, the child looks for one that has a ready-made link with the word to be memorized. And the statement that among the cards given, 'nothing works' to help remember the stimulus offered, is one of the most typical of a child of this age. Whereas the child easily memorizes a given word with the help of a picture which makes up a ready complex

with the word, the child proves unable to make use of any sign having linked it to the given word with the aid of the auxiliary verbal structure.

2　In tests where meaningless figures (Zankov) were presented as auxiliary aids for memorizing, we very frequently obtained not a refusal to make use of them, and not an attempt to link them with the given word by artificial means, but attempts to turn these figures into direct reflections of the given word, a drawing of it.

Thus, in Zankov's tests shape *a* in figure 7.5,[59] presented as a reminder of the word 'bucket', was turned upside down by the child, and served to remind it of the word only when shape *b* really began to resemble a bucket: in the same way, shape *c* became the sign of the word 'bench' only when turned upside down as in *d*. In all these cases the auxiliary figure was not linked to the given meaning by any type of indirect link, but proved to be a direct, immediate drawing of it. It follows then, that the introduction of meaningless figures into the test did not only stimulate (as we might have supposed) the child's transition from the use of already formed links to the creation of new ones, but led to a diametrically opposed result: to the child's urge to see the given figure as the direct, albeit schematic, description of one or another object and to the refusal to memorize when this was impossible.

3　A similar phenomenon was as a rule apparent in tests with small children, where concrete-meaning pictures, not immediately related to the word presented, served as auxiliary stimuli. Tests carried out by Yussevich showed that in a great number of cases this auxiliary picture was also not used as a sign: the child looked at it trying to see the object that had to be remembered. When asked to remember the word 'sun' with the help of a picture showing an axe, the child did it very easily, pointing to a small yellow spot in the drawing and saying 'There it is, the sun'. The complex instrumental nature of the operation is replaced by an elementary attempt to directly create an 'eidotoid' reflection of the contents present in the auxiliary sign. Thus in both cases we can also not speak of the child's reproducing the given word through memory – any more than when we name the original upon glancing at a photograph.

All these facts show that at this stage of development the word links up with the sign following completely different laws than in the case of developed sign operation. It is

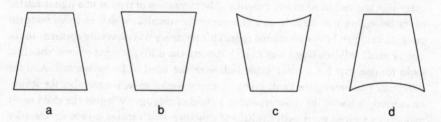

a　　　　　b　　　　　c　　　　　d

Figure 7.5

in this connection that all psychological processes included in indirect operation, as, for instance, the selection of an auxiliary sign or the process of recollection and restoration of a filled-out meaning, proceed here in a fundamentally different way; and it is this fact that stands as the fundamental verification and confirmation that the intermediate stage of development between the elementary and fully instrumented processes actually has its own laws of connections and relations, out of which the finished indirect operation will develop fully only later.

Special tests enabled us to make a more detailed study of this *natural history of the sign*. The study of the use of signs by the child and of the development of this form of activity could not but lead us to investigate how sign activity appears in the child. This problem was the subject of special studies. They may be divided into four series:

1   Research related to how sign meaning originates in the child during experimentally organized games with objects.
2   Research pertaining to the tie between sign and meaning and between word and object.
3   Studies of the statements made by the child when explaining why a given object is called by a given word (according to the clinical method of Piaget).
4   Investigation by means of choice-reaction (N. G. Morozova).

If we sum up the results of these studies negatively, we are led to the general conclusion that sign activity makes its appearance in the child differently from complex habits, discoveries or inventions. The child neither invents, nor does it learn this form of activity. Intellectualist and mechanist theories are both equally erroneous, although the training of habits as well as intellectual 'discoveries' are not infrequently interwoven with the history of the child's use of signs; however, they do not determine the inner development of this process, they are incorporated only as auxiliary, subordinate, secondary components of its structure.

*Sign operations are the result of a complex process of development, in the full sense of the word.* At the beginning of this process, one may observe transitional, mixed forms that combine both natural and cultural components of child behaviour. We called these forms the stage of child primitiveness or the natural history of the sign. In contrast to naturalistic theories of games, our experiments lead us to the conclusion that play constitutes the main avenue of the child's cultural development and, in particular, of the development of the child's symbolic activity.

Experiments show that both in plan and in speech the child is far from consciously realizing the relativity of the sign operation or of the arbitrarily established connection of sign and meaning. In order to become an object's (word's) sign, the stimulus finds support in the properties of the designated object itself. Not 'everything can represent everything' for the child in this game. The objects' real properties and their sign meanings come into complex structural interaction during play. Thus, for the child, the word is linked to the object through the latter's properties and is incorporated in one structure, common to it. That is why the child in our experiments refuses to call the floor a mirror (it cannot walk on a mirror), but has no qualms at transforming a chair into a train, using its properties in play, i.e. manipulating it as if it were a train. When asked to call a lamp 'table' and vice versa, the child refuses, because one 'can't write on a lamp, or turn on a table'. To change (or swap) meanings for the child means to change the properties of objects.

We can think of nothing more obviously underlining the fact that at the very beginning of speech the child sees no connection between sign and meaning, nor does it begin to become conscious of this connection for quite some time. Further experiments show that the 'function of naming' (Nennfunktion) is not the creation of a single discovery, but has its own natural history, and that probably at the beginning of speech formation the child does not discover that every object has its own name, but rather learns new ways of dealing with them – and that is what gives them names.

Thus, the relations between sign and meaning which, because of their similar way of functioning and thanks to their external resemblance, begin at an early stage to remind us of the corresponding ties in the adult, are really by their inner nature psychological features of quite a different kind. To put the mastering of this relation at the very beginning of the child's cultural development means to ignore the complex history of inner formation of this relation, a history at least a whole decade long.

## The further development of sign operations

We have described the child's sign operations in both structural and genetic roots; it would, however, be incorrect to think that instrumentation with the help of certain outer signs is the permanent form of the higher psychological functions; a careful genetic analysis convinces us of exactly the reverse and makes us think that this form of behaviour, too, is merely a stage in the history of psychological development, a stage growing from primitive systems and presupposing a transition at later stages to considerably more complex psychological formations.

The observations made earlier concerning the development of indirect memorizing underline an extremely peculiar fact: if, at the beginning, indirect operations proceeded exclusively with the help and use of external signs, at the late stages of development we observe that this outer instrumentation ceases to be the only operation by way of which the higher psychological mechanisms master the task before them. Experiments show that not only the forms of use of signs change here, but that the very operation's structure undergoes radical changes. The essential quality of this change might be expressed by saying that from an external-instrumented operation the process becomes an inner-reconstructed operation. This is expressed in that the child begins to memorize the given material principally in the same way as those described above, but without turning to outer signs, which from that minute on are no longer required. The entire operation of indirect memorizing takes place now as a purely inner process; judging from external appearances, it does not seem to differ in any way from the primary forms of direct memorizing. In fact, if we judge *only* from external appearances we will be under the impression that the child has simply begun to memorize more and better, has somehow perfected and developed its memory and, most important of all, has reverted to the method of direct memorizing which our experiment forced it to abandon. However, this is only illusory: development, as often happens, proceeds here not in a circle, but in a spiral, passing through one and the same point at each new revolution at a higher level.

We call this withdrawal of the operation within, this reconstruction of the higher psychological functions related to new structural changes, the process of interiorization, meaning, mainly, the following: the fact that at their first stages, the higher psychological functions are built as outer forms of behaviour and find support in the outer sign is by no means accidental; on the contrary, it is determined by the very psychological nature of the higher function which, as we have mentioned above, does not appear as a direct continuation of elementary processes but is a *social method of behaviour applied by itself to itself.*

This transfer of social means of behaviour inside the system of individual forms of adaptation is far from being a purely mechanical operation; it is not accomplished automatically, but is related to a structural and functional change of the entire operation, and it stands as a special stage in the development of the higher forms of behaviour. Transferred to the sphere of individual behaviour, complex forms of co-operation now begin to function according to the laws of that primitive whole, an organic part of which they now constitute. Between the one statement, that the higher psychological functions (of which the use of signs is an inalienable part) originate in the process of co-operation and social intercourse, and the second statement, that these functions develop from primitive roots on the basis of lower or elementary functions, i.e. between the sociogenesis of higher functions and their natural history, there exists a contradiction that is not logical but genetic in character. The transition from the collective form of behaviour to the individual at first lowers the level of the whole operation, since it becomes incorporated in the system of primitive functions, thus acquiring qualities common to all functions of this level. Social forms of behaviour are more complicated and are in advance in their development in the child; when, however, they become individual, they are 'lowered' and begin to function according to simpler laws. Egocentric speech *per se*, for instance, is structurally lower than normal speech, but as a stage in the development of thought it is higher than social speech in the child of the same age; that may be the reason why Piaget regards it as the predecessor of socialized speech and not as a form derived from it.

Thus we proceed to the conclusion that every higher psychological function inevitably begins by bearing a character of external activity. In the beginning the sign, as a rule, is an external auxiliary stimulus, an external means of autostimulation. This is conditioned by two causes: first, by the fact that the roots of this operation are found in the collective form of behaviour which always belong to the sphere of external activity, and, second, because of the primitive laws of the individual sphere of behaviour which, in their development, have not yet become separated from external activity, are not set apart from direct perception and external action (for instance, from practical thought in the child); yet the laws of primitive behaviour state that the child masters its external activity earlier and with less difficulty than inner processes.

Herein lies the reason for this operation not becoming at once an inner process of behaviour when being transformed from an *inter-psychological* to an *intra-psychological* operation. For a long time, it continues to exist and *to change* as an external form of activity, before definitively turning inward. For many functions, this stage of external sign lasts forever as the final stage of their development. But other functions go further in their development and gradually become inner functions. They take on the character of inner processes as a result of a prolonged development. Their transfer inward is coupled once more to changes in their laws of activity, and they are again incorporated into a new system where new laws rule.

We cannot dwell on the details of this transition of higher functions from the system of external activity to the system of inner activity. We are forced to omit many related events in this development, and we shall only attempt, albeit briefly, to touch on some of the principal moments connected with this inward transition of higher functions.

The fact of 'interiorization' of the sign operation was experimentally traced by us in two situations: in mass tests with children of different ages, and individually by means of prolonged experimenting with one child. In the work carried out by Leont'ev in our laboratories, a great number of children, aged from seven years to adolescence, underwent tests pertaining to direct and indirect memorizing. The change in the quantity of filled-in elements, in both cases, resulted in two lines that demonstrate the dynamics of sign operations over the course of the entire process of child development. The figure given below[60] illustrates the line of development of direct and indirect memorizing in children of various ages. Several things are at once evident: the way these two lines are situated in relation to each other is not accidental, but displays a certain order. Quite clearly, the line of direct memorizing is situated below that of indirect memorizing, and both show a certain tendency to grow according to the age of the child. This growth, however, displays an irregularity at the different stages of child development, and if we witness up to the ages of ten to 11 a particularly rapid *growth of outward indirect memorizing* which the lower line noticeably lags behind, this period stands as a turning point after which the growth of *outward direct memory* is particularly dynamic and which overtakes in pace the line of development of the outward instrumented operation.

An analysis of this diagram, which we have called the 'parallelogram of development' and which remains constant in all tests, shows that it is conditioned by forms that play a primary role in the development of the child's higher psychological processes. If the first stage of the child's development was characterized by the ability to mediate its memory only by turning to certain external methods (hence, the sharp rise of the upper line), and all memorizing without the aid of external signs remained in essence a direct and almost mechanical kind of keeping in mind, then at the second stage a leap forward occurs: the development of outward sign operations, generally speaking, reaches its limit, but now the child *begins to reconstruct the inner process of remembering, unaided by outward signs. The 'natural' process becomes indirect*, the child begins to apply certain inner methods, and the sharp rise in the lower curve indicates this turning point.

In the development of inwardly mediated operations, the phase of application of outer signs plays a decisive role. The child proceeds to inward sign processes because it has already gone through the phase when these processes were on the outside. We are convinced of this by a series of individual experiments. Measuring in these the coefficient of 'natural' memorizing in the child , we carried out a series of experiments with outwardly instrumented memorizing, and then once again checked the operations which are not supported by the application of outer signs. The results, shown in figure 2,[61] illustrate the fact that even in experiments with a mentally retarded child, we obtain, first, a considerable growth of outwardly instrumented and then of 'direct' memorizing which, after this intermediate series of tests, renders a double or triple effect, transferring, as corroborated by analysis, the methods of outward sign operation to inner processes.

In all the operations described we observe a two-pronged process. On the one hand, the natural process undergoes radical reconstruction, being transformed into an indirect, instrumented act; and on the other hand, the sign operation itself changes, ceasing to be external and becoming transformed into the most complex inner psychological systems. This two-fold change is symbolized in our diagram by the turning point of both curves, meeting in one point and indicating the inner dependence of both these processes.

We are present at what is actually a process of the greatest psychological importance: what was an outward sign operation, i.e. a certain cultural method of self-control from without, is now *transformed into a new intra-psychological layer* and gives birth to a new psychological system, incomparably superior in content, and cultural–psychological in genesis.

The process of 'interiorization' of cultural forms of behaviour, which we have just touched upon, is related to radical changes in the activity of the most important psychological functions, to the reconstruction of psychological activity on the basis of sign operations. On the one hand, natural psychological processes as we see them in animals, actually cease to exist as such, being incorporated in this system of behaviour, now reconstructed on a cultural–psychological basis so as to form a new entity. This new entity must by definition include these former elementary functions which, however, continue to exist in subordinate forms acting now according to new laws characteristic of this whole system. On the other hand, the operation *per se* of the use of external signs is also radically reconstructed. Formerly a decisively important operation in young children, it is replaced here by essentially different forms. The inwardly instrumented process begins to make use of entirely new connections and methods unlike those that were characteristic of the outward sign operation. The process here undergoes alterations analogous to those observed in the child's transition from 'outward' speech to 'inward'. As a result of the process of interiorization of the higher psychological operation, we have a new structure, a new function of formerly applied methods and an entirely new composition of psychological processes.

It would be most superficial to suppose that the further reconstruction of the higher psychological process, under the influence of the use of signs, takes place on the basis of the inward transfer of the entire ready-made sign operation. It would be equally incorrect to think that, in the development of the system of higher psychological processes, we have a simple superimposition of a higher stage over a lower and the simultaneous existence of two relatively independent forms of behaviour – natural and instrumented. Actually, as a result of the 'interiorization' of the cultural operation, we find a qualitatively new combination of systems that sharply distinguishes human psychology from the elementary functions of animal behaviour. These most complex interlacements are, generally speaking, as yet little known, and at present we can point to only a few of their principal and most characteristic features.

During the process of 'interiorization', i.e. the inward transfer of functions, there occurs a complex reconstruction of their entire structure. Experiments reveal that the following moments, characteristic of this reconstruction, are essential: (1) the substitution of functions; (2) the alteration of natural functions (or of the elementary processes forming a basis for, and constituting a part of, the higher function); (3) the appearance of new psychological functional systems (or systems of functions) which assume the role in the general structure of behaviour that was previously performed by separate functions.

Briefly, these three interconnected aspects may be explained by the example of the changes that occur in the higher functions of memory in the process of 'interiorization'. Even in the simplest forms of indirect memorizing, the fact of the substitution of functions is quite obviously apparent. Binet was not wrong when he called the mnemotechnique of the memorizing of a row of numbers the replica of numerical memory.[62] Experiments show that neither the power nor level of development of memory constitutes the decisive factor in memorizing of that sort but, rather, the activity of combination, building and changing of structures, the perception of relations, thought in the broad sense, and other processes which in this case take the place of memory *per se* and determine the structure of this activity. With the inward transfer of activity, this substitution of functions in itself leads to the verbalization of memory and, connected with it, to memorizing with the aid of concepts. Thanks to this substitution of functions, the elementary process of memorizing is moved from the place it first occupied, and yet is not fully cut off from the new operation, but uses its central position in the psychological structure and occupies a new place in relation to the entire new system of co-acting functions. Entering into this new system, it begins to function according to the laws of the whole of which it is now a part.

As a result of all these changes, the new function of memory (which has now become an inner indirect process) corresponds only in name to the elementary processes of memorizing; in its inner essence it is a new specific formation with its own special laws.

## 5  Methods for the study of higher psychological functions

The methods of the contemporary psychological experiment have always been closely tied to the general basic questions of psychological theory and have essentially always been the reflection of the way in which the principally important psychological problems were solved. Because of this, criticism of the main views concerning the essence and development of psychological processes must inevitably result in a re-examination of the basic principles of the methods of research.

The two schools of psychology described above as the school of pure spiritualism, on the one hand, and that of pure naturalism, on the other, led to the creation of two absolutely independent methods of psychological research; in due time they both acquired a certain degree of finality and both must become the subject of complete revision as soon as their philosophic basis undergoes criticism.

Thus, if the first of these saw a specific object for psychological research in the states of consciousness, proposing that these higher forms were a special property of the human spirit, closed to further analysis, then pure phenomenology, inner description and self-observation could be the only adequate methods for psychological studies. One aspect, however, proved to be fatal to spiritual attempts to create a method for the study of psychological processes: the higher psychological functions always evaded spiritualistic attempts to establish their origin and structure. They proved once and for all to be beyond the grasp of spiritualistic description *because* of their socio-historic genesis and indirect structure. These methods found a particularly unsuitable soil in child psychology, and it may be said that they suffered defeat in that field even before their philosophic premises were subjected to criticism and revision.

The second group of psychological systems proved to be considerably more stable in the sphere of child psychology. Starting from the presumption that the higher forms of child behaviour are actually the uninterrupted continuation of the forms already known through the study of animals (differing from them in their greater complexity but basically remaining the same in structure), this system found that the mechanism of responsive movement to external stimulation from environment, already well known in zoopsychology and physiology, was fully suitable as the basic mechanism of child behaviour. This relation S→R was preserved, as these psychologists assumed, both in the simplest and in the most complex acts of behaviour, and being a universal scheme guaranteed thus the preservation of the unity of psychological studies encompassing a considerable field.

Obviously, this generalized concept of structure acquired a concrete character in the research methods which these authors considered adequate for their purposes. These methods consist historically in the simple transfer of methods applied in animal physiology and psychology to child psychology; they became generally accepted over the past decade in the majority of psychological laboratories, a decade of great progress in psychological experiments. Directed primarily at the study of those

primitive or complex responses by which the organism adapts itself to its environment, these methods always were in the type of structure already known in experiments on simple reflexes; offering the subject a stimulus, the psychologist diligently
studied the reactions and regarded his task as completed if these were described in
sufficient detail and with the objectivity of natural science.

This method, however, had two very doubtful aspects: first, *though objective, it was
not objectivizing*: the psychologist's vital problem, that of uncovering and bringing to
light the hidden psychological mechanisms with the help of which complex reactions
were achieved, was here left unsolved; if the method was adequate for the study of
simple reflectory acts, it was not so in the case of attempts to understand the structure
of complex psychological processes. The inner methods by which the processes were
carried out remained hidden, not brought to light, and the psychologist was forced
willy-nilly to turn to the subject's verbal answers if he wished to know something
more definite about these processes.

The second defect prevailing in the methods of 'stimulus reaction' in experimental
child psychology was undoubtedly its *antigenetic attitude*. Approaching functions, that
differed in complexity, and different stages in the child's history with one and the
same experimental scheme, and repeating (on the child) tests that had been applied
to animals, this method was fated to ignore development *per se* related to the
appearance of qualitatively new formations and the interaction of psychological
functions in principally new relations. Following Wundt in the stability of the
methods and the repetitions of one and the same experiment in possibly constant
conditions, this method of studying 'reactive' behaviour once and for all cuts itself off
from the possibility of studying inter-relations specific to development.

Lastly, and we find this point important, any method built on these lines *proves
inadequate for the very problems facing the study of the higher psychological functions*; while
disclosing the reactive mechanism, it describes merely the subordinate category
present in all processes, including the elementary psychological and thus, *a priori*,
makes its study meaningless and fruitless, actually brushing aside what is characteristic of the higher psychological systems, what distinguishes them from the elementary and what makes them what they are. The peculiarity of the genesis, structure and
functioning of these higher psychological processes remained, thus, quite beyond the
grasp of this elementary psychological method.

In all our studies we followed a basically different route. We established, in our
studies of child development, that the latter proceeded along lines leading to a radical
alteration of the very structure of child behaviour, and that at each new stage the child
changes not only the form of its reaction, but carries out this reaction to a considerable
extent by new ways, drawing on new 'instruments' of behaviour and replacing one
psychological function by another. A prolonged analysis made it possible for us to
establish that development follows, first of all, a direction leading to the *indirect*
character of those psychological operations which, at the first stages, were achieved
through direct forms of adaptation. The growing complexity and development of
forms of child behaviour are reflected in the change in the means used for fulfilling the

task, in the inclusion of formerly 'uninterested' psychological systems in the operation, and in the corresponding reconstruction of psychological processes. It can readily be seen that, as indicated above, an essential mechanism of this reconstruction is to be found in the creation and employment of a number of artificial stimuli that play an auxiliary role and permit man to master his own behaviour, at first from without and later by more complex inner operations.

It can be understood that, when the structure of psychological development is such, the process can no longer be expressed by the simple S→R scheme and the method of the simple study of reactive responses ceases to be adequate to the complexity and peculiarity of the process studied; this method, which so easily registers the subject's response, proves useless when the main problem becomes the study of the means and methods by the aid of which the subject is able to organize his behaviour in those concrete forms which are most adequate to the given task.

Directing all our attention to the study of just these (outer or inner) means of behaviour, we must undertake a radical revision of the very method of psychological experiment.

We regard the functional method of two-fold stimulation [usually referred to as 'functional *method of double stimulation*' – eds] as most adequate to our task. Seeking to study the inner structure of the higher psychological processes, we do not limit ourselves to the usual method of offering the subject simple stimuli (no matter whether elementary stimuli or complex tasks) to which we expect a direct response; we simultaneously offer a second series of stimuli which must play a functionally special role, serving as a means by which the subject can organize his own behaviour. In this way, we study the *process of accomplishing a task by the aid of certain auxiliary means*, and the whole psychological structure of the act thus proves to be within our reach over the entire course of its development and in all the variety of each of its phases. Examples of our experiments, noted above, show that this way of *bringing auxiliary means of behaviour* to the surface permits the tracing of the entire genesis of the most complex forms of higher psychological processes.

Whether we are studying the development of memorizing in the child, furnishing it with external auxiliary means for this task and observing the degree and character of indirect mastering of the task, or whether we use this method in studying how the child organizes its active attention with the aid of certain external means, or whether we are tracing the development of infant calculation, making the child manipulate some outer objects and applying methods either suggested to the child or 'invented' by it – in all cases we follow one principal route, studying *not only the final effect of the operation, but its specific psychological structure*. In all these cases the psychological structure of the developing process appears with much greater richness and variety than in the classic method of the simple 'S→R' experiment.

We believe two points are worthy of particular mention. If the method of 'stimuli reaction' were an *objective* psychological method, limiting its studies only to those processes which in man's behaviour were already external, then our method may in all truth be qualified as *objectivizing*: its main attention focuses immediately on inner psychological methods and structures hidden from direct observation. And considering the study of these to be its task, by bringing to the surface the auxiliary operations with the help of which the subject masters this or the other problem, it brings them within reach of objective study; in other words, it objectivizes them. We regard the objectivization of inner psychological processes as incomparably more correct and adequate, where the goals of psychological research are concerned, than the method of studying ready objective responses, for only the former guarantees scientific research the actual exposure of specific forms of higher behaviour as opposed to subordinate forms.

In one respect the method we applied differs sharply from those that prevailed in contemporary child psychology. Whereas the experiment was usually isolated from the comparative–genetic method of study, focusing only on the relatively stable forms of behaviour, while the comparative–genetic method was usually detached from the experiment, we follow a reverse course combining both these lines of research in an integral *experimental–genetic method*. By employing the method of two-fold stimulation, we are able to offer the subject tasks geared to differing phases of development and to provoke in reduced form those processes of mastering tasks which allow us to trace, in the experiment, consecutive stages of psychological development. By shifting the difficulty of our requirements, exposing the methods by which the task is mastered, and by prolonging our experiment over a number of consecutive series, we find ourselves capable of tracing in laboratory conditions the *process of development in all its basic features* and, hence, of arriving at an analysis of the factors that take part in it. By including and excluding speech from the operation, by giving the subject signs and means which he previously never used, by depriving the already developed subject of these signs, we obtained a sufficiently comprehensive idea of separate stages of development, their typical peculiarities, sequence, and also the main structural laws of the higher psychological systems.

With the application of a series of experimental–genetic methods, the psychology of childhood for the first time poses a number of concrete questions pertaining to the genesis of the higher psychological structures and to the structure of their genesis itself.

In our experimental researches there is no mandatory need to proceed each time by presenting our subject with ready-made external means with the help of which he must solve a given problem. The basic outline of our tests does not suffer in the least if, instead of giving the child ready-made external means, we wait until it applies spontaneously some kind of auxiliary method, incorporating in its operation some kind of auxiliary system of symbols.

A considerable part of our experiments was carried out following the above method. When asking our subject to memorize something (stimulus), we suggest that he draw something to make the subject to be memorized more easily kept in mind (auxiliary symbol). We thus created conditions for the reconstruction of the psychological process of memorizing and the application of given auxiliary means. Without furnishing the child with ready-made symbols, we were able to follow in the spontaneous unfolding of the methods applied, how all the essential mechanisms of the child's complex symbolic activities were manifested.

The best examples, perhaps, of this method of active instrumentation, are our tests with the use of *speech* and the reconstruction, with its help, of the whole structure of child behaviour.

If speech was usually observed either as a system of reactions (behaviourists) or as a means leading to the comprehension of the subject's inner world (subjectivists), we regard speech as a system of auxiliary symbols, i.e. means that help the child to reconstruct its own behaviour. Observations pertaining to the genesis and active application of these means simultaneously allow us to trace the actual social roots of these higher psychological processes and to furnish an analysis of the part played by indirect operations at various stages of child development.

Everything we have said concerning the specific character of the method we applied leads to one conclusion: this method makes it possible to extricate ourselves from the predicament in which psychology has found itself due to the collision of the spiritualistic and mechanistic concepts. While the first of these inclined psychologists to a simple description of spontaneous behaviour, considered as a special and irreducible form of 'vital processes', and while the second led to the study of *reactive* behaviour which in essence represented an experimental mechanism, already present at the lowest stages of the genetic ladder, our approach to the issue leads us to the study of a special form of human behaviour, differing both from the spontaneous and the reactive processes. We see this particular form in those indirect (higher) psychological functions which arose historically (as opposed to being the product of the free spirit) and which transferred behaviour from elementary to the higher forms, creating from the elementary forms of animal behaviour the complex behaviour of civilized man.

## 6 Conclusions

### The problem of functional systems

We have come to the end of the exhausting study of the main aspects of the evolution of practical intellect in the child and of the development of its symbolic activity. We must now only group together and generalize the conclusions which our research has led us to reach. We must sum up theoretically our analysis of the problem of development of practical intellect and point out such important theoretic and methodic conclusions which may be drawn from a series of such investigations, each of which is devoted to one or another particular problem.

If we attempt to embrace in one glance everything that has been said until now concerning the evolution of practical intellect in the child, we may note that the basic content of this evolution boils down to the following: instead of one and, what is more, one simple function of practical intellect, as observed in the child prior to its mastering speech, there appears in the process of development another form of behaviour, complex in content, multiple and composed of different functions.

As our studies show, there occurs not only an inner reconstruction and perfecting of separate functions in the process of psychological development in the child, but the intra-functional ties and relations are also altered in the most radical way. As a result of these changes, new *psychological systems* appear which unite in complex co-operation and in complex combinations various separate elementary functions. Lacking a better definition, we call these psychological systems, these units of a higher order that take the place of homogeneous, isolated elementary functions the *higher psychological functions*.

Everything that has been said up to now compels one to acknowledge that the real psychological function which, in the process of child development, replaces its elementary practical intellectual operations, cannot be defined otherwise than as a psychological system. This concept includes the complex combination of symbolic and practical activity which we have consistently insisted upon, the new co-relation of single functions characteristic of man's practical intellect, and the new unity which this heterogeneous whole is brought to in the process of development.

Thus, we arrive at a conclusion diametrically opposed to that reached by Thorndike in his investigation of intellect. As is well known, Thorndike's starting point is the assumption that higher psychological functions are nothing else but the further development, by way of quantitative growth, of associative connections that are of the same nature as those at the basis of elementary processes. In his opinion, phylogenesis, as well as ontogenesis, displays a principal identity of the psychological nature of the ties underlying the lower and higher processes.

All our investigations contradict this assumption. They compel us to acknowledge that ties of a different nature characterize the specific new formations which we call psychological systems or higher psychological functions. Since Thorndike's concept is, as he personally admitted, directed against the traditional dualism in the teachings of the lower and higher forms of behaviour, and since the problem of overcoming this traditional dualism is one of the fundamental methodological and theoretical problems of modern scientific psychology, we must dwell on the question as to what kind of answer to this problem (dualism or the unity of higher and lower functions) can be furnished in the light of our experimental studies.

But first we must clarify one point so as to prevent any misunderstanding from arising. Objections against Thorndike's theory could be directed primarily along lines which in this case are not our prime source of interest, that is, an exposure of the general incompetence of the associative point of view and of the entire mechanistic concept of intellectual development maintained and based on this viewpoint. We do not intend to touch on that issue here, for our interests lie in a different area. It matters little whether or not we acknowledge the associative or the structural characer of psychological functions, for the main problem remains no less vital: can the higher psychological functions be equated to the lower ones in their essentials, basic laws; are they only a more complex and intricate expression of the same laws that prevail in the lower forms, or are they in their very essence, constitution and method of activity the result of the effect of new laws unknown to the elementary forms of behaviour?

We are of the opinion that the solution of this problem is related to that change of principle viewpoint in contemporary psychology upon which Lewin[63] insists and which he defines as the transition from the 'phenotypical to the conditional–genetic' point of view. Further, we believe that psychological analysis, penetrating beyond the external manifestation of phenomena and revealing the inner structure of psychological processes and, particularly, the analysis of the development of higher forms, compels us to acknowledge *the unity, but not the identity, of higher and lower psychological functions.*

That the problem of the dualism of lower and higher functions continues to exist during the transition from the associative to the structural point of view, is confirmed by the fact that a non-stop argument is going on among structural psychologists concerning two different outlooks on the nature of the higher processes. Some insist on the acknowledgement of two different types of psychological processes and arrive at a strict division of two principal forms of activity, one of which is usually determined as a responsive type and the other as a spontaneous type of activity, the decisive point of which is that it originates in the given individual. They defend the assumption that in psychology we are compelled to proceed from a dualistic understanding of both processes in principle. As they put it, a living creature is not only a system that meets with stimuli, but also a system that pursues aims (Ch. Bühler).

An opposing point of view is presented by those who are against a sharp division of the higher (spontaneous activity) and lower (responsive activity) processes. They attempt to demonstrate that the clear-cut dualism, the metaphysical opposition between the two types of activity which is usually stressed, in reality is non-existent. They try to reveal the responsive character of many aspects of the spontaneous forms of behaviour and, in responsive processes, the active character of aspects depending upon the inner structure of the system itself. They show that in so-called spontaneous processes the organism's behaviour also depends on the character of stimulus and, vice versa, in responsive processes behaviour also depends on the inner structure and state of the system itself. Some of them, as for instance Lewin, see the solution of this problem in the concept of 'needs', i.e. in the fact that objects of the external world may have a definite relation to needs. They may have a positive or negative 'Aufforderungscharakter'.[64]

We see thus that the refutation of the associative theory and the adopting of the structural point of view does not by itself solve the problem without calling for a special investigation, but rather evades it. True, the new point of view helps overcome the metaphysical character of traditional psychological dualism and acknowledges the principal unity of higher and lower functions as related to inner and external features active in both processes. But inevitably there arises here two new problems to which we find no principal answer in the solution usually offered.

The first problem is that the external and inner elements, although of necessity present in both types of processes, may differ in their specific part in each given case and, consequently, may in a qualitative manner determine the whole process of behaviour. Must we or must we not separate the higher processes as compared to the lower – not metaphysically, but empirically? And the second problem manifests itself in the fact that the division between spontaneous and responsive forms of behaviour may not coincide with the division between actions guided chiefly by inner needs and actions guided by outer stimuli.

### The use of tools in animal and human behaviour

Investigations show that genetically, functionally and structurally the higher processes are so considerably specific that they must be grouped in a special class; but the separation of higher and lower functions does not coincide with the division of the two types of activity mentioned above. We can speak of a higher form of behaviour whenever a person masters his own behavioural processes (in the first place, when the person can control his reactions). The individual, subjecting the process of his own responses to his will, thus enters into a principally new relation with the environment, arrives at a new functional use of environmental elements as stimuli signs, by means of which relying on external means, he guides and regulates his own behaviour externally masters himself externally forcing the stimuli signs to influence him and to provoke and stimulate the desired responses. Inner regulation of purposeful activity originates an external regulation. Responsive action provoked and organized by man himself ceases to be responsive and becomes purposeful.

In this sense, the phylogenetic history of man's practical intellect is closely tied, not only to mastering nature, but also to mastering himself. The history of labour and that of speech can scarcely be understood without each other. Man not only invented tools, by means of which he conquered nature, but he invented also stimuli that motivated and regulated his own behaviour and by means of which he subjugated his own forces to his will. This becomes apparent at the earliest stages of the development of man.

'Thus, on Borneo and the Celebes,' says Bücher,[65] 'special sticks made to dig the soil were found, each having a small stick attached to its top part. When the digging stick is used as a hoe to sow rice, the small stick produces a sound.' This sound is something like a work call or command, the aim of which is to produce a rhythmic pattern to regulate work. The sound of the small stick, fixed atop the hoe stick, replaces the human voice or, at any rate, performs an analogous function.

This intertwining of sign and tool which found its concrete symbolic expression in a primitive hoeing stick shows how early the sign (and later, its highest form, the word) begins to participate in the use of tools by man, and how early it begins to fulfil a highly specific function, to be compared with nothing else in the general structure of these operations that stand at the very beginning of the development of human labour. This stick is fundamentally different from that used by apes, although without doubt they are related to each other genetically. If we ask ourselves in what does this fundamental psychological difference between man's tool and that of an animal rest, we must answer this question with yet another question, first formulated by Köhler in connection with his discussion of a chimpanzee's activities, activities geared to the future and guided by a notion of the external conditions that must manifest themselves in the near or distant future. Köhler asks: to what limitation of capacities in the chimpanzee must we ascribe the fact that they do not demonstrate even the slightest element of cultural development, this notwithstanding evidence of them manifesting many elements usually found only in civilization (even if they be the most primitive)?

'The most primitive man,' continues Köhler, further developing his thought, 'makes a stick to dig with even when he does not intend to start digging immediately, when the objective conditions for the use of tools are not as yet apparent in any tangible way. The fact that he makes the tool in advance is without the least doubt related to the beginning of culture.'[66]

The activity of man, as it appeared in the process of historico-cultural development of behaviour, is a free activity, i.e. not depending on direct needs and the immediately perceived situation; it is an activity geared to the future. In contrast, as Köhler noted elsewhere, apes are to a much greater extent slaves of their field of vision than adult human beings. All this must have a foundation, and obviously this foundation is at the same time the most reliable criterion for the genetic, functional and structural division between the two types of activity mentioned above. But our studies induce us to advance, instead of a metaphysical foundation for this division, a historical one which is also in full harmony with the facts noted by Köhler in the behaviour of a chimpanzee. Thus, there are two types of activity between which the psychologist must discriminate in principle: one is the behaviour of animals, the other that of man; activity as a product of biological evolution and activity originating in the process of man's historical development.

The temporality of life, cultural development, work – in short, everything that distinguishes man from animals in the psychological field – all this is intimately related to the fact that, parallel to his conquest of nature over the course of his historical development, man also mastered his own self, his own behaviour. The stick mentioned by Bücher is a stick for future use. This is already a work tool. As Friedrich Engels so aptly put it, 'labour created man himself',[67] i.e. created the higher psychological functions which distinguish man as man. Primitive man, using his stick, by means of outer sign masters the processes of his own behaviour and subordinates his activity to the aim which he forces external objects to serve: tool, soil, rice.

In this sense, we may once more touch on Koffka's remark, briefly noted earlier. He asks: is there any sense in calling the actions of a chimpanzee in Köhler's experiments volitional actions? From the point of view of old psychology, this activity, being non-instinctive, non-automatized and, what is more, intelligent, must without doubt be classed as volitional action. But new psychology answers this question in the negative – and with reason. In that sense, Koffka is absolutely right.

Only man's action, subordinated to his will power, can be qualified as volitional action.

In his excellent analysis of the psychology of purposeful activity, Lewin makes a clear-cut definition of free and volitional intention as a product of the historico-cultural development of behaviour and as a specific feature of man's psychology. He says:

> The fact that man displays extraordinary freedom in what concerns the formation of any, even the most senseless intention, is astounding in itself . . . This freedom is characteristic of cultural man. It is incomparably less characteristic of a child and, probably, of primitive man, too; there is reason to believe that this, more than his highly developed intellect, distinguishes man from the animals which stand closest to him. This division corresponds to the problem of self-control (Beherrschung).

The development of this 'freedom of action', as we have tried to show above, is in direct functional dependence on the use of signs. The specific world–action relation which we have constantly been studying, occupies a central place in the ontogenesis of practical intellect in man, this notwithstanding the fact that in the field of higher functions ontogenesis repeats phylogenesis to an even lesser degree than in the field of elementary functions. Anyone who from this point of view follows the development of free action in the child will agree with K. Bühler's statement that the history of the development of child volition has not yet been written. In order to lay the foundations of this history we must first of all establish this relation between word and action, which lies at the beginnings of the formation of the child's will. Simultaneously this will signify the first resolute step along the way to the solution of the problem of the two types of human activity which we have mentioned above.

### Word and action

To certain psychologists the ancient biblical 'In the beginning was the Word' retains all its fascination. New investigations, however, do not leave any doubt as to the fact that the word does not stand at the beginning of the development of the child's mind.

As Bühler correctly notes along the same lines: 'It was said that speech stands at the source of man's coming to be; perhaps this is true, but prior to speech there is instrumental thinking (Werkzeugdenken)'. Practical intellect is genetically more ancient than verbal; action precedes the word, even intelligent action precedes the intelligent word. Now, however, while repeating this thought, very true in itself, there is a tendency to overestimate action at the word's expense. The most common approach is to conceive the relation between word and action (independence of action from the word and primacy of action) characteristic of early age, as remaining thus during all the following stages of development and throughout life. Bühler is more cautious than most others, but he too expresses the general opinion, formulating this thought as follows: 'In man's later life, too, his technical, instrumental thinking is related to speech and ideas to a much lesser degree than other forms of thought'.[68]

This certitude is based on a false assumption that the first relations between isolated functions remain unchanged throughout the process of development. Meanwhile, investigation shows the opposite. At each step it makes us admit that the entire history of the development of higher psychological functions is nothing else than the alteration of primary interfunctional relations and ties, and the appearance and development of new psychological functional systems. This, among other things, applies one hundred per cent to our subject of interest, i.e. the interfunctional relation between word and action.

Together with Gutzmann,[69] we say: 'Even if we, following Goethe, refute the "word's" high value *per se*, that is, the "sounding" word's,[70] and if we translate together with him the biblical dictum as "in the beginning was the deed", it is nevertheless possible to read this verse (understanding it from the point of view of historical development) thus: "*in the beginning* was the deed"'.

But Gutzmann makes a different mistake. Objecting on legitimate ground to Liepmann's[71] doctrine of apraxy, which treats the relation between action and speech and their disturbance in apraxy and aphasia as the relation of the general to the particular, Gutzmann adopts a position that presents the word and action as being completely independent of each other. Liepmann sees aphasia only as a particular case of apraxy, and speech, as a specific type of movement, is only a particular case of action in general. Gutzmann quite justly objects to this concept which merges the word, as a specific function, with the general notion of action. He points out that only action as a more general concept can embrace, on the one hand, expressive movement (speech) and, on the other, actions as co-ordinative, parallel, co-ordinate, co-relative and more particular concepts. To conceive of speech as a partial case of action means to lean upon a philosophically and psychologically erroneous point of view/definition of the concept of action.

This concept, according to which speech and action are logically parallel and independent processes, inevitably leads to an antigenetic point of view, the repudiation of development, to a metaphysical affirmation of the parallelism and, hence, the absence of meeting, of speech and action, as an eternal law of nature, and finally, to an attitude that ignores the capacity for changeability of a system's functional ties and relations. Gutzmann, as he admits himself, adopts the viewpoint of historical development for a minute but only in order to distinguish between what occurred first and what later. He changes nothing in the biblical dictum on the beginning of things except the logical accent. He is interested in what came first and what followed later, what belongs to the more primitive elementary lower forms of behaviour and what should be classed among the more developed complex and higher functions. 'Speech', says he, 'always signifies a higher stage of man's development than even the supreme expression of action – the deed (die Tat).'[72]

But at the same time Gutzmann, like the majority of authors, adopts an attitude of formal logic. He looks upon the relation of speech to action as an object, not as a process; he sees it as static, not dynamic in motion; he considers it as eternal and unchangeable, although it is historical and at every stage of development takes on a different concrete form. All our investigations in this field lead us to believe that there cannot exist one single formula to embrace the great multiformity of these relations between speech and action at all stages of development and in forms of disintegration. The real dialectical character of development of functional systems cannot be adequately reflected in any one constructive, formal, logical, scheme of relation of concepts – neither in Liepmann's nor in Gutzmann's, for both ignore the *movement* of concepts and processes, the changeability of relations, the dynamics and dialectics of *development* underlying them.

'Practically accomplished action as such,' says Gutzmann formulating his thought, 'has nothing in common with speech, even if we take this word in its broadest sense'.[73] If this approach is true for the beginning of development and characterizes the primary stages in the development of action, it becomes fundamentally false when applied to the later stages of the same process. It reflects one aspect but not the process as a whole. Therefore the theoretical and clinical conclusions which may be drawn from this approach are true for only a very limited sphere, namely the sphere of the first stages of development of the relations we are interested in; and to portray them as characteristic of the process as a whole means to fall inevitably into an irreconcilable contradiction with factual data pertaining to the development and disintegration of higher forms of action. Let us dwell on this contradiction between theory and facts.

Gutzmann sees the basic difference between act and word in the fact that a volitional act, which he, like Wundt, considers as an affect, 'is a clearly expressed unilateral personal attitude of the acting individual to the outer world';[74] the communication of inner states, so characteristic of speech and all types of expressive movements, sinks here into the background and is of a secondary significance.

> While the inner character of an action is chiefly personal and egocentric (even in the case of altruistic purposes), the nature of an expressive action is the opposite. Even when following a selfish purpose, it displays, as it were, a kind of altruism, or, using a notion from Comte's doctrine[75] so as to separate it from the usual meaning of this word, a kind of tuism (Tuismus): it is 'tuistic', it inevitably ['eminently' – eds] is of a social character.[76]

But the most remarkable point of what occurs during the process of development of action and word is bypassed: the appearance of *egocentric* speech and *tuistic* action, the transformation of the social method of behaviour into a function of individual adaptation, the inner reorganization of action by means of the word, the social nature of all higher psychological functions, including practical action in its highest forms. It is not astonishing, then, that a volitional act is equated here to affect, with the difference that it leads to external changes that destroy the affect itself. Self-control as the essential inner moment of a volitional action remains beyond the experimenter's field of vision. The new relation of action to personality which arises thanks to the word and leads to the mastering of action; the new attitude of the acting individual to the outer world, manifested in free action directed and guided by the word – all this does not appear at the beginning of the process of development and is therefore not taken into consideration at all.

Yet we were able to observe on a factual basis how, in the process of development, the child's action becomes social, and how, in losing speech because of aphasia, its practical action falls to the level of its elementary zoopsychological form.

He who pays no attention to these facts inevitably presents the psychological nature of speech and of action in a false light, for the source of their changes rests in their functional junction. Anyone who ignores this fundamental fact and who, having the purity of concept classification as his purpose, tries to represent speech and action as two never-meeting parallels, willy-nilly limits the real scope of both concepts because this scope of content is rooted first and foremost in the ties of both of them.

Gutzmann limits speech to expressive functions, communication of inner states, communicative activity. The entire individual–psychological aspect of speech, all the word's reformative inner activity are simply ignored. If this parallel and independent relation between speech and act were preserved throughout the entire process of development, speech would be powerless to change anything in behaviour. The affective aspect of the word is mechanically excluded, therefore there inevitably arises an underestimation of volitional action, action in its highest forms, that is, action tied to the word.

The essence of the matter, as demonstrated in investigations of these ties between word and action in child-age and in cases of aphasia, lies in the fact that speech lifts action to its highest stage, action that was previously independent of it. Both the development and the disintegration of higher forms of activity corroborate this fact. Contrary to Liepmann's concept of aphasia as a particular case of apraxy, Gutzmann asserts that 'apraxical disorder must be placed parallel to aphasia'.[77] It is not difficult to see in this a direct continuation of his fundamental ideas concerning the independence of action and speech. But clinical data pertaining to speech contradict this point of view. The disorder of higher forms of action tied to the word, the disintegration of these higher forms, coupled to a cutting off of the action and its functioning according to independent primitive laws, in fact, the reversion to a more primitive organization of action during aphasia and its fundamentally important sinking to a lower genetic level, something we were able to observe in all our experiments – all this shows that the pathological disintegration of action and speech, as in their genetic construction, does not proceed along two independent, never-meeting parallel lines.

We have, it seems, dwelt sufficiently on this problem in the previous treatment of our topic; as a matter of fact, our entire article was devoted to this problem. Now it is only a question of concentrating its contents into one concise formula which would express with the greatest possible exactness the essence of everything we have found in our clinical and experimental investigations of higher psychological functions in their development and disintegration, and, in particular, in investigations of practical intellect.

We cannot dwell, as should be sufficiently obvious from the preceding passages, on either the evangelical or Goethean formula, no matter which word we accentuate. But we must remark that all these formulae, Gutzmann's included, necessarily require a continuation. Each speaks about what occurred at the beginning. But what happened later? The beginning is only a beginning, i.e. the starting point of movement. The process of development *per se*, however, must by necessity include a denial of this starting point and movement toward higher forms of action lying not at the beginning but at the end of the whole process. How does this process occur? The attempt to answer this question induced us to write this article. In it we have tried to show how the *word*, becoming intellectualized and developing on the basis of *action*, lifts this action to a supreme level, subjects the child to its power, stamps it with the seal of will. But since we wanted to express all this in one short formula, in one sentence, we might put it thus: if *at the beginning* of development there stands the act, independent of the word, then at the end of it there stands the word which becomes the act, the word which makes man's action free.

## Notes

This is the English language original given to Michael Cole by Alexander Luria in the early 1970s for publication by an international publisher. This publication did not take place, and the manuscript was conveyed by its owner Professor Cole for publication in the present volume. Judging by a number of characteristics, the manuscript was designated to appear in the *Handbook of Child Psychology* (C. Murchison, ed.), but was never published. A remark mentioning that a manuscript of the present title was sent to the *Handbook* in 1930 appears in Vygotsky's bibliography of 1934 (see *Myshlenie i rech*, 1934, p. 322). A version appeared in Russian in Volume 6 of *Sobranie Sochinenii* of Vygotsky in 1984 (see Van der Veer and Valsiner, 1991, p. 188). All through these notes, we will make comparisons between the present English text and the Russian version (henceforth referred to as such), indicating discrepancies and editorial changes traceable in the two. In some cases, the corresponding Russian expression is inserted into the present text, and the English phrasing altered accordingly (as marked by editorial comments). In accordance with the designation in Vygotsky's *Myshlenie i rech*, the co-authorship of Alexander Luria is restored in the present printing.

1   This quote seems to be taken from Carl Stumpf's speech at the first meeting of the Berlin Society for Child Psychology, and is reported on p. 1 of Groos, K. 1921: *Das Seelenleben des Kindes*. Berlin: Reuther & Reichard.

2   In the English manuscript, 'evolves' was replaced by 'is presented' by an editor. We adhere to the original which is matched in the Russian version (p. 7).

3   An editor's change to 'recent experimenters' is changed back to the original 'new investigators', which matches the Russian version (p. 8).

4   An editor of the English manuscript had inserted 'activity' after 'child', which is eliminated (also absent in the Russian version, p. 8).

5   Refers to pp. 48–9 of Bühler, K. 1929: *Abriss der geistigen Entwicklung des Kindes* (4th and 5th enlarged edn). Leipzig: Quelle & Meyer.

6   Ibid., p. 51.

7   Ibid., p. 51.

8   Refers to Lipmann, O. and Bogen, H. 1923: *Naive Physik*. Leipzig: J. A. Barth.

9   An editor of the English manuscript had inserted 'is due' here; we revert to 'proceeds due' as it also fits with the idea in the Russian version (p. 10 – *prodvigaetsia vpered*).

10  See p. 89 of Lipmann and Bogen (1923).

11  See p. 100 of Lipmann and Bogen (1923). However, the authors italicized the word 'behaviour' and used 'learning' instead of 'teaching'.

12  The reference to the book (unidentified here) by (Luise?) Schlüter is absent from the Russian version, p. 11.

13  Reference here is made to Brainard, P. P. 1930: The mentality of a child compared with that of apes. *Journal of Genetic Psychology*, 37, 268–92.

14  Brainard, 1930, p. 289: 'A three-year-old child has approximately the same difficulties in solving the problems as did Köhler's apes'.

15  Reference is made to the research group of M. Ia. Basov (or Bassow, in German transliteration). For further information about the work of Basov and his research group, see Valsiner, J. 1988: *Developmental Psychology in the Soviet Union*. Brighton: Harvester Press (ch. 5); as well as a series of special issues of *Soviet Psychology* (1991, 29, No.'s 5 and 6) by the present editors.

16  S. A. Shapiro and E. D. Gerke (or Guerke, as given here) were Mikhail Basov's co-workers, whose experimental techniques served as one of the bases for Vygotsky's notion of 'method of double stimulation'. The reference in the text is to Shapiro, S. A. and Gerke, E. D. 1930: The process of adaptation to environmental conditions in a child's behaviour. In M. Ia. Basov (ed.), *Ocherednyie problemy pedologii* (pp. 73–111). Moscow-Leningrad: Gosudarstvennoe Izdatel'stvo. In English translation see *Soviet Psychology*, 1991, 29, 6, 44–90.

17  Shapiro and Gerke, 1991, p. 56.

18  Ibid., p. 89.

19  Guillaume, P. and Meyerson, I. 1930: Recherches sur l'usage de l'instrument chez les singes. I: Le probleme du détour. *Journal de Psychologie*, 27, 177–236.

20  Here is the first major discrepancy between the English original text printed here and the Russian version. The English original text continues directly to the next sub-part, while the Russian version of 1984 includes a number of pages that are word-for-word repetitions of parts of text that occurs later. Most probably these repetitions were a result of editorial manipulation of the Russian text in the 1970s/1980s, since the following exact repetitions occur (references to the pages of the published Russian version): pp. 14–15 are a repetition of pp. 69–70; pp. 15–16 of pp. 74–5 and pp. 16–17 of pp. 71–2.

21  This is a reference to Yerkes, R. M. and Learned, B. W. 1925: *Chimpanzee Intelligence and its Vocal Expressions*. Baltimore: Williams & Wilkins.

22  See pp. 135–6 of Stern, W. 1927: *Psychologie der frühen Kindheit*. Leipzig: Verlag von Quelle und Meyer.

23  In the English manuscript, an editor had introduced 'tools' instead of implements; in the present version the original wording is restored. In the Russian text (p. 22), the word used is *orudie*.

24  Roza E. Levina was one of the few co-workers closely related to the tradition of Vygotsky and Luria (see Levina, R. E. and Morozova, N. G. 1984: Memories of L. S. Vygotsky. *Defektologia*, 5, 81–6). Being mostly interested in defectology, Levina performed experiments with children that bridged the difference between the work of Shapiro and Gerke [see note 16] and Vygotsky's theoretical insights. The particular kind of experiment referred to here can be found described in Levina, R. E. 1968: Ideas of L. S. Vygotsky about the planning speech of the child. *Voprosy psikhologii*, 14, 4, 105–15; English translation under the same title in J. V. Wertsch (ed.) 1981: *The Concept of Activity in Soviet Psychology* (pp. 279–99). Armonk, NY: M. E. Sharpe.

25    The word 'inculcation' is used in the English original; the Russian version gives the meaning as 're-construction ['perestroika'] of the laws ['zakonov'] of the visual field' (p. 23).

26    In the Russian version: *opredelennaia gruppa detei* with the connotation of 'special' (rather than 'given'). See Russian version, p. 23.

27    The use of 'moments' here is retained along the wording of the original English manuscript (also corroborated by the Russian text, p. 23); a better meaning here would be 'periods'.

28    In Russian *rechevoye myshlenie*, i.e. thinking with the help of (and on the basis of) speech.

29    Watson, J. B. 1924: *Psychology from the Standpoint of a Behaviorist*. Philadelphia: J. B. Lippincott – Chapter 9: The genesis and retention of explicit and implicit language habits. See especially pp. 343–56.

30    The work of Sir Henry Head (1861–1940) in neurology [e.g. see Head, H. 1920: *Studies in Neurology*. London: Frowde, Hodder & Stoughton.] was a relevant source for Vygotsky and Luria. The reference here is probably to Head, H. 1926: *Aphasia and Kindred Disorders of Speech*. 2 vols. Cambridge: Cambridge University Press.

31    Given as in the original English text, fits the Russian (*v geneticheskom plane*) meaning 'from the viewpoint of development'.

32    In the Russian version: *slozhnyie i neorganizovannyie massivy praksicheskikh deistvii*.

33    In the Russian version, the code-switching to German 'werden' (to become) has been replaced by Russian *protsess stanovlenia* (p. 27).

34    Allusion here seems to be to the Köhler-type experiments with children, who use speech concurrently with action (see references in notes 16 and 24).

35    Clarified on the basis of the Russian version, p. 34.

36    In the Russian version (p. 36): *funktsia otrazhenia i sozdanie slepka s situatsii*.

37    In the original manuscript, reference (in footnote) is made to Köhler's article in French: 'W. Koehler. La perception humaine. Journal de Psychologie, 1929'. The accurate bibliographical reference of this article is *Journal de Psychologie*, 1930, 27, 1–2, 5–30. (It appears with the correct year of publication also in the text of the Russian version, p. 38.)

38    In the Russian version (p. 39) the reference to Stern is dated 1922. The issue referred to – personal construction of perceptual images – is treated in Stern, W. 1919: *Die menschliche persönlichkeit*. Leipzig: J. A. Barth. For English-language summary, see: Stern, W. 1938: *General Psychology from the Personalistic Standpoint*. New York: MacMillan (pp. 179–83).

39    'In these tests we used Stern's original pictures which, owing to their dynamic qualities, allowed for an adequate perception by the child in pantomime form' [original footnote].

40    The text from here until the next sub-heading ('The separation of the primary unity of the sensori-motor functions') is absent from the Russian version (p. 41). Instead, a Russian editorial footnote asks the reader to return to chapter 1, where the following text is indeed reproduced on pp. 17 (4th paragraph) – 18 (except for the last paragraph).

41    Lia Solomonovna Gueshelina (born 1892) is described in a commentary to the Russian version (p. 348) as 'a pedagogue, a specialist in pre-school education'.

42    Refers to Jaensch, E. R. 1923: *Über den Aufbau der Wahrnemungswelt und ihre Struktur im Jugendalter*. Leipzig: Barth.

43    In the original manuscript, reference is made in a footnote to: 'A. R. Luria. Die methode der abbildenden Motorik. Psychologische Forschung, Bd. 12, 1929'; followed by a reference to Luria's 'Affection, conflict and will. New York: Liveright, 1931'. These

references are eliminated from the Russian version (p. 43). The correct bibliographic references to these works are Luria, A. R. 1929: Die Methode der abbildende Motorik bei Kommunikation der Systeme und ihre Anwendung auf die Affektpsychologie. *Psychologische Forschung*, 12, 127–79; and Luria, A. R. 1932: *The Nature of Human Conflicts, or Emotion, Conflict and Will*. New York: Liveright.

44 In the Russian version, the 'we' form of reference is preserved (p. 43 – while Alexander Luria's role in co-writing the text is eliminated). The experiments referred to here were performed by Luria, and the given form of reference to them indicates the co-written – by Vygotsky and Luria – nature of this manuscript. Undoubtedly, though, Luria played the role of the second author in this text.

45 In the original manuscript, reference is here made (in a footnote): 'A detailed analysis of the corresponding stages of mastering signs is described by N. G. Morozova in her article "A psychological analysis of the reaction of choice", in Proceedings of the Psychological Laboratory, Academy of Communist Education'. This footnote is not included in the corresponding locus in the Russian version of text (p. 45). This direction of Morozova's experimental work was directly related with Alexander Luria's investigations (see note 43 for Luria, 1932, p. 388).

46 The following compositional division (usual in Russian texts of the 1920s) does not appear in the Russian version of the text in a corresponding location (p. 46).

47 In the Russian version, the reference is made to G. Kafka (p. 47).

48 We have been unable to locate this reference.

49 Footnote in the original manuscript: 'With the transition to these artificially established demands, the emotional centre of the whole situation is shifted *from the aim* to the *solution of the task*. In essence, the situation of the "task" (Aufgabe) in experiments with apes exists only in the eyes of the experimenter: as far as the animal is concerned there exists only the bait and obstacles standing in the way of possessing it. The child strives, above all, to solve the given problem, thus entering a world of entirely different purpose-relations. Due to the possibility of forming quasi-needs, the child proves to be capable of *breaking down* the operation, transforming each of its separate parts into an independent problem which he formulates himself with the help of speech.' (This footnote, without italics and the use of the German 'Aufgabe', also appears in the Russian version, p. 49).

50 This sentence is corrected on the basis of the idea as expressed in the Russian text (p. 56).

51 Figures A, B and C are absent from the Russian version (p. 57).

52 In the Russian version (p. 58) instead of plural ('our laboratories') the singular ('our laboratory') is used.

53 In the Russian version (p. 60), the expression is 'ourselves and our colleagues'.

54 This scheme is absent from the Russian version (p. 63).

55 Here in the Russian version (p. 63) the singular form ('our laboratory') is used. In the original manuscript, the footnote reads: 'See A. N. Leont'ev, The development of memory. Proceedings of the Psychological Laboratory of the Academy of Communist Education, No. 5, 1930.' In the Russian version, this reference is substituted by reference to Leont'ev's book Development of Memory. Moscow, 1931 (p. 349). The full bibliographic reference of the latter is: Leont'ev, A. N. 1931: *Razvitie pamiati. Eksperimental'noe issledovanie vysshikh psikhologicheskikh funkcij*. Moscow-Leningrad: Uchpedgiz.

56 In the Russian text: 'our laboratory'.

57 Reference to Ernst Cassirer is absent from the corresponding locus in the Russian text (p. 66). The reference is to the classic work by Cassirer: Cassirer, E. 1929/1977: *The Philosophy*

*of Symbolic Forms. Vol. 3: The phenomenology of knowledge.* New Haven: Yale University Press. Kant's facultas signatrix is mentioned on p. 210 of this book in the chapter 'Toward a pathology of the symbolic consciousness'.

58   These schemes are absent in the Russian version (p. 67).

59   These schemes are also absent in the Russian version (p. 68).

60   The figure is missing from both the English manuscript (with a handwritten note 'see Russian original') and the Russian version (p. 72). In the latter, an editorial footnote refers the reader to A. N. Leont'ev's *Selected Psychological Investigations*, vol. 1, Moscow, 1983 (pp. 55, 56, 58). Quite likely, this and the next figure were similar to the figure given as table 11.2 in chapter 11 of this reader.

61   This figure is also missing from both English and Russian versions.

62   Refers to Binet, A. 1894: *Psychologie des grands calculateurs et joueurs d'échec.* Paris: Librairie Hachette.

63   See Lewin, K. 1926: Vorbemerkungen über die psychische Kräfte und Energien und über die Struktur der Seele. *Psychologische Forschung*, 7, 294–329.

64   Usually known in English as 'valence' or 'demand character'. The Russian text (p. 83) does not provide the German term, but its Russian literary translation (*kharakter povelevania*).

65   K. Bühler in the Russian version (p. 84). The reference should be to Bücher, K. 1899: *Arbeit und Rhythmus.* Leipzig: B. G. Teubner.

66   Refers to p. 3 of Köhler, W. 1922: Zur Psychologie des Schimpansen. *Psychologische Forschung*, 1, 2–46.

67   Refers to p. 444 of Engels, F. 1925/1978: *Dialektik der Natur.* Berlin: Dietz Verlag.

68   The authors repeat the quotes from Bühler (1929) given in the first chapter in a slightly different translation (see note 5). We corrected a mistake (also present in the Russian edition, p. 86) in the second quote. It had 'other forms of speech' instead of the correct 'other forms of thought'.

69   Reference here is to p. 72 of Gutzmann, H. 1922: Psychologie der Sprache. In G. Kafka (ed.) *Handbuch der vergleichenden Psychologie*, vol. 2 (pp. 1–90). München: Ernst Reinhardt.

70   In German the difference here is between 'Wort' and 'Lautwort'.

71   The English manuscript had Lipmann (Otto), but the reference is to Liepmann (Hugo). See Cassirer (1929/1977) for a discussion of Liepmann's findings.

72   See p. 72 of Gutzmann (1922) (see note 69).

73   Ibid., p. 72.

74   Ibid., p. 68.

75   In the Russian version, the name of Auguste Comte is not mentioned on the corresponding page (p. 88).

76   Ibid., pp. 68–9.

77   Ibid., pp. 71–2.

# 8

# The socialist alteration of man

## Lev Vygotsky

Scientific psychology has established as its basic thesis the fact that the modern psychological human type is a product of two evolutionary lines. On the one hand, this modern type of human being developed in a lengthy process of biological evolution from which the biological species *homo sapiens* has arisen, with all its inherent characteristics from the point of view of body structure, the functions of various organs and certain types of reflexes and instinctive activity, which have become hereditarily fixed and which are passed on from generation to generation.

But together with the beginning of social and historical human life and the fundamental changes in the conditions to which he had to adapt himself, the very character of the subsequent course of human evolution also changed very radically. As far as one is able to judge on the basis of the available factual material, which has been obtained mainly by comparing biological types of primitive peoples at the most primitive stages of their cultural development with representatives of the most culturally advanced races, as far as this question can be resolved by contemporary psychological theory, there are strong reasons to suppose that the biological human type has changed remarkably little during the course of the historical development of man. It is not, of course, that biological evolution has come to a stop and that the species 'man' is a stable, unchangeable, constant quantity, but rather that the basic laws and the essential factors which direct the process of biological evolution have receded to the background and have either completely fallen away or have become a reduced or sub-dominant part of new and more complex laws governing human social development.

Indeed, the struggle for existence and natural selection, the two driving forces of biological evolution within the animal world, lose their decisive importance as soon as we pass on to the historical development of man. New laws, which regulate the course of human history and which cover the entire process of the material and mental development of human society, now take their place.

As an individual only exists as a social being, as a member of some social group within whose context he follows the road of his historical development, the composition of his personality and the structure of his behaviour turn out to be a quantity which is dependent on social evolution and whose main aspects are determined by the latter. Already in primitive societies, which are only just taking their first steps along the road of their historical development, the entire psychological makeup of individuals can be seen to depend directly on the development of technology, the degree of development of the production forces and on the structure of that social group to which the individual belongs. Research in the field of ethnic psychology has provided incontrovertible proof that both of these factors, whose intrinsic interdependence has been established by the theory of historical materialism, are the decisive factors of the whole psychology of primitive man.

Nowhere else, according to Plekhanov,[1] does that dependence of consciousness on the way of life manifest itself in a more obvious and direct manner as it does in the life of primitive man. This is due to the fact that the factors which mediate between technological and psychological progress are very meagre and primitive and this is the reason why this dependence can be observed almost in the raw. But a much more complicated relationship between these two factors can be observed in a highly developed society which has acquired a complex class structure. Here the influence of the basis on the psychological superstructure of man turns out to be not direct, but mediated by a large number of very complex material and spiritual factors. But even here, the basic law of historical human development, which proclaims that human beings are created by the society in which they live and that it represents the determining factor in the formation of their personalities, remains in force.

In the same way as the life of a society does not represent a single and uniform whole, and society is subdivided into different classes, so, during any given historical period, the composition of human personalities cannot be said to represent something homogeneous and uniform, and psychology must take into account the basic fact that the general thesis which has been formulated just now, can have only one direct conclusion, to confirm the class character, class nature and class distinctions which are responsible for the formation of human types. The various internal contradictions which are to be found in different social systems find their expression both in the type of personality and in the structure of human psychology in that historical period.

In his classic descriptions of the early period of capitalism, Marx frequently dwells on the subject of the corruption of the human personality which is brought about by the growth of capitalist industrial society. On one extreme end of society, the division between intellectual and physical labour, the separation between town and country, the ruthless exploitation of child and female labour, poverty and the impossibility of a free and full development of full human potential, and on the other extreme, idleness and luxury; not only does all this result in the single human type becoming differentiated and fragmented into several separate social class types which stand in sharp contrast to one another, but also in the corruption and distortion of the human personality and its subjection to unsuitable, one-sided development *within all these different variants of the human type.*

'Along with the division of labour', says Engels, 'man himself became subdivided.'[2] According to Ryazanov, 'every form of material production specifies some social division of labour, and this is responsible for the spiritual division of labour. Beginning already with the corruption of primitive society, we can observe selection of a number of spiritual and organizational functions into special species and subspecies within the scheme of the social division of labour'.[3] Engels further says:

Already the very first major division of labour, the division of town from country, sentenced the rural population to millennia of mental torpor, and the city dwellers to enslavement, each by his particular work. It destroyed the basis for spiritual development for the former, or physical development for the latter. If a peasant is master of his land and the craftsman of his craft, then in no lesser degree the land rules over the peasant and the craft over the craftsman. The division of labour has caused man himself to become subdivided. All remaining physical and spiritual faculties are sacrificed for the sake of developing just one type of activity.

This degeneration of man increases at the same rate as the division of labour, which reaches its highest level in manufacture. Manufacture breaks up craftsmanship into fractional operations and assigns each of them to a separate worker as his life vocation and chains him down to a specific fractional operation, to a specific tool of labour for the rest of his life . . .

And it is not only workers, but also the classes who exploit them directly or indirectly, who become enslaved by the instruments of their activities, as a result of the division of labour: the petty bourgeois, by his capital and desire for profit; the lawyer by his ossified juridical ideas which rule over him like an independent force; 'the educated classes' in general, by their particular local limitations and one-sidedness, their physical shortcomings and spiritual myopia. They are crippled by their education which trains them for a certain specialty, by their lifelong enslavery to this specialty, even if this specialty is doing nothing at all.[4]

This is what Engels wrote in 'Anti-Dühring'. We have to proceed from the basic assumption that intellectual production is determined by the form of material production.

So, for example, a different form of spiritual production than the type which was prevalent during the Middle Ages fits in with capitalism. Each historically defined form of material production has its corresponding form of spiritual production, and this, in its turn, signifies that human psychology, which is the direct instrument of this intellectual production, assumes its specific form at a certain stage of development.[5]

This crippling of human beings, this one-sided and distorted development of his various capabilities which Engels describes, and which appeared together with the division of town and country, is growing at an enormous rate due to the influence of the technological division of labour. Engels writes:

All the knowledge, the insight and the will which both the independent peasant and craftsman develop albeit on a small scale, like the savage who makes the whole art of war consist of the exercise of his personal cunning – these faculties are now required only for the workshop as a whole. The intellectual potencies of production make them expand in one direction, because they vanish in many others. What is lost by the detail labourers ['Teilarbeiter'] is concentrated in the capital that employs them. It is as a result of the division of labour in manufacture that the labourer is brought face to face with the intellectual potencies of the material process of production, as the property of another, and as a ruling power. This process of separation begins in simple co-operation, where the capitalist represents to the single workman the oneness and the will of the social labour ['Arbeitskörpers']. It is developed in manufacture which cripples the labourer into a detail labourer. It is completed in large scale industry, which separates science as a productive potential from labour and presses it into the service of capital.[6]

As a result of the advance of capitalism, the development of material production simultaneously brought with it the progressive division of labour and the constantly growing distorted development of the human potential. If 'in manufacture and manual labour the worker makes use of his tools, then in a factory he becomes the servant of the machine'. Marx says that in the former case he initiates the movement of his tool, but here he is forced to follow its movement. The workers turn into 'living extensions of machines', and what results is a 'dismal monotony of the endless torment of labour', which Marx [1890/1962, p. 445] says is the characteristic feature of that period in the development of capitalism which he is describing. He is tethered to a specific function, and according to Marx [ibid., p. 381], this turns him 'from a worker into an abnormality and artificially ['treibhausmäsig'] fosters him in just one special skill whilst suppressing all the remaining wealth of his productive inclinations and talents'.

In our times, child labour represents a particularly horrifying example of the disfigurement of human psychological development. In the pursuit of cheap labour and due to the extreme simplification of the separate functions which the workers have to carry out, large scale recruitment of children becomes possible and this results in a retarded, or a wholly one-sided and distorted development occurring at the most impressionable age when the personality of the person is being formed. Marx's classic research is full of examples of 'intellectual barrenness', 'physical and intellectual degradation', 'transformation of immature human beings into machines for the production of surplus value' [ibid., pp. 421–2], and he presents [ibid., p. 514] a vivid picture of the whole process which results in a situation where 'the worker exists for the sake of the production process, and not the production process for the sake of the worker'.

However, all these negative factors do not give a full picture of how the process of human development is influenced by the speedy growth of industry. All these adverse influences are not inherent in large scale industry as such, but in its capitalist organization, which is based on the exploitation of enormous masses of the population and which has resulted in a situation where, instead of every new step toward the conquest of nature by human beings, every new level in the development of the production forces of the society, has not just failed to raise humanity as a whole and each individual human personality to a higher level, but has led to an ever deeper degradation of the human personality and its growth potential.

Whilst observing the crippling effects of the process of progressing civilization upon human beings, philosophers like Rousseau and Tolstoy could not see any other solution than a return to the integral and pure human nature. According to Tolstoy, our ideal is not ahead of us but behind us. In this sense, from the point of view of this reactionary romanticism, the primitive periods of the development of human society appear as that ideal toward which humanity should be striving. And really, a deeper analysis of the economic and historical tendencies which regulate the development of capitalism, shows that this crippling process of human nature which was discussed above, is inherent not only in the very fact of the growth of large scale industry, but in the society's specific capitalist form of organization.

The most fundamental and important contradiction in this whole social structure consists of the fact that within it, under relentless pressure, forces are evolving and preconditions are being created for its destruction and replacement with a new order, which is based on the absence of man's exploitation of man. More than once, Marx demonstrates how labour by itself or large scale industry by itself does not necessarily have to cripple human nature, as a follower of Rousseau or Tolstoy would assume, but, on the contrary, *it contains within itself endless possibilities for the development of the human personality.*

He says, 'As can be ascertained from the particulars given by Robert Owen, a seed of a future educational system has grown, which will combine productive labour with schooling and physical education for all children above a certain age, not only as a method of increasing social production, but as the only method of producing well rounded educated human beings' [ibid., pp. 507–8]. So the participation of children in manufacturing, which under the capitalist system, particularly during the period of growth of capitalism described, is the source of physical and intellectual degradation, contains seeds for a future educational system *in itself* and may well turn out to be a higher form of creation of a new type of human being. The growth of large scale industry *in itself* makes it necessary to work out a new type of human labour and a new type of human being who would be capable of carrying out these new forms of work. 'The nature of large scale industry stipulates a changing work; a continual changing of functions and an all-round mobility for the worker', says Marx. 'The individual who has been turned into a fraction, the simple bearer of a fractional social function, would be replaced by a fully developed individual for whom the various social functions represent alternating forms of his activities' [ibid., pp. 511–12].

So it appears that not only will the combination of manufacturing labour with education prove to be a means of creating all-round developed people, but that it will also mean that the type of person who will be required to work in this highly developed manufacturing process, will differ substantially from the type of person who used to be the product of production work during the early period of capitalist development. In this respect the end of the capitalist period presents a striking antithesis to its beginning. If in the beginning the individual was transformed into a fraction, into the executor of a fractional function, into a live extension of the machine, then at the end of it, the very requirements of manufacturing require an all-round developed, flexible person, who would be capable of changing the forms of work, and of organizing the production process and controlling it.

No matter which one of the individual features which characterize the human psychological type during either the early or the late periods of the development of capitalism we select, everywhere we will encounter a double meaning and a double character of each critical feature. The source of the degradation of the personality in the capitalist form of manufacturing, also contains within itself the potential for an infinite growth of personality.

To provide an example, let us conclude by examining labour situations where both sexes and all ages have to work together. 'The composition of the whole staff of employees from persons of both sexes and all ages . . .', says Marx, 'must, on the contrary, under appropriate circumstances, turn into a source of humane development' [ibid., p. 514].

From this it can be seen that the growth of large scale industry contains within itself hidden potential for the development of the human personality and that it is only the capitalist form of organization of the industrial process which is responsible for the fact that all these forces exert a one-sided and crippling influence, which retards personal development.

In one of his early works, Marx says that if psychology wishes to become a really meaningful science, it will have to learn to read the history book of material industry which embodies 'the essential powers of man', and which itself is a concrete embodiment of human psychology.[7] As it happens, the whole internal tragedy of capitalism consists in the fact that at the time when this objective, i.e. thing-orientated, psychology of man, which contained within itself infinite potential for mastery over nature and development of his own nature, was growing at a fast pace, his actual spiritual life was degrading and went through the process which Engels so graphically depicts as the crippling of man.

But the essence of this whole matter consists of the fact that this double influence of factors inherent in large scale industry on human personal development, this internal contradiction of the capitalist system, cannot be resolved without the destruction of the capitalist system of organization of industry. In this sense, the partial contradiction which we have already mentioned, between the growing power of man and his degradation which is growing in parallel, between his increasing mastery over nature and freedom on the one hand, and his slavery and the growing dependence on things produced by him, on the other – we wish to reiterate that this contradiction represents only one part of a much more general and all-encompassing contradiction which lies at the base of the whole capitalist system. This general contradiction between the development of the production forces and the social order which was in correspondence with the level of development of these production forces, is being resolved by the socialist revolution and a transition to a new social order and a new form of organization of social relationships.

*Alongside this process, a change in the human personality and an alteration of man himself must inevitably take place.* This alteration has three basic roots. The first of these consists of the very fact of the destruction of the capitalist forms of organization and production and the forms of human social and spiritual life which will rise on their foundation. Along with the withering away of the capitalist order, all the forces which oppress man and which cause him to become enslaved by machines and which interfere with his free development will also fall away, disappear and be destroyed. Along with the liberation of the many millions of human beings from suppression, will come the liberation of the human personality from its fetters which curb its development. This is the first source – the liberation of man.

The second source from which springs the alteration of man resides in fact that at the same time as the old fetters disappear, an enormous positive potential present in large scale industry, the ever growing power of humans over nature, will be liberated and become operative. All the features discussed above, the most shining example being the entirely new form of creating a future based on the combination of physical and intellectual work, will lose their dual character and will change the course of their influence in a fundamental way. Whereas earlier, their actions were directed *against* people, now they begin to work *for their sake*. From their previous role as obstacles, they now turn into powerful moving forces of the development of human personality.

Finally, the third source which initiates the alteration of man is change in the very social relationships between persons. If the relationships between people undergo a change, then along with them the ideas, standards of behaviour, requirements and tastes are also bound to change. As has been ascertained by psychological research, the human personality is formed basically under the influence of social relations, i.e. the system which it is a part of, from the earliest childhood onward. 'My relationship to my environment', says Marx, 'is my consciousness.'[8] A fundamental change of the whole system of these relationships which man is a part of, will also inevitably lead to a change in consciousness, a change in man's whole behaviour.

It is education which should play the central role in the transformation of man – this road of conscious social formation of new generations, the basic form to alter the historical human type. *New generations and new forms of their education represent the main route which history will follow whilst creating the new type of man.* In this sense, the role of social and polytechnical education is extraordinarily important. As it happens, the basic ideas which underpin polytechnical education, consist of an attempt to overcome the division between physical and intellectual work and to reunite thinking and work which have been torn asunder during the process of capitalist development.

According to Marx, polytechnical education provides familiarity with the general scientific principles of all the production processes and, at the same time, it teaches children and adolescents practical skills which makes it possible for them to operate basic tools used in all industries. Krupskaja formulates this idea in the following way:

A polytechnical school can be distinguished from a trade school by the fact that it focuses on the interpretation of work processes, on the development of the ability to unify theory and practice and in the ability to understand the interdependence of certain phenomena, whereas the centre of gravity in a trade school is directed toward providing the pupils with labour skills.[9]

Collectivism, the unification of intellectual and physical labour, a change in the relationships between the sexes, the abolition of the gap between physical and intellectual development, these are the key aspects of that alteration of man which is the subject of our discussion. And the result of achieving this, the crowning glory of this whole process of transforming human nature, should be the appearance of this higher form of human freedom which Marx describes in the following way: 'Only in community [with others has each] individual the means of cultivating his gifts in all directions: only in community therefore, is personal freedom possible.'[10] Just like all human society, the individual personality must make this leap forward from the realm of necessity to the sphere of freedom, as described by Engels.

Whenever the alteration of man and the creation of a new, higher level of human personality and conduct is under discussion, it is inevitable that ideas about a new type of human being connected with Nietzsche's theory of the superman are mentioned. Proceeding from the perfectly true assumption that evolution did not stop with man and that the modern type of human being represents nothing more than a bridge, a transitional form leading to a higher type, that evolution did not exhaust its possibilities when it created man and that the modern type of personality is not the highest achievement and the last word in the process of development, Nietzsche concluded that a new creature can arise during the process of evolution, a superman, who will have the same relation to contemporary man, as contemporary man has to the ape.

However, Nietzsche imagined that the development of this higher type of man was subject to the same law of biological evolution, the struggle for life and selection based on the survival of the fittest, which prevails in the animal world. It is for this reason that the ideal of power, the self assertion of the human personality in all the fullness of its instinctive power and ambition, rugged individualism and outstanding men and women, formed, according to Nietzsche, the road to the creation of a superman.

This theory is erroneous, because it ignores the fact that the laws of historical evolution of man differ fundamentally from the laws of biological evolution and that the basic difference between these two processes consists of the fact that a human being evolves and develops as a historical, social being. Only a raising of all of humanity to a higher level in social life, the liberation of all of humanity, can lead to the formation of a new type of man.

However, this change in human behaviour, this change of the human personality, must inevitably lead to further evolution of man and to the alteration of the *biological type of man*. Having mastered the processes which determine his own nature, man who is struggling with old age and diseases, undoubtedly will rise to a higher level and transform the very biological organization of human beings. But this is the source of the greatest historical paradox of human development, that this biological transformation of the human type which is mainly achieved through science, social education and the rationalization of the entire way of life, does *not represent a prerequisite, but instead is a result of the social liberation of man.*

In this sense Engels, who had examined the process of evolution from the ape to man, said that it is labour which created man.[11] Proceeding from this, one could say that new forms of labour will create the new man and that this new man will resemble the old kind of man, 'the old Adam', in name only, in the same way as, according to Spinoza's great statement, a dog, the barking animal, resembles the heavenly constellation Dog.[12]

## Notes

First published as Vygotsky, L. 1930: Socialisticheskaja peredelka cheloveka. VARNITSO, 3, 36–44. VARNITSO was the journal of the All-Union Association of Workers in Science and Technics for the Furthering of the Socialist Edification in the USSR (Vsesojuznaja Assotsiatsija Rabotnikov Nauki i Tekhniki dlja Sodejstvija Socialisticheskomu Stroitel'stvu v SSSR). Somehow, the paper was published under Vygotsky's original name, i.e. spelled with 'd'.

1  Probably refers to Plekhanov, G. V. 1922: *Ocherki po istorii materializma.* Moscow.

2  Refers to p. 272 of Engels, F. 1894/1978: *Herrn Eugen Dühring's Umwälzung der Wissenschaft* [Anti-Dühring]. Berlin: Dietz Verlag.

3  It is unclear to which book Vygotsky is referring.

4  Refers to pp. 271–2 of Engels 1894/1978. See also pp. 381 and 445 of Marx, K. 1890/1962: *Das Kapital* [*The Capital*] (4th edn). Berlin: Dietz Verlag.

5  Similar passages can be found all over Marx's and Engels' works, but this exact passage we haven't been able to locate.

6  A curious mistake. The text attributed to Engels can be found on p. 382 of Marx, K. 1890/1962: *Das Kapital* [*The Capital*] (4th edn). Berlin: Dietz Verlag.

7  'We see how the history of *industry* and the established *objective* existence of industry are the *open* book of *man's essential powers*, the perceptibly existing human *psychology . . . a psychology* for which this book, the part of history existing in the most perceptible and accessible form, remains a closed book, cannot become a genuine, comprehensive and real science.' See pp. 302–03 of *Marx – Engels Collected Works. Vol. 3: Economic and Philosophical Manuscripts.* New York: International Publishers (1975).

8  Refers to p. 30 of Marx, K. and Engels, F. 1846/1978: *Die deutsche Ideologie* [*The German Ideology*]. Berlin: Dietz Verlag.

9  Lenin's wife, N. K. Krupskaja, devoted much attention to educational matters. In her book *Vospitanie molodezhi v Leninskom dukhe* [*Education of the Youth in the Spirit of Lenin*] she discussed contemporary international experiments with labour schools (Arbeitsschule) in the light of Marx's ideal of the polytechnic education. See Krupskaja, N. K. 1925/1989: *Vospitanie molodezhi v Leninskom dukhe.* Moscow: Pedagogika. We haven't been able to establish the exact source of the present citation.

10   See p. 74 of Marx and Engels (1846/1978).

11   See pp. 444–55 of Engels, F. 1925/1978: *Dialektik der Natur* [*Dialectics of Nature*]. Berlin: Dietz Verlag.

12   One of Vygotsky's favourite quotations from Spinoza's *The Ethics*. See p. 61 of Spinoza, B. de 1677/1955: *On the improvement of the understanding. The ethics. Correspondence*. New York: Dover. 'The old Adam' may be an implicit reference to Marx's (1890/1962, p. 118) use of this expression.

# 9
# The development of thinking and concept formation in adolescence

*Lev Vygotsky*

*Content of the lesson*

The theory of the purely quantitative evolution of thinking in adolescence and a criticism of this theory. – Evolution of the form and content of thinking in adolescence. – Theory of the development of higher psychological functions and the problem of intellectual development of the adolescent. – The formation of concepts regarded as the main factor characterizing adolescent psychology. – Methods of studying these concepts. – Ach's and Rimat's studies. – Functional methodology of double stimulation and the investigation of concept formation. – Investigation of the concept formation process. – Three stages in the development of the concept formation process: the stage of syncretic images; the stage of concrete complexes and the stage of potential concepts. – The structure and process of the formation of real concepts. – Changes in the content of thinking in connection with concept formation. – Comparative studies of the thinking structures in children and in adolescents.

*Study plan for the lesson*

1  Read the text and make up a plan and summary of the whole chapter.
2  Making use of the concept definition method, compare the answers to the same questions (about a number of different concrete and abstract concepts) given by a pre-school, a school age and an adolescent child and analyse these answers in the light of the account given in this chapter.
3  Study the three stages in the formation of concepts in the thinking process of a young child, a pre-school child, a school age child and an adolescent which are described in the text of the project.
4  Look for the presence of syncretism in the pre-school child's explanations, of verbal syncretism in the school age child's statement and for the disappearance of these phenomena in the adolescent's answers.

5 Think about what conclusions can be drawn, based on the data obtained about the particular features of the intellectual development of adolescents, which might serve as a basis for an educational methodology, from the point of view of thinking content and form.

6 Using the method of completion of sentences by subordinate clauses after 'because . . .', 'although . . .', etc., determine at what stage *full* control of logical modes of thinking is achieved.

I

Currently, the history of thought development in adolescence, the age of transition, also finds itself in a somewhat transitional stage between old concepts and a new level of understanding of the process of intellectual maturation which has been formulated on the basis of new theoretical approaches to the psychological nature of speech and thinking, and on the development and functional and structural inter-relation of these processes. At the present time, in an article devoted to the study of adolescent thinking, paedology at the time of puberty is able to overcome the basic and fundamental prejudices and the disastrous misunderstandings which stand in the way of the development of accurate ideas about the crisis accompanying intellectual maturation which makes up the substance of adolescent thought development. This error is generally expressed in the statement that there is nothing fundamentally new in adolescent thinking as compared with the thought processes of the younger child. Some writers even take the extreme view, in defending the idea that puberty does not really mark the appearance of any sort of new intellectual operation in the thinking sphere which cannot already be found in a three-year-old child.

Looking at it from this point of view, the development of thinking has no central place in the maturation process. The vital momentous transformations which occur in literally all parts of the adolescent's organism and personality during this crucial period, the uncovering of new deep layers of his personality and the development of the higher forms of his organic and cultural life – all this, when looked at from this perspective, does not in any way affect adolescent thinking. All these changes occur in other areas and spheres of the personality. The result is that the role of intellectual changes in the overall process of the maturation crisis in adolescence are disparaged and presented as having no significance.

Firstly, if one were to follow this point of view consistently, the very process of the intellectual changes which occur at this age is reduced to a simple quantitative accumulation of the same particular features which are already present in the thinking of a three year old and to a further purely quantitative growth to which, strictly speaking, the word 'development' can not really be applied.

In recent times this point of view has been most consistently followed by Ch. Bühler in her theory of adolescence in which, among others, a continuing, orderly development of the intellect during the period of pubescence is ascertained. This theory assigns an extremely insignificant role to the intellect within the overall system of these transformations and in the general structure of the processes which exemplify maturation, without recognizing the enormous positive significance of intellectual development for the fundamental and most profound transformation of the whole personality system of the adolescent. 'Generally speaking', says this author,

> one can surmise that during puberty a more marked separation of dialectic and abstract thinking from perception occurs. For the belief that any intellectual operation only appears for the first time during the age of puberty belongs to those tales which child psychology has discredited. All possibilities for the later development of thinking are essentially already present in a child of three or four.[1]

To support these ideas, the author refers to K. Bühler's study, which pursues the point of view that the most essential features of intellectual development, in the sense of a gradual ripening of the basic intellectual processes, take shape already at a very early age. Ch. Bühler thinks that the difference between thinking in young children and of adolescents is the fact that in the case of the child, visual perception and thinking are generally much more closely affiliated. She says:

> A child rarely thinks in purely verbal or abstract terms. Even very talkative and verbally gifted children always proceed from a starting point of some concrete experience, and in cases where they are *just* carried away by a desire to speak, they generally *chatter away* without thinking. The mechanism is being exercised, without seemingly pursuing any other function. Furthermore, the fact that children draw conclusions and make judgements solely within the confines of their own concrete experience, and that their plans, in relation to their own short-term goals, are enclosed in a tight circle of visual perception, is well accepted and has given rise to the false assumption that children are completely incapable of abstract thinking.
>
> This opinion has long since been refuted as it has been possible to establish that, from a very early age, a child perceives, whilst abstracting and selecting, and mentally rounds out with a kind of hazy general content, concepts such as good, bad, sweet, etc., as well as being able to develop other concepts through abstraction, to draw conclusions, etc. However, there can be no doubt that, in large measure, all these things are closely dependent on his visual perceptions and impressions.[2]

In adolescents, on the contrary, thinking becomes less constrained and less concrete than the sensory source on which it is based. Therefore we observe that the rejection of the idea of any essential changes in the intellectual development of the adolescent, inevitably leads to an affirmation of a process of simple growth of the intellect during puberty and its growing independence from sensory material. One way in which this idea could be formulated is that adolescent thinking acquires a sort of new quality in comparison with the thinking of young children as it becomes less concrete and furthermore, it intensifies and becomes strengthened, it increases and grows when compared with the thinking of a three year old; however, not a single intellectual function has its origin during this entire transitional period and therefore thinking itself is not of any critical or decisive importance for the adolescent's development in general, and it appears to occupy only an extremely insignificant place in the overall system during this critical period of maturation.

This view has to be considered the most traditional one and, unfortunately, is also the most widespread and the one which is not interpreted critically by the majority of contemporary theories of adolescence. Nonetheless, in the light of contemporary scientific data regarding adolescent psychology, this opinion strikes us as profoundly inadequate; its roots reach way back to old fashioned research, which dealt with nothing but the most external, superficial and obvious features, i.e. the change in the emotional state, among all the psychological changes taking place in a child undergoing the metamorphosis to adolescence.

In this sense, traditional adolescent psychology has a tendency to see the emotional changes as the central core and principal content of the whole crisis and to contrapose the development of the adolescent's emotional life with the intellectual development of a school aged child. It seems to us that when the question is put in this way, everything appears turned on its head, and everything regarded in the light of that theory seems to us to be turned inside out: it is precisely when we see young children as the very emotional creatures which they are, in whose whole being emotion plays a pre-eminent role, that the adolescent appears to us, above all, as a thinking being. The traditional view is expressed most comprehensively and, at the same time, most concisely by Giese. He says: 'Whilst the psychological development of a child before puberty primarily includes the functions of the senses, memory store, intellect and attention, the period of puberty is characterized by the development of an emotional life'.[3]

The logical course followed by this point of view leads to the banal approach to adolescents which tends to ascribe the entire psychological aspect of maturation to their heightened emotional state, dreaminess, outbursts and other such semi-dream-like products of emotional life. The fact that the period of puberty is a time of striking growth of intellectual development and that, for the first time during that period thinking comes to the fore, not only remains unnoticed when this question is formulated in such a way, but it even takes on a mysterious and inexplicable hue in the light of this theory.

Other writers also hold the same view, for example Kroh who, like Bühler, regards all the variations found in adolescent thinking from that of younger children to be due to the fact that the visual basis of thinking which plays such an important role in childhood, recedes into the background during the period of puberty. This author derogates the importance of this difference even more, when, with good cause, he points out that often, between the concrete and the abstract forms of thinking, a transitional fleeting stage in the development process which is characteristic for adolescence manifests itself. This writer gives the fullest positive expression to this theory, shared by Bühler, when he writes: 'We cannot expect a school aged child to progress to entirely new forms of thinking in the area of judgement. Differentiation, subtlety, a significant degree of self-assurance and awareness in the use of forms of expression already available at an earlier stage, should also be regarded as most essential challenges of development at this stage'.[4]

Kroh then summarizes the same point of view which brings together the development of the thinking process and the subsequent refinement of the previously existing forms in the following way:

> To summarize what has been discussed so far, we can establish that both in the realm of the systems which process perceptions (selection, set, categorical perception and processing classification) and in the sphere of logical connections (concept, judgement, inference, criticism), no completely new forms of psychological functions and actions appear in children of school age. All these are in existence earlier, but during school age they undergo considerable development, which can be seen in their being used in a more differentiated, subtle and frequently even more conscious fashion.

If one is to render the meaning of this theory in one sentence, one could say that the appearance of new shades of nuances, more specialized and cognizant application contributes to the differences found in the thinking process of an adolescent as compared with that of a child.

Essentially the same view is developed in our literature by Rubinstein, who systematically considers all changes in the realm of thinking which occur during adolescence to be a continuation of a journey along a trail which has already been blazed in the thinking of the young child. In this respect Rubinstein is in complete agreement with Bühler.

Whilst rejecting Meumann's stand, who believes that the ability to draw conclusions only fully develops in children at the age of 14, Rubinstein declares that not a single form of intellectual activity, not even the ability to draw conclusions, makes it appearance for the first time in adolescence. This writer claims that the view which proclaims that, in the sphere of mental development, childhood can be differentiated from youth by the fact that the central thinking action, namely the ability to draw conclusions in the true sense of the word, only appears in adolescence, is entirely false. In actual fact, this is entirely untrue. There is no doubt that the central thinking process, including the ability to draw conclusions, is already to be found in children.

The only difference between the thinking of a child and that of an adolescent, is that what we as adults understand to be objectively immaterial, circumstantial and superficial, children interpret as essential qualities. 'It is only in adolescence that the major premises as well as the personal definitions and judgements begin to be furnished with essential attributes and, in any case, the framework of the tendency to find them and not to be simply guided by the first superficial feature, becomes clearly apparent.'[5]

So the whole difference can be ascribed to the fact that among children and adolescents the same modes of thinking are provided with a different content. Rubinstein even talks about an expansion of awareness. In children, these forms are filled with non-material attributes; in adolescents a tendency to fill them with material attributes first appears. Therefore, the whole difference is in the material, in the content and in the filling. The forms remain the same and, at best, undergo a process of further development and consolidation. Among such new shades and nuances, Rubinstein includes the ability to think to the point, a markedly increased steadfastness in the direction of the thinking process, greater flexibility, a wider scope and mobility of thought and other similar characteristics.

The reason why this theory is of particular interest can easily be seen from the retort which its author directs toward all those who have a tendency to deny that a sharp rise and intensification occurs in the mental development of adolescents and young people. This is how Rubinstein defends the idea that the intellectual development of the adolescent is characterized by just such a marked improvement and intensification:

> Observations of fact point to this and theoretical considerations lead us in the same direction, otherwise we would have to assume that the influx of new experiences, of new content and new relationships contributes nothing at all and that the causes remain without effects. Thus, one has to look for typical signs of an intensification of mental development not only in the appearance of new interests and inquiry, but also in the deepening and broadening of old ones, in their range and in the entire reach of life's concerns.

In this speculation Rubinstein exhibits the same internal contradiction which, in equal measure, is present in all the theories which want to deny the appearance of anything essentially new in the thinking process during the period of sexual maturation. However, all writers who deny the emergence of new forms of thinking in adolescence, agree about one thing, namely that the amplification of this process of thinking, its content and the material with which it operates, the objectives towards which it strives, in other words the adolescent's thinking from the point of view of its contents, are undergoing a real revolution.

## II

This gap in the evolution of form and content of the process of thinking is very characteristic of any dualistic and metaphysical psychological system incapable of formulating an evolutionary theory of the forms and content in thinking in a dialectically unified manner. This fact is so deeply symptomatic, that the most consistently idealist system of adolescent psychology which is developed in Spranger's book, passes over in complete silence the subject of the development of thinking during adolescence.[6]

Not a single chapter in the book is devoted to this problem, but at the same time the entire book, which is dominated by one prevalent idea, is given over to the discovery of the process which, according to Spranger, forms the basis of maturation and which is called the adolescent's growing into the culture of his time. One chapter after another is devoted to the examination of how the content of adolescent thinking changes, how this thinking obtains completely new material and how it infiltrates entirely new cultural spheres. For Spranger, the adolescent's penetration into the spheres of law and politics, professional life and morality, science and ideology, all make up the central core of the maturation process, but the adolescent's intellectual functions themselves, the patterns of thought, its composition, structure and the type of activity which is part of his intellectual operations, remain constant and timeless.

When one gives these theories some more careful consideration, it is difficult to get rid of the sensation that they are based on a very rough, simplistic and psychologically elementary concept of form and content in the thinking process. According to this concept, the relationship between the form and the content of thinking are quite reminiscent of the relationship between a vessel and the liquid which it contains: the same mechanical filling of an empty, hollow form, the same prospect of filling up the same unchanging form with ever new content, the same internal incoherence, mechanical contraposition of the vessel and the liquid, i.e. the form and the substance filling it.

From the point of view of this theory, the profound revolution in the content of the adolescent's thinking which is wholly renewing itself at all points, is in no way connected with the development of those intellectual operations which are indispensable for the formation of any sort of thinking process.

According to many writers, this revolution occurs either from the outside, in such a way that the same unchangeable forms of thinking, always duplicating themselves at every new stage of development depending on the level of enriched experience and wider association with the environment, are being replenished with ever new content, or the driving mechanism of this revolution is concealed beneath a veil of thought in the adolescent's emotional life. It is capable of mechanically plugging in this thought into a completely new system and directing it, like a simple mechanism, towards a new content.

In both cases the evolution of the thinking content turns out to be an unbridgeable chasm which keeps the evolution of intellectual forms apart. The fact that, without exception, any theory which consistently strives in this direction comes up against such internal contradictions, can be easily demonstrated by the plain example that not a single one of the above mentioned theories denies – and cannot deny – that a profound and fundamental revolution in the realm of the content of adolescent thinking, and a complete renewal of the entire material composition which fills up the empty forms, does indeed take place.

So, Bühler, who finds all the basic intellectual operations peculiar to adolescents already present in a three year old, confines her statement to the purely formal aspect of the problem in question. As far as the content of thinking is concerned she would, of course, refuse to take seriously any statement which would maintain that, in the realm of content of adolescent thinking, nothing evolves which is significantly new in comparison with what is already present in the thinking process of a three-year-old child.

So Bühler cannot deny the fact that only with the advent of adolescence, a transition to a formal logical thinking process is achieved. She refers to Ormian's painstaking study in this field, who was able to demonstrate that a turning point towards a strictly formal mode of thinking can only be observed at about 11 years of age.[7] As far as the content of thinking is concerned she, too, like Spranger, devotes a significant part of her work to the elucidation of new layers of ethical contents, religious concepts and the rudiments of ideology in adolescent development.

In exactly the same way, Kroh points out the fact that, along with the new variations which he associates with the development of thinking during school age, it is only in adolescence that the ability to handle logical concepts manifests itself. Referring to Berger's study, which deals with the problem of categorical perception and its pedagogic significance, he comes to the conclusion that the perceiving and regulating function of psychological categories first appears in an explicit fashion in experiences and memories only during puberty.

It seems, therefore, that all the writers agree that, whilst they all deny the presence of any new configurations in the realm of intellectual forms, any investigator is forced to admit that there occurs a situation of complete renewal of the entire content of the thinking process during adolescence.

The reason why we have analysed and criticized this point of view in such detail is that without overthrowing it decisively, without disclosure of this theoretical foundation and without contrasting it with new points of view, we can see no other way of finding a methodological and theoretical key to the whole problem of the development of thinking in adolescence. This is why, for us, to understand the details of the theoretical foundations on which all these different (albeit similar from the point of view of their central essence) theories are constructed is of primary importance.

## III

As has been mentioned above, the main cause of this theoretical muddle is the gap between the evolution of form and content of thinking. In its turn, this gap is a result of another fundamental failing of the older psychology and child psychology in particular, namely that until recently child psychology had no real scientific concept of the nature of the higher psychological functions.

The observed phenomenon where higher psychological functions are not seen simply as a continuation of the basic functions and their automatic combination, but as an intrinsically new psychological creation whose development follows very special rules and which conforms to entirely different natural laws, has till now not succeeded in becoming part of child psychology.

Higher psychological functions are the product of the historical development of humanity and its phylogenetic plan, but they also have their special ontogenic record. This history of the development of higher forms of behaviour reveals a direct and close dependence on the organic and biological development of the child and on the growth of his elementary psycho-physiological functions. But in this instance, association and dependence are not one and the same thing.

It is for this reason that in our study we must demarcate the line of development of higher forms of behaviour in the ontogenetic sphere and trace it along all the stages of its conformity to natural laws, not forgetting for one moment about its association with the general organic development of the child. At the beginning of our course, we had already developed the idea that human behaviour in its present form is not only the product of biological evolution, which has resulted in the creation of a human type with all its existing psycho-physiological functions, but is equally a product of a historical development of behaviour or cultural development. Behavioural development did not stop at the beginning of the history of human existence, but neither did it simply continue along the same road as the biological development of behaviour.

The historical development of behaviour was an organic part of the whole process of human social development and fundamentally it conformed to those natural laws which define the progress of historical human development in general. Similarly, in the ontogeny of the development of a child, we should be able to distinguish both lines of the development of behaviour, albeit represented in an interlocked way and in a complicated dynamic synthesis. However, a study which would fully correspond to the real complexity of this synthesis and which would not, at all costs, strive to simplify the issue, would necessarily have to take into account the whole distinctive framework of higher forms of behaviour which are the product of child development. In contrast to Spranger, serious scientific studies show that during cultural behavioural development not only did the content of the thinking process undergo a change but its form did as well, and new mechanisms, new functions, new operations, new spheres of activity, unknown at earlier stages of historical development, were coming into being and falling into place. In the same way, the process of the child's cultural development does not simply include the process of growing into one or other cultural sphere, and does not only represent the filling up of thought with ever new cultural content, but, alongside the development of the content, involves a step by step development of the form of thinking, as well as those higher forms and spheres of activity which originated in the historical past and whose development makes up the necessary conditions for this process of growing into culture.

In actual fact, any truly serious study brings home to us the reality of the unity and indivisibility of form and content, i.e. structure and function, and it shows how any new step forward in the realm of development of the content of thinking, is also inextricably linked with the acquisition of new mechanisms of behaviour and with the raising of intellectual operations to a higher stage.

Certain contents can only be adequately represented with the help of certain forms. Thus, the content of our dreams cannot be adequately expressed in the form of logical thinking, or in the form of logical connections and attitudes, and it is inseparably linked with pertinent archaic, ancient, primitive forms or ways of thinking. And the opposite is true as well: the content of one or other science, the adoption of a complex system, for example mastery of modern algebra, does not suggest a straightforward filling up with appropriate contents of the same forms which already exist in a three-year-old child; this new content cannot come into being without new forms. The dialectical unity of form and content in the evolution of thinking is the beginning and end of contemporary scientific theory of speech and thought.

Actually, is it not rather puzzling from the point of view of theories (outlined above) which deny that adolescent thinking reaches a new qualitative stage, that contemporary research has worked out standards for mental development which require, like, for example, in the case of the Binet–Simon tests (in the version of Burt–Blonsky),[8] a description and explanation of a painting from a child of 12, solutions to some major problems in life from a 13-year old, a definition of abstract terms from a 14-year-old adolescent, at the age of 15 the pointing out of differences between abstract terms, and at 16 years old the ability to grasp the meaning of a philosophical argument?

Is it possible for these empirically established symptoms of intellectual development to become comprehensible from the point of view of a theory which allows for nothing more than new variations arising in adolescent thinking? From the point of view of nuances, how is one to account for the circumstance where the average 16-year-old adolescent reaches the stage of mental development where the understanding of the meaning of a philosophical argument can serve as a significant indicator and symptom?

Only an inability to distinguish between the evolution of elementary and higher functions of thinking and between forms of intellectual activity which are chiefly biologically conditioned and those which are mainly historically derived, could lead one to deny a qualitatively new stage in the development of adolescent intellect. It is perfectly true that new elementary functions do not appear in adolescence. This situation, as has been rightly pointed out by K. Bühler, is fully confirmed by biological data in relation to the increase in weight of the brain. Edinger, one of the outstanding brain experts, has formulated the following general thesis: 'Anyone who knows the brain structure in the animal domain will have become convinced that the appearance of any new skills is always connected with the appearance of new parts of the brain or with the enlargement of existing ones'.[9]

Edinger's thesis, which he developed for the phylogeny of the psyche, is now frequently and readily applied to ontology as well, in an attempt to grasp the parallelism between the development of the brain, as far as this is testified to by its increase in weight, and the appearance of new skills. But it is often overlooked that the parallelism can only apply to elementary functions and abilities which are the product of biological behavioural evolution like the brain itself; but, as it happens, the essence of historical evolution of behaviour is precisely dependent on the appearance of new skills, which are not connected with the development of new parts of the brain nor with the growth of existing ones.

There are good reasons to assume that the historical development of behaviour from its primitive form to the most complex and highest, did not occur as a result of the development of new parts of the brain or the growth of existing ones. This is the essential characteristic of adolescence, as it is, for the most part, the age of cultural development and the development of higher psychological functions. Blonsky is absolutely correct when he makes the following comment about it: 'The period of the eruption of permanent teeth can be regarded as the child's civilizing age, the era when he acquires a store of contemporary knowledge, beginning with the ability to write and when he comes into contact with modern technology. Civilization is still much too recent an acquisition of humanity for it to be hereditary'.[10]

So it would be unreasonable to expect the evolution of higher psychological functions to progress in a parallel manner with the development of the brain, which is mainly brought about by hereditary forces. According to Pfister's findings, the brain doubles its original weight during the first nine months and it trebles it by the end of the third year; however, throughout the entire developmental period, the brain only quadruples in size. 'One of the phenomena of child psychology', says Bühler, 'fully concurs with this finding. The child acquires *all the basic mental functions* during the first three or four years of life, but never again during the rest of his life does he achieve the same sort of mental progress as, for example, during the time he is learning how to speak.'[11]

We wish to emphasize again that this parallelism can only apply to the maturing of the elementary functions which are the product of biological evolution and which emerge along with the growth of the brain and its parts. It is for this reason that we must agree with Bühler's thesis only to a limited extent when he says: 'We dare to hope that some day we will be able to discover physiological grounds for every major stage of progress in the mental life of a normal child within the development of the structure of the large brain.'[12]

We feel bound to put a restriction on this thesis because it is basically applicable to changes in the development of the psyche which are determined by heredity, but the complex syntheses which take place during the process of a child's or adolescent's cultural development have their roots in other factors, and these, above all, include social relationships, cultural development and children's and adolescents' work activities.

Granted, some people hold the view that the most profound intellectual leaps observed during this transitional period are due to an intensification of the development of the brain which occurs during adolescence. Blonsky's hypothesis states that 'the milk tooth stage of childhood, in contrast to the preceding and the following stages, is not characterized by any intensive development of thought and speech, but rather it is a phase of the development of motor and co-ordination skills and emotions.' Blonsky links this phenomenon with the fact that during the milk tooth stage, intensive growth of the spinal cord and cerebellum occurs, in contrast with the toothless and school age stages, which are mainly characterized by intensive cortical (intellectual) development. Observations of the dramatic transformation of the forehead in the pre-pubertal age, lead this author to the conclusion that during school age the primary site of development is to be found in the frontal part of the cerebral cortex. However, based on the same evidence which Blonsky relies on and which he, himself, calls shaky and not very reliable, we feel justified in drawing conclusions about the intensive development of the brain only in relation to the pre-pubertal, i.e. primary school age.

But there are no factual data available to support these proposals with respect to the age of puberty or adolescents. It is true that, according to the findings of Vyazemsky,[13] quite a significant increase in the weight of the brain can be observed at age 14–15, then after a brief pause and slackening, slight new rises at age 17–19 and 19–20 occur. But if we take the latest data into account, we will see that there is only an insignificant increase in the weight of the brain during the whole period of development from age 14–20. So, we have to look for new ways of explaining the intensive intellectual development which takes place during the period of puberty.

As a result, the changeover from research largely based on external phenomena and on phenotypical likeness to a more profound investigation of the genetic, functional and structural nature of thinking for the different age groups, inevitably forces us to reject the traditional view, which tends to identify adolescent thinking with that of a three year old. And that is not all: even that part of those theories which admits the existence of qualitative differences between the thinking processes of a young child and that of an adolescent, makes the mistake of listing first the positive achievement, and only later the really new phenomena which emerge during that period.

As can be seen from new research data, the assertion that the abstract is out of touch with the concrete and the hypothetical with the visual in adolescent thinking is incorrect; the dynamics of thinking during this period are not characterized by the fact that the connections between intellect and its material base where it originates are severed, but rather by the emergence of a completely new form of relationship between the abstract and the concrete aspects of the thinking process, a new form of fusion or synthesis, and we now see such elementary, long since crystallized functions like the child's visual thought, perception or practical intellect in a completely new way.

This is why Bühler's and some other theories prove untenable not only in respect to what they deny, but also in what they affirm, not only in their negative aspect, but in the positive parts as well. The opposite is also true: not only do completely new and hitherto non-existing complex synthetic forms, absolutely unknown to a three year old, appear in the adolescent's thinking process, but even these elementary primitive forms which the child acquires already at the age of three, transform themselves into entirely new principles during adolescence. It is not only that new forms appear during the period of puberty, but it is precisely on account of their appearance that the old ones are transformed according to a completely new principle.

So, whilst summarizing what has been discussed above, we come to the conclusion that the most serious methodological weakness to be found in traditional theory consists of the flagrant internal contradiction between the affirmation of a profound revolution which is taking place in the realm of the content of the adolescent thinking process, and the refutation of any sort of real breakthrough in the evolution of its intellectual function, in its inability to correlate form and content in the development of thinking.

As we have attempted to demonstrate, this rift is, in its turn, caused by the inability to distinguish between two lines in the development of behaviour, i.e. the line of development of the elementary and that of the higher psychological functions. At the present time we feel we are in a position to formulate the main idea which has constantly guided our critical investigations, based on the conclusions which we have drawn.

We could say that this fatal rift between form and content inevitably stems from the situation that the evolution of the thought content is always considered to be a process of cultural development which, first and foremost, is conditioned by historical and social factors, whereas development of the form is normally looked upon as a biological process conditioned by the level of the child's organic maturation and parallel to the increase in the weight of the brain. When we talk about the content of the thinking process and the changes which it undergoes, we have in mind a historically variable, socially conditioned quantity which originates in the process of cultural development; but when we are discussing the forms of thinking and their dynamics, because of the misunderstandings arising from traditional psychology, we usually mean either metaphysically inert psychic functions or biologically conditioned, organically generated forms of activity.

So a great chasm continues to gape between these two concepts. The historical and the biological aspect of the child's development end up separated from one another and it is impossible to build a bridge of any sort between them, which might help us unite facts and data pertaining to the dynamics of form in the thinking process with the facts or data about the dynamics of the content which fills this form.

It is only with the introduction of the principles of higher forms of behaviour which are the product of historical evolution, and the marking out of a particular line of historical development, or the development of higher psychological function in the ontogeny of behaviour, that it will become possible to fill in this abyss, to throw a bridge across it and to begin to study the dynamics of form and content of the thinking process in their dialectic unity. We can then correlate the dynamics of content and form through their common historical character which, in equal measure, will identify both the content of our thoughts and their higher psychological functions.

Therefore, to proceed from these ideas, which in their totality comprise the principles of the child's cultural development expounded by us elsewhere, we can find the key for a correct formulation and thus a correct solution to the problem of the development of adolescent thinking.

## IV

According to a number of research findings, the key to the whole problem of the development of thinking during adolescence is the established fact that an adolescent masters the process of concept formation for the first time and that he progresses to a new and higher form of intellectual activity, i.e. to thinking in concepts.

This central phenomenon of the entire adolescent period and the underestimation of the significance of the intellectual development of the adolescent, the tendency inherent in the majority of contemporary theories of adolescence to relegate the changes which have an intellectual character to the background, as compared with the emotional and other aspects of this age group, can be explained, firstly, by the fact that the formation of concepts is an extremely complex process which, by no means, can be considered to be analogous to the simple maturation of elementary intellectual functions, and for this reason resists any attempt to explain it by using superficial examples or rough eye estimates. The changes which occur in the thinking process of an adolescent who has mastered thinking in concepts, are to a large extent changes of an internal, intimate, structural nature, frequently not externally visible in any clear way and not always evident to an outside observer.

And if we are to limit ourselves only to such externally observable changes, we will have to agree with those researchers who suggest that nothing appears for the first time in adolescent thinking and that it just grows quantitatively, in a constant and gradual way, filling up with continually new content and becoming ever more accurate, more logical and closer to reality. But one only needs to proceed from a purely external observation to an internal investigation in depth to see this whole teaching crumble to dust. As has been mentioned already, the formation of concepts takes centre stage in the whole developmental process of thinking during the period of puberty. This process is indeed a herald of revolutionary changes to come, both in the realm of content as well as in that of forms of thinking. We have already discussed the fact that from the methodological point of view, the rift between the form and the content of thinking which underpins the majority of theories like an unspoken premise, is untenable. The reality is that form and content in the thinking process represent two aspects of one single integral process, two aspects which are internally bound up with one another by an essential, not an accidental bond.

There exist particular types of thought contents which can be properly understood, assimilated and perceived and are generally conceivable only in certain forms of intellectual activity. But there are also other contents which cannot be adequately reproduced in the same form, but require different forms of thinking which, together, make up one indivisible whole. So, for example, the contents of our dreams cannot be adequately communicated within the system of logically singular verbalization, within the forms of verbal, logical intellect; any attempt to reproduce the content of a dream through imagery in the form of logical speech, inevitably results in a misrepresentation of that content.

The same applies to scientific knowledge; for example mathematics, natural sciences and social sciences cannot be adequately communicated and represented in any other way except in the form of logical verbal thought. Content, therefore, turns out to be closely bound up with form, and when we say that the adolescent achieves a higher level in his thinking process and masters the art of concept formation, we are certainly pointing out a new domain of forms of intellectual activity and an equally new world of thought content which, at that time, unfolds for the adolescent.

So, by the very presence of the formation of concepts, we find a solution to the contradiction between the abrupt changes in the thought content and the immobility of its forms during adolescence which had inevitably arisen in several of the theories which were examined above. A number of contemporary studies bring us to the incontrovertible conclusion that it is precisely the formation of concepts which constitutes the basic core around which all the essential changes in adolescent thinking congregate.

Ach, the author of one of the most interesting studies on the formation of concepts, whose book dominates a whole era of research related to this problem, whilst attempting to elaborate the complex picture of the ontogeny of the formation of concepts, picks out the age of adolescence as being just such a borderline critical moment which marks a decisive qualitative turning point in the development of the thinking process. This is what he says:

> We are able to establish one more swiftly passing phase in the process of the intellectualization of mental development. As a rule, it tends to coincide with the period of puberty. Up to the time of sexual maturity, the child often lacks the ability to form abstract concepts, as, for example, has been demonstrated by Eng's observations. But thanks to the influence of instruction, using educational material which, for the most part, necessarily consists of general concepts which express some sort of laws or rules, attention tends to turn more and more in the direction of abstract associations under the influence of speech and thus results in the *formation of abstract concepts*.[14]

As the two basic factors leading up to the formation of abstract concepts, Ach mentions, on the one hand, the influence of the material of assimilated learning and, on the other, the guiding influence of speech on the adolescent's consciousness. He cites Gregor's studies, which have shown the enormous influence of learning on the development of abstract thinking.

This gives us an indication of the genetic role of the new content which is now becoming part of the adolescent's thinking process, and which obliges him to progress towards new forms and faces him with problems which are soluble only with the help of formed concepts. On the other hand, functional changes in the direction of awareness which are achieved with the help of speech also appear. A climax in the development of thinking and the progression to conceptual thinking is thus brought about, both by a change of function, and by the new problems which now face the adolescent's thought process in connection with the necessity of having to master new abstract material.

According to Ach, as a result of the progression to this higher stage, both the process of intellectualization and the progression to conceptual thinking, increasingly narrow down the orbit of visual thinking and thinking in images. This brings about atrophy of the type of thought inherent in childhood, which now the child has to abandon and replace with the creation of a completely new form or type of intellect.

In connection with this, Ach points out a problem to which we intend to return in the next section. He asks whether this reality of the progression from imagistic thinking to conceptual thinking may not be responsible for the circumstance that the eidetic tendency, investigated by Jaensch, is much less frequently encountered in this age group than in childhood.[15]

## V

Until recent times, the main difficulty in the area of concept investigation was that no proper experimental methods had been devised which could be used for attempting a deeper analysis of the process of the formation of concepts and studies of its psychological nature.

All the traditional methods of investigating concepts fall into two basic groups. A typical example of methodology belonging to the first group is the so-called definition method and all its indirect variations. This method is characterized by the investigation of the child's already functional and formed concepts by verbal definition of their content. It is precisely this method which has been adopted by the majority of test-based research. Despite its wide use, this method suffers from two basic shortcomings which make it impossible to rely on it in cases where a deep investigation of the process is called for.

1   It deals with the result of a previously completed process of concept formation, with a finished product, but does not catch the dynamics of this process, its development, nor its course, beginning and end. This is rather an investigation of a product than of a process which has led up to the formation of this product. Because of this, when we define ready made concepts, very often we are dealing not so much with the child's thought process, as with a replica, a reproduction of ready made information and definitions apprehended ready made. When we analyse the definition given by the child for this or that concept, we frequently learn much more about the child's awareness, experience and the level of his speech development than about his thinking in the true sense of the word.

2   The definition method operates almost exclusively by using words, forgetting that, particularly for a child, a concept is closely linked with sensory material, from whose perception and reworking process it comes into being; both the sensory material and the word are indispensable features of the process of concept formation, and words which are cut off from this material transform this whole process of the definition of the concept into a purely verbal plan which is not natural for a child. It is for this reason that, when this method is used, one is hardly ever able to establish the relationships which exist between the meaning which the child assigns to the word using a purely verbal definition, and its true, real meaning which corresponds to the word in the process of its living relationships with the objective reality which it signifies.

For all this, the most essential thing for a concept, i.e. its relationship to reality, remains unexplored; we tried to get near the meaning of a word by using another word, and what we get as a result of this operation can sooner be applied to relationships which exist between separate adopted verbal clusters than to a true reflection of childish concepts.

The second group of methods includes those for the study of abstractions which attempt to overcome the shortcomings of the purely verbal definition method, and which try to understand the psychological functions and processes which lie at the foundation of the concept formation process and the sorting out of the visual experience from which concepts arise. They all present the child with the problem of selecting any general feature from a number of concrete impressions, of segregating and abstracting this feature or attribute from a number of others which are merged with it in the process of perception, and to generalize the characteristic which is common to a large number of impressions.

This set of methods has the drawback that in place of the complex synthetic process, they substitute an elementary one which is part of it and ignore the role of words or signs in the process of concept formation, by which means they infinitely oversimplify the very process of abstraction, treating it as if it were outside the special and characteristic relationship which the concept formation process happens to have with words which represent the central distinctive signs of the entire process. So it appears that traditional methods of research into concepts are both equally characterized by a withdrawal of the word from the objective material – they operate either with words but without the objective material, or with the objective material but without words.

A great step forward in the field of research into concepts was the creation of an experimental method which made a successful attempt to reflect the process of concept formation, which includes both these features, i.e. material on the basis of which the concept is developed, and the word, which helps it to come into existence.

We will not dwell upon the complex history of the development of this new method of research into concepts; suffice it to say that when it was introduced, a whole new world opened up for the researchers – they began to study not just ready made concepts, but the very process of their formation. In particular this method, in the form in which it was used by Ach, can justifiably be called a synthetic–genetic method, as it investigates the process of the establishment of the concept, the synthesization of a number of signs which make it up and the process of its development.

The underlying principle of this method is the introduction into the experiment of non-existent words, which are initially meaningless to the subject and which are not connected with the child's earlier experiences, and also of artificial concepts which are specially constructed for experimental purposes by combining a number of features never found in the realm of our normal concepts, and which are given meaning during speech in this particular association. So, for example, in Ach's experiments the word 'Gazun', which, to begin with, the subject finds meaningless, gradually acquires meaning in the course of experience and begins to carry a meaning which amounts to something big and heavy; or the word 'fal' begins to signify something small and light.

In the process of acquiring experience before the experiment, the whole routine of trying to make sense of the meaningless word, the acquisition of a meaning for the word and the working out of the concept begins. Thanks to the introduction of non-existent words and artificial concepts, this method frees itself of one of the most serious weaknesses which pervade other methods, namely, it does not assume any previous experience or knowledge and therefore, in this respect, it puts young children on a par with adults for the purposes of solving the problem which faces the experimental subject.

Ach applied his method in exactly the same way to a five year old and to an adult, putting them on a par with one another from the point of view of their knowledge. As a result, his method is also applicable to adults and allows the investigation of the process of concept formation in its pure form.

One of the main faults of the definition method is that the concept breaks away from its natural connection and it is examined in a congealed static form, outside its association with real thought processes in which it is normally found and in which it originates and resides. The experimenter takes an isolated word and the child is supposed to define it, but this definition of an extracted, isolated word which is taken in a congealed form does not, in the least, tell us how it is understood in action, how the child manages it in a living situation of problem solving and how he uses it when a real live need arises.

According to Ach, this ignoring of the functional factor is, in essence, a refusal to take into consideration that a concept does not live in isolation and that it does not represent a congealed immovable phenomenon, but on the contrary, it is always found within a living, more or less complex thinking process and it always fulfils either a communicative, an interpretative or a comprehending function, or attempts to solve a problem.

But the new method does not suffer from this shortcoming, as it gives a central place to precisely these functional aspects of concept formation. It approaches a concept in connection with one or other problem or requirement generated by the thinking process, in connection with comprehension or communication, in a direction or problem solving situation which cannot be implemented without concepts being formed. All these things taken together mark this new method as an important and valuable tool for understanding the development of concepts. And even though Ach himself did not devote any special study to the question of concept formation in adolescence, nevertheless, whilst relying on the results of his investigations, he could not have failed to notice the dual revolution, embracing both the content and form of thought, which occurs during the period of the adolescent's intellectual development and signifies the transition to thinking in concepts.

# VI

Rimat devoted a special, very thoroughly elaborated study to the process of concept formation in adolescence, which he conducted with the help of a slightly modified version of Ach's method. The basic conclusion reached as a result of this research can be summarized by saying that concept formation appears only with the coming of adolescence and up till that time it is inaccessible to a child. 'We can say with certainty', he writes, 'that only beginning at the age of 12 a marked improvement in the ability to independently form general objective concepts appears. I think that it is important to take account of this fact. *Thinking in concepts which is a function remote from visual experiences, makes demands which exceed a child's psychological capabilities . . . until the 12th year of life.*'[16]

We are not going to go into the methods used in carrying out this experiment, nor into any other theoretical conclusions and results which its author was able to draw from it. We are going to limit ourselves to pointing out the basic result which indicates that despite the views of some psychologists, who disallow the appearance of any new intellectual function in adolescence and who maintain that every child of three is already in possession of all the intellectual operations which make up the adolescent's thinking process – despite this assertion, specific investigations show that only after the age of 12, i.e. only at the beginning of the pubescent period and after the end of the primary school age, do the processes which lead to the formation of concepts and abstract thinking begin to develop in children.

One of the basic conclusions we can draw from Ach's and Rimat's studies, is to refute the associative point of view in relation to concept formation. Ach's investigation has shown that no matter how numerous and durable the associative connections among various verbal signs and various objects might be, just this fact alone is an entirely inadequate cause for concept formation to occur. Therefore, the old idea that a concept arises purely by following an associative path due to the greatest reinforcements of certain associative connections which correspond to attributes common to a number of objects, and the weakening of other associations which correspond to attributes in which these objects differ, has not been confirmed by experimental evidence.

Ach's experiments have shown that the process of concept formation always has a productive rather than reproductive character. The concept comes into being and is formed through a complex operation which is directed toward a solution of a problem, and the presence of only external circumstances and a mechanical establishment of a connection between a word and an object is not sufficient cause for it to come into being. Along with the establishment of this non-associative and productive character of the process of concept formation, these experiments have led to another, no less important conclusion, namely the establishment of a fundamental factor defining the whole course of this process in general. According to Ach, this factor is the so-called determining tendency.

Ach assigns this term to the tendency which regulates the course of our conceptions and actions, which originates in our notion of a goal for whose attainment all the striving of this trend is directed, beginning with the problem toward whose solution all the observed activity is directed. Before Ach, psychologists differentiated between two basic tendencies which are subordinated to the flow of our perception, the reproductive or associative tendency and the persevering tendency. The first of these signifies the tendency, in the succession of ideas, to evoke those which were associatively connected with information from earlier experiences; the second points to the tendency of each conception to keep returning and repeatedly to infiltrate the tide of conceptions.

In his earlier investigations Ach has demonstrated that both these tendencies are insufficient grounds for explaining both the purposeful and consciously regulated thinking acts which are directed toward solving problems, and that these are regulated, not so much by reproduction of concepts according to an associative connection and the tendency of each conception to infiltrate the consciousness again and again, but rather by a particular determining tendency which originates from a conception of a goal. In his investigation of concepts, Ach again demonstrates that the central feature without which no new concept can arise, is the regulating action of the determining tendency, which originates from the problem which the experimental subject is presented with.

So, according to Ach's scheme, concept formation is not formed according to a chain of associations, where one link calls up and brings along with it the next one to which it is connected by association, but rather according to a type of purposeful process which consists of a number of operations which play a role of means in relationship to the solution to the basic problem. The learning by heart of words and the association of them with objects, in itself does not lead to concept formation; it is necessary for the experimental subject to be faced with a problem, which cannot be solved any other way except with the help of concept formation, in order for this process to be set in motion.

As has already been mentioned above, Ach made a great stride forward in comparison with former researchers, in the sense that the processes of concept formation were included within the structure of a resolution of a particular problem, and in the sense that the functional meaning and the role of this feature were investigated. However, this is not enough, because the objective which is the problem in itself, of course, makes up the one absolutely necessary feature for the process, which is functionally linked with its solution, to arise; pre-school and primary school children have goals as well, but neither a child from this latter age group nor from the former, nor generally speaking (as has already been said) any child below the age of 12, who is perfectly capable of realizing that a problem exists, is, however, as yet capable of working out a new concept.

And even Ach himself also showed in his studies that pre-school children, whilst trying to solve a problem with which they are faced, differ from adults and adolescents in their approach, not because they apprehend the goal more or less fully or correctly, but because they go about developing the whole process of attempting to solve the problem in a totally different manner. In a complex experimental investigation of concept formation in pre-school children, which we discuss below, Usnadze has demonstrated that a pre-school child attacks problems in precisely this functional matter in exactly the same way as an adult when the latter is operating with concepts, but the child solves these problems in a completely different way. Just like the adult, the child uses words as a tool; therefore, for him words are linked with the function of communication in exactly the same way as for an adult.

It therefore appears that it is not the problem itself, the goal or the determining tendencies which result from it, that condition the essential genetic differences between thinking in images and other forms of thinking in the adult as opposed to the young child, but some other factors which have not been mentioned by this researcher.

Usnadze drew particular attention to one of the functional aspects which Ach's investigations had brought to the fore, i.e. the instant of communication, of mutual understanding among people with the aid of speech. 'Words serve as a tool for mutual understanding among people', says Usnadze,

> It is precisely this circumstance which plays the decisive role in concept formation: when the necessity of mutual understanding arises, a specific sound complex takes on a specific meaning and so it becomes a word or a concept. Without this functional aspect of mutual understanding it would not be possible for any sound complex to become the carrier of any meaning whatsoever and no concept could be formed.[17]

It is a known fact that contact between a child and his surroundings is established extremely early; right from the very start the child grows up in an ambient atmosphere of speech and he himself begins to apply the mechanism of speech already during the second year of his life. 'There is no doubt that these are not senseless sound complexes, but real words, and as he matures, he learns how to associate more differentiated meanings with them.'[18] But at the same time we are certain that children reach the stage of socialization of thinking, which is necessary for the working out of fully developed concepts, relatively late.

> So, we can see that, on the one hand, the fully fledged concepts which assume a higher level of socialization of the child's thinking process, develop relatively late, while, on the other hand, children begin to use words and to reach the stage of mutual understanding with adults and among themselves by using them relatively early. Therefore, it is clear that words which have not yet reached the stage of fully developed concepts, take over the function of the latter and can serve as a means of communication between speaking individuals. A special investigation of the appropriate age group should tell us how these forms of thinking which have to be interpreted not so much as concepts but as their functional equivalents, develop and how they manage to reach the stage which can be considered to represent fully developed thinking.[19]

Usnadze's entire study shows that these forms of thinking which amount to functional equivalents of thinking in concepts, differ sharply (from the qualitative and structural point of view) from the more developed thinking of an adolescent or an adult. At the same time, this difference cannot be based on the factor suggested by Ach, because it is precisely from the functional point of view, in the sense of providing solutions to particular problems, and in the sense of determining tendencies which originate in goal conceptions, that these forms, as Usnadze has shown, amount to equivalent concepts.

So we end up with the following situation: it turns out that the problem and the goal conceptions which arise from it are accessible to a child at relatively early stages of his development; it is precisely because both in a child and in the adult the problems of understanding and communication are principally identical that the functional equivalents of concepts in children develop extremely early; but even though the problems are identical and the functional features equivalent, the forms of thinking themselves which function during the process of problem solving, are fundamentally different in children and in adults, because of their composition, their structure and by the way they operate.

It becomes obvious that it is not the problem, and the goal conception which is part of it, that in themselves determine and regulate the whole process, but some new factor which Ach had ignored; it is also evident that the problem, and the determining tendencies which are connected with it, cannot adequately explain the genetic and structural differences which we can observe in the functionally equivalent forms of thinking among children and adults.

The general goal cannot provide the answer to this. Granted that without the existence of a goal there cannot be any goal directed action, yet the presence of this goal cannot in any way explain the whole process of reaching it in its development and its structure. In Ach's own words, due to earlier actions, the goal and the determining tendencies which it engenders, set the process in motion, but do not regulate it; the presence of the goal and of the problems is a necessary but insufficient cause for goal directed activity to arise; no goal directed activity can arise, without the presence of a goal or a problem which sets this process in motion and gives it direction.

But the presence of a goal and a problem do not yet guarantee that a genuinely goal directed activity will be brought to life and, in any case, it does not possess any magical powers to define and regulate the process and structure of such activity. Both the child's and the adult's experiences are full of numerous incidents where, at certain stages of development, the individual is faced with unanswered questions, unresolved or incompletely worked out problems, or unattained or unattainable goals, without, however, any guarantee of success merely as a result of their being there. As a general rule it seems that we should use the goal as a starting point, but without limiting ourselves to it, in cases where an attempt to explain the nature of the psychological process which leads to problem solving is involved.

The goal, as has already been said, cannot explain the process. The most important and basic problem connected with the process of concept formation and the process of goal directed activity as a whole is the problem of the means used to carry out some psychological operation, to accomplish some goal directed activity.

In the same way as we cannot give a satisfactory explanation of human goal directed activity, labour, by saying that it is elicited by certain goals and certain problems which human beings encounter, and must explain it by referring to tool use and the application of special means without which labour activity could not come into being, in the same way the problem of the means by which man masters the process of his own behaviour is the central problem encountered when we attempt to explain all the higher forms of behaviour.

Investigations, which we are not going to discuss here, have shown that all higher psychological functions are united by one common characteristic, namely that they are mediated processes, i.e. that they incorporate in their structure, as the central and basic part of the process in general, the use of the sign as a basic means for directing and mastering the psychological processes.

In the context of the problem of concept formation with which we are concerned here, this sign is represented by words which play the role of instruments of concept formation and later become its symbols. The only way of ever discovering the key to understanding the process of concept formation, is to study the functional use of words and their development and the varied forms of their usage, multifarious, quantitatively distinct at different ages, but genetically related to one another.

The main weakness in Ach's method is that it does not allow us to explain the genetic process of concept formation, but only confirms the presence or absence of this process. By the way that the experiment is organized, the assumption that the means with whose help the concepts are formed, i.e. the experimental words which play the role of signs, which are given at the very beginning, become a constant quality which does not change throughout the whole course of the experiment and, in addition, the way that they are to be used is stipulated in the instructions beforehand; the words do not appear in the role of signs from the very beginning and they do not principally differ from any other number of stimuli produced by objects with which they are affiliated and which appear in the course of the experiment; for the sake of his critical and polemical ambitions, in an attempt to prove that a simple associative connection between words and objects is insufficient grounds for the emergence of meaning, and that the meaning of a word or concept is not equal to the associative connection between a sound complex and a number of objects, Ach retains the traditional course of the whole process of concept formation in its entirety and he subordinates it to the well recognized scheme which can be expressed in the following way: from the bottom up and from separate concrete objects to a few concepts which embrace their meaning.

However, as Ach himself admits, an experimental course such as this sharply contradicts the real path of the process of concept formation which, as we shall see below, is by no means constructed on the basis of a number of associative chains. Quoting the now famous statement by Vogel, it is not equivalent to climbing up the concept pyramid and to a transition from the concrete to the ever more abstract.

This is exactly one of the fundamental results to which Ach's and Rimat's investigations had led them; it disclosed the inaccuracy of the associative approach to the concept formation process, pointed to the productive and creative character of the concept, explained the fundamental role of the functional aspect of concept formation, underlined the fact that only where a specific need or demand for a concept exists, only during the course of some intelligent activity directed toward the attainment of a specific goal or the solution of a particular problem, can a concept come into being and take form.

These studies, having once and for all buried the idea of a mechanical conception of concept formation, nevertheless did not manage to disclose the essential genetic, functional and structural nature of this process, and strayed onto the path of purely teleological explanation of these higher functions, which essentially can be reduced to the assertion that the goal itself, with the aid of determining tendencies, creates an appropriate and goal directed activity, and that the problem contains the solution within itself.

As already pointed out, apart from being generally philosophically and methodologically unsound, from the purely factual point of view this kind of explanation leads to insoluble contradictions and to the impossibility of explaining why, even though the functional aspects of problems and goals are identical, the forms of thinking which make it possible for the child to solve these problems, are fundamentally dissimilar at every age.

Looking from this vantage point, the fact that thinking forms undergo development appears entirely incomprehensible. This is why Ach's and Rimat's experiments, which undoubtedly began a new epoch in the study of concepts, have nevertheless left this problem completely open, in terms of its causal and dynamic solution, and an experimental study should have investigated the concept formation process during its development in its causal and dynamic conditionality.

## VII

In our attempt to solve this problem, we relied on a particular method of experimental investigation, which can be described as the functional method of double stimulation. The essential feature of this method is that it investigates the development and activity of higher psychological functions using two groups of stimuli, each of which plays a different role in relationship to the behaviour of the experimental subject. One group of stimuli has the function of a task toward which the activity of the experimental subject is directed, whilst the other takes on the function of signs which help to organize this activity.

At this stage we have no intention of providing a detailed description of how this method was applied to the investigation of the process of concept formation, as this has already been done by our colleague Sakharov;[20] we will merely limit ourselves to pointing out the basic features which may be of fundamental importance in connection with everything which has been discussed above in a general way. Because the object of this experiment was to discover the role of words and the character of their functional usage in the process of concept formation, in a certain sense this whole experiment had to be designed in the opposite way to Ach's experiment.

The beginning of Ach's study shows the period of learning by heart, which consists of the experimental subject (who has not yet been given a problem by the researcher but possesses all the means, i.e. words which are necessary for the solution of the ensuing problem), memorizing the names of all the objects put in front of him, by picking them up one by one and examining them.

Thus, the problem is not presented at the very beginning but is introduced later, which results in a turning point occurring in the whole course of the experiment. However, the means (words) are given right from the start, but in a direct associative connection with the stimuli objects. As it happens, by using the method of double stimulation, both these aspects are resolved in reverse manner. The problem is fully disclosed to the experimental subject from the very start of the experiment and it remains unchanged throughout every stage of the experiment.

We do this because we proceed from the assumption that the formulation of this problem and the emergence of the goal are necessary prerequisites for the process as a whole to come into being; but the means are introduced into the problem gradually, along with every new attempt on the part of the experimental subject to solve the problem in a situation where the previously provided words prove insufficient; the period of learning by heart is not there at all. So, by converting the means required for solving the problem, i.e. the stimuli signs or words into a variable quantity, and making the problem into a constant quantity, we are able to investigate how the experimental subject uses these signs as means to guide his intellectual operations, and how, depending on the way that these words are used, the process of concept formation as a whole emerges and develops from its functional application.

At the same time we consider one aspect (discussed in detail below) to be most significant and of primary importance within the context of this investigation, namely that when the experiment is organized in this way, the concept pyramid ends up standing on its head. The process of the solution of the experimental problem corresponds to the real genetic process of concept formation, which, as we will see below, is not constructed in a mechanically quantitative way like Galton's collective photograph, by a gradual transition from the concrete to the abstract, but is one where the movement downwards, from the general to the particular, from the top of the pyramid to its base, is just as characteristic as is the reverse process of ascending to the heights of abstract thinking.

Finally, the functional aspect discussed by Ach is also of primary importance; the concept is examined not in its static and isolated state, but within living, thinking processes and problem solving situations in such a way, that the investigation as a whole breaks up into a number of separate stages, each of which includes the investigation of the concept in action, in one of its functional applications within the thinking process. At the beginning we have the process of the working out of the concept, then the process of transferring the worked out concept to new tasks, then using the concept in the process of free association and, finally, the application of the new concept to the drawing of conclusions [making of judgements] and the definition of newly worked out concepts.

The experimental process proceeds as follows: on a special board divided into separate sections, rows of shapes of different colour, form, height and size are arranged in front of the experimental subject in a random manner. All these shapes are depicted in a schematic way in figure 9.1. Figures, on the reverse side of which the experimental subject reads a meaningless word, are uncovered one at a time in front of him.

The subject is asked to move all the shapes on to the next section of the board which he considers to have the same word written on them; after every attempt by the subject to solve the problem, whilst checking him, the experimenter uncovers a new figure which carries either the same name as one previously uncovered, but different from it in a number of ways and the same in a number of others, or is marked with a different attribute, whilst again being similar to a previously uncovered figure in some respects and different from it in some others.

It can be seen that after each new attempt at a solution, the number of uncovered shapes is increased and along with it the number of attributes which denote them, and, depending on this basic factor, it becomes possible for the experimenter to follow the changes in the character of the solution to the problem, which remains constant at all stages of the experiment. Every word is placed on shapes which refer to one and the same general experimental concept, denoted by that particular word.

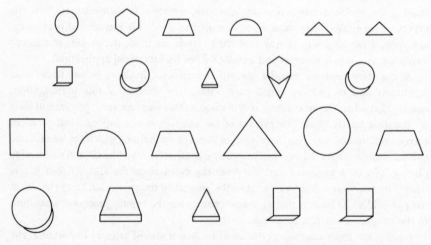

**Figure 9.1** Investigation of concept formation.

## VIII

In our laboratory, a number of investigations dealing with concept formation were initiated by Sakharov and continued and completed by us in co-operation with Kotelova and Pashkovskaya.[21] These investigations involved about 300 persons in all, children, adolescents and adults, and also persons suffering from various pathological disorders in their intellectual and speech functions.

The basic conclusions which these investigations have led us to, are directly related to a subject which is presently of great interest to us. Whilst observing the genetic process of concept formation in different age groups, and comparing and appraising this process which takes place under exactly the same conditions in a child, an adolescent child and an adult, based on these experimental investigations we were able to explain the fundamental laws which govern the development of this process.

The basic conclusion of our investigation in the genetic context can be formulated as a general rule, which says that the roots of development of the processes which afterwards lead to concept formation, reach back to early childhood, but they reach maturity only in adolescence, and those intellectual functions which form and develop are the ones which, in their particular combinations, make up the psychological basis of the process of concept formation. It is only when the child turns into an adolescent, that the final transition into the realm of thinking in concepts can occur.

Before this age we find special intellectual phenomena which appear superficially to resemble real concepts, and a cursory analysis may result in this superficial resemblance being taken as a sign of the presence of true concepts already at a very early age. These intellectual aspects really do appear comparable to the true concepts which, in their functional capacity, tend to mature considerably later.

This must mean that they fulfil a similar function to that of concepts in solving similar problems, but an experimental analysis reveals that these equivalents of our concepts, in their psychological nature, their composition, their structure and the type of function they perform, have the same relationship to the latter as an embryo to the mature organism. To identify one with the other would be to ignore the lengthy process of development and to place an equals sign between its beginning and its final stage.

It is no exaggeration to say that to identify the intellectual operations which appear in adolescence with the thinking of a three-year-old child, as has been done by many psychologists, would be just as unsound as to deny that the secondary school age is the age of puberty because elements of future sexuality, the partial ingredients of the future drive, can already be observed in infancy.

Below we will take the opportunity to make a more detailed comparison between true concepts which appear in adolescence and analogous phenomena which can be found in the thinking of pre-school and school children. By this comparison we will be able to establish that which is really new and original in the realm of adolescent thinking, and that which promotes concept formation into the centre of psychological changes which comprise the substance of the completion of maturation. But first we wish to explain, in the most general terms, the psychological nature of the process of concept formation and to disclose why it is that not until the age of puberty is it possible to master this process.

Experimental investigations of the process of concept formation have revealed that the functional use of words or other signs as means for actively directing attention, the breakdown and apportionment of attributes and abstracting and synthesizing them, is a basic and indispensable part of the process as a whole. The formation of a concept or the acquisition of meaning by a word results from a complex dynamic activity (operation by word or sign), in which all the basic intellectual functions take part in their peculiar combinations.

In view of this we may formulate a basic thesis, to which we are led by this investigation; it shows that concept formation is a particular, distinctive process of thinking and that the most likely factor to shed light on the development of this new kind of thinking, is neither association as supposed by many writers, nor directed attention as suggested by Müller,[22] nor judgement and idea working in concert, as Bühler's theory of concept formation suggests, nor the determining tendency which Ach points out; all these factors and all the processes take part in concept formation, but not a single one of them encompasses the determining and essential feature which could adequately explain the appearance of a new form of thinking, which is qualitatively original and not comparable to any other elementary intellectual operations.

We would like to reiterate that not a single one of these processes undergoes any kind of noticeable change during adolescence, because none of the elementary intellectual functions appear for the first time and can be regarded as a really new acquisition in adolescence. As far as the elementary functions are concerned, the opinion of many psychologists discussed above is perfectly justified. They maintain that nothing really fundamentally new makes its appearance in an adolescent's intellect in comparison with what is already present in a child, and that what we are observing is a continuous, regular development of the same functions which were established and matured a lot earlier.

The process of concept formation cannot be reduced to associations, attention, conception, judgement and determining tendencies, even though all these functions are indispensable in order for this synthesis to occur, which, in effect, amounts to the process of concept formation. The most essential feature of this process, as the investigations have disclosed, is the functional use of signs or words as means with which the adolescent takes charge of his own psychological processes, and with whose aid he masters the flow of his own psychological processes and directs their activity for the purpose of solving the problems he is faced with.

All the commonly discussed elementary psychological functions take part in the process of concept formation, but they do so in a completely different form, not so much as independent processes which develop according to the rules of their individual logic, but ones which are mediated by signs or words, processes which are directed toward the solution of a specific problem and which end up in new combinations, a new synthesis, and it is only as part of this synthesis that every one of those partial processes is capable of achieving its true functional significance.

Applied to the problem of concept development, it means that neither the accumulation of associations, nor the development of the range and reliability of attention, the accumulation of groups of conceptions nor the determining tendencies – not a single one of these processes on its own, no matter how far it has progressed in its development, is able to bring about the process of concept formation and, therefore, not one of the processes is a developmental factor which can be regarded as a fundamental and essential agent determining concept formation. Concepts cannot exist without words and thinking in concepts is not possible outside verbal thinking, and the new, essential, central feature of the entire process, which should basically be regarded as the primary cause responsible for concept development, is the specific use of words and the functional application of signs as means for concept formation.

Whilst discussing the methods used in our investigations, we mentioned that just stating the problem and the creation of a requirement for concepts cannot be regarded as sufficient grounds for the induction of this process, because even though such conditions are able to initiate the process, they cannot guarantee its implementation for the solution of the problem. And regarding the goal as the driving force which plays a decisive role in the process of concept formation, also fails to explain fully the real causal, dynamic and genetic relationships and associations which form the basis of this complex process, in the same way as it would be difficult to explain the flight of a cannon ball from the vantage point of its final target.

This final target, in so far as it is consciously taken into account beforehand by he who is aiming the cannon is, of course, part of the general aggregate of features which determine the real trajectory of the cannon ball; in exactly the same way the character of the problem and the goal facing the adolescent, which is attainable only with the help of concept formation, undoubtedly comprise one of the functional aspects without which we would not be able to give a complete scientific explanation of the whole process of concept formation. It is precisely because of the presence of the problems raised, the reality of the created and stimulating necessity and the goals which are being put before him, that the social environment stimulates and encourages the adolescent to make this decisive step forward in the development of his thinking.

In contrast to the process of maturation of instincts and inborn drives, the impelling force which determines the start of any process or initiates any evolving mechanism of behaviour and propels it forward along the path of further development, is not to be found inside, but outside the adolescent and, in this sense, the problems thrown up in front of the maturing adolescent by the society around him, which are connected with the process of growing into the cultural, professional and social life of adults, are extremely important functional aspects which continually depend on the reciprocal conditionality and the organic coherence and internal unity of form and content in the development of thinking.

In our discussion of the general factors connected with cultural development in adolescence outlined below, we will have to consider the long established and scientifically observed fact that where the environment fails to present appropriate problems, does not come up with new requirements and does not stimulate and create development of the intellect with the help of new goals, the adolescent's thinking does not develop according to all the available potential, and it does not reach its higher forms, or only achieves them at an exceptionally late stage.

It would therefore be wrong to ignore completely or even to underestimate the importance of the functional aspect of life's problems as one of the real and powerful factors which fuel and guide the whole process of intellectual development in adolescence; but it would be just as mistaken to perceive in this functional aspect a causal–dynamic explanation, and to treat it as a revelation of the very mechanism of development and the genetic key to the problem of the development of concepts.

The problem facing this investigation is to discover the inner link between these two aspects and to reveal concept formation which is genetically linked to adolescence, as a function of the social and cultural development of the adolescent and which includes both the content and the mechanism of thinking. A new significative use of words, i.e. its use as a means of concept formation – all these things amount to the most likely psychological reasons for the intellectual revolution which takes place on the boundary of childhood and adolescence.

If there is no sign at this time of any new basic functions, which are totally unlike any previously observed ones, it would still be incorrect to conclude that no changes are taking place in these basic functions. They are being incorporated into a new structure, entering a new synthesis and becoming part of a new complex entity as subordinate instances, whose laws also define the fate of each of their individual parts. The process of concept formation entails a mastery of the course of one's own psychological processes with the help of the functional use of words or signs as part of its basic and central substance. This mastery of the processes of one's own behaviour is only able to reach the final stage of its development in adolescence, supported by other factors.

Experimental results have shown that concept formation is not the same thing as the development of any other habit, no matter how complicated. Experimental investigations of concept formation in adults, as well as the light we have been able to shed upon these processes during childhood, and studies of their disintegration in cases of pathological disturbances of intellectual activity, bring us to the conclusion that the hypothesis regarding the identification of the psychological nature of higher intellectual processes with the elementary and purely associative processes of the formation of connections or habits, which has been suggested and developed by Thorndike, is in sharp contradiction with factual data about the composition, functional structure and genesis of the process of concept formation.

Accordingly, these investigations disclose that the process of concept formation, like any other higher form of intellectual activity, is not just an exceptionally more complex lower form quantitatively, and that it differs from the purely associative activity not by the number of associations, but that it represents a new, basically different type of activity which cannot be reduced to just any range of associative connections qualitatively, and where the fundamental difference can be said to be a result of the transition from indirect intellectual processes to operations which are mediated by signs.

The significative structure (connected with active use of signs) which represents the general rule guiding the formation of higher forms of behaviour, is not identical with the associative structure of elementary processes. The mere accumulation of associative connections can never result in the appearance of a higher form of intellectual activity. It is impossible to explain the real differences in the higher forms of thinking on the basis of quantitative changes in association. In his theory of the nature of intellect, Thorndike maintains that 'the higher forms of intellectual operations are identical to the purely associative activity or the formation of associations and they depend on physiological associations of the same type, but they require a much greater number of them'.[23]

From this point of view, the difference between the adolescent intellect and that of a child, can be reduced entirely to the number of associations. To quote Thorndike, 'a person who has a greater, higher or better intellect than another, in the final analysis differs from the latter not by the fact that he possesses a new kind of physiological process, but simply due to a larger number of associations of the most ordinary sort'.

As has already been said above, this hypothesis cannot be confirmed by experimental analysis of the process of concept formation, or by studying concept development, or by the picture presented by cases where they are in a state of disintegration. Thorndike's position which proclaims that 'it appears that both the phylogenesis and the ontogenesis of intellect show that selection, analysis, abstraction, generalization and reflection originate as a direct result of an increase in the number of associations', cannot be confirmed by experimentally organized and carefully investigated ontogenesis of concepts in children and adolescents. This investigation of the ontogenesis of concepts shows that development from lower to higher planes does not follow the road of a quantitative increase in associations, but is achieved by qualitatively new formations; in particular, speech, which is one of the basic features of the higher forms of intellectual activity, is included not in an associative manner like a function with a parallel course, but in a functional way, like a means which is utilized in a rational manner.

Speech itself is not based on purely associative connections but requires a basically different relationship between signs and the structure of intellectual processes, which happens to be very characteristic of higher intellectual operations as a whole. The phylogenesis of intellect, as far as this can be ascertained on the basis of psychological studies of primitive man and his thinking processes, also fails to shed any light on the developmental path from lower to higher forms, as was assumed by Thorndike, through a quantitative increase of associations, at least in its historical part. Following the famous investigations by Köhler, Yerkes and others, there is no reason to expect that the biological evolution of the intellect will be able to affirm the identical nature of thinking and associations.

## IX

If one were to attempt to make any schematic inferences from our research, they would basically reveal that the road which leads to concept development consists of three intrinsic stages, each of which, in its turn, can also be subdivided into several separate parts or phases.

The first stage of concept formation which most frequently can be observed in young children's behaviour, is the appearance of an as yet unorganized and unregulated quantity, an ability to distinguish a mass of random objects, at a time when the child is faced with a problem which we, as adults, normally manage to solve by forming a new concept. This stockpile of objects picked out by the child, which is consolidated without any adequate inner substance, without any sufficient inherent similarity and relationship between its constituent parts, presupposes a diffuse, non-directed dissemination of the meaning of words, or their equivalent signs, to a number of superficially connected, but intrinsically disconnected elements in the child's experience.

At this stage of development, the meaning of a word conjures up a not-fully defined, unorganized syncretic chain of separate objects, connected with one another in certain ways in the child's imagination and perception, and forming one combined image. The decisive role in the formation of this image is played by the syncretism of the child's perception or action, and for this reason the image tends to be extremely unstable.

It is a well known fact that children reveal this kind of tendency to correlate the most diverse and unconnected elements on the basis of a single impression in their perception, thinking and also in their actions, creating from them a closed, consolidated image; Claparède has named this tendency the syncretism of childhood perception, and Blonsky called it the disconnected coherence of childish thinking. Elsewhere, we have already described this same phenomenon as the tendency on the part of the child to replace the lack of objective associations by an abundance of subjective connections, and to take the association of impressions and thoughts for associations between things. Of course, this over-production of subjective associations has an enormous significance as a factor in the subsequent development of childish thinking, as it constitutes the basis for any further process of selection of the applicable realities and connections which can be verified in practice. Superficially, the meaning of some words uttered by children who have reached a certain stage in their conceptual development can, indeed, remind one of the meaning of words uttered by adults.

Children are able to communicate with adults by using words which have certain meanings; within this superabundance of syncretic associations and the unregulated syncretic stockpiles of themes which have been formed with the help of words, objective connections are also reflected to a great degree, in so far as they correspond to the connections between the child's impressions and perceptions. Therefore, in many instances, the meaning of the words which children utter can partially coincide with the meanings these same words have acquired in adult speech, particularly when they refer to the real objects of the child's surroundings.

In this way children's words often conform in meaning to those of adults or, more precisely, the meaning of one and the same word can often coincide in one and the same real object in the speech of children and adults, and this fact proves sufficient grounds for mutual understanding between them. But the psychological path which leads up to the point of understanding in the thinking of adults and children is totally different, and even in cases where the meaning of a child's words partially coincides with that of an adult, it is due to completely different, unique operations, and it is a product of the syncretic mixture of images which are the source of children's words.

In its turn, this stage in the process of the formation of concepts in children can be divided into three phases, which we had the opportunity to investigate in detail.

The first phase of the creation of the syncretic image or stockpile of objects which correspond to the meaning of a word, fully coincides with the period of trial and error in childish thinking. The child then takes up a group of new objects at random, and this is accompanied by individual trials which replace one another when their inaccuracy becomes apparent.

This phase is succeeded by a second one, where the spatial arrangement of shapes in the staged conditions of our experiment and, what is more, purely syncretic laws of perception of the visual field and the organization of childish perception, play a decisive role. The syncretic image or the stockpile of objects forms, on the basis of space and time, meetings between individual elements, or indirect contact, or some other more complicated relationship arising between them within the process of indirect perception. But what remains essential for this particular period is that the child is guided, not by objective association which he discovers in things, but by subjective connections suggested to him by his own perceptions. The objects begin gradually to line up and are gathered under one general meaning, not because of any prevalent features which are inherent in them or been singled out by the child, but because of the similarities between them in the child's perception.

Finally, the third and leading phase of this stage, one which signifies its end and the transition to the second stage in concept formation; this is the phase where the syncretic image, which is equivalent to the concept, emerges on a more complex basis and is dependent on the ability to gather specimens from various groups, which have previously already become unified in the child's perception, under a single meaning.

In this way, every one of the separate elements of the new syncretic series or stockpile represents some group of objects previously unified in the child's perception, but all of them taken together are in no way intrinsically connected with one another, and they represent the same kind of disjointed connectedness as in the stockpile, as was the case with the concept equivalents during the two previous phases.

The only difference and complication is due to the fact that the associations which children utilize to form the meaning of a new word, stem not just from one single perception but, it seems, from a two-stage processing of the syncretic associations; first of all syncretic groups are formed, from which individual specimens subsequently emerge and become syncretically united all over again. At this stage it is no longer the plane, the perspective, the double series of associations, or the double structure of the groups which can explain the meaning of the child's words, but these double series and double structures are still unable to rise above the formulation of the unregulated quantity or, speaking metaphorically, the stockpile.

A child who, by virtue of having reached this third phase, completes the entire first stage in the development of concepts, and gives up the stockpile which has hitherto represented the basic form of the meaning of words, proceeds to the second stage which, conditionally, we call the stage of the formation of complexes.

# X

The second important stage in the development of concepts includes many types of this generically identical mode of thinking which vary greatly from the functional, structural and genetic points of view. This manner of thinking, as well as all the remaining ones, leads to the creation of associations, to the establishment of relationships between different actual experiences, to the unification and generalization of individual themes and to the regulation and systematization of the child's entire previous experience.

But the manner of the unification of different real objects into general groups, the character of the connections which becomes established during this process, the structure of the affinities which arise on the basis of such thinking, which is characterized by the relationship of each individual object having become part of the composition of the group, to the group as a whole – all this is fundamentally different by its nature and the manner of its operation from thinking in concepts, which only develops at the time of puberty.

There is no more appropriate way in which we could have identified this particular mode of thinking than by naming it 'thinking in complexes'. This means that the generalizations which are achieved with the help of this mode of thinking, by its structure, represent complexes of individual real objects or things, which are already united not only because of the subjective associations which can be established in the child's imagination, but on the basis of objective connections, which actually exist between these objects.

If, as was said above, the first stage in the development of thinking is characterized by the building of syncretic images, which in a child are the equivalent of our concepts, so the second stage is characterized by the building of complexes which have the same functional significance. This represents a new step forward along the path leading to the mastery of concepts, and a new stage in the development of the child's thought process, which stands head and shoulders above the one which precedes it. Without question it signifies considerable progress in the life of the child. This transition to a higher type of thinking consists of the fact that in place of the 'disjointed connectedness', which lies at the foundation of the syncretic image, the child begins to unify similar objects into a common group and finally to combine them according to the rules of objective connections which he is able to discover in things.

The child who is in the process of evolving this type of thinking, is able to overcome his egocentrism[24] to some extent. He gives up taking the connections from his own experience for the actual connections between things and he takes a decisive step forward along the road of rejecting syncretism and along the path of success of objective thinking.

Thinking in complexes is by its nature associative thinking and, at the same time, objective thinking. These are the two essential features which raise it high above the previous stage, but at the same time this connectedness in its turn and this objectivity are still not the connectedness and objectivity which characterize thinking in concepts achieved finally by the adolescent.

The difference of this second stage of concept development from the third and final one, which contains the whole ontogenesis of concepts, lies in the fact that the complexes formed at this stage are built according to entirely different laws of thinking than those which apply to concepts. As has already been mentioned, they reflect objective connections, but in a different form and manner than in concepts.

Adult speech also shows many remnants of thinking in complexes. The best example to illustrate this basic law of the structure of various types of thought complex in our speech is the family name. Every family name, for example 'the Petrovs', includes this kind of complex of individual themes, which is the nearest thing to the complex character of childish thinking. In a certain sense, one might say that at this stage of his development, it is as if a child thinks in family names, or to put it another way, from his point of view the world of individual themes coalesces and organizes itself into groups of separate, but mutually affiliated, family names.

This idea could be formulated in yet another way by saying that the meaning of words at this stage of development can be defined most accurately as the family names of objects which have been combined into complexes or groups.

For the formation of a complex, the most essential underlying feature is a concrete and factual connection between the separate elements which are part of its composition, rather than an abstract and logical one. And so we can never decide whether a certain person has anything to do with the family name Petrov, and whether he can be called by that name, based simply on the logical relationship with the other carriers of the same family name. This question can only be resolved on the basis of a factual affiliation or a factual kinship between people.

The complex is founded on factual associations which can be revealed through direct experience. It is for this reason that this complex represents, first of all, an actual unification of a group of objects according to their mutual actual proximity, and all remaining aspects of this way of thinking are a result of this. The most important of these can be described as follows: as such complexes lie in the realm of concrete and factual thinking and not in the abstract and logical sphere, they do not diverge from the unity of these associations which constitute the support on which their very existence depends.

A complex, like a concept, is a generalization or blend of various real heterogeneous themes. But the association with whose help this generalization is formed, can be of many different types. Any association can result in the inclusion in the complex of a certain element, as long as it is available, and this is the most characteristic feature of the complex building process. Whilst associations of a single type which are logically identical to one another form the foundation of concepts, the ones found at the root of complexes include many varied factual associations, which frequently have nothing at all to do with one another. In a concept, the objects are generalized according to one feature, but in a complex they are based on various factual grounds. Therefore, material and uniform associations and affiliations between objects are reflected in concepts, whilst complexes present factual, random and concrete ones.

The diversity of associations which underpin complexes constitutes their main difference from concepts, which are characterized by the uniformity of the associations which make them up. This means that each individual object incorporated in the generalized concept is included in this generalization on an identical basis with all the other objects. All these elements are connected to the whole by associations of the same type, expressed in a concept and, through it, unified by a single image.

In contrast to this, every element of a complex can be connected with the whole by the most diversified associations, expressed in the complex and with separate elements which make up its composition. Basically, in concepts, these associations represent the relationship between the general and the particular, and the particular with another particular via the general. In a complex, these associations can vary just as much as any factual contiguity and factual semblance of the most diverse objects which are found in any real relationship with one another.

In our investigations we have mapped out five basic forms of complex systems which make up the basis of generalizations which arise in the child's thought process at this stage of development.

The first type of complex we have named the associative one, because any associative connection with any one of the attributes which a child may notice in an object which is part of the experiment, makes up its essence and forms the nucleus of the future complex. The child is able to build a whole complex around this nucleus and to include within it the most diverse objects; some because they have an identical colour to this object, others, because of their shape, still others, due to their size and so on, or perhaps because of some distinctive feature which attracts the child's attention. Any actual relationship which the child discovers, any associative connection between the nucleus and the element of the complex, is enough reason for the child to include this object in a group selected by him, and for it to be designated by a common family name.

These elements can also exist in a totally disunited state. The only principle guiding the process of their generalization is their factual affiliation with the primary nucleus of the complex. At the same time, their connection with the latter can be any associative link. An element may turn out to have an affiliation with the nucleus of a future complex because of its colour and another because of its form, etc. If one takes into account that this connection can be the most incongruous one, not only because of its attributes, but also because of the character of the very relationship between the two objects, it will become clear how variegated, disorderly, inadequately systematized and not properly unified is the alternation of the multitudes of material features revealed every time in the process of thinking in complexes, albeit it is based on objective connections. And at the roots of this multitude, there can be found not merely a consistent identification of the attributes, but also their similarities and contrasts and their associations by mere contact, etc., but always and without fail, a real association.

For a child, finding himself at this stage of development, words cease to be signifiers of separate objects or proper names. For him, they have now become family names. During this period, to provide a child with a word, means to point out a family of things which are intimately connected with one another according to a great variety of types of kinship. To call an object by a proper name as understood by the child is to relegate it to a specific real complex with which it is associated. For a child, to name an object at this stage means to give it a family name.

## XI

The second phase in the development of thinking in complexes is formed by the joining up of objects and actual impressions of things into special groups which, because of their structure, remind one, above all, of what is commonly referred to as collections. Here, various real objects become unified on the basis of a mutual complementing of one another according to some feature, and they form a single whole which consists of different, mutually complementary parts. It is precisely this heterogeneity of their composition and the mutual process of completion and joining together using a collection, which characterizes this stage in the development of thinking.

Under experimental conditions, the child selects other shapes to match a given standard and which differ from the given pattern in their colour, form, size or some other way. However, he does not pick them out in a chaotic and random fashion, but is guided by some attribute marking this difference and a complementary aspect of this attribute which is contained in the model and apprehended by him as grounds for the unification. The collection which comes into being as a result of this assembly, forms an assortment of various objects which differ according to colour or shape, and represent a selection of the basic colours or the basic shapes which are to be found among the experimental material.

An essential difference between this form of thinking in complexes and associative complexes is that recurring examples of objects with the same attribute are not included in the collection. It is as if individual examples representative of the whole group are selected from each group of objects. It is association by contrast rather than by similarity which is observed here. It is true that this form of thinking frequently goes together with the associative form described above. In such cases we have a collection which is put together on the basis of different attributes. The child does not consistently hold up the principle which he has designated as the foundation of complex formation in the process of putting together the collection, but he combines different attributes by association, and he still puts each attribute at the base of the collection.

This lengthy and persistent phase in the development of childish thinking has very deep roots in the entire range of actual, visual and practical experience of the child. In his visual and practical thinking, the child always deals with specific collections of things which complement each other, as well as with a specific whole. The most frequent form of generalization of actual experience the child learns from his visual experience. It includes the incorporation of individual objects into a collection and the selection of mutually complementary subjects which are significant from the practical point of view and functionally belong together. A cup, a saucer and a spoon make up a unified set, which also includes a fork, a knife, spoons and plates; the child's clothes as well, all these things are examples of natural complex collections which the child comes up against in his daily life.

Because of this, it becomes natural and obvious for the child to construct such complex collections in his verbal thinking, by matching objects and concrete groups according to the attributes of their functional supplementary function. Furthermore, it appears that such forms of complex formations which are structured on collections, can also play an extremely important role in the thinking of adults, particularly in the thinking of nervous and mental patients. Often, when an adult speaks about crockery or clothing, in his actual expressions he has in mind not so much the parallel abstract concept, as the corresponding sets of actual objects which comprise the collection.

If, for the most part, emotional subjective associations between experiences which the child perceives as associations between things, form the basis of syncretic images, and if the recurring and obtrusive similarity of attributes of separate objects is the foundation of the associative complex, then the collection is based on associations and relationships between things which are established by the practical active and visual experience of the child. One could even say that a complex collection is a generalization of things according to their complicity in a single practical operation, on the basis of their functional co-operation.

But, at this moment, all three of these different forms of thinking are of interest to us, not so much for their own sakes, but rather as different genetic paths leading towards one goal – the formation of concepts.

## XII

If one is to follow the logic of experimental analysis, one should place the chain complex, which is also an indispensable stage in the process of the child's ascent to mastering concepts, after the second phase in the development of thinking in complexes in children.

The chain complex is constructed according to the principle of a dynamic, temporary unification of individual links into a single chain and of the transmission of meaning along the separate links of this chain. This type of complex is usually represented in an experimental situation in the following way: the child matches one or several objects which have some definite associative relationship with a given model; after that the child continues to select real objects into a single complex, but at this stage following some other peripheral attribute of a previously selected object, an attribute which is not at all present in the pattern.

For example, the child matches several angular shapes to the pattern, which is a yellow triangle, and then if the last of these selected shapes happens to be blue, he matches up other blue shapes, for example half circles or circles with it. And this again proves sufficient reason in order to incorporate a new attribute and to select further objects, now using the attribute of roundness. During the process of complex formation, there is a continuous transfer of one attribute to another.

In the same way, the meaning of words moves along the links of the complex chain. Every link is connected on one side with the previous link, and on the other with the following one, and the most important distinction of this type of complex can be described by the fact that the character of the association or the manner of the connection of the same link with the preceding and the following one can be entirely different.

Yet again we find that associative connections between separate concrete elements form the basis of the complex, but this time the associative connection is not required to connect every individual link with the standard. Each link, whilst becoming part of the complex, turns into the same sort of varied member of this complex like the pattern itself, and whilst following an associative attribute it may again become the centre of attraction for a number of real objects.

Here we can see very clearly to what extent thinking in complexes can have a visual–concrete and figurative character. An object, when it is included in a complex due to its associative attributes, becomes part of it as a given real object with all its attributes, but by no means as a carrier of only one defined attribute by whose virtue it has been accepted into this particular complex. This latter attribute is not segregated by the child from all the remaining ones. It does not play any specific role in comparison with all the others. It does not stand out because of its functional meaning and it remains equal among equals, one amongst many other attributes.

At this stage we can take the opportunity to discover the really tangible and essential peculiarity of the whole realm of thinking in complexes, which differentiates it from concept thinking. This peculiarity consists of the fact that, in contrast to concepts, there is an absence of any hierarchical connections and hierarchical relationships between attributes in complexes. All the attributes are basically equal in their functional meaning. The relation of the general to the particular, i.e. of the complex to each separate concrete element entering into its composition, and the relationships of the elements to each other, as well as the principles governing the structure of the whole generalization process, differ significantly from all the features found within the concept structure.

In a chain complex, the structural centre can be entirely absent. The individual concrete elements are able to form relationships with each other, whilst bypassing the central element or standard. It is therefore possible for them to have nothing in common with any of the other elements, but they can nevertheless belong to the same complex just on the basis of having a common attribute with some other element, and this other element, in its turn, is connected with a third one, etc. But the first and third elements may not have any other connection between them except that they both, each according to its own attribute, have a connection with the second one.

Therefore, we feel justified in considering the chain complex to represent the purest form of thinking in complexes because, in contrast to the associative complex, where some sort of centre capable of being filled with a paradigm can still be observed, this complex is devoid of any such centre. This means that the connection between the separate elements in the associative complex still comes into being through some element which is common to them all and which forms the centre of the complex, and such a centre is not present in the chain complex. Any connection within it exists only inasmuch as it is viable to bring together any separate elements. The end of the chain may have nothing in common with its beginning. It is enough, in order for them to be able to belong to one complex, to be held and tied together by intermediate connecting links.

So, in attempting to characterize the relationship of the separate concrete elements with the complex in general, we might say that in contrast to concepts, the concrete element becomes part of a complex as a real visible unit with all its factual attributes and connections. A complex does not stand above its elements, like a concept stands above the real objects which are to become a part of it. In fact, a complex blends together with real objects which are becoming part of its composition and which are connected with one another.

This blending of the general and the particular and of the complex and the element, this psychological amalgam, according to Werner,[25] constitutes the most essential feature of thinking in complexes in general and of the chain complex in particular. Due to this fact the complex is, to all intents and purposes, inseparable from the actual group in which the objects are unified and which blends directly with this visual group, and frequently can take on a highly indefinite and somewhat diffuse character.

These connections themselves pass from one to another imperceptibly and the very character and type of these associations undergo minute changes. Most of the time a distant similarity or a very superficial point of contact between the attributes proves sufficient reason for actual connections to occur. A coming together of attributes frequently occurs not so much because of any real similarities between them, but rather because of a distant, vague impression of some common properties which they share. What emerges is what we call the fourth phase in the development of thinking in complexes, or the diffuse complex under the conditions of experimental analysis.

# XIII

The essential distinguishing feature of the fourth type of complex is that the attribute itself which unifies separate concrete elements and complexes by means of associations, appears diffuse (becoming less defined), dispersed and vague, and the resulting complex has to unify graphically concrete groups of images or objects by means of diffuse, indefinite associations. For example, to match the given pattern, in this case a yellow triangle, the child will pick up not just other triangles, but trapezium shaped objects as well, as they remind him of triangles, but with their apexes cut off. Later, squares are matched up with trapezia, hexagons with squares, half-circles and, finally even circles, with the hexagons. And in the same way as here, the shape which is perceived as the basic attribute becomes diffuse and indefinite; sometimes the colours run into each other in cases where a diffuse colour attribute has become incorporated into the complex. The child then selects green objects to match up with yellow ones, blue ones are matched with the green, and black with blue.

This form of thinking in complexes, which is so extremely persistent and important in the natural conditions of child development, is of great interest in experimental analysis because it clearly reveals one more very essential feature of thinking in complexes, namely, the vagueness of its outlines and its fundamental lack of any boundaries.

Just like the ancient biblical clan which, whilst representing a perfect family unit, dreamt of multiplying and becoming numberless like the stars in the sky and like the sands of the seashore, in an identical way, the diffuse complex in the thinking of children represents the same kind of family unit of things, which includes boundless opportunities for expansion and incorporation of more and more new, but quite concrete, objects into the original clan.

If the collection complex manifests itself in the natural life of children primarily in the form of generalizations based on functional similarities of individual objects, then the life prototype and natural analogy of the diffuse complex in the development of childhood thinking are seen in the generalizations which the child creates precisely in those realms of his thinking which do not easily submit to practical scrutiny, or in other words, in the non-visual and non-practical realms of thinking. We know what unexpected combinations, frequently incomprehensible to an adult, what fairy tales of thought, what risky generalizations and what diffuse transitions the child can sometimes come up with when he begins to reason or think beyond the bounds of his visual, objective, circumscribed little world and his practical running experience.

At this stage the child enters the world of diffuse generalizations, where attributes shift and oscillate and imperceptibly pass from one into another. There are no hard contours to be found here. This is the domain of limitless complexes, which frequently show astonishing universality in the associations they are able to orchestrate.

Meanwhile, after analysing this complex carefully, one becomes convinced that the principle which guides its structure is the same principle as that which directs the building of limited concrete complexes. Both here and there, the child does not go beyond the limits of real factual associations between individual objects of the visual image. The whole difference lies in the fact that, as this complex unifies things which are found outside the child's practical knowledge, these associations have to form on the basis of unreliable, indefinite and shifting attributes.

## XIV

To complete the picture of the development of thinking in complexes, it only remains for us to pause and examine its one last remaining form, which plays an important part in the child's thinking process, both under experimental and under real life conditions. This form throws a shaft of light in both directions as, on the one hand, it illuminates for us all the child's past stages of thinking in complexes, and on the other, serves as a bridge to a new and higher stage, namely the formation of concepts.

We have called this type of complex a pseudoconcept,[26] because we have before us a generalization process which comes into being in the child's thinking, which outwardly reminds us of concepts which adults use in their intellectual activities but which, at the same time, inwardly, in its psychological nature, represents something completely different from a concept in the true sense of the word.

If we proceed to analyse with care this last stage in the development of thinking in complexes, we will see that what we have is a complex generalization of a number of real themes which, from the phenotypical point of view, i.e. in their external appearance and the totality of their external features, conform to concepts completely, but which, by no means, can be considered to be concepts because of their genetic nature, the conditions in which they come into being and the development and causal dynamic associations which underlie them. When we observe them from the outside, what we see is a concept, but from the inside they are complexes. It is for this reason that we have given them the name of pseudoconcepts.

Under experimental conditions, a child creates a pseudoconcept every time he picks up a number of objects which could be selected and combined with one another on the basis of some abstract ideas, and matches them up with the given pattern. Consequently, such a generalization could just as easily be a result of a concept, but in reality, in children, it appears as a result of thinking in complexes.

It is only in the final analysis that the complex generalization can be seen to coincide with a generalization based on a concept. For example, a child matches all the triangles available in the experimental material to the given pattern, i.e. the yellow triangle. This group could have been put together as a result of abstract thinking. But, in actual fact, as our investigations have shown and experimental analysis has confirmed, the child has combined the objects because of their concrete, factual, visual connections, on the basis of simple association. He has only managed to build a limited associative complex; he has arrived at the same point, but all the time he has travelled along a different road.

This type of complex and this form of visual thinking dominate a child's real thinking both from the functional and from the genetic point of view. It is for this reason that we feel compelled to investigate, in somewhat more detail, this central matter relating to the process of conceptual development in children, a chasm which divides thinking in complexes from thinking in concepts and which, at the same time, binds both of these genetic stages of concept formation together.

## XV

First of all it is important to note that in a child's real life thinking process, among all the other types of thinking in complexes found in pre-school children, pseudoconcepts comprise the most widespread, dominant and often almost exclusive form. The prevalence of this form of thinking in complexes has a deep functional base and a deep functional meaning. The circumstance which is responsible for this widespread and almost exclusive predominance of this form, is the fact that childhood complexes which correspond to the meaning of words, do not develop freely and spontaneously along the lines marked out by the child himself, but in certain definite directions which have been predetermined for the developmental process of the complex by previously established meanings which have been assigned to the words in adult speech.

It is only under experimental conditions that we are able to liberate the child from this steering influence of words from our language, and to allow the child to instil the words with meaning and to create complex generalizations following his own free judgement. This fact accounts for the enormous significance of the experiment which permits us to reveal a child's own activity involved in the acquisition of adult language. The experiment shows us how children's language might have turned out and to what generalizations the child's thinking might have aspired, were he not guided by the language he hears in the world around him, which predetermines the range of real subjects of which the meaning of a given word can be applied.

Objections could be raised to the effect that our use of the conditional case speaks rather against than in favour of this experiment. For, after all, in reality a child is not free during the process of development of meanings which he acquires from adult speech. But we are able to counter this objection by pointing out that what this experiment teaches us is not limited to that which might occur if the child were free from the guiding influence of adult speech, and were to work out his own generalizations independently and freely. The experiment reveals to us the real continuing active discipline the child employs in the creation of generalization, which is not easily apparent to a superficial observer and which does not disappear, but only conceals itself and acquires a very complicated means of expression due to the guiding influence of the speech of people around him.

The child's thinking process, directed by an established and constant meaning of words, does not change the basic laws of its activity. These laws achieve distinct expression only in those specific circumstances where the real development of the child's thinking process takes place.

The speech of the people surrounding the child, with its established, constant meanings, predetermines the path which the development of the child's generalizations can take. It limits the child's individual actions and directs them down specific, strictly defined channels. But the child, whilst travelling along this defined predetermined path, continues to think in ways peculiar to the stage of development of intellect where he happens to be at that time. By engaging the child in verbal communication, an adult can influence the further progress of this generalization process, as well as the end and outcome of that journey which will be the result of the child's generalizations. But adults cannot pass on their method of thinking to children. A child assimilates ready-made meanings of words from adults, but he does not have to select actual themes for the complexes himself.

The paths of dissemination and transmission of the meaning of words are given to him by people around him in the process of verbal communication. But a child cannot immediately assimilate the adult's way of thinking and he acquires a product which looks like the adult product, but which is acquired by means of completely different intellectual operations and is reached by a particular method of thinking. This is what we call the pseudoconcept. To all appearances, what one gets is something which practically coincides with the meaning adults ascribe to words, but effectively it is profoundly different.

But it would be a big mistake to view the duality found in this end product as causing any discord or a breach in the child's thinking process. Such discord or breaches exist only in the eyes of an observer who happens to be investigating this process from two different vantage points. For the child himself, complexes which are equivalents of adult concepts, i.e. pseudoconcepts, do exist. After all, we can easily imagine cases of this type where, quite frequently, we have observed the following during the process of experimental concept forming: a child creates a complex with all the features from the structural, functional and genetic points of view which are typical for thinking in complexes, but the end product of this process of thinking in complexes coincides with a generalization which could also have been constructed on the basis of thinking in concepts.

Due to this coincidence of the end result or end product of thinking, it becomes extermely difficult for the investigator to distinguish what he is actually dealing with, thinking in complexes or thinking in concepts. This disguised form of thinking in complexes which arises because of the superficial likeness between pseudoconcepts and real concepts, is an important obstacle in the way of genetic analysis of the thinking process.

It is precisely this circumstance which is responsible for the fact that many investigators have developed the erroneous idea which we have discussed at the beginning of this chapter. The superficial likeness which can be observed between the thinking of a three year old and that of an adult, the practical coincidences of word meanings used by children and adults which make verbal communication and mutual understanding between children and adults possible, and the functional equivalence of complexes and concepts, have all been responsible for leading investigators to draw false conclusions which proclaim that in the thinking of a three year old there is already present – albeit in a still immature form – the full range of forms of adult intellectual activity and that, consequently, no essential breakthrough or decisive new strides toward the mastery of concepts occurs in adolescence. It is quite obvious where such a mistaken idea originated. At a very young age a child assimilates a large number of words whose meanings for him coincide with the same meanings which adults give him. This ability to understand one another gives rise to the impression that *the end point in the development of the meaning of a word coincides with the starting point*, that the ready-made meaning is given right at the beginning and that, consequently, there is no room for development. Anyone who identifies a concept with the meaning of a word (as Ach does) will inevitably reach this wrong conclusion, which is based on an illusion.

To be able to find the border which divides the pseudoconcept from a real concept promises to be a very difficult task and one which is inaccessible to purely formal phenotypical analysis. If one is to make judgements purely on the basis of external likeness, then the pseudoconcept looks as much like a real concept as a whale looks like a fish. But if one accepts the theory of the 'origin of the species' of intellectual and animal forms, then, without question, the pseudoconcept must be assigned to the realm of thinking in complexes, in the same way as the whale is classified as a mammal.

So, our analysis has led us to the conclusion that an internal contradiction is present in the pseudoconcept, the most widespread concrete form of thinking in complexes in children, which is imprinted on its very name and which, on the one hand, is the greatest problem and obstacle we face in our attempts to investigate it from the scientific point of view, and on the other, underlines its enormous functional and genetic significance as the most important determining factor in the process of development of thinking in children. The essence of this contradiction is the existence of a complex in the form of a pseudoconcept which, from the functional point of view, is equivalent to a concept in so far as an adult who becomes involved in a situation of verbal communication and mutual understanding with a child, is unaware of the difference between this complex and a concept.

Consequently, what we have is a complex which coincides with concepts from the practical point of view and which, in effect, includes the same range of concrete themes as the concept. What we have is a shadow of a concept, its contours. As one author has expressed it metaphorically, what we have is an image which 'can in no way be understood as a simple sign for a concept. Rather, it is a picture, a mental drawing of the concept, a little story told about it'.[27] On the other hand, we have a complex, i.e. a generalization which is based on entirely different laws than those of a real concept.

We have already discussed above how this real contradiction arises in the first place and what conditions it. We have seen that the language of adults who surround the child with its constant definitions, determines the path of development of a child's generalization process and the range of complex systems. A child does not select a meaning for a word. It is given to him in the process of verbal communication with adults. A child does not construct his complexes freely. He acquires them in a pre-fabricated state during the process of interpreting the speech of other people. He is not able to select individual concrete elements freely and to incorporate them in one of the complexes. He receives a number of ready made things which have already been generalized by the given word.

He does not assign a given word to a given objective group spontaneously, and he transfers its meaning from object to object, thus widening the range of the objects which are included in the complex. All he does is to emulate adult speech and assimilates the already established objective definitions of words which are given to him ready made. To put it more simply, a child does not create his speech, but rather assimilates the ready-made speech of adults around him. This about sums it up. It also includes the fact that a child does not himself create complexes which correspond to the meaning by common words and designations. This is the reason why his complexes coincide with adult concepts and this is also why a pseudoconcept or a concept–complex comes into being.

But we have also pointed out already that, whilst conforming in its external form with a concept and in the attainable thinking ramifications and its end product, by no means does a child associate himself with the adults' method of thinking in the type of intellectual operations which help him to arrive at the pseudoconcept. This is the reason why the pseudoconcept achieves such an enormous functional importance, as a specific dualistic, internally contradictory form of the childhood thinking process. Were it not that pseudoconcepts constitute the principal form of thinking in children, their complexes and adult concepts would take off in completely different directions, as tends to happen in an experimental situation where a child is not bound by the imposed meanings of words.

Mutual understanding using words and verbal communication between adults and children would then become impossible. This communication is only possible because, in reality, children's complexes do coincide with adult concepts and are able to make contact. Concepts and mental pictures of concepts turn out to be functionally equivalent, as has already been pointed out, and as a result, a very important circumstance is created which allocates an immense functional significance to the pseudoconcept, in that a child who is thinking in complexes and an adult who is thinking in concepts are able to establish a state of mutual understanding and verbal communication because, in effect, their thinking is able to make contact in the overlapping complexes–concepts.

We have said already at the beginning of this chapter that the whole difficulty of the genetic problem of concepts in childhood lies in attempting to understand the internal contradiction which is inherent in children's concepts. From the very earliest days of his development, words become the means of communication and mutual understanding between children and adults. As Ach has demonstrated, it is precisely because of this functional factor of mutual understanding by using words, that the precise meaning of words comes into being, and that they become the carriers of concepts. Without this functional factor of mutual understanding, says Usnadze, no sound complex could ever become a carrier of any meaning whatsoever, and no concepts of any kind could be formed.

But it is well known that verbal understanding and verbal contact between adults and children appears extremely early and this fact, as has already been pointed out, causes many researchers to assume that concepts develop just as easily. Meanwhile, as we have stated above whilst citing Usnadze's belief, fully fledged concepts develop relatively late in children's thinking, whilst mutual verbal understanding between children and adults is established very early on.

'It is clear', says Usnadze, 'that words which have not yet reached the stage of fully developed concepts, take over the function of the latter and can serve as a means of communication between speaking individuals.'[28] So the researchers is faced with the problem of discovering the principles behind the development of these forms of thinking, which should be regarded not as concepts, but as their functional equivalents. This contradiction between the late development of concepts and the early development of verbal understanding finds its real resolution in pseudoconcepts, as a form of thinking in complexes which synchronizes the processes of thinking and understanding between children and adults.

Thus, we have been able to discover both the causes and the meaning of this exceptionally important form of thinking in complexes in children. Now it only remains for us to comment on the subject of the genetic significance of this final stage in the development of childhood thinking. At this stage, it is perfectly understandable why, in the light of this dualistic functional nature of the pseudoconcept described above, this stage in the development of children's thinking acquires an entirely exceptional genetic significance. It serves as a connecting link between thinking in complexes and thinking in concepts. It connects these two important stages in the development of children's thinking. It reveals to us the process of the making of children's concepts. Owing to the contradiction inherent in it whilst it is a complex, it already contains the nucleus of a future concept which is developing inside it. Thus, verbal communication with adults becomes a powerful moving force and a vital factor in the development of concepts in children. For a child, the transition from thinking in complexes to thinking in concepts is accomplished imperceptibly, because the pseudoconcepts already practically coincide with adult concepts.

So, a peculiar genetic situation is created which is more likely to illustrate a general rule than the exception in the intellectual development of children. The peculiarity of this genetic situation is due to the fact that at this time a child begins to make actual use of, and to operate with, concepts before he becomes consciously aware of their existence. In children, the concept in itself and for others develops before the concept for himself. The concept in itself and for others is already present in a pseudoconcept and is the basic genetic prerequisite for the development of concepts in the true sense of the word.[29]

Therefore, a pseudoconcept is regarded as a special phase in the development of thinking in complexes in children, and it concludes the whole second stage and leads into the third stage in the development of thinking in children, at the same time serving as a connecting link between them. It represents a bridge which is erected between the realms of concrete visual–figurative and abstract thinking in children.

## XVI

By having described this last concluding phase in the development of thinking in complexes in children, we have exhausted a whole epoch of conceptual development. In a general overview we do not intend to reiterate any of its distinctive features which we kept pointing out along the way whilst analysing each separate form of thinking in complexes. We think that in our analysis we have managed to depict sufficiently clearly thinking in complexes from below as well as from above, having discovered the signs which distinguish it from syncretic images, on the one hand, and from concepts, on the other.

The absence of unity of associations, the absence of hierarchies and the concrete visible character of the connections underlying it, the special relationship among the individual elements and the universal law which determines the structure of generalizations as a whole, have passed before us in all their distinctiveness and in all their striking variety, including both lower and higher types of generalizations. We have been able to observe the logical substance of different types of thinking in complexes, with a clarity only made possible by the experiment. For this reason we feel that we have to indicate certain features of our experimental analysis which, if misunderstood, might give rise to incorrect conclusions about what has been said above.

An experimentally elicited process of concept formation is never a mirror reflection of the actual genetic process of development as it occurs in real life. However, we do not consider this to be a drawback, but rather an enormous advantage of experimental analysis. Experimental analysis allows us to discover the very essence of the genetic process of concept formation in a theoretical form. It provides us with the key to a real understanding and insight into the actual process of concept formation as it takes place in a child's real life conditions.

It is for this reason that dialectical thinking does not set the logical and the historical methods of study against each other. According to Engels' famous definition,

> The logical method of research . . . is the same as the historical method, except that it is free from the historical form and from interfering accidents. The logical thought process starts at the same point as history and its subsequent development will be nothing more than a reflection of the historical process in an abstract and theoretically consistent form; an adjusted reflection, but one which is adjusted according to the laws which the real course of history itself has taught us, because each moment in the development can be studied at its most mature stage, in its classic form.[30]

If we apply this general methodological position to our actual investigation, we can say that the basic forms of concrete thinking which we have discussed, represent the most significant moments of development at their most mature stages and their classic form, and in their pure aspect brought to its logical conclusion. In a real process of development, they would be found in a complicated and mixed state and, as is suggested by experimental analysis, their logical description represents a reflection of the real process of conceptual development in its abstract form.

Therefore, the most significant moments in the process of conceptual development revealed by our experimental analysis should be viewed by us from the historical point of view, and should be perceived as reflections of the most significant stages which occur in the actual process of development of children's thinking. At this point, historical evaluation becomes the key to the logical conception of concepts. The developmental point of view becomes the starting point for the clarification of the process as a whole and also of each of its individual moments.

As it has, quite correctly, been pointed out by Krueger, one of the founders of contemporary 'developmental psychology', inevitably a purely morphological investigation of complicated psychological phenomena and manifestations without genetic analysis, is bound to be imperfect. 'Purely morphological analysis', says Krueger,

> at best turns out imperfect. The more complicated are the processes being studied, the more likely are they to rely more heavily on earlier experience as their precondition, and the more they require a clear-cut statement of the problem at hand, a methodical comparison and, from the point of view of the inevitability of development, conceptual associations, even in cases where nothing more than the elements of activity which are contained in one single section of consciousness are involved.[31]

A purely morphological study, as Krueger shows, is all the more impossible where there is a higher level of organization and differentiation of psychological phenomena.

> Without a genetic analysis and synthesis, without a general comparative study of the previous history of some whole and its constituent parts, we cannot even decide what we

should regard as its elementary constituents and the bearers of essential connections. Only a comparative study of a large number of genetic cross-sections can, step by step, reveal to us the real framework and connections between individual psychological structures.

Development is the key to the understanding of any higher forms of being. 'The highest genetic law', says Gesell,

> seems to be the following: each process of development in the present bases itself on a past development. Development is not just a simple function, which can be adequately summed up as the X of hereditary components plus the Y of environmental components. It is rather a historic complex, which at each stage reflects the past which forms part and parcel of it. To put it another way, the artificial duality of heredity and environment is misleading. It conceals from us the fact that development is an uninterrupted, self-conditioning process and not a puppet controlled by the pulling of two strings.[32]

So it turns out that an experimental analysis of concept formation inevitably brings us very close to functional and genetic analysis. Therefore, following a morphological analysis, we should attempt to bring closer together the main forms of thinking in complexes, and the forms of thinking which are actually found in the process of development in children which we have discovered. We should attempt to include a historical perspective and a genetic point of view in our experimental analysis. On the other hand, we ought to try to shed some light on the actual process of development of children's thinking, using the data which we have obtained in the process of experimental analysis. Such a gathering together of the experimental and the genetic analyses, and the experimental data and reality, will inevitably lead us away from morphological analysis of thinking in complexes towards an investigation of complexes in action, in their actual functional significance and in their real genetic structure.

The main problem facing us, therefore, is the bringing closer together of the morphological and functional, or experimental and genetic, analyses. Our task is to use the facts observed in the process of actual development to verify the data obtained from experimental analysis and to illuminate the actual process of conceptual development by using these data.

## XVII

We might summarize in the following way the basic conclusion to be drawn from our study of the second stage of conceptual development: a child at the age of thinking in complexes thinks about the same things as an adult (the same subjects) from the point of view of the meaning of words, thus making communication possible between them, but he thinks about the same things in a different way, using a different process and employing different intellectual functions.

If this theory is really correct, then it should be possible to verify it functionally. This means that if we examine adult concepts and children's complexes in action, the differences in their psychological nature should become clearly apparent. If children's complexes are different from concepts, it would mean that the activity of thinking in complexes would manifest itself in a different way than the activity of conceptual thinking. We therefore wish, at this stage, to carry out a brief comparison between the results of our investigation and other data established by psychological research regarding the characteristics of children's thinking, and the development of primitive thinking in general, and by applying an operational test, to subject the properties of thinking in complexes which we have discovered to a functional verification.

The first phenomenon from the history of development of children's thinking which, for our purposes here, attracts our attention, is the well known process of transfer of meaning of a child's first words by a purely associative route. If we can find out which groups of objects are included and how the child combines them during the transfer of meaning of his first words, then we can see a mixed example of what we, in our experiments, have called the associative complex and the syncretic image. We will use an example which we have borrowed from Idelberger.

> On day 251, Idelberger's son uses the word 'wauwau' for a china figure of a little girl on the sideboard, which he likes to play with. On day 307 he uses the same word 'wauwau' for a dog which is barking outside, as well as for a portrait of his grandparents, his rocking horse and the wall clock. On day 331, for a fur stole with a dog's head and also for another stole without a dog's head. At the same time his attention is particularly drawn to the glass eyes. On day 334, the same name is given to a squeaky rubber toy manikin and on day 396, to the black studs on his father's shirt. On day 433 the child utters the same word when he sees a string of pearls and also when he looks at a bath thermometer.

After having analysed this example, Werner concludes that the child designates by the word 'wauwau' a great number of objects which can be classified in the following way: firstly, dogs and toy dogs, then small oblong objects which are reminiscent of dolls like the rubber manikin, the bath thermometer, etc., and secondly, studs, pearls, etc., as small objects. This assortment is based on the attribute of an oblong shape or a shining surface which is reminiscent of eyes.[33]

Thus we can see that the association of separate concrete objects in children happens according to the complex principle and the entire first chapter in the history of the development of word use in children is filled with such natural complexes.

In a well known example often cited the child, at first, calls a duck swimming in a pond 'quack', then he applies the same name to any liquid substance, including tea and the milk in his own bottle. Then, one day he notices an eagle depicted on a coin, and the coin is also called by the same name, and this proves sufficient reason to call all round objects reminiscent of coins by the same name after that.[34] Here we have a typical example of a chain complex, where each object is incorporated into the complex exclusively on the basis of a known common attribute with another element, but the essential character of this attribute can be subject to endless variation.

This complex nature of children's thinking is responsible for the appearance of one of its peculiar qualities, namely, that the same word can have completely different meanings in different situations, i.e. they can depict different objects, and in exceptional circumstances which are of particular interest to us, a child can use the same word to combine even opposite meanings, if only they can be related to one another in the same way as a knife and fork.

A child who uses the word 'before' to express a chronological relationship of 'before' and also 'after', or the word 'tomorrow' in the sense of depicting both the day after and the day before, is exhibiting a full analogy with the fact, long ago noticed by investigators, that in ancient languages like Hebrew, Chinese and Latin, the same word contained quite opposite meanings. For example, the Romans used the same word for high and deep. This kind of co-existence of opposite meanings in one word can only be possible as a result of thinking in complexes, where each concrete object, whilst being incorporated in a complex, does not, by this very fact, blend with the other elements of the complex, but retains all of its concrete independence.

## XVIII

One additional and extremely interesting characteristic of children's thinking exists which may serve as an excellent test for a functional verification of thinking in complexes. In children who already have reached a higher level of development than those discussed above, thinking in complexes may already take on the character of pseudoconcepts. However, because the nature of a pseudoconcept is that of a complex, it should reveal differences in its activity despite its external resemblance to real concepts.

For a long time now, researchers have noticed one extremely interesting characteristic of thinking, first described by Lévy-Bruhl in relationship to primitive societies, then by Storch in mental patients and by Piaget in relationship to children. This characteristic of primitive thinking, which apparently typifies the attributes of thinking in its early genetic stages, is generally referred to as 'participation'. What is understood by this term is the relationship which primitive thought creates between two objects or two phenomena, which are regarded as either being identical or having a very strong influence on one another without, however, the existence of any spatial contact nor any sort of other intelligible causal relationship between them.

Piaget, who accepts the cited definition, himself contributes very profound observations related to this type of participation in the thinking of children, i.e. the establishment of such relationships between different objects and actions by children, which otherwise would seem absolutely incomprehensible from the logical point of view, and which do not have any foundations in any objective relationships between things.[35]

Lévy-Bruhl cites the following case as the most striking example of this kind of participation in the thinking of primitive man: according to Von den Steinen, the northern Brazilian tribe Bororo prides itself on the fact that members of the tribe can be found among the arara or red parrots. 'This does not only mean', says Lévy-Bruhl, 'that after their deaths they become araras, and not just that the araras are Bororos in metamorphosis . . . the question is about something entirely different. According to Von den Steinen, who did not want to believe it, but who had to make sure because of the categorical confirmation he received from them, "the Bororos coolly confirm that they *indeed are* araras, in the same way as if a caterpillar were to say that it is a butterfly". This is not a name which they have appropriated for themselves nor a kinship on which they insist. What they understand by it, is an essential identity.'[36]

Storch, who has subjected some of the archaically primitive thinking found in schizophrenia to meticulous analysis, has also been able to disclose the same phenomenon of participation in the thinking of psychotics.[37] However, we think that up till now, the phenomenon of participation itself has not received a sufficiently convincing psychological explanation. In our opinion this has happened for two reasons.

Firstly, because whilst investigating the particular association which primitive thinking makes between different things, the researchers have, as a rule, studied this phenomenon exclusively from the point of view of its content, as an independent feature, at the same time ignoring those functions, those forms of thinking and those intellectual operations with which similar associations are determined and worked out. Usually, the investigators have studied the finished product and not the actual process of how the given product has come into being. This is the reason why the product of primitive thinking itself has taken on a mysterious and nebulous character in their eyes.

The second complication which arises in connection with attempts to provide a correct psychological explanation for this phenomenon, must be considered to be the fact that the researchers do not bring these participation phenomena in close enough contact with all the other associations and relationships which are established by primitive thinking. As a rule, these associations only ever fall into the researchers' field of vision as a result of their exclusive nature, when they happen to deviate blatantly from our habitual logical mode of thinking. The Bororos' assertion that they are red parrots, seems so absurd from our usual viewpoint, that it immediately attracts the attention of the investigators.

Meanwhile, a careful analysis of those associations created by primitive thinking and which do not outwardly deviate from our logic, reaffirms that the same essential mechanism of thinking in complexes lies at the foundations of both types of associations.

If one takes account of the fact that a child at a given stage of development has mastered thinking in complexes, that words for him are means for the designation of complexes containing concrete objects, and that the pseudoconcept is the basic form he uses for generalizations and associations which he is in the process of establishing, then it will become absolutely clear that, with logical inevitability, participation is destined to be the product of such thinking in complexes, i.e. associations and relationships between things must arise in this thinking process which would be impossible and unthinkable from the point of view of conceptual thinking.

In actual fact, we understand perfectly well that identical things can be incorporated into different complexes according to their own different actual attributes and that, consequently, they may end up having the most varied names and designations depending on which complex they belong to.

On several occasions during our experimental investigations we have had the opportunity to observe this type of participation, i.e. the simultaneous allocation of some actual object to two or more complexes, thus resulting in one object ending up with several names. In such cases not only is participation not exceptional, but rather it becomes the rule for thinking in complexes, and we would consider it a miracle if such associations, impossible from the point of view of our logical thinking and which are given this name, did not become apparent at every step of the way in the process of primitive thinking.

In equal measure, the key to the understanding of participation in the thinking processes of primitive people should also be seen in the fact that this primitive thinking is not carried on in concepts, that its character is of the complex type and that, consequently, in these languages, words have an entirely different functional application and are used in different ways, and are not simply a means for the creation and carrying of concepts, but that they play a role similar to that of a family name used for the naming of groups of real objects which have been combined according to a known factual kinship.

This type of thinking in complexes, as it has quite rightly been called by Werner, just like in children, should inevitably result in such an interweaving of complexes which would then generate participation. At the foundation of this thinking process lies a visual group of real objects. Werner's excellent analysis of this primitive thinking process has convinced us that the key to the understanding of the phenomenon of participation is to be found in the peculiar combination of speech and thinking which characterizes a given stage in the historical development of human intellect.

Finally, as Storch has convincingly demonstrated, schizophrenic thinking also has such a complex character. In the thinking of schizophrenics, we see a multitude of peculiar motives and tendencies, about which Storch remarks that 'they all have one feature in common, namely that they can be related to the primitive stage of thinking . . . The individual notions in the thinking of these patients, are combined in *complex aggregate attributes*'.[38] The schizophrenic regresses from conceptual thinking to a more primitive thinking stage which, according to Bleuler, is characterized by an abundant use of images and symbols. 'It may well be', says Storch, 'that the most distinguished feature of primitive thinking is that in place of abstract concepts, the *full concrete images* are used.'[39]

It is precisely in this that Thurnwald sees the basic characteristic of the thinking of primitive people. 'The thinking of primitive man', he says, 'makes use of aggregate global impressions of phenomena . . . They think in entirely concrete images as they are presented by reality.'[40] These visual and collective formations which replace concepts in the forefront of the thinking process in schizophrenics, are images analogous to concepts which substitute for our logical categorical structures in the primitive stages (Storch).

Therefore, it seems that participation is a general formal symptom of the primitive stage in the development of thinking, as observed in the thinking of psychotics, primitive people and in children, specifically a symptom of thinking in complexes, even when the exceptional singularity which differentiates each of these three types of thinking is taken into account, and that the mechanism of thinking in complexes and the functional use of words as familial insignia or names always underpins this phenomenon.

It is for this reason that we do not think that Lévy-Bruhl's interpretation of participation is correct, because whilst analysing the meaning of the Bororos' assertion that they are, in effect, red parrots, Lévy-Bruhl constantly uses concepts taken from our own logic, and he assumes that this assertion signifies the identical nature or sameness of beings in primitive thinking. In our opinion, no more profoundly erroneous interpretation of this phenomenon is possible. If the Bororos really did indeed think in logical concepts, then their assertion could not be understood in any other way than in this sense.

However, since words are not carriers of concepts for the Bororos, but only represent familial designations of concrete objects, then, for them, this assertion must have a completely different meaning. The word arara, with which they designate red parrots and under which they classify themselves, is a common name within a certain complex to which both birds and people relate. This assertion does not signify an identification of parrots with people, in the same way as the assertion that two people go under the same family name and are related to one another does not indicate the sameness of these two beings.

## XIX

But if we turn to the history of the development of our speech, we will see that the mechanism of thinking in complexes, with all its inherent characteristics, is the basis of the development of our language. The first thing that we can learn from contemporary linguistics is that, according to Peterson,[41] it is essential to distinguish between the meaning of a word or expression and its objective reference,[42] i.e. the objects which this word or expression indicates.

There can be one meaning and various objects and, vice versa, there can be various meanings and only one object. Whether we say 'the victor at Jena' or 'the vanquished of Waterloo' the person we are talking about (Napoleon) is one and the same in both cases. But the meaning of the two expressions is different. Some words, for example personal names, have only one function, namely to denote an object. So contemporary linguistics does make a distinction between the meaning and the objective reference of words.

If we apply this to the problem under scrutiny, of thinking in complexes in children, we could say that children's words coincide with adult words in their objective references, i.e. they indicate the same objects and refer to the same range of phenomena. But they do not coincide in their meaning.

This coincidence in the objective reference and the lack of it in the meanings of words, which we have discovered to be the most essential characteristic of thinking in complexes in children, can again be said to be the rule and not the exception in language development. We mentioned above, whilst summing up the most significant result of our research, that from the point of view of the meaning of a word, children think the same as adults, i.e. about the same objects, and that as a result mutual understanding becomes possible, but that they think about the same content in a different way, using a different method and different intellectual operations.

The same formula, in its entirety, can also be applied both to the history of the development and the psychology of language in general. Here, at every step of the way, we find factual confirmation and proof which convince us of the validity of this proposition. In order for words to be able to coincide in their objective reference, it is necessary for them to denote the same object. But they may denote the same object by different means.

A typical example of such a coincidence of the objective reference co-existing with a non-coincidence of the thought operations which are at the basis of the meaning of the word, is the presence of synonyms in every language. In Russian the words 'luna' ['moon'] and 'mesjac' ['moon'] depict the same object, but they depict it in a different way which is contained in the history of the development of each of the words. 'Luna' is by its origin connected with a Latin word, which means 'capricious', 'changeable', 'whimsical'. The person who gave the moon this name obviously wanted to emphasize the inconstancy of its form, its transition from one phase into another, as the most essential difference from the other heavenly bodies.

The meaning of the word 'mesjac' is connected with the meaning of 'izmerjat' ['to measure']. 'Mesjac' means 'measuring instrument'. The person who gave the moon this name wished to refer to it by emphasizing another property, namely, that by means of the measurement of the lunar phases, one can calculate [the passage of] time.

In a similar fashion, as regards the words used by children and adults, one could say that they are also synonyms in the sense that they depict the same object. They are names for the same things and thus they coincide in their nominative function, but the thought operations underlying them are different. The manner in which a child and an adult arrive at this naming of things, that operation by which they think about a given object and the meaning of the word which is equivalent to this operation, turn out to be essentially different in the two instances.

In exactly the same way, the same objects in different languages coincide in their nominative function, but in different languages the same object may be named after completely different features. In Russian the word 'portnoj' ['tailor'] developed from the old-Russian 'port' – a piece of tissue, cloth, coverlet. In French and German the same subject is referred to after a different feature – the word 'to cut'.[43]

'So' – to formulate this proposition – it is important to differentiate two aspects of what is commonly referred to as the meaning of a word: the meaning of the expression in the proper sense of the word and its function as a *name*, [which] relates to this or some other object, its *objective reference*.' From this it becomes clear that when the meaning of a word is being discussed, it is necessary to differentiate the meaning of a word in the proper sense of the word from the denotation of an object which is inherent in this word (Schor).

We think that the differentiation of the meaning of a word and its relationship to certain objects, the distinction between the meaning and the name of the word, provides us with the key to the correct analysis of the development of thinking in children in its early stages. With good reason Schor observes that the difference between these two aspects, the meaning or content of an expression and the object which it denotes in the so-called meaning of a word, manifests itself clearly in the vocabulary of children. Children's words can coincide in their objective reference with adult words and fail to do so in their meaning.[44]

If we turn to the history of the development of words in every language and to the transfer of the meaning of the word, we will see, as strange as this may appear at first glance, that in the process of development words change their meanings in the same way as they do in the case of children. Just like in the example we cited above, where a large number of the most varied, and from our point of view, not comparable objects were given the same name 'wauwau' by the child, we find similar transfers of meaning occurring in the history of the development of words, which indicates that they are based on a mechanism of thinking in complexes, that words are used and applied here in a different manner than in mature thinking using concepts.

Let us take the history of the Russian word 'sutki' ['24 hours'] as an example. Originally it signified a 'shov' ['seam'], the place where two pieces of tissue are united, something woven together. Then it began to signify every junction, a corner in a cottage, the place where two walls come together. Further, it acquired the metaphorical sense of 'sumerki' ['twilight'], the junction of day and night, and after that, it covered the period from twilight to twilight or the time period that includes morning and evening twilight. It began to signify a day and a night, that is, 'sutki' in the real sense of that word. Thus we see that in the historical development of this word such diverse phenomena as a seam, a corner in a cottage, twilight and 24 hours, are combined into a single complex according to the same visual characteristic used by the child to combine different objects into one complex.

'Anyone who begins to investigate the questions of etymology for the first time is struck by the vapidity and triviality of some of the expressions which are tied to the name of certain objects', says Schor. Why do both 'svin'ja' ['swine'] and 'zhenshchina' ['woman'] mean 'one who gives birth', why are both 'medved' ['bear'] and 'bober' ['beaver'] called 'burymi' ['brown'], why should 'izmerjajuschij' ['the measuring one'] refer to exactly the moon, 'revushcij' ['howler'] to a 'byk' ['bull'], 'koljuchij' ['thorny'] to a 'bor' ['forest']? If one were to investigate the history of these words, it would become apparent that it is not logical necessity and not even associations which have become established in concepts which have given rise to them, but purely imagistic concrete complexes and associations of the very same type we were able to observe in children's thinking. Some sort of concrete feature is singled out, after which the object gets its name.

'Korova' ['cow'] means 'rogataja' ['horned'], but in other languages analogous words emerged from the same root which also mean 'horned', but indicate the goat, the deer or other horned animals. 'Mysh' ['mouse'] means 'thief', 'bull' means howler, 'doch' ['daughter'] means milkmaid, 'ditja' ['child'] and 'deva' ['maiden'] are connected with the word 'doit' ['to milk'] and designated a 'sucker' or a 'wet nurse'.

If we examine the laws which govern the coming together of families of words, we will see that new phenomena and objects are named after one attribute which is not an essential feature from the point of view of logic, and which does not logically express the essence of the phenomenon in question. It never happens that a name which is only just emerging becomes a concept. Therefore, from a logical point of view, on the one hand, the name proves inadequate as it turns out to be too narrow, and on the other, it is too wide. Thus, for example, 'the horned one' as a name for a cow or 'thief' for a mouse are too narrow, in that the ideas of a cow and a mouse are not exhausted by the attributes which are contained in these names.

On the other hand they are too wide because the same names may be applicable to many other objects as well. It is for this reason that, in the history of language, what we observe is a constant, uninterrupted struggle between conceptual thinking and primordial thinking in complexes. The complex name chosen because of a certain attribute, contradicts the concept it depicts and, as a result, a struggle between the concept and the image which underpins the word ensues. Then the image becomes erased, is forgotten and effaced from the speaker's consciousness and the connection between the sound and the concept as the meaning of the word becomes incomprehensible to us.

For example, nowadays no speaker of Russian who uses the word 'okno' ['window'] knows that it signifies the place to which one looks or the place where light passes through, and that it does not include any suggestion not only of a frame, etc., but not even the concept of an aperture. Still we commonly use the word 'okno' to denote a frame with glass panes and completely forget the word's etymological connection with the word 'oko' ['eye'].

In the same way 'chernila' ['ink'] once denoted writing fluid and indicated its external attribute – the black colour.[45] The person who called this substance 'chernila' included it into the complex of black things in a purely associative way. But nowadays this in no way prevents us from talking about red, green or blue ink, forgetting that from a perceptual point of view such a word combination is absurd.

If we turn to the transfer of names, then we will see that they are transferred by association, by contiguity or by similarity in reverse, i.e. not according to logical thinking, but according to the laws of thinking in complexes. Even now, whilst creating new words, we observe a large number of extremely interesting processes of such complex allocation of a wide variety of objects to one single group. For example, when we speak about the neck of a bottle, a table leg, a door handle or the arm of a river we are carrying out precisely this kind of complex allocation of objects to one general group.

The essence of this kind of name transfer is that the function carried out by the word is neither semasiological nor interpretative. Here, the word fulfils a nominative or indicative function. It denotes, names a thing. In other words, in this case a word is not a sign for some meaning with which it is bound up in the act of thinking, but a perceptually given thing which is associatively connected to another perceptually given thing. And in so far as the name is bound up with the thing which it designates by association, so, as a rule, the transfer of the name takes place according to various associations, which it would prove impossible to reconstruct without intimate knowledge of the historical circumstances of the act of the transfer of this name.

What this means is that entirely concrete factual connections underpin such transfers as the complexes which are created in the thinking of children. If we apply this idea to children's speech, we could say that when a child understands adult speech, something occurs akin to what we pointed out in the examples cited above. Whilst pronouncing the same word, a child and an adult are referring to the same person or object, to Napoleon for example, but one of them thinks of Napoleon as the victor at Jena, whilst the other, as the vanquished at Waterloo.

According to Potebnya's wonderful statement, language is a means for understanding oneself.[46] It is for this reason that we must study the function which is carried out by language or speech in relationship to children's own thinking, and we should point out here that, aided by speech, a child understands himself differently than he understands an adult through the same speech. This means that the thinking operations which a child carries out with the aid of speech do not coincide with the operations carried out in the thinking of an adult when he pronounces one and the same word.

We have already cited the opinion of one writer who says that the first word cannot be viewed as a simple sign for the concept. Rather, it is an image, a picture, a mental drawing of the concept, a little story told about it.[47] In actual fact it is an artistic creation. Because of this it has a concrete complex character and it can, simultaneously, depict several objects which can well be related to one and the same complex.

It is more correct to put it in the following way: when a person names an object with the aid of such a picture/concept, he allocates it to a certain complex, combines it into a single group with a large number of other objects. Pogodin[48] is fully justified in saying about the origin of the word 'veslo' ['oar'] in the word 'vesti' ['to lead/drive'] that 'veslo' might have been more appropriately used for a boat, as a means of transportation, or a pack horse, or a carriage. We see that all these objects belong as it were to a single complex [of the kind] we also observe in the thinking of the child.

## XX

The language of deaf and dumb children, for whom the basic motive which leads to the formation of children's pseudoconcepts is absent, presents an extremely interesting example of pure thinking in complexes. We have pointed out above that the circumstance which is the determining factor in the formation of pseudoconcepts in children, is that a child does not create his complexes freely, by combining objects into integral groups, but that he finds words already tied to definite groups of objects in adult expressions. This is the reason why a child's complex coincides with concepts in adult thinking in its physical affiliation. A child and an adult who understand one another when they utter the word 'dog', relate this word to the same object, having in mind the same real content, but at the same time one of them is thinking of the concrete complex of dogs, whilst the other's thought is the abstract concept about a dog.

In the language of deaf and dumb children this situation loses its impact because they are deprived of the possibility of verbal contact with adults and, left to themselves, they are able to form complexes which are freely designated by the same word. Thanks to this context, it is in their thinking that the characteristics of thinking in complexes come to the fore with particular distinctness and clarity.

Thus, in the language of the deaf and dumb, a tooth can have three separate meanings. These are white, stone and tooth. These different names are combined in one complex which requires the addition of another demonstrative or figurative gesture in order to define the objective reference of the given meaning. These two word functions in the language of the deaf and dumb are, as it were, separate. The deaf and dumb person shows a tooth and then either points to its surface or makes a throwing gesture with his hand and thus indicates which object the word has to be related to.

We also observe an extremely interesting phenomenon at every step of the way in the adult thinking process. It is that even though the formation of concepts and their use is accessible to the adult thinking process, most of this thinking is not devoted to such activities.

If we examine the most primitive forms of human thinking as they appear in dreams, there we will see this primeval, primitive mechanism of thinking in complexes, expressed in visual fusion, condensation and transfer of images. Investigation of the generalizations which can be observed in dreams, as is rightly pointed out by Kretschmer, provides the key to the proper understanding of primitive thinking and does away with the prejudice that generalization in thinking only appears in its most developed form, i.e. in the form of concepts.

We could point to Jaensch's studies, which have shown that particular generalizations or combinations of images do exist in the sphere of purely visual thinking, and which can, as it were, be regarded as concrete analogues of concepts or visual concepts, and which Jaensch refers to as meaningful compositions and fluxion. In adult thinking we often observe a transition from conceptual thinking to concrete, complex and transitional thinking.

Pseudoconcepts are not the sole and exclusive property of children. Our own everyday life is very frequently dominated by thinking in pseudoconcepts. From the point of view of dialectical logic the concepts which appear in our ordinary speech cannot be seen as concepts in the strict sense of the word. They rather represent general ideas about things. However, there is no doubt that they exemplify a transitional stage which leads from complexes and pseudoconcepts to a real concepts in the dialectical sense.

## XXI

The process of thinking in complexes as observed in children, described above, represents only the fountainhead of the history of conceptual development. But the development of concepts in children also has a second source. This second source comprises the third major stage in the development of children's thinking, which, like the second one, can, in its turn, be divided into several separate phases or steps. In this sense, the pseudoconcept which we examined above, constitutes a transitional stage between thinking in complexes and the second source or root of the development of concepts in children.

We have already mentioned that the process of development of concepts in children is presented in our account in the way in which it has been revealed in the artificial conditions of experimental analysis. These artificial conditions show the process of conceptual development in its logical sequence and, therefore, this inevitably deviates from the actual process of conceptual development. This is the reason why the sequence of individual stages and separate phases within each stage do not coincide in the actual process of children's development of concepts and in our depiction of it.

Whilst examining the question which concerns us here, we have attempted to follow its genetic route at all times, but we have also tried to present some of the individual genetic aspects in their most matured and classical form, and this has sometimes made it necessary to deviate from the complicated, twisting and, at times, zigzagging road along which the actual development of children's concepts has to meander.

So, once again, whilst passing on to the description of the third and last stage in the development of children's concepts, we have to point out that, in reality, the first phases of the third stage do not necessarily start immediately the moment thinking in complexes has completed its full cycle of development. On the contrary, we have seen that the higher forms of thinking in complexes, in the guise of pseudoconcepts, represent such a transitional form, where our everyday thinking, based on ordinary speech, often lingers.

Meanwhile, the primary elements of these forms, which we will now describe, predate the formation of pseudoconcepts considerably, but from the point of view of their logical essence, they represent, as has been said above, the second and, as it were, independent source in the history of conceptual development and, as we shall now be able to see, they fulfil a completely different genetic function, i.e. they play a different role in the process of conceptual development in children.

The most characteristic feature of the process of thinking in complexes which we have described above, is the milestone of the establishment of associations and relationships which constitute this type of thinking. At this stage a child's thinking assembles the individual perceived objects into complexes and assembles them into specific groups, in this way laying the foundations for the integration of unco-ordinated impressions and taking the first steps along the road towards generalization of the unco-ordinated elements of experience.

But a concept in its natural developed state presupposes not just the unification and generalization of separate concrete elements of experience, but also postulates the segregation, abstraction and isolation of the individual elements and the ability to regard these segregated, abstract elements outside the framework of the concrete and factual associations which they are given by experience.

Thinking in complexes turns out to be inept in this respect. It is totally imbued with an excess or an overproduction of associations and a dearth of abstractions. The process of the segregation of attributes in thinking in complexes is exceptionally ineffectual. Meanwhile, as we have said, an authentic concept is dependent on the processes of analysis to the same extent as on the processes of synthesis. Both stratification and assembly, in equal measure, are indispensable internal factors in the building of a concept. Analysis and synthesis, according to Goethe's famous words, assume the existence of the other, like breathing in and breathing out.[49] All this applies in equal measure not just to thinking in general, but to the building of each individual concept as well.

If we wanted to analyse the actual process of development of thinking in children we would, of course, be able to find neither a separate isolated line of development of the function of complex formation, nor a separate line of development of the function of stratification of the whole into its separate elements.

In actual fact both are seen in a combined, intermingled state and it is only in the interests of scientific analysis that we are presenting these two lines as separate, in an attempt to examine each of them with the greatest possible degree of accuracy. However, this distinction of the two lines should not simply be viewed as a conventional method used in our analysis, which we could replace at will with any other method. On the contrary, it is rooted in the very nature of things, because the psychological nature of each of these functions is fundamentally different.

So, it can be seen that the genetic function of the third stage in the development of children's thinking is the development of stratification, analysis and abstraction. In this respect the first phase of this third stage is strikingly close to the pseudoconcept. The unification of different concrete objects is accomplished because of the maximum similarity between its various elements. But because this similarity can never be complete, we end up with an extremely interesting situation from the psychological point of view, namely, that where his attention is concerned, the child may well create unfairly auspicious conditions for the various attributes of a given object.

These attributes, which in their entirety reflect maximum resemblance to the model which has been provided, tend to attract the focus of the child's attention and, as a result, undergo the process of segregation and abstraction from all the remaining attributes, which remain on the periphery of his attention. Here, for the first time, we can observe, with some degree of clarity, the appearance of that process of abstraction whose nature is often difficult to discern, due to the fact that what has been abstracted is an entire, insufficiently intrinsically stratified group of attributes, which sometimes is nothing more than a product of a vague impression of the presence of common characteristics, and not a clear-cut segregation process of individual traits.

But, at least, a breach in the realm of children's integral perception has been opened. The attributes have been divided into two unequal parts, and the two processes, which Külpe's school has named positive and negative abstraction, have been identified. The concrete object no longer enters the complex and becomes part of the generalization with all its attributes and all its factual completeness intact, but on entering the complex, it leaves part of its attributes outside the door and thus becomes impoverished; however, on the other hand, the attributes which have served as the basis for its inclusion in the complex, stand out particularly boldly in the child's thinking. This generalization which the child creates on the basis of maximum likeness, can, simultaneously, be considered to be a more impoverished and a more enriched process than the pseudoconcept. It is richer than the pseudoconcept because it is constructed on a selection of what is important and essential from a general group of perceived traits. It is poorer than the pseudoconcept because the associations upon which this construction rests are extremely poor, and they can be reduced to nothing more than a vague impression of the presence of common characteristics or of maximum likeness.

## XXII

The second phase in the same process of development of concepts is the phase which could be called the period of potential concepts. Under experimental conditions, a child who finds himself in this phase of his development, as a rule, picks out a group of objects which have been generalized by him according to one common attribute. Yet again, we have before us a picture which, at first glance, is very reminiscent of pseudoconcepts and which could, judging by its outer appearance, be taken for a proper concept in the real sense. An identical product might have been obtained by an adult thinking in concepts. Its deceptive appearance and its superficial resemblance to a real concept show that the potential concept and the pseudoconcept are related. But they are essentially dissimilar by nature.

It was Groos who first introduced to psychology the distinction between real and potential concepts, and he made this distinction the starting point for his analysis of concepts. 'A "potential" concept', says Groos,

> need not be more than an effect of habit. As such, in its most elementary form, it amounts to the fact that we 'expect', or to be more precise, we '*set our minds*' on similar causes eliciting *similar general impressions* . . . If a 'potential' concept really is anything like what has just been described, namely a 'set' to focus on what is routine, then one can say that it can already be observed in children at a very early stage . . . I believe it to be an indispensable precondition for the formation of intellectual judgements, but on its own it does not contain *anything intellectual*.[50]

So this potential concept can be considered a pre-intellectual phenomenon, which makes its appearance in the history of development of thinking at a very early stage.

From this viewpoint, the majority of contemporary psychologists agree that the potential concept in the form in which we have just described it, can already be found in the thinking of animals. In this sense, we fully agree with Kroh, who rejects the generally accepted opinion that abstraction can only be observed for the first time in adolescense. 'Isolating abstraction', he says, 'is a tendency already observed in animals . . .'.

And, indeed, special experiments with domestic chickens to investigate abstraction processes of shapes and colours have revealed that, if not the potential concept as such, then something very much like it, which includes the isolating or separating off of individual attributes, takes place at very early stages in the behavioural development of animals.

From this point of view, Groos is quite right when he interprets the potential concept as the tendency to react in a habitual manner and refuses to see in it any sign of development in children's thinking, and reckons that, from the genetic point of view, it is just one of the pre-intellectual processes. Our first potential concepts, he says, are pre-intellectual. The activity of these potential concepts can be explained without taking any logical processes into account. In this case 'the relationship between a word and what we call its meaning, can sometimes be a simple association which does not contain any real semantic relations'.[51]

If we examine a child's first words, we see that indeed, in their meaning, they approach potential concepts. These concepts can be seen to be potential, firstly, because of their practical relation to a certain range of objects, and secondly, because of the process of isolating abstraction which makes up their fundamental characteristic. They are concepts of probability which have not yet realized this probability. They are not yet a concept, but are something that can become one.

In this connection, Bühler points out a perfectly valid analogy between a child's use of one of his usual words at the sight of a new object, and an ape's recognition that many things resemble a stick if they are found in circumstances where a stick proves to be useful and which, in different circumstances, would not remind him of it at all.[52] Köhler's experiments with tool using chimpanzees have shown that once the ape has used a stick as a tool to achieve his goal, he will extend the function of the tool to other objects which have something in common with the stick and are able to carry out its function.

The superficial resemblance to our concepts is striking. Such a phenomenon does, indeed, deserve the name of a potential concept. Köhler interprets the relevant results of his observations of chimpanzees in the following way. 'If one were to maintain', he says,

> that the stick in the visual field acquired a specific functional value for certain situations, and that this meaning will extend to all the other objects, whatever they might be, but which have, from the point of view of form and texture, certain objective traits in common with the stick, this leads us to the only view consistent with the behaviour observed in the animals.[53]

These experiments have shown that an ape begins to use the brim of a straw hat, shoes, a piece of wire, straw or a towel as a stick, i.e. the most varied objects, which have an oblong shape and which, in their external appearance, may serve as a substitute for a stick. So, to a certain extent, we can see that here, too, a process of generalization of a whole range of concrete objects occurs.

But the difference between this and Groos's potential concept lies in the fact that the latter talks about similar impressions, whilst here we are concerned with similar functional meaning. There, the potential concept is worked out in the realm of visual thinking, here, in the sphere of practically functional thinking. It is a well known fact that, according to Werner, these types of motor concepts or dynamic concepts, and according to Köhler, such functional values, can be observed in the thinking of children for a long time, right up to school age. It is known that the definition of concepts in children carries this kind of functional character. For a child, to define an object or a concept is tantamount to assigning a name to what the object does or, more often, what one can do with the aid of this object.

All the same, when the question concerns the definition of abstract concepts, this definition emerges as a concrete, usually active situation looming in the foreground, equivalent to the child's conception of the word in question. In his investigation of thinking and speech, Messer provides a strikingly apt definition of this kind of abstract concept, formulated by a child who had just started going to school. 'Reason', said the child, 'is when one is very hot and doesn't drink water'.[54] This type of concrete and, at the same time, functional meaning forms the natural psychological foundation of a potential concept.

It should be mentioned that, already at the stage of thinking in complexes, these types of potential concepts play an extremely important role, and they frequently merge during the formation of complexes. So, for example, as we have demonstrated above, in the associative complex and in many other types of complex, the building of the complex presupposes a selection of a certain attribute which is common to various elements. Granted, the fact that this attribute is highly unstable and is soon replaced by another attribute and that it, in no way, can be considered to be some privileged trait in comparison with all the remaining ones, is characteristic for pure thinking in complexes. This is not characteristic of potential concepts. Here, the given attribute which serves as the basis for the object's inclusion in a certain common group, is viewed as a privileged attribute which has been abstracted from the concrete group of attributes with which it is bound up in practice.

Let us remember that similar potential concepts play an extremely important role in the history of development of the words we use. Above, we gave many examples of how each new word comes into being on the basis of the segregation of some single attribute which has attracted our attention, and which then serves as a foundation for the construction of a generalization of a number of objects called or designated by the same word. Frequently, such potential concepts remain permanently at a given stage of their development and never progress to a real concept. But, in any case, they do play an extremely important role in the process of development of children's concepts. The significance of this role can be demonstrated in the fact that here, for the first time, by abstracting different attributes, the child transcends the physical situation and the concrete association of attributes, and by so doing creates the necessary precondition for a new combination of these attributes by applying a new principle. It is only by mastering the process of abstraction, together with the development of thinking in complexes, that the child is able to reach a stage where he can form real concepts. And it is this ability to form real concepts that constitutes the fourth and last phase in the development of thinking in children.

The concept is reached when a number of abstracted attributes are re-synthesized and the newly acquired abstract syntheses become the basic form of thinking, and when the child then applies this to the comprehension and interpretation of surrounding reality. At the same time, as has already been pointed out above, our study shows that the decisive role in the process of real concept formation belongs to words. It is precisely by using words that a child is able to focus his attention on certain attributes in an arbitrary manner, to synthesize them with the aid of words, and also to symbolize the abstract concept with words and to use it like a sign, on a higher level than any of the others which human thought has ever created.

It is a fact that the role of words is already prominent at the stage of thinking in complexes. Thinking in complexes, in the sense in which we have described it above, is impossible without words, which play the role of family names which unify groups of effect-related objects. In this respect, in contrast to a number of other writers, we are making a distinction between thinking in complexes as a given stage in the development of verbal thinking and that wordless, visual type of thinking which characterizes animal perceptions and which other authors, such as Werner, also designate as belonging to the complex type because of its tendency to amalgamate separate impressions contained within it.

In this sense, these writers tend to put an equals sign between the processes of condensation and transference as they appear in our dreams, and the thinking in complexes of primitive people,[55] which is one of the higher forms of verbal thinking and a product of a long standing historical evolution of human intellect and the definitive predecessor of concept thinking. Some authorities, among them Volkelt, go even further and tend to identify the complex, emotion-like thinking observed in spiders with that of the primitive verbal thinking of the human child.[56]

From our own point of view, there is a fundamental difference between these two phenomena, which separates the natural form of thinking, a product of biological evolution, from the historically evolved form of human intellect. However, by acknowledging that words also play a decisive role in thinking in complexes, we are not, in any way, obliged to identify the role that words play in thinking in complexes with their role in concept thinking.

On the contrary, first and foremost, we see the very distinction between complexes and concepts to be due to the fact that one generalization is the result of the use of words, whilst in the other it comes into being as a result of an entirely different functional application of the same word. A word is a sign. One can use this sign in different ways, it can be applied in a different way. It can serve as a means for various intellectual operations and it is precisely these different functional methods of using words, the different intellectual operations which are carried out with words, which are responsible for the fundamental distinction between complexes and concepts.


## XXIII


In relation to the subject which concerns us, the most important genetic conclusion to be drawn from our whole investigation is the basic thesis which states that it is only in adolescence that a child is able to reach the stage of concept thinking and to realize the third stage in the development of his intellect.

During the course of experiments designed to investigate adolescent thinking, we had the opportunity to observe how, along with the intellectual maturation process, the primitive forms of syncretic thinking and thinking in complexes progressively recede into the background, how potential concepts are observed less and less frequently in thinking and how, sporadically at first, then more and more frequently, the subject begins to create real concepts in his thinking process.

However, one must not imagine this process – of changeover of the various forms of thinking and separate phases in its development – as a purely mechanical process, where each new phase ensues only when the previous one is entirely over and has been accomplished. The picture of this developmental process turns out to be much more complicated. Various genetic forms exist just like strata of diverse geological epochs exist inside the Earth's crust. This situation is not the exception but rather the rule for behavioural development as a whole. We know that human behaviour does not constantly function only at the upper or highest levels of its development. The most recent forms of human behaviour, which have made their appearance in human history only in recent times, live side by side with the most ancient ones, and the daily variations of the different forms of behaviour, as Blonsky has so beautifully demonstrated, essentially reproduce the history of behavioural development throughout the ages.

The same is true in relation to the development of thinking in children. Here, too, a child who is in the process of mastering a higher form of thinking in concepts, by no means just abandons the more elementary forms. For a long time they still continue to be the dominant forms of thinking, both from the quantitative and the steering points of view in the whole range of his experience. As we have mentioned above, even an adult does not always think in concepts. Quite commonly, his thinking is carried out on the level of complexes, and sometimes it even descends to more elementary and more primitive forms.

But often the concepts themselves as well, both in adolescents and adults, do not rise above the level of pseudoconcepts, particularly where their use is limited solely to the realm of everyday experience, and even though they have all the attributes of concepts from the formal logical point of view, nonetheless they cannot be considered as concepts from the perspective of dialectical logic and they amount to nothing more than general ideas, i.e. complexes.

Therefore, adolescence cannot be said to be the age of culmination, but rather the age of crisis and maturation of thinking. Just as in all other respects, this age is also one of transition as regards the higher forms of thinking accessible to the human mind. This transitional character of adolescent thinking becomes particularly obvious when we observe its significance, not so much in a finished state, but in action and when we subject it to a functional test, for it is in action and in their application when these phenomena reveal their true psychological nature. At the same time, whilst investigating concepts in action, we have also uncovered a certain extremely important psychological rule, which underpins this new form of thinking and which sheds light on the character of intellectual activity in adolescence in general, and on the development of the adolescent's personality and his view of the world, as we hope to demonstrate below.

In this respect, the first thing that should be mentioned is the profound discrepancy which this experiment revealed between the formation of a concept and its verbal definition. This variance remains in force not only in adolescent thinking, but also in that of adults, sometimes even during the most highly elaborate thinking process. The presence of the concept and the awareness of it do not concur either in respect to the moment of its appearance, nor in respect to its activity. The former may appear earlier and function independently of the latter. The ability to analyse reality with the aid of concepts comes into being much earlier than the ability to analyse the concepts themselves.

This has been graphically demonstrated in experiments with adolescents, where, more often than not, the divergence between words and actions in the formation of concepts is the most characteristic feature of the age group, which points to the transitory nature of this thinking process. The adolescent forms a concept and is able to apply it correctly in a specific situation, but as soon as a verbal definition of the concept is required, this same thinking encounters the most serious problems and the definition of the concept ends up much more limited than its living application. In this we see direct confirmation that concepts do not arise simply as a result of logical processing of some elements of experience, or that the child does not think up his concepts himself, but that they come into being by a different route, and it is only later on that he becomes aware of them and subjects them to logical treatment.

At this stage another characteristic feature of the application of concepts in adolescence comes to light. The essence of this characteristic is that the adolescent tends to use concepts in a visual situation. At the time when this concept has not yet become detached from the concrete, visually perceived situation, it is able to guide the adolescent's thinking perfectly. The process of transferring the concept, i.e. applying it to other, completely different things, proves to be a lot more problematic, as when the segregated signs which have been synthesized into concepts, meet up with other signs in an entirely different concrete environment, and when they themselves are given in entirely different concrete proportions. When the visual or specific situation changes, the application of a concept which has been worked out in a different situation can become extremely problematic. However, as a rule, in the end the adolescent does manage to accomplish this transition even during the first stage of the maturation of his thinking.

The process of defining such a concept presents a much more complicated problem, when the concept breaks away from the specific situation in which it has been worked out and when it completely ceases to be guided by concrete impressions and begins to operate within a completely abstract scheme. At this stage the verbal definition of the concept and the ability to become conscious of it and to define it, presents marked difficulties and in the course of the experiment it can be observed very frequently how the child or adolescent who has, in effect, already managed to solve the problem of concept formation, regresses to a more primitive stage when he attempts to define the ready formed concept, and begins to list various concrete objects which this concept includes in this specific situation whilst attempting to define it.

So this is how it happens that an adolescent can use a word as a concept and define it as a complex. This is an extremely characteristic form of thinking found in adolescence, which oscillates between thinking in complexes and thinking in concepts. But the greatest problems encountered by the adolescent and which he is usually only able to overcome towards the very end of adolescence, is the further transference of the sense or meaning of the worked out concept to ever new concrete situations, which he also contemplates within an abstract scheme.

This road from the abstract to the concrete proves to be no less difficult than the ascending road from the concrete to the abstract had been in its own time.

## XXIV

By now the experimental results leave us in no doubt whatsoever that the usual picture of how concepts are formed, as traditional psychology had drawn it (having slavishly reproduced this depiction from the formal logical description of the concept formation process), bears no resemblance to reality. The concept formation process as traditional psychology depicts it could be summarized in the following way: a number of concrete ideas form the foundation of a concept.

Let us take an example, says one of the psychologists – the concept of a tree. It arises from a number of similar ideas about a tree. 'A concept comes into being from the ideas of single similar objects.'[57] He continues by introducing a scheme which explains the concept formation process and presents it in the following way. Let us assume that I had the chance to observe three different trees. The notions I have of these three trees can be broken up into their constituent parts, each representing the shape, colour or size of each tree. The remaining constituent parts of these images turn out to be the same.

Assimilation should now take place between the like parts of these ideas and as a result, a general idea about the given attribute will be formed. Then, because of the synthesis which occurs among these ideas, one general idea or concept of a tree comes into being.

So it can be seen that looking from this point of view concepts are formed in the same way as in Galton's collective photograph, where we get a family portrait of various individuals who belong to the same family. We know that the technique of this photograph is based on the fact that images of individual members of the family were printed on a single plate. These images are superimposed upon one another in such a way that similar and frequently recurring features, common to many members of the family, stand out in sharp, marked relief whilst random, individual features, which are different among the various members of the family, obliterate and suppress one another by this overlaying process.

In this way segregation of similar features is achieved, and it is the totality of these segregated common attributes of a number of similar objects and features which, according to traditional views, results in a concept in the true sense. One cannot imagine any claims more false from the point of view of the active process of development of concepts than this logicized picture, drawn with the aid of the scheme described above.

As a matter of fact, as has been noted by psychologists a long time ago and as our experiments demonstrate with crystal clarity, the adolescent's concept formation process never follows the logical route of the process of concept formation which this traditional scheme has described. Vogel's investigations have revealed that a child

obviously does not enter the realm of abstract concepts from a starting point of individual species and rising to higher ones. On the contrary, at first he uses the most general concepts. And he reaches those which are in the middle ground, not by the path of abstraction from below upwards, but by determining them from above. A child's idea develops by passing from the undifferentiated to the differentiated, and not the other way round. Thinking develops by passing from genus to species variety, and not the other way round.[58]

According to Vogel's illustrative representation, thinking almost always moves up and down within a pyramid of concepts but only rarely in a horizontal direction. At one time this thesis was considered to be revolutionary by the traditional psychological science of concept formation. Instead of the former idea, according to which concepts came into being as a result of a simple process of segregation of similar attributes from a number of concrete objects, the process of concept formation was now presented to the researcher in its real complexity, as a complicated process of the movement of thinking within a pyramid of concepts, which was shifting continually from the general to the particular and from the particular to the general.

Recently, Bühler also formulated a theory of the origin of concepts,[59] in which, just like Vogel before him, he tends to reject traditional ideas about the development of concepts by means of the segregation of similar attributes. He distinguishes between two genetic sources in the formation of concepts. The first source is when the child assembles his ideas into segregated groups, and then the groups blend with each other into complicated associative bonds, which form between the various groups of these ideas and between their separate elements which make up each group.

The second genetic source of concepts Bühler considers to be the function of judgement. As a result of thinking and the already formed judgemental process, a child arrives at the stage of being able to form concepts, and Bühler sees weighty evidence for this in the fact that words which define concepts are able to reproduce the child's ready made judgement which refers to these concepts very easily, as we ourselves have quite often had occasion to observe during associative experiments involving children.[60]

Obviously, judgement turns out to be something very elementary and the natural logical place for the concept, according to Bühler, is judgement. The idea and judgement co-operate in the process of concept formation. Thus the process of concept formation develops from two directions – from the general and the particular – more or less simultaneously.

The fact that the first word which a child utters is indeed a general designation and it is only much later that particular and concrete designations tend to appear in the speech of a child, strongly confirms this. Of course, a child learns the word 'flower' earlier than the names of individual flowers and even if, due to some particular circumstances affecting his speech development, he should learn some particular name earlier and he comes across the word 'rose' before the generic name 'flower', then he will use this word and apply it not just in relation to a rose, but to all flowers, i.e. he will use this particular name as if it were a general one.

In this sense Bühler is quite right when he says that the process of development of concepts does not consist of the ascent of the pyramid of concepts from below, but that the process of concept formation proceeds from two directions, like the method of cutting a tunnel.[61] One must admit that all this poses an extremely important and difficult problem for psychology. This problem is, that by accepting the fact that a child learns the general and the most abstract name earlier than the concrete one, many psychologists have found it necessary to re-evaluate the traditional view according to which abstract thinking develops comparatively late, namely at the time of sexual maturation.

These psychologists, who have based themselves on the quite correct observation of the succession of general and concrete names in the child's development, have come to a wrong conclusion by assuming that at the same time as general names appear in children's speech, i.e. very, very early, the existence of abstract concepts can also be ascertained.

For example, such is Ch. Bühler's theory and we can see that this results in an erroneous view according to which adolescent thinking does not undergo any special changes and does not boast any great achievements. According to the theory nothing principally new, in comparison with what we already observe in the intellectual activity of a three-year-old child, appears in adolescent thinking.

In our next section we shall take the opportunity to discuss this question in more detail. For now, let us say only that the use of general words does not yet in any way presuppose an equally early mastery of abstract thinking because, as we have already demonstrated throughout the present chapter, a child uses the same words as the adult and applies these words to the same range of objects, but nevertheless thinks about that object totally differently, in an unrelated manner, to that of an adult. Therefore when, at a very early age, a child applies these words, which in adult speech signify abstract thinking in its most theoretical forms, they do not, by any means, signify the same thing in the child's thinking.

Let us remember that words heard in children's speech coincide with words used by adults according to their physical affiliation but not according to their meaning, therefore we have no reason to assume that abstract thinking is present in a child's mind just because he makes use of abstract words. As we will attempt to demonstrate in our next section, a child who uses abstract words at the same time thinks about the corresponding object in a decidedly concrete way. One thing, at least, is certain, namely that the old idea about concept formation, analogous to the story of how the collective photograph was made, does not in any way correspond either to any actual psychological observations or to any data obtained from experimental analysis.

Bühler's second conjecture which has been fully confirmed by experimental data is also beyond doubt. Concepts do, indeed, have their natural place in judgements and conclusions, and they function as constituent parts of the latter. A child who reacts by answering 'big' when the word 'house' is mentioned, or when he hears the word 'tree' answers 'apples grow there', is really providing proof that the concept exists only as an integral and inseparable part of the general framework of a judgement.

Just as the word can exist only as part of a whole sentence and just as, from the psychological point of view, sentences appear in a child's development earlier than separate isolated words, so, in the same way, judgement also appears in the thinking of a child earlier than individual concepts which have been set apart from it. It is for this reason, according to Bühler, that the concept cannot simply be a product of association.[62] Associative connections of separate elements constitute a necessary prerequisite, but at the same time one which is inadequate for the formation of concepts. It is this double root of concepts, both in the processes of ideas and the processes of judgement which, in Bühler's opinion, is the genetic key to the correct understanding of the processes of concept formation.

In our experiments we did, indeed, have the chance to observe both of these aspects which Bühler mentions. However, we do not agree with the conclusion he draws about the double root of concepts. Already Lindner noticed that the most general concepts are mastered by children relatively early.[63] In this sense, there is no doubt that very early in life a child learns how to use these same general names correctly. It is also true that the development of his concepts is not accomplished as a result of a successful ascent of the pyramid. In our experiments we were frequently able to observe how a child, when given a model, proceeds to match up with it a number of figures provided for him and which bear the same name as the model and, by doing so, he widens the supposed meaning of the word, and uses it in a very general sense and not, by any means, as a concrete or differentiated name.

We have also seen how a concept can come into being as a result of thinking and finds its organic natural place in the judgemental process. In this sense, the experiment completely confirmed the theory, according to which concepts do not arise mechanically, like a collective photograph of concrete objects; in this case, the brain functions like a camera which makes collective snapshots, and thinking is not included in the simple arrangement of these snapshots; and the reverse is true, the thinking processes, both visual and practical thinking, appear a long time before any concepts are formed, and the concepts themselves are the product of a long and complicated process of development of thinking in children.

As we have said above, a concept arises during a process of an intellectual operation and it is not formed by the action of a play of associations. A special blend of all the elementary intellectual functions take part in its creation and the crucial aspect of this whole operation is the functional use of words as means for the voluntary control of attention, abstraction and segregation of individual attributes and their synthesis and symbolization by the use of signs.

On many occasions, during the course of our experiment, we had the opportunity to observe how the primary function of words, which could be called the indicative function as the word is depicting a definite object or a definite attribute, appears to have an earlier genetic origin than the significative function which supersedes many of the visual impressions and signifies them. As in the conditions of our experiment the meaning of the intially senseless word referred to the visual situation, we could then observe how word meaning develops when such a meaning is made available. We were able to study this relationship of the word to specific attributes in a living situation, and to observe how once it is perceived, segregated and synthesized, it acquires the sense and meaning of a word, becomes a concept, and then how these concepts are elaborated and transferred to other specific situations and finally, how they are consciously grasped.

Concepts are always formed during a process of finding a solution to some problem facing the adolescent's thinking process. The creation of the concept is dependent on a solution to this problem being found. Therefore the question of the double root in the formation of a concept has not been presented by Bühler in a sufficiently precise manner. In actual fact, the development of concepts tends to move along two main channels.

We have attempted to demonstrate how in its development, the function of complexing or associating of a number of separate objects by a family name which is common to the whole group, is the basic form of thinking in complexes observed in children and how, in parallel fashion, potential concepts which are based on the process of segregation of certain common attributes, form a second channel in the development of concepts.

Both of these forms represent real double roots in the process of concept formation. But we do not consider the roots of concepts described by Bühler to be real, but merely apparent ones, and this is the reason why. In fact, the prototype of a concept in the form of associative groups, and the design of concepts in the memory is, of course, a natural process which has no connection with words, and is related to that thinking in complexes which we discussed above, and which manifests itself in visual thinking which is in no way connected with words. We can find detailed analogies of these associative complexes of individual ideas in our dreams or in the thinking of animals, but as we have already demonstrated above, it is not these amalgamations of ideas which form the basis of concepts, but complexes which are formed on the basis of word applications.

So we think that Bühler's first mistake consists of ignoring the role of words in these complex amalgamations, which are the forerunners of concepts, as well as the attempt to deduce the concept from the purely inborn natural form of processing of impressions, disregarding the historical nature of the concept, ignoring the role of words and a reluctance to acknowledge the difference between a natural complex, which arises in the memory and has been represented in Jaensch's visual concepts, and other complexes which arise as a result of a highly developed verbal type of thinking. Bühler, too, makes the same mistake by ascertaining the presence of a second root for concepts which he discovers in the judgemental processes found in thinking.

This statement of Bühler's, on the one hand, brings us back to the logisizing point of view, according to which a concept is formed on the basis of reflection and is a product of logical judgement. But we have already seen to what extent both the history of concepts in our everyday language and the history of children's concepts deviate from the road which has been prescribed by logic. On the other hand, whilst designating thinking as the root of concepts, Bühler once again ignores the difference between various forms of thinking, and in particular between the biological and the historical, the natural and the cultural elements, the lower and the higher non-verbal and verbal forms of thinking.

In fact, if a concept develops from a judgement, i.e. from an act of thinking, then the question about what distinguishes a concept from a product of visual or practical–functional thinking comes to mind. Yet again, the subject of words which are crucial to the formation of concepts is passed over in silence by Bühler and is excluded when factors which contribute to concept formation are being analysed, and as a result it becomes incomprehensible how two such different processes as judgement and the complexing of ideas can lead to the formation of concepts. It is inevitable that Bühler ends up drawing a wrong conclusion from such wrong assumptions, which, as we have already pointed out on several occasions, says that concept thinking is already present in a three-year-old child and that therefore nothing basically new, as far as the development of concepts is concerned, occurs during adolescence as compared with a three year old.

This researcher, deceived by external appearances, fails to take into account the profound dissimilarity, despite their superficial resemblance, of the causal–dynamic connections and associations of two types of thinking so completely different from the genetic, functional and structural points of view.

Our own experiments have led us to an essentially different conclusion. They show that a concept develops from syncretic images and associations, thinking in complexes and from potential concepts when, based on the use of a word as a means of concept formation, a particular significative structure comes into being which we feel justified in calling a concept in the true sense of the word.

## XXV

So, as a result of our investigations, we have found that an adolescent makes an extremely crucial stride on the road of his intellectual development during the period of sexual maturation. He passes from thinking in complexes to thinking in concepts. The formation of concepts and the ability to operate with them constitute the essentially new acquisitions of this age. And the adolescent intellect finds something more than a simple continuation of the former lines of his behaviour in concepts.

A concept is not just an enriched and internally joined associative group. It represents a qualitatively new phenomenon which cannot be reduced to more elementary processes which are characteristic of the early stages of development in the intellect. Concept thinking is a new form of intellectual activity, a new mode of conduct, a new intellectual mechanism.

The intellect is able to find a new and unprecedented *modus operandi* in this particular activity and a new function becomes available within the system of intellectual functions which is distinctive both in its composition and structure as well as in the way it functions.

The traditional view which tends to deny the appearance of any essentially new phenomena in the intellectual sphere during adolescence, and which attempts to regard adolescent thinking simply as an ongoing, amplified and deeper version of the thinking of a three year old, as can best be seen from Ch. Bühler's remarks, essentially fails to notice the qualitative difference between concepts and complexes and syncretic images.

This view is based on a purely quantitative conception of the development of intellect, surprisingly near to Thorndike's theory, according to which the higher forms of thinking can be distinguished from elementary functions only quantitatively, according to the number of associative connections which form part of their composition. It is precisely because such a view dominates traditional adolescent psychology, that we have found it necessary to trace the whole process of development of thinking with great care and to show the three different qualitative milestones which this road has to pass.

Throughout this study we have borne the primary subject in mind, that of adolescent thinking. However, we used continuously the method of genetic cross-sections whilst investigating thinking, in the same way as a research anatomist takes cross-sections at various stages of development of an organ and is able to determine the process of development from one stage to the next by comparing these cross-sections.

According to Gesell's correct observation, the method of genetic cross-sectioning is becoming the predominant method of studying behaviour and its development in contemporary child psychology.[64] The previous method – the description of some particular features of behaviour at various ages – has generally resulted in a static characterization, a mere listing of a number of peculiarities, attributes and distinguishing features observed in the thinking process in the given stage of development.

This resulted in a situation where the static characterization usually supplanted the dynamic examination of the age period in question. The idea of development was being lost sight of and the given form which may have been characteristic for a given age, was assumed to be stable, immutable and always equal to itself. Both thinking and behaviour at every age were being examined more like a thing than a process, at rest and not in motion. Meanwhile, the essence of every form of thinking can only reveal itself when we begin to interpret it as a distinct organically necessary moment in the complicated and integrated process of development. The only adequate technique for uncovering its essential qualities is the method of genetic cross-sectioning, to be used in comparative genetic studies of behaviour at different stages of its development.

This is exactly what we have tried to do in our attempts to elucidate the peculiar nature of adolescent thinking. We were not merely interested in compiling a list of the peculiar features of adolescent thinking, or an inventory of expressions of intellectual activity found in adolescents, nor in a simple enumeration of the forms of thinking in their quantitative relationships with one another. First and foremost we wanted to establish what is essentially new in adolescence in the development of thought and what it brings with it; we were interested in adolescent thinking in the making. Our objective consisted of trying to capture the process of crisis and maturation of thinking which makes up the basic content of the whole age period in question.

In order to achieve this we have had to describe adolescent thinking and to compare it with earlier stages in the development of thinking, to discover transitions between one form and another and by using comparisons to establish the nature of the decisive change, the fundamental reconstruction and radical reorganization which takes place in adolescent thinking. For this purpose we had to take cross-sections, as it were, at various stages of the process of development of thinking and, all the time following a comparative genetic path, to attempt to establish connections among these cross-sections and to restore the actual dynamic process which takes place when thinking passes from one stage to another.

And in future we intend to proceed in exactly the same way, as the comparative–genetic approach to investigation and the genetic cross-section method is the basic and principal method of carrying out studies in child psychology.

It is true that when we subjected the results of our comparative study to a functional test, we always made use not only of data referring to the ontogeny of thinking, but also of its phylogenetic development and its disintegration and involution in disease. In this we were at all times guided by the principle of the unity of higher forms of intellectual activity, regardless of the variety of processes in which it may find its actual expression. We have made the assumption that the basic laws governing the structure and activity of thinking and the basic patterns which control it remain the same in both the normal and the pathological state, but that these patterns manifest themselves in different forms of concrete expression depending on the different circumstances.

Just as contemporary pathologists regard disease as life in particular changed circumstances, so we feel we have the right to regard any thinking activity which is affected by various disorders as a manifestation of the general patterns of thinking in special circumstances brought about by the illness.

Modern psychoneurology is now firmly convinced that development is the key to the understanding of the loss and involution of psychological functions, and that investigations into the loss and disintegration of these functions is the key to the understanding of their structure and development. So general and pathological psychology can shed light on one another providing both are built on genetic foundations.

The comparison of ontogenetic and phylogenetic data has not, for one moment, led us to accept the idea of biogenetic parallelism, or to suppose that we would be able to find in the history of child development a repetition and recapitulation of those forms of thinking which were dominant during past stages of human history. Throughout, we were guided by the same comparative method, about which Groos has quite rightly said that its goal is not just in finding similarity, but also in establishing differences. 'Just like everywhere else', he says, 'in this instance the word "comparison" does not only imply the segregation of coincidental features, but even more so, looking for variations in the similarities.'[65]

This is why we have never identified the process of concrete thinking in children with the process of concrete thinking in the history of the development of the human race. What we were concerned with throughout this study was to reach as full an explanation as possible of the nature of the phenomenon which was the main objective of our investigation. And it is precisely this nature which manifests itself in the multifarious associations and forms of essentially the same kind of thinking.

To say that logical thinking appears at a certain age in the development of human history and that it appears at a certain stage of a child's development, only amounts to a confirmation of an incontestable truth, but at the same time, it does not, in any way, mean that the person holding these beliefs is accepting the point of view of biogenetic parallelism. In the same way, a comparative analysis of thinking in complexes in its phylogenetic and ontogenetic aspects does not, in the least, assume the idea of a parallelism between various processes, nor the idea of the sameness of different forms.

We have made a special attempt to underline one aspect of the phenomenon under study, and this aspect stands out in the best possible way in this type of comparative study of various manifestations of the same form of thinking. This aspect is the unity of form and content in concepts. It is because the form aspect and the content aspect are united in concepts, that the transition to thinking in concepts signifies a real revolution in the thinking process of a child.

## Notes

This text formed part of chapter 10 of Vygotsky, L. S. 1931: *Pedologija podrostka* [*Paedology of the Adolescent*]. Moscow-Leningrad: Uchebno-Pedagogicheskoe Izdatel'stvo. Paragraphs five to 24 were with slight alterations republished in his *Myshlenie i rech'* [*Thinking and Speech*] (1934). As can be seen from its general format the book was intended to be used as a textbook for the (correspondence) courses at Moscow University. For a textbook *Pedologija podrostka* was surprisingly lopsided: the chapter from which this text is taken, for instance, covered no less than 130 pages, whereas other chapters totalled a meagre 15 pages. It seems, then, that Vygotsky used the textbook to publish the results of those investigations that were in the focus of his scientific interests at that time. A large part of the empirical work which is at the basis of his chapter was carried out by L. S. Sakharov, to whose memory the book was dedicated. Its theoretical orientation owes much to the work of Groos, Werner, Ach and others as Vygotsky himself acknowledges.

1   Refers to p. 126 of Bühler, Ch. 1929: *Das Seelenleben des Jugendlichen* (5th edn). Jena: Fischer.

2   Ibid., pp. 126–7.

3   See p. 389 of Giese, F. 1922: Kinderpsychologie. In G. Kafka (ed.) *Handbuch der vergleichenden Psychologie* vol. 1 (pp. 323–518). München: Reinhardt.

4   This and the other quotes from Kroh are probably from Kroh, O. 1922: *Subjektive Anschauungsbilder bei Jugendlichen*. Göttingen: Van den hoek & Ruprecht. Vygotsky may also have used a Russian translation of one of Kroh's articles. See Kroh, O. 1931: Intellektual'noe razvitie v period sozrevanija. In I. Ariamov (ed.), *Pedologija junosti*. Moscow.

5   Rubinstein, Moisej Matveevich (1878–1953). This and the following quote were probably taken from Rubinstein, M. M. and Ignat'ev, V. E. 1926: *Psikhologija, pedagogika i gigiena junosti*. Moscow: Mir. Vygotsky recommended this book for further reading.

6  Refers to Spranger, E. 1927: *Psychologie des Jugendalters*. Jena: Fischer.

7  See p. 127 of Ch. Bühler (1929).

8  Sir Cyril Burt's version of the Binet–Simon test was adapted for Russian use by P. P. Blonsky.

9  Refers to p. 522 of Edinger, L. 1911: *Vorlesungen über den Bau der nervösen Zentralorgane der Menschen und der Tiere*. Leipzig: Quelle und Meyer.

10  This quote and the other reference to Blonsky were probably taken from Blonsky, P. P. 1925: *Pedologija*. Moscow: Rabotnik Prosveshchenija.

11  Refers to p. 17 of Bühler, K. 1918: *Die geistige Entwicklung des Kindes*. Jena: Fischer. Bühler mentions Pfister's findings.

12.  Ibid., p. 15.

13  We have not been able to locate N. V. Vyazemsky's book.

14  Refers to pp. 338–9 of Ach, N. 1921: *Uber die Begriffsbildung. Eine experimentelle Untersuchung*. Bamberg: C. C. Buchners Verlag.

15  Ibid., pp. 339–40. The reference is to Jaensch, E. R. 1923: *Über den Aufbau der Wahrnehmungswelt und ihre Struktur im Jugendalter*. Leipzig: Barth.

16  Refers to pp. 96–7 of Rimat, F. 1925: Intelligenzuntersuchungen anschliessend an die Ach'sche Suchmethode. *Untersuchungen zur Psychologie, Philosophie und Pädagogik*, 5, 1–116.

17  Refers to p. 139 of Usnadze, D. 1930: Die Begriffsbildung im vorschulpflichtigen Alter. *Zeitschrift für angewandte Psychologie*, 34, 138–212.

18  Ibid., p. 139.

19  Ibid., p. 140.

20  See chapter 6 of this reader.

21  The empirical results of the investigations carried out by Sakharov and (later) Kotelova and Pashkovskaya were never independently published and the present chapter is the most detailed description we have.

22  Refers to Müller, G. E. 1913: Zur Analyse der Gedächtnistätigkeit und des Vorstellungsverlaufes. *Zeitschrift für Psychologie und Physiologie der Sinnesorgane. Ergänzungsband 8*. Leipzig: Barth.

23  Vygotsky suggests that this and the following quotes come from Thorndike, E. L. 1911/1965: *Animal Intelligence. Experimental Studies*. New York-London: Hafner Publishing Company. Unfortunately, these quotes cannot be found in that book, nor in several other books by Thorndike which we checked. Very similar ones, though, abound in several of Thorndike's books.

24  It is interesting to see that Vygotsky assumes some role for the concept of childhood egocentrism. In his preface to the Russian edition of two of Piaget's books he severely criticized the concept and its theoretical background in psychoanalysis. See Vygotsky, L. S. 1932: Foreword. In J. Piaget, *Rech i myshlenie rebenka* (pp. 3–54). Moscow-Leningrad: Uchpedgiz.

25  See pp. 44–7 of Werner, H. 1933: *Einführung in die Entwicklungspsychologie*. Leipzig: Barth.

26  The term 'pseudoconcept' – as well as many other of the stages in concept formation and the names attached to it in this chapter – is not original with Vygotsky. The term is used by the Sterns ('Scheinbegriff' or 'Pseudobegriff') and the idea dates back to at least Ament. See Stern, C. and Stern, W. 1928/1981: *Die Kindersprache*. Darmstadt: Wissenschaftliche Buchgesellschaft.

27  We have been unable to establish the identity of this author.

28  Repeats the quote given earlier. See p. 140 of Usnadze (1930).

29 The terms 'concept in itself', 'concept for others' and 'concept for himself' were inspired by Vygotsky's reading of Hegel.

30 Refers to Engels' (1859/1964) review of Marx's 'Zur Kritik der politischen Ökonomie'. See p. 475 of *Marx Engels Werke, vol. 13*. Berlin: Dietz Verlag.

31 Refers to pp. 99–100 and 149 of Krueger, F. 1915: Über Entwicklungspsychologie, ihre sachliche und geschichtliche Notwendigkeit. In F. Krueger (ed.) *Arbeiten zur Entwicklungspsychologie, vol. 1*. Leipzig: Engelmann.

32 Refers to p. 218 of Gesell, A. 1932: *Pedologija rannogo vozrasta*. Moscow-Leningrad: Giz.

33 Idelberger's example and Werner's discussion of it can be found on pp. 245–6 of Werner, H. 1933: *Einführung in die Entwicklungstheorie* (2nd edn). Leipzig: Barth.

34 The 'well known example' dates back to an example given by Darwin and Romanes and was indeed frequently quoted in the 1920s. See, for example, p. 187 of Stern, C. and Stern, W. 1928/1981: *Die Kindersprache*. Darmstadt: Wissenschaftliche Buchgesellschaft.

35 See especially chapter 4 of Piaget, J. 1926: *La représentation du monde chez l'enfant*. Paris: Alcan.

36 Refers to pp. 77–8 of Lévy-Bruhl, L. 1922: *Les fonctions mentales dans les sociétés inférieures* (5th edn). Paris: Alcan.

37 See pp. 31–4 of Storch, A. 1922: *Das archaisch-primitive Erleben und Denken der Schizophrenen*. Berlin: Julius Springer.

38 Ibid., pp. 8–9.

39 Ibid., p. 9.

40 The lines are taken from two different papers by Thurnwald published in the journal *Antropos* in 1917/1918 and 1919/1920 respectively. Vygotsky is quoting them from p. 9 of Storch (1922).

41 Refers to Peterson, M. N. 1930: *Sintaksis russkogo jazyka*. Moscow: Bjuro Zaochnogo Obuchenija pri Pedfake 2-go MGU.

42 With 'objective reference' (*predmetnoe otnesenie*) Vygotsky indicates what is now technically called the 'extension' of a concept. The 'meaning' (*znachenie*) of a word in Peterson's sense would now be called 'intension'.

43 The French and German words are 'tailleur' (from 'tailler') and 'Schneider' (from 'schneiden'), respectively.

44 We have been unable to identify this author.

45 In Russian the root of the word 'chernila' is connected with the word for black ['chernyj'].

46 Refers to Potebnya, A. A. 1922: *Mysl' i jazyk*. Odeassa: Gosudarstvennoe Izdatel'stvo Ukrainy.

47 See note 27.

48 Pogodin, A. L. (1872–1947), Russian historian, linguist and psychologist. Vygotsky apparently makes use of his 'Jazyk kak tvorchestvo' ['Language as creativity']. This information is taken from the first volume of Vygotsky's Collected Works where it is added: 'After 1919 he was an emigrant'. Until recently such lapidarian statements served to brand people as ideological enemies.

49 Refers to Goethe's words 'den nur beide zusammen, wie Aus- und Einatmen, machen das Leben der Wissenschaft'. See p. 56 of Morris, M. (ed.) (MDCXL) *Goethes sämtliche Werke. Bnd. 39. Schriften zur Naturwissenschaft 1*. Stuttgart-Berlin: Gotta'sche Buchhandlung Nachfolger.

50 Refers to pp. 196–7 of Groos, K. 1921: *Das Seelenleben des Kindes* (5th edn). Berlin: Verlag von Reuther & Reichard.

51  Although this text covers Groos' discussion very adequately, it doesn't seem to be a literal quote. See especially p. 202 of Groos (1921).

52  See p. 57 of Bühler, K. 1929: *Abriss der geistigen Entwicklung des Kindes* (4th and 5th enlarged edn). Leipzig: Quelle und Meyer.

53  Refers to p. 26 of Köhler, W. 1921: *Intelligenzprüfungen an Menschenaffen*. Berlin: Springer.

54  Refers to p. 204 of Groos (1921) where Messer's example is given. It was taken by Groos from Messer, A. 1900: *Kritische Untersuchungen über Denken, Sprechen und Sprachunterricht*. Berlin: Reuther & Reichard. The assumption is that it is unhealthy to drink (cold) water when one is hot.

55  'This type of primitive thinking', says Kretschmer, 'is also called *complex thinking* (Preuss), to the extent that complexes of images which merge and become blended into conglomerates do still represent the sharply demarcated and abstract concepts'. Accordingly, all writers agree that what they are seeing in this type of thinking is 'a first, imagistic stage of the concept' [original footnote]. The quotation is from p. 79 of Kretschmer, E. 1922/1950: *Medizinische Psychologie* (10th improved and enlarged edn). Stuttgart: G. Thieme Verlag.

56  Refers to Volkelt, H. 1912: *Über die Vorstellungen der Tiere. Ein Beitrag zur Entwicklungspsychologie*. Doctoral dissertation, Leipzig.

57  We have been unable to establish the identity of this psychologist.

58  Refers to p. 27 of Vogel, P. 1911: *Untersuchungen über die Denkbeziehungen in den Urteilen des Kindes*. Doctoral dissertation, Giessen.

59  Refers to pp. 260–70 of Bühler, K. (1918). See also pp. 135–45 of Bühler, K. (1929).

60  See pp. 264–5 of Bühler (1918), where he argues that concepts cannot be solely based on associations, but form and depend upon a comprehensive system of knowledge. Thus, the concept 'house' is not just the invariant part of all houses the child has seen, but forms part of an interconnected system of judgements. Children will, for example, often react to the word 'house' with the words 'they are big', that is, each concept leads to a number of judgements or propositions. Concepts, then, are embedded in a system of propositions. This is even more true in Bühler's view of scientific or academic concepts such as 'mammal'.

61  Ibid., p. 137.

62  Ibid., pp. 264–5. The examples in the preceding paragraph concerning the house and the tree can be found on p. 265.

63  Refers to p. 341 of Lindner, G. 1882: Beobachtungen und Bemerkungen über die Entwicklung der Sprache des Kindes. *Kosmos*, 6, 321–42.

64  Refers to Gesell, A. 1930: *Umstvennoe razvitie rebenka*. Moscow-Leningrad: Giz; or to Gesell, A. 1932: *Pedologija rannogo vozrasta*. Moscow-Leningrad: Giz.

65  Refers to p. 7 of Groos (1921).

# 10

# Imagination and creativity of the adolescent

## Lev Vygotsky

*Contents of the lesson*

The problem of imagination and creativity in the light of psychopathology. –
Imagination and thinking in adolescence. – The eidetic problem in adolescence. –
Concrete and abstract imagination in adolescence. – The problem of concrete thinking and the formation of 'visual concepts'. – Comparative studies of imagination in
childhood and in adolescence. – Creative imagination in adolescence. – Creative
imagination as a synthesis of emotion and thinking.

*Plan of study*

1  Read the text of the lesson and devise a plan and a summary of the whole chapter.
2  Draw any conclusions from the data referring to the development of the imagination in adolescence which may have educational applications.
3  Analyse the research material on any subject and select the aspects which are
   dependent on creative imagination.


## I

Cassirer[1] describes a patient exhibiting a complex disorder of the higher intellectual
functions whom he had the opportunity to observe in the Frankfurt Neurological
Institute. This patient was able to repeat any sentence without any problem but, in
his version of the sentence, he was capable of communicating only real and concrete
situations which directly corresponded to his concrete, sensory experience.

Once, during a conversation which took place on a nice sunny day, when he was
asked to repeat the sentence 'Today the weather is bad and it is raining', he could not
bring himself to carry out this request. The first words were uttered easily and
confidently, but then he became confused, stopped speaking and could not bring
himself to finish the sentence in the way it had been given to him. He kept on
changing over to another form, which corresponded to the observed reality.

Another patient in the same institute, whose entire right side was severely paralysed, and as a result of which he had lost the use of his right hand, was unable to repeat the sentence 'I can write well with my right hand'. He substituted the correct word 'left' for the incorrect word 'right' every single time.

Other patients who also suffered from complicated disorders of different, but equally high intellectual functions structured on speech and thinking in concepts, also exhibited a clear and total dependence on direct concrete perceptions. One of these patients was perfectly able to make use of any everyday objects correctly, so long as he encountered them in a familiar situation and under the right conditions, but he would become totally unable to do so when the circumstances changed. So, for example, he used his spoon and drinking glass like any normal person whilst eating his dinner, but at other times he performed completely senseless actions with the very same objects.

Another patient who was incapable of pouring himself a glass of water when asked to do so, was able to perform this operation without the slightest difficulty when he was driven to it by thirst. In all these cases, what strikes one is the complete dependence of behaviour, thinking, perception and action on a given real situation, which manifests itself according to strict conformity to a systematic law, every time the higher intellectual functions become disturbed, when the mechanism of thinking in concepts breaks down and its place is taken by a more ancient, genetic mechanism of concrete thinking.

What we see in these cases, in a clear, sharp and extremely graphic form, we may regard as representing a complete antithesis to fantasy and creativity. If we wanted to find a form of behaviour in which there is a complete absence of any elements of imagination and creativity, we would have to quote the above example. A person who is capable of pouring himself a glass of water from a carafe when thirst motivates him to do so, but who is incapable of performing the same action at another time, or a person who cannot repeat a sentence which says that the weather is bad when the weather is good – all this tells us a lot which is significant and fundamental for the understanding of what underlies fantasy and creativity, and what links them to those higher intellectual functions which have become disturbed and disrupted in such cases.

We can even say that the behaviour observed in these patients strikes us, above all, by the fact that it is not free. The person cannot do something which is not directly motivated by an actual situation. What appears to be beyond his ability is to create a situation or to modify it in such a way as to become free of the immediate influence of external and internal stimuli.

As has already been mentioned above, pathological cases are of interest to us only as long as they illuminate the same laws which apply to normal behavioural development. Pathology is the key to understanding development and development is the key to the understanding of pathological changes. So in this case we are able to observe the same zero point of imagination and creativity in the process of behavioural development as that which is present in young children and in primitive man.

Both of these find themselves at a stage of development where the normal state expresses itself in this mechanism of unfreedom and where behaviour is totally dependent on an actual situation, this being completely determined by the external environment and wholly subservient to the stimuli which happen to be present and which, in the cases cited above, is regarded as a pathological symptom.

Lewin,[2] who has recently devoted a number of studies to how intentions are formed, turns his attention to the extremely interesting problem of freedom in forming any kind of resolution. 'In its own right this is a most curious state of events', he says,

> that a human being has this amazing degree of freedom in the sense of having the opportunity to carry out many types of determined actions, even totally meaningless ones. This freedom characterizes civilized human beings. It is accessible to children and, it seems, to primitive man as well, but to a much lesser degree and is probably the single factor which, to a much greater degree than his higher intellect, differentiates a human being from its closest relatives in the animal world. It appears that this difference goes together with the problem of mastery over one's own behaviour.

The behaviour of the patients we described above strikes one precisely by the inability to form any resolutions. It is not surprising then that, as has already been said, this phenomenon can be observed most frequently in cases where higher intellectual functions, which are the seat of thinking in concepts, have been disrupted. This is most clearly seen in cases of aphasia, a disorder which results from disturbed verbal activity and thinking in concepts.

In the course of our research we had the opportunity to observe how patients with similar conditions are faced with extreme difficulties which, from their point of view, are insoluble. As has been pointed out by Head, the same situation arises when an aphasic is asked to perform a task which can be started from either end, and he is unable to solve the problem because he cannot find a starting point and does not know where to begin. This starting point must be chosen at will, and for him this is precisely the main source of the difficulty.[3] During our studies we have frequently been able to observe how difficult it is for certain aphasics to repeat a sentence which contains an indefinite statement from the point of view of a concrete concept.

For example, a patient who is perfectly able to repeat dozens of other sentences correctly, cannot repeat the phrase 'Snow is black'. He is incapable of solving this problem, despite repeated requests on the part of the experimenter for him to repeat the phrase.

The same difficulties are encountered by this type of patient when, in reply to a given word, he is asked to say what this thing is not or what it cannot do. The aphasic manages to solve the opposite problem easily, and he solves this problem as well if he is allowed to formulate his answer in the following way: 'Snow is never black'. But simply to name the wrong colour, the wrong attribute or the wrong action, proves beyond his powers. When the aphasic is asked to name a wrong colour or action when looking at some real object which is of a different colour or which performs some other action, the question becomes even more difficult. To transfer the attributes of various things, to replace one with another, to form combinations of attributes and actions, proves an impossible task. He is firmly and solidly tethered to the situation which he perceives in a concrete manner and he cannot step outside its confines.

We have already discussed above how thinking in concepts is connected with freedom and purposefulness of action. Gelb formulates the same idea in a paradoxical but quite correct manner, when he recalls Herder's thesis which says that the language of thinking is the language of freedom. Gelb develops this idea further when he says: 'It is only man who is capable of doing something which is senseless'.[4] And this is absolutely true. An animal is incapable of carrying out any action which is meaningless in the context of an actual situation. Animals perform only those actions which are motivated by internal motives or an external stimulus. But they are incapable of performing actions which, from the point of view of their situation, are arbitrary, premeditated, free or senseless.

Incidentally, it must be said that for a long time, both in philosophical arguments about free will and in everyday thinking, our ability to do something meaningless, absolutely useless and which is elicited neither by external or internal circumstances, has usually been regarded as the clearest indication of the wilfulness of resolve and freedom of the action which is being performed. It is for this reason that the aphasic's inability to perform a senseless action at the same time amounts to an inability to perform a free action.

We think that the examples we have given will suffice to illustrate the straight-forward idea that imagination and creativity are linked to a free reworking of various elements of experience, freely combined, and which, as a precondition, without fail, require the level of inner freedom of thought, action and cognizing which only he who has mastered thinking in concepts can achieve. So it is not without reason that imagination and creativity disappear when this function is affected.

## II

We have quite deliberately prefaced our examination of fantasy and creativity in adolescence with this short psychopathological excursion. At the same time, right from the start, we have been guided by the wish to underline precisely and clealy that this problem requires a completely new formulation in the light of our basic understanding of adolescent psychology, which is opposite to that which can be regarded as the traditional and generally accepted one in the field of adolescent psychology.

The traditional point of view regards this function as being the central and vital function of the entire psychological development of the adolescent. It places imagi-nation in the foreground of the adolescent's entire intellectual life. Using it as a starting point, it attempts to subordinate all the remaining aspects of adolescent behaviour to this basic function, which it regards as the primary and independent manifestation of all the fundamental and dominant factors of all aspects of psychology during the age of puberty. What happens during this period, is not just that the adolescent experiences a severe distortion of the relative proportion of things, and that the structures of the intellectual functions are transmitted in an inaccurate form, but that the very process of imagination and creativity acquires a wrong interpretation.

This false interpretation of fantasy is due to it being viewed one-sidedly, as a function which is linked to emotional life, the life of inclinations and sentiments; but its other side, which is linked to intellectual life, remains obscure. But, as Pushkin has aptly remarked, 'imagination is as necessary in geometry as it is in poetry'.[5] Everything that necessitates artistic transformation of reality, everything that leads to inventiveness and the creation of anything new, requires the indispensable participation of fantasy. In this sense some writers quite rightly contrapose fantasy as creative imagination to memory as reproductive imagery.

Besides, everything which is essentially new in the development of fantasy in adolescence, consists of the fact that the adolescent's imagination forms a close link with thinking in concepts; it, as it were, becomes intellectualized, is then included into the system of intellectual activity and begins to perform a completely new function in a new structure of the personality. In his study, Ribot drew a curve of the development of imagination in adolescents and pointed out that the age of puberty is characterized by the fact that the curve of development of the imagination, which hitherto had followed a separate course from the curve of intellectual development, begins to approach the latter and follows a parallel route.[6]

If we have managed to define the development of adolescent thinking satisfactorily as a transition from rational to intellectual thinking, and if we have also detailed correctly the intellectualization of these functions as memory, concentration, visual perception and wilful action, then, following the same logical consistency, we ought to be able to draw the same conclusion as regards fantasy. That is that fantasy is not really a primary, independent and leading function in the development of adolescent psychology, and its development is a consequence of the function of concept formation, an end result which completes and implements all the complicated processes of change which the adolescent's whole intellectual life has to overcome.

Up till now, the question of the nature of imagination in adolescence still remains a controversial subject among psychologists belonging to different schools of thought. Many writers, such as Ch. Bühler, point to the fact that, along with the transition to abstract thinking, as if at the opposite pole, a reservoir of all the elements of his concrete thinking begins to take shape within the adolescent's fantasy.[7] In this instance, fantasy is not only regarded as a function which is independent of thinking in concepts, but even as a quite opposite function. Whilst thinking in concepts is characterized by its existence in the realm of the abstract and general, imagination exists in the concrete sphere. And fantasy in adolescence, whilst being inferior in the sphere of productivity as compared with the mature fantasy of an adult, nevertheless is superior to the latter in its intensity and originality; we feel we have the right to ask whether this writer considers fantasy to be a function which is diametrically opposed to intellect.

In this respect the fate of the so-called eidetic images, recently investigated by Jaensch and his school,[8] are of great interest. Generally, the name of eidetic images is given to those visual representations which the child is able to create with hallucinatory clarity after perceiving some visual situation or picture.

In the same way as when an adult, after fixing his gaze for several seconds upon a red square, sees its after-image in its complementary colour on a grey or white background, the child when looking at a picture for a short time, continues to see the same picture on an empty screen after the picture has been removed. This amounts to a kind of prolonged inertia of a visual stimulus which continues to function after the source of the impulse has disappeared. In the same way as a loud sound appears to continue in our ears for some time after we have actually ceased to perceive it, the child's eye, as it were, retains the trace and continuing echo of a vivid visual stimulus for some time afterwards.

At this stage we are not so much concerned with the problem of discussing the details of eidetic imagery or with all the facts discovered by experimental research. For our purposes suffice it to say that, according to Jaensch's findings, these imagistic visual perceptions can be considered as a kind of transitional stage between perceptions and conceptions. These tend to disappear at the end of childhood, while they are still in the process of development, but they do not disappear completely and are transformed into a visual base for our conceptions on the one hand, and on the other, become constituent parts of our perceptions. According to some writers, these eidetic images occur most frequently during adolescence.

As these phenomena provide evidence about the visual, concrete and sensory character of memory and thinking, and as they are the basic ingredients of a representational perception of the world and representational thinking about reality, immediately doubts come to mind whether they could really be regarded as distinguishing characteristic features of the adolescent age. Recently, this question has been reassessed by several researchers, who have been able to confirm that, indeed, eidetic visual images are typical in childhood and, in particular, that we are justified in thinking that they are most characteristic of very early childhood. A very young child can be described as an eidetic, in the sense that his memories, imagination and thinking can still directly reproduce real perceptions in the fullness of the original experience, the full richness of their tangible details and with the vividness of a hallucination.

Eidetic images tend to disappear during the transition to thinking in concepts, and we had to assume, *a priori*, that they will have disappeared by the time of puberty, as this period marks the transition from the visual, concrete mode of thinking to an abstract thinking in concepts.

Jaensch has established that eidetic images dominated the primitive stages of human culture not only in the ontogenetic, but also in the phylogenetic development of memory. However, together with the cultural development of our thinking, these phenomena gradually disappeared, their place taken by abstract thinking, and they have survived in the primitive forms of thinking only in children. 'In the course of further development . . .' says Jaensch,

> the meanings of words became more general and abstract. It appears that the eidetic tendency receded to the background in step with the interest in concrete images, and the change in the character of language resulted in the eidetic inclinations being driven back still further. In the case of civilized mankind, the driving back of this tendency may have been the result of civilized language which brought with it general word meanings which, in contrast to the individual word meanings in primitive languages, rather limit than facilitate the attention paid to sensory given facts.[9]

In the same way as in the genetic plan, the development of language and the transition to thinking in concepts, in their time, resulted in the atrophy of eidetic features; similarly, in the adolescent's development, the period of puberty is characterized by two internally linked moments, i.e. the intensification of abstract thinking and the disappearance of eidetic visual images.

Until now, the question of when eidetic images reach their peak has produced wide disagreement among various writers. Whilst some say that its culmination is reached in early childhood, others place the peak of the curve in adolescence, whilst a third group think that it occurs somewhere between the two, around early school age. Recently, however, it has finally become firmly established that what is observed in adolescence is not a steep rise, but rather a sharp fall in the growth of development of visual images. The change which occurs in the adolescent's intellectual activity is very closely linked with the change in the life of his conceptions. It cannot be emphasized strongly enough that subjective visual images are not symptomatic of the period of sexual maturation, but are essential attributes of childhood, as has been confirmed by Kroh, the eminent researcher in the field of eidetic imagery.[10]

This is a cardinal statement, as attempts to turn these eidetic images into symptoms of the age of puberty are being renewed over and over again. To counter this, it must be pointed out that even the earliest experiments of this author have uncovered a strong decline in the development curve of these images at the time of puberty. Other experiments have shown that the maximum frequency of eidetic phenomena decreases somewhere between 11 and 12 years of age, and it falls further with the advent of puberty.

'This is why', says Kroh, 'we must decisively reject any attempt to regard visual images as being symptomatic of the age of puberty or as resulting directly from the psychological lability of that age.' At the same time, it must be kept in mind that these visual images do not disappear immediately, but survive, as a rule, for quite a long time into the age of puberty. But the realm where these images arise becomes more and more circumscribed and specialized, and can basically be explained in relationship to the prevailing interests.

In the previous chapter we have already discussed the fundamental changes which occur in the memory during adolescence; we tried to show that memory progresses from eidetic images to a form of logical memory and that internal mnemotechnics become the principal and basic form of memory in adolescents. Therefore, what is characteristic of eidetic images, is that they do not disappear from the sphere of the adolescent's intellectual activity entirely, but shift to another sector of the same sphere, as it were. After ceasing to be the basic form of the memory process, they begin to serve imagination and fantasy and, in this way, they change the nature of their basic psychological function.

Quite rightly, Kroh points out that during adolescence so-called daydreams and fancies, which take up the middle ground between a real dream and abstract thought, begin to make their appearance. In these daydreams, the adolescent usually weaves a long epic poem, where the separate parts are connected with one another, which remains more or less consistent over long periods of time and which contains separate peripeteias, situations and episodes. It amounts to a creative dream vision, which is conceived by the adolescent's imagination and which he experiences when awake. So the adolescent's daydreams, this type of dream visionary thinking, often becomes involved with visual eidetic images, which are evoked spontaneously.

'It is for this reason', says Kroh, 'that, during the early stages of puberty, the spontaneous visual images often appear even when the arbitrarily evoked images have completely ceased to happen.' And when asked what he considers to be the main reason for the disappearance of the eidetic images from the memory sphere, and their displacement to the realm of imagination, which is the fundamental factor responsible for the changes in the psychological function which occur in these spheres, Kroh replies, in complete accord with Jaensch's views, that both in the spheres of ontogeny and phylogeny, it is language which, in the process of becoming the means for the formation of concepts, the autonomization of speech and thinking in concepts, constitutes the main reason.

Both essential and inessential elements, in a disunited form, mixed up with eidetic images, can be found in the concepts of an adolescent. Therefore Kroh's general conclusion, which is that subjective visual images begin to disappear at about 15 to 16 years of age, fully corresponds to his own theory that, at the same time, concepts begin to replace the former images.

So we seem to have reached a conclusion which appears to confirm the traditional point of view which establishes the concrete character of the imagination in adolescence. We should also remember that, when the eidetic images in children were investigated, the presence of elements linking these images with fantasy was already confirmed. The eidetic image does not always appear as the precise and accurate effect of the percept which has elicited it. Very frequently this percept undergoes a change and is reworked in the process of its eidetic reconstruction. The underlying cause of the eidetic tendency is not just the visual stimulation, but we also find in eidetic images the complicated function of revision of the visual conception, the selection of interesting material and even a distinctive process of generalization.

One of Jaensch's important contributions is the discovery of visual concepts, i.e. of such generalizing visual eidetic images which, as it were, are analogous to our concepts in the sphere of concrete thinking. The enormous significance of this concrete thinking process cannot be exaggerated, and Jaensch is perfectly correct when he says that the intellectualism which used to dominate education, tended to develop the child in only one direction, and its approach was one-sided, because it regarded him primarily as a logician and logicized the entire system of his psychological operations.

There is no doubt that, to a great extent, adolescent thinking still remains in the domain of concrete thinking, and this concrete thinking also survives at higher levels of development, even in adulthood. Many writers identify this process of concrete thinking with imagination, but in actual fact it seems that what we are observing here is a visual reworking of concrete sensory images, and, after all, this has always been considered the basic characteristic feature of imagination.

## III

The traditional view of fantasy regards it as an integral and distinctive feature, the visual part of the images which it contains. Researchers usually point out that, as applied to adolescence, all those elements of concrete, imagistic, visual conceptions of reality, which are being progressively banished from the sphere of the adolescent's abstract thinking, tend to congregate within the realm of fantasy. We have already seen that, strictly speaking, such a statement is not completely true, even though it appears to have been confirmed by a number of facts which speak in its favour.

It would not be quite correct to regard the function of fantasy as an exclusively visual, imagistic and concrete activity. Quite rightly, it has been pointed out that the same sort of visual quality is also characteristic of the imagery of memory. On the other hand, activity of a schematic or barely visual type is also present in fantasy. 'If we limit fantasy exclusively to the realm of visual conceptions', says Lindworsky, 'and remove any aspects of thinking from it, then it would not be possible to describe a poetic creation as a product of the activity of fantasy'.[11] In exactly the same way, Meumann disagrees with Lau's point of view, who saw the difference between fantasy and thinking in the fact that the former operates in visual images and does not contain any elements of abstract thinking.

'Elements of abstract thinking', says Meumann, *are never absent* from our images and perceptions.'[12] And there is no way in which they could not be there, because in an adult the entire conceptual material exists in a form which has been reworked by abstract thinking. Wundt has also expressed the same idea when he objected to fantasy being regarded as simply the work of visual conceptions.

Indeed, as we shall see later on, one of the essential changes which fantasy undergoes in adolescence is its liberation from purely concrete, imagistic features and, at the same time, its infiltration by elements of abstract thinking.

We have already said that one essential characteristic of adolescence is the rapprochement between fantasy and thinking, and the imagination begining to rely on concepts. But this rapprochement does not signify complete absorption of fantasy by thinking. Both functions approach each other, but they do not merge, Müller-Freienfels' formulation that productive fantasy and thinking are one and the same thing,[13] has not been verified by the actual situation. As we shall see later, there are many features which characterize fantasy and corresponding experiences which differentiate fantasy from thinking.

So our problem remains to discover the peculiar relationships between the abstract and the concrete aspects which are characteristic of imagination in adolescence. From a certain viewpoint, what we have in the adolescent's imagination is, indeed, as it were, a collection of all the elements of concrete visual thinking which recede to the background in his thinking. In order to understand the meaning of the concrete aspect of adolescent fantasy correctly, we must take into consideration the connections which exist between adolescent imagination and childhood play.

From the genetic point of view, imagination in adolescence is the successor to child play. According to one psychologist's apt statement,[14]

A child, despite all his enthusiasm, is perfectly able to keep apart in his mind the world he invents during his play from the real one, and naturally he looks for support for the imagined objects and relationships in the palpable real objects of real life. It is precisely this support he seeks which differentiates the child's play from fantasizing. As the child grows up it gives up play. He replaces play with imagination. When a child who is growing up gives up playing, what he is doing, strictly speaking, is giving up nothing more than the search for this support in real objects. In place of play, he now gives himself over to fantasy. He builds castles in the air and creates what is called daydreams.

Clearly, fantasy, as the successor to childish play, has only recently broken away from the support which it was able to find in tangible and concrete objects in real life. It is for this reason that it is eager to find support in concrete conceptions which stand for these real objects. Images, eidetic pictures and visual conceptions begin to play the same role in the imagination as a doll representing a child, or a chair representing a steam engine, in childish play. This is the source of the striving of the adolescent's fantasy to have the backing of concrete sensory material and of the tendency towards figurativeness and use of visual images. But it is equally noteworthy that this use of visual images and this figurativeness have changed their function completely. They have ceased to be a support for memory and thinking, and have passed on to the sphere of fantasy.

A striking example of such a tendency towards concretization can be found in Wassermann's novel *The Maurizius Case*.[15] One of the novel's heroes, a 16-year-old boy, reflects on the unjust sentence given to Maurizius, who has been locked up in prison for 18 years due to a legal error. The thought of this unjustly sentenced man takes over the adolescent's mind and here, in a state of agitation, whilst thinking about the fate of this man, the boy's inflamed brain draws pictures, whilst at the same time Etzel desires nothing more than it should function in a logical way.

> He is thinking. His inflamed brain draws pictures, but at the same time Etzel demands nothing more than it should think in a logical way. But it is not always possible to make the thinking apparatus fulfil its basic function. He calculates that eighteen years and five months equals two hundred and twenty one months or approximately six thousand six hundred and thirty days and six thousand six hundred and thirty nights. It is very important to differentiate between them: days are one thing and a nights, quite another. But at this instant he stops imagining things and all that remains is an incomprehensible number; it is as if he is standing in front of an ant hill and is attempting to count the crawling insects. He makes an effort to make sense of all this, and he wants to fill this number with meaning – with six thousand six hundred and thirty steps – but this proves too difficult; a match box with six thousand six hundred and thirty matches – hopeless; a purse with six thousand six hundred and thirty pfennigs – he cannot do it; a train with six thousand six hundred and thirty carriages – unnatural; a stack of six thousand six hundred and thirty sheets (note: sheets and not pages, as two pages of each sheet correspond to a day and a night).
>
> And here, at last, he will achieve a visual conception; he takes down a pile of books from the shelf; the first book has one hundred and fifty sheets, the second one – one hundred and twenty five, the third – two hundred and ten; not a single one of them has more than two hundred and sixty; he has misjudged the resources; having piled up twenty three volumes, he has managed to obtain only four thousand two hundred and twenty sheets. Dumbfounded, he abandons this activity. Just to think that every single day lived has to be added on. His own life hardly comprises five thousand nine hundred days and how long it seems to him, how slowly it has been progressing; another week seemed to him like a forced march along country roads, another day seemed to stick to his body like tar, which could not be pulled off.
>
> And at the same time, while he slept, read, went to school, played, talked with people and made plans, winter came and went, spring came, the sun shone, it rained, evening came, morning followed, and all this time he was there; time came, time went, and all the time he was there, always there, always there. Etzel had not even been born yet (infinite, mysterious word, and suddenly he was born), the first, the second, the five hundredth, the two thousand two hundred and thirty seventh day, even that one was over, but all the time he remained there.[16]

Using this example, it can clearly be seen how tightly adolescent fantasy is still bound up with the concrete support which it finds in sensory conceptions. In this sense the genetic fate of visual or concrete thinking is of great interest. Visual thinking does not completely disappear from the intellectual life of the adolescent along with the appearance of abstract thinking. It only moves to another place, goes off into into the fantasy sphere, partly undergoes a change under the influence of abstract thinking and then, like any other function, rises to a higher level.

Special investigations of the relationship which exists between visual thinking carried out with eidetic pictures and intellect, have at first produced contradictory results. The researchers found that a predominance of visual thinking and ideational tendencies was characteristic of mentally retarded and primitive children. On the other hand, other researchers found these phenomena present in mentally gifted subjects. However, Schmitz's[17] last investigation has shown that no simple relationship between the intellect and eidetic tendencies can be ascertained. A strongly expressed eidetic tendency can co-exist with any level of intellectual development. However, another, more detailed investigation has shown that a timely development of concrete thinking is an indispensable condition for the raising of the thinking process to a higher level.

This writer quite rightly refers to Ziehen's[18] research which has established that it is precisely gifted children who remain for longer on the level of concrete conceptions than non-gifted ones; it seems as if the intellect had to start developing by first becoming satiated with visual contemplation and thus building a concrete foundation for the further development of abstract thinking.

## IV

In this respect, research carried out in the field of the so-called visual concepts is of particular interest. Recently, special investigations of the formation of concepts in visual thinking were carried out in Jaensch's school. What these researchers understand by the formation of concepts in visual thinking is the peculiar fusion, combination and cohesion of images into new formations which are analogous to our concepts. These investigations were carried out using information about eidetic images, which are considered to be eminently suitable subjects for such research.

To reiterate, an eidetic image is a visual conception which, as it were, is seen by the eye on a blank screen placed in front of the subject, in a similar way to when we see a green square after fixating on a red square with our eyes. The subject is then shown several similar pictures or representations, which have some similar features but also some different ones. Next, whatever the subject sees when the eidetic image appears under the influence of not just one, but several, similar representations is examined. The results have revealed that, during this procedure, the eidetic image is never built up mechanically like Galton's photographic plate, which selects similar features and obliterates the dissimilar ones. The eidetic image never selects similar and regularly repeated features whilst the different ones are concealed. The experiments show that the eidetic image creates a new whole, a new combination and a new image from several concrete impressions. The researchers have described two basic types of such visual concepts.

The first type is based on the so-called fluxion, where the eidetic image represents a dynamic combination of a number of separate concrete impressions. The eidetic sees one of a number of objects presented to him on a screen. The object then begins to change its contours and turns into a different but similar object. An image changes into another, then into a third, and sometimes during this process a whole cycle is completed, where all the objects join in a dynamic change of the image which represents each of the separate objects in turn.

As an example, the subject is presented with some red carnations and a rose which are all the same size. At first the subject sees the last flower exhibited. Then its contours and shape become obliterated and they blend into an indistinct coloured spot which appears like something half way between two presented colours. When the subject is shown two other flowers, at first what he sees is an image of the rose which then proceeds to change into a red spot. Gradually, it acquires a yellow tinge. In this way one object changes into another. The investigators quite rightly point out that the intermediate image which appears at that time is still, to a certain extent, close to the picture which traditional logic perceives as the underlying structure of a concept, because, in reality, the spot-like images described above contain some features common to both individual objects.

In this respect it would prove extremely revealing to turn one's attention to the question of what this conceptual formation would actually come to, were it to follow the schemes set up for it by formal logic. Some sort of vague, shapeless spot, devoid of any individuality or similarity with the real object, is what the visual image generated by two similar flowers turns into. A concept of formal logic represents precisely such a spot, which 'sees the function of a concept as a loss of a number of characteristics and ascribes its formation to the auspicious gift of oblivion'.

In contrast to this barren picture, an integration of images of the fluxion type conveys the full richness of reality and whilst, in actual fact, this coloured spot does nothing more than reveal a loss of attributes as compared with reality, fluxions do, indeed, produce new formations and new shapes, whose essence lies in the fact that the features of individual objects combine in a new synthesis which had not been revealed in advance. An image of a leaf which is evoked following the presentation of several similar leaves may serve as an example of fluxion. This image keeps moving and keeps shifting constantly backwards and forwards whilst it changes its form.

Another process of combining images in visual thinking is composition. This combination consists of the subject forming a new, sensible whole which is constructed according to a known usable attribute selected from various features of concrete objects. Thus, for example, the subject is shown a representation of a dachshund and another of a donkey. What the subject sees on the screen is a gundog. Composition can be differentiated from fluxion in that, here, the combination of images is given not in a moving, oscillating form, but in a form which is restrained and steady. For example, if the subject is shown representations of three different houses, he ends up seeing one house with the different features of all the three images presented to him.

These investigations carried out by Jaensch and Schweicher graphically demonstrate the extent to which the idea that concepts originate simply as a result of simple addition or combination of images is without foundation. Jaensch's visual concept is a combination of images. But a concept in the real sense of the word is not a combination of images, but a combination of assessments, a certain system composed of them. The most important difference between the two is that in the former what we have is a first hand and in the latter a mediated knowledge and assessment of the object.

Using Hegel's famous distinction, one could say that in the sphere of visual thinking we are concerned with a product of sense, whilst in the realm of abstract thinking we are concerned with a product of intellect. A child's thinking is governed by sense. An adolescent's thinking is intellectual thinking. One of the most difficult problems encountered by experimental psychology, the problem of non-visual thinking, can be solved when the concept is understood in this definitive way. A concept is, as it were, a condensation of assessments, a key to a whole complex consisting of them, their infrastructure. This makes it quite clear that concepts have a non-visual character and that they come into being by a different path than simply by way of various combinations of conceptions.

The research we have just discussed has finally done away with the possibility of the presence of anything resembling real concepts in the process of visual thinking. The highest point which a combination of conceptions can reach is fluxion and composition. At the same time, we have to agree entirely with the writers who maintain that we ought to regard visual thinking as a peculiar form of thinking which is very important in the development of the intellect. Our observations have convinced us that visual thinking, whose development breaks off when concepts begin to form, continues to function in the realm of fantasy, where it begins to play a significant role. But even here, as we shall see later, it does not continue to exist in its former cast, exclusively as visual thinking. It undergoes a vigorous transformation under the influence of concepts, which cannot be excluded from the activity of imagination. Once again the statement we have discussed above, which claims that for human beings to think without words is to have to rely on words after all, has been proved correct.

## V

What then does this essential difference between adolescent fantasy and the fantasy of a child amount to, and what new features can be observed at this time?

When we pointed out that a child's play turns into adolescent fantasy, we had already described the most essential part of it. So, despite the concrete and real elements which are still found in it, the adolescent's imagination is nevertheless different from child's play, in that it breaks its links with real objects. Its foundations remain concrete, but are of a less visual character than those of a child. However, we feel that attention should be drawn to the progressively abstract character of the adolescent's fantasy.

There is a widely held view which maintains that a child does possess a well developed fantasy and that early childhood is the time of the flowering of fantasy. Despite its extreme prevalence, this opinion turns out to be incorrect. As Wundt quite rightly points out, children's fantasy turns out not to be as extensive as it has been thought to be. On the contrary, it does not take very much to satisfy it. Days on end can be filled with thoughts about a horse drawing a cart. And, at the same time, the imagined scenes hardly differ at all from reality.

A similar activity in an adult would signify a complete absence of fantasy. A child's vivid fantasy is conditioned not so much by the richness of his ideas, but by the fact that it is accompanied by a greater intensity and is more likely to arouse his emotions. Wundt tends to interpret this aspect in an extreme way and maintains that one can say that a child totally lacks synthesizing fantasy. One can dispute this last statement, however the truth of the basic thesis, that children's fantasy is considerably more impoverished than the fantasy of adolescents, and that it is only because of its greater susceptibility to emotional arousal, the intensity of experience and the absence of critical judgement, that it occupies a more prominent place in the child's behaviour, can be ascertained; this is also the reason why it appears to us richer and more developed than it really is. For the same reason we can observe that by becoming more abstract, rather than poorer, the adolescent's fantasy is enriched compared with that of a child.

Wundt is right when he points out the extreme poverty of the creative aspects of children's fantasy. From this point of view adolescent fantasy becomes more creative than children's. It is perfectly true that, according to Bühler,[19] the adolescent's fantasy is not productive in the same sense as the word is used in relation to adults. The very fact of the late appearance of artistic creativity testifies to this. According to these researchers, among all the artistic creations in adolescence, the only one which can be considered as a creation which he is able to invent for himself is an ideal love. But, at the same time, the writers note the extreme prevalence of creativity which involves the keeping of diaries and poetry writing. 'It is startling', she says, 'how people without any talent for poetry begin to write poetry in adolescence.' It is obvious that this phenomenon is not accidental and that the inner drive for creative expression and the inner tendency for productivity is a distinguishing feature of the adolescent age.

By the way, we do not detect any contradiction in the two statements we have just discussed. Adolescent fantasy appears creative when it is compared with children's fantasy, but by no means can it be considered productive in comparison with adult fantasy. This is because the creative character does not become an inherent part of it until adolescence. This explains why it has a rudimentary character and does not yet represent full-scale creativity. Bühler is quite right when she points out that this adolescent fantasy is tightly bound up with the new needs which make their appearance in adolescence and as a result of which the image takes on specific characteristic features and an emotional tone. This is how adolescent fantasy creates.

Later, we will have another chance to discuss in more detail the question of the link which fantasy maintains with needs and emotions. But now we are interested in another problem, namely, the relationship between adolescent fantasy and intellect. Bühler maintains that experience would make one suppose that in adolescence abstract thinking and visual thinking stand apart from one another. They do not yet co-operate in any sort of creative activity. Internal images, coloured by emotion and intensely experienced, follow one upon another, but without in any way being influenced by creative thinking in the form of selection or association. For thinking creates in an abstract fashion, without any visual component whatsoever.

So, if one is to take this statement in the context of its genetic plan and to adjust it by taking development into account, it will not be seen to contradict the theory stated above, which says that it is precisely the rapprochement of intellect and imagination which distinguishes the adolescent age. As Ribot has shown, the two lines of development, which had hitherto run separately, now meet at one point at this age and after that they continue tightly bound together. But precisely because this meeting, this rapprochement, only happened in adolescence for the very first time, they do not lead immediately to a complete fusion or a full co-operation between the two functions, and an alienation of the thinking process and imagination, which Bühler has described, is the result.

In the meantime, we have seen that many writers attempt, not so much to establish this division between thinking and imagination in adolescence, as to find characteristics which separate thinking from imagination. Meumann ascribes this difference to the fact that the activity of imagination focuses our attention primarily on the content of the conceptions and thoughts, whilst in thinking it is focused on the logical relationships which result from it. 'The activity of fantasy', he says, 'consists of the fact that we actually take an interest in the content of an image or thought *as such* . . . and break up existing connections between images and thoughts to create new combinations.'[20]

After all, the goal of our thinking activity is the establishment of logical relationships amidst the contents of our thoughts. From our point of view, such a definition does not differentiate clearly enough between imagination and thinking. And what is more, we do not think it possible to draw such a precise demarcation line. This is conditioned by the very situation which consists of the fact that, as it happens, the essential change which the adolescent's imagination undergoes, is the external rapprochement with thinking in concepts. Just like all the other functions which we discussed in the previous chapter, the adolescent imagination experiences basic changes and it becomes transformed with the aid of a new infrastructure under the influence of thinking in concepts.

It is possible to illustrate the internal dependence of the imagination on thinking in concepts using the examples from the behaviour of aphasic patients which we cited at the beginning of this chapter. Along with loss of speech, as a means for the formation of concepts, imagination also disappears. The following is another extremely curious feature, namely that in aphasics we very often observe an inability to use or comprehend metaphors and any words used in a figurative sense. We have already seen that it is only during adolescence that thinking aided by metaphors becomes accessible. The schoolboy still finds it very difficult to associate a proverb with an ordinary sentence with the same meaning.

It is very significant that a similar disruption also occurs in aphasia. One of our experimental subjects who suffered from aphasia was totally incapable of understanding any symbolical expressions. When he was asked what was meant when a person was described as having golden hands, he would reply: 'This means that he knows how to melt down gold'. He would usually reduce any figurative expression to an absurdity. To be able to understand a metaphor was beyond him. He also found it impossible to associate a proverb or any allegorical expression with a sentence which expressed the same idea in a direct form.

Here we are able to see a full analogy with the example cited at the beginning of this chapter, which, as we have already said, testifies that, together with the disappearance of thinking in concepts, imagination also tends to vanish completely. This is quite understandable. We have seen that this zero point of imagination, this absolute absence of fantasy, can be observed because the person is unable to divert his attention from the concrete situation, to transform it creatively, to re-group the attributes and to free himself from the influence of the actual situation.

In exactly the same way, we can see how in the present example the aphasic cannot free himself from the concrete literal meaning of the word, and how he is not able to combine the different concrete situations into a new image in any creative way. In order to be able to do this, a certain detachment from the actual situation is required and this detachment, as we have seen above, can only be provided by thinking in concepts. Thus, it is conceptual thinking which is the main factor which conditions the prospect of creative fantasy in adolescence.

It would, however, be a mistake to suppose that, because of this, fantasy blends completely with abstract thinking and that it loses its visual character. But it is exactly this peculiar relationship between abstract and concrete aspects that we consider to be the main characteristic feature of fantasy in adolescence. This can be explained further by saying that purely concrete thinking which is devoid of any concepts, also lacks completely any trace of fantasy. For the first time the formation of concepts brings with it a release from the concrete situation and a likelihood of a creative reworking and transformation of its elements.

# VI

But one of the characteristic features of imagination is that it does not stop developing at this stage and that, from its standpoint, abstraction is only a transitory link in the chain, a stage along the road of development, or simply a leap forward in the process of its movement towards the concrete. From our point of view, imagination is a creative transforming activity which moves from one form of concreteness to another. But the mere movement from a given concrete form to a newly created form of it and the very feasibility of a creative construction, is only possible with the help of abstraction. So abstraction is incorporated into the process of imagination as an indispensable constituent part, but it does not form its centre. The movement from the concrete through the abstract to the construction of a new form of a concrete image, is the path which describes imagination in the adolescent age.

In connection with this, Lindworsky[21] points to a number of features which differentiate fantasy from thinking. According to him, what distinguishes fantasy from the point of view of its characteristic attributes, is the relative novelty of the created results. However, we think that it is not the novelty for its own sake which differentiates this process, but the novelty of the concrete image arising as a result of the activity of fantasy, and the novelty of the idea embodied in it. In this sense we think that Erdmann's[22] definition, when he says that fantasy creates images of unperceived objects, is nearer the truth.

It is the creative character of concrete expression and the construction of a new image which exemplify fantasy. Its culminating point is the achievement of a concrete form, but this form can only be attained with the help of abstraction. An adolescent's fantasy moves from the concrete visual image through a concept to an imaginary image. In this respect we do not agree with Lindworsky, who attributes the characteristic difference between fantasy and thinking to the absence of a defined problem. He does, however, make a reservation that the absence of a defined problem should not be confused with the involuntariness of fantasy.

He shows that, within the process of fantasy, free will does influence the development of conceptions to a significant degree. We think that what is especially typical in adolescence is the transition from a passive and imitative type of childish fantasy, mentioned by Meumann and others, to an active and creative fantasy characteristic of the adolescent age.

But we think the most essential feature of fantasy during adolescence is its bifurcation into a subjective and an objective imagination. Strictly speaking, fantasy only begins to take shape during adolescence. In this respect we agree with Wundt's assertion that children completely lack the combining type of fantasy. This is true in the sense that, for the first time, the adolescent begins to select and visualize this form as a special function. A strictly select function related to imagination does not yet exist in childhood. But an adolescent is aware that his subjective fantasy is subjective, and he also recognizes the actual boundaries of his objective fantasy, which is working in rapport with his thinking.

As we have already said above, the separation of subjective and objective features and the creation of opposite poles within the personality and world view, are characteristic of the adolescent age. And the same sort of dissociation of subjective and objective features is also typical of adolescent fantasy.

It is as if fantasy branches out into two separate channels. On the one hand, it begins to serve the goal of bringing satisfaction to the emotional side of life, all the needs, moods and feelings which fill the adolescent's being. It turns into a subjective activity which gives personal satisfaction and is reminiscent of child's play. As a previously cited psychologist so aptly remarks: 'It is, by no means, a happy person who indulges in fantasies, but rather an unsatisfied one'.[23] An unsatisfied desire acts as a stimulus for fantasy. Our fantasy represents the realization of desire, a correction of unsatisfying reality.

This is the reason why almost all writers agree in pointing out the one character-istic of adolescent fantasy, namely that, for the first time, it turns its attention to the intimate realm of his experience, normally hidden from other people, and thus becomes an exclusively subjective form of thinking, thinking exclusively for oneself. A child makes no attempt to hide his play, but an adolescent conceals his fantasies and safeguards them from other people's eyes. Our author is right in saying that he conceals them like his most precious secret and is more likely to admit to any wrongdoings than to reveal his fantasies. It is just this reticent aspect of fantasy which points to the fact that it is tightly bound up with inner desires, incentives, attractions and emotions within the adolescent's personality, and that it is beginning to serve this whole side of his life. In this respect, the association of fantasy with emotion is extremely significant.

We know that different emotions always activate in us a certain definite flow of ideas. Our feeling strives to cast itself into the mould of certain images where it finds an expression and release. Therefore it is to be expected that the different images may prove to be powerful means for calling forth, exciting and relieving different feelings. This is the essence of the close bond which exists between lyric poetry and the feelings of the person reading it. And the subjective value of fantasy also consists of this. It is a long time now since our attention has been called to the fact that, as Goethe expressed it, feelings do not deceive, it is judgements which deceive. When, with the help of fantasy, we construct some sorts of unreal images, the latter are not real, but the feeling which they evoke is experienced as being real. When the poet says: 'I will dissolve in tears over this fiction',[24] he realizes that this figment is something unreal, but his tears belong to the realm of reality. In this way an adolescent finds a means of expressing his rich inner emotional life and his impulses in fantasy.

But it is also in fantasy that he is able to discover an effective means of finding a direction for this emotional life and for taking charge of it. Similar to the way in which an adult overcomes his feelings during the reading of a literary work, say of a lyric poem, the adolescent clarifies, reveals to himself and incorporates his emotions and his longings in creative images. The unexpressed part of his life finds its expression in creative images.

We therefore feel justified in saying that the creative images which the adolescent fantasy engenders, fulfil the same function for him as a work of literature does for an adult. This kind of creative work is strictly for oneself. But also for oneself are the poems and novels, the dramatic performances and tragedies, and the elegies and sonnets composed and created in the mind. In this respect Spranger quite correctly contrasts adolescent fantasy with childish fantasy. He says that even though the adolescent can still be considered to be still half way a child, his fantasy is of a completely different sort than that of a child. It gradually comes closer to the conscious illusion of adults. Spranger illustrates this difference between childish fantasy and adolescent imagination in the following way: 'Childish fantasy', he says, 'is a dialogue with things, whereas adolescent fantasy is a monologue with things.' An adolescent is aware that his fantasy is a subjective activity. A child is still not able to differentiate his fantasy from the things with which he is playing.[25]

Alongside this channel which fantasy follows, primarily serving the adolescent's emotional sphere, the adolescent fantasy also develops along another channel of purely objective creativity. We have already said that, where creation of some sort of new concrete structure, a new picture of reality, of a creative embodiment of some sort of idea, becomes indispensable for the process of understanding or the process of practical activity, there we find fantasy coming to the fore as a basic function. It is with the help of fantasy that not just literary works, but all the scientific inventions and technical achievements are created. Fantasy is one of the manifestations of creative activity of man, and this is especially true in adolescence, when the rapprochement with thinking in concepts occurs, and it undergoes significant development in this objective aspect.

It would not be right to suppose that these two channels which the development of fantasy in adolescence follows actually diverge. On the contrary, both the concrete and abstract aspects, as well as the subjective and objective ones, are frequently found in a state of complex interlacement with each other. Objective expression may be coloured by vivid emotional tones, but subjective fantasies are also often observed within the sphere of objective creativity. To illustrate the rapprochement of both of these channels in the development of the imagination, we should like to point out that it is, precisely, within the realm of his fantasy that, for the first time, the adolescent has a chance to discover the course his life is to take. His strivings and obscure drives are cast in the mould of specific images. In his fantasy, he anticipates his future and consequently also comes closer to its creative construction and realization.

## VII

With this, we feel we can conclude the cycle of our discussion of adolescent psychology. We started by examining the most crucial change which occurs in adolescence. We have established that a whole new and complicated world of new longings, strivings, motives and interests is created following puberty, that new moving forces drive the adolescent's thinking process forward and that new problems open up before us.

Later we saw how these new problems lead to the development of the central and leading function of the entire psychological development, i.e. to the formation of concepts, and how a great number of entirely new psychological functions come into being as a result of the formation of concepts, how the adolescent's perception, memory, concentration and practical activity are transformed as a result of the new reigning principles, and, most important of all, how they become part of a new structure and how gradually new bases for higher syntheses of personality and world view become established. And now, whilst subjecting imagination to an analysis, we are, once again, able to see how these new forms of behaviour, which have their origins during the time of puberty and the yearnings which are bound up with it, begin to serve the adolescent's emotional strivings, how the adolescent's emotional and intellectual aspects of behaviour achieve their synthesis in his creative imagination, and how longings and thinking become combined in a complicated new way, in the activity connected with the creative imagination.

## Test problems for lessons 9–12

Answer the following questions in writing, giving reasons for your answers:

1 What are the basic stages of adolescence and the interests which characterize each stage?
2 What are the basic stages in the development of the formation of concepts and what basic changes in the content and form of thinking occur in connection with the formation of concepts during adolescence?
3 What are the most important changes in the functions of perception, memory, concentration and practical intellect which occur during adolescence; what does the link between these changes and the function of formation of concepts consist of and how can this connection be explained in the light of our knowledge about hysteria, aphasia and schizophrenia?

## Notes

This text was chapter 12 of Vygotsky, L. S. 1931: *Pedologija podrostka* [*Paedology of the Adolescent*]. Moscow-Leningrad: Uchebno-Pedagogicheskoe Izdatel'stvo. Parts of it (from part 2) have been translated into English on the basis of the Russian edition of Vygotsky's Collected Works (Vol. 4, Moscow, 1984). See Vygotsky, L. S. 1991: Imagination and creativity in the adolescent. *Soviet Psychology*, 29, 1, 73–88. It is crucial to consider that the inclusion of *Pedologija podrostka* in the 1984 edition was itself abridged and its (abridged) translation into English was based on that version. The translation included here is made from the first Russian original published in 1931.

1 Here Vygotsky gives examples taken directly from pp. 295–6 of Cassirer, E. 1929: *Philosophie der symbolischen Formen Vol. 3: Phänomenologie der Erkenntnis*. Berlin: Bruno Cassirer Verlag [or in English: from p. 254 of *The Philosophy of Symbolic Forms Vol. 3: The phenomenology of knowledge*. New Haven, Ct: Yale University Press]. The Frankfurt Neurological Institute was the location of much of the neuropsychological work of Kurt Goldstein and Adhemar Gelb.
2 We have been unable to trace the reference to Lewin.

3   This reference to Henry Head's patient is made via Cassirer (1929, footnote 64 on p. 245 of English version). Cassirer quotes the words of Head's patient No. 10: 'When you asked me to do this first . . . I couldn't do it. I couldn't get the starting point. I knew where all the things were in the room, but I had difficulty in getting a starting point when it came to setting them down on a plan. You made me point out on the plan, and it was quite easy because you had done it.'

4   We have been unable to find Gelb's text.

5   'Voobrazhenie stol' zhe potrebno v geometrii kak i v poezii.' The citation is not exact. It should be 'Vdokhnovenie nuzhno v poezii, kak i v geometrii' ['Inspiration is as necessary in poetry as it is in geometry']. See p. 491 of Pushkin, A. S. 1825/1984: O stat'jakh Kjukhel'bekera v al'manakhe 'Mnemozina'. In S. A. Pushkin, Sobranie Sochinenji v Odnom Tome. Moscow: Khudozhestvennaja Literatura.

6   The curve is on p. 140 of Ribot, Th. 1926: Essai sur l'imagination créatrice. Paris: Felix Alcan. Ribot claimed that imagination develops when the child is around three years old and develops a considerable time before the intellect. The first period in childhood is, consequently, one of non-rational imagination. As soon as reason has reached the same level as imagination the latter gets rationalized. This can happen in either of two ways. The first, most frequent, case is that of a gradual decline of imagination. Life becomes more prosaic, as Ribot says, and only in rare cases imagination is still used. The second, and more happy, case we find when imagination becomes transformed by reason and turns into intellectual imagination. This is the case of creative scientists, poets, etc. Ribot believed that a similar development could be found in human history.

7   See pp. 128–9 of Bühler, Ch. 1929: Das Seelenleben des Jugendlichen (5th improved edn). Jena: Gustav Fischer.

8   Refers to the work of E. R. Jaensch, W. Jaensch, H. Freiling, F. Reich and others. See Jaensch, E. R. 1923: Über den Aufbau der Wahrnehmungswelt und ihre Struktur im Jugendalter. Leipzig: Barth; Jaensch, E. R. 1933: Die Eidetik und die typologische Forschungsmethode (3d edn). Leipzig: Quelle and Meyer. In English see Jaensch, E. R. 1930: Eidetic Imagery and Typological Methods of Investigation. New York: Harcourt, Brace and Co.

9   See p. 238 of Jaensch, E. R. (1923).

10  Oswald Kroh was a leading German child psychologist who belonged to Jaensch's school. In Vygotsky's Collected Works (in Russian) we find references to five different works by Kroh (one in Russian, four in German) all of which are rather difficult to locate. The most likely source for this and the following citations is Kroh, O. 1922: Subjektive Anschauungsbilder bei Jugendlichen. Göttingen: Van den hoek & Ruprecht.

11  This is probably quoted from Lindworsky, J. 1925: Methoden der Phantasieforschung. In E. Abderhalden (ed.) Handbuch der biologischen Arbeitsmethoden, vol. 6. Vienna: Fischer.

12  Refers to pp. 239–40 of Meumann, E. 1907: Vorlesungen zur Einführung in die experimentelle Pädagogik und ihre psychologischen Grundlagen, Bd. 1. Leipzig: Verlag von Wilhelm Engelmann.

13  See Müller-Freienfels, R. 1925: Grundzüge einer Lebenspsychologie. Vol. 2: Das Denken und die Phantasie (2nd edn). Leipzig: Barth.

14  We have been unable to establish the identity of this author.

15  The original German novel by Jakob Wassermann – Der Fall Maurizius – was published in Berlin in 1928 (S. Fischer Verlag).

16  The present translation was made from the Russian edition published in Leningrad, 1929.

17  We have not been able to trace this publication.

18  See Ziehen, Th. 1898: *Die Ideenassoziation des Kindes*. Berlin: Reuther & Reichard.
19  This and the next two paragraphs paraphrase pp. 135–8 of Bühler, Ch. (1929). The quotation is taken from p. 138. In the Russian original Vygotsky mixes up Charlotte Bühler with her husband Karl Bühler by writing 'Bühler is quite right when *he* says' etc.
20  See p. 239 of Meumann (1907).
21  Cf. pp. 240–5 of Lindworsky, J. 1931: *Experimentelle Psychologie* (5th improved edn). Munich: Kösel & Pustet.
22  This is possibly a reference to Erdmann, K. O. 1925: *Die Bedeutung des Wortes*. Leipzig: Haessel.
23  See note 14.
24  'Nad vymyslom slezami obol'jus''. Line from Pushkin's poem 'Elegija' (1830). See p. 100 of Pushkin, A. S. 1984: *Sobranie Sochinenij v Odnom Tome*. Moscow: Khudozhestvennaja Literatura.
25  The quotation and explanation are taken from pp. 53–4 of Spranger, E. 1925: *Psychologie des Jugendalters*. Leipzig: Quelle & Meyer.

# 11

# The development of voluntary attention in the child

*Aleksej Leont'ev*

The problem of the nature and mechanism of voluntary attention and the general questions of the voluntary behaviour of man belong to one of the least accessible fields of the science of psychology. The difficulties associated with the problem of voluntary acts arise, undoubtedly, from the fact that the main principles upon which the scientific study of higher forms of behaviour are built have not been sufficiently worked out. The first important step towards the construction of a scientific theory of voluntary attention is made when we refuse to regard the higher forms of attention as immobile, completed phenomena, subject to direct research, and, instead of that, proceed to their genetic study.

The idea of development alone, taken as a methodological principle, cannot, of course, determine the direction to be taken by the research work. The conception of development may be interpreted variously. We may regard development either as the result of the unfolding of forces inherent in the nature of the given creature, or as the result of a concrete process of interaction of the organism and the environment. According to the point of view we choose, differences will be found in the comprehension of the phenomena studied, and, consequently, in the main method of research. Even in the latter case, however, when the development of the higher psychological functions is regarded as a result of interaction, there still remains a fundamental question – the question of the central factor determining this interaction.

If, on the one hand, we can take the genetic point of view as a sufficiently established one in contemporary psychology, on the other hand, the question of the principal factor lying at the basis of man's psychological development has also been decided in the main.

In particular, and in connection with the development of voluntary behaviour, the role of this factor, that is, the specific part played by the social environment of man, has more than once been indicated in psychology, and there exists a number of fully worked-out theories on this subject. Blondel's theory of will and Ribot's theory of voluntary attention are especially interesting in this connection.[1] Until lately, however, these theories had no place in the great psychological systems, and did not constitute an organic part of any one integral structure, which, creating this whole, would at the same time acquire significance as a part of the whole. In this respect the fate of Ribot's theory of attention is typical. In present-day psychology this theory is shown persistently from one side only, that is, as a 'motor' theory, while the other, and from our point of view much more important side – bringing out the sociogenetic conception of voluntary attention – remains in the background. Obviously, it does not find a sufficiently wide response in present-day psychological thought.

The social nature of voluntary attention is constantly being emphasized, but this does not mean that attention is actually being examined from this point of view. 'Both voluntary and involuntary attention are the result of the dominant process, *of choice* between disturbing factors,' says one of the most recent writers on this subject.

> If this choice is conditioned chiefly by *peripheral causes* (intensity of irritation) or internal organic causes, we speak of *involuntary attention*. If this choice is conditioned chiefly by *central* causes, which are expressed, so to speak, in the routine work of associative nerve routes, we speak of *voluntary* attention.
>
> It is clear, then, that voluntary attention arose as the result of the development of social relations, and is the product of social connections and environment. (Dobrinin, 1928; original emphasis)

Are the actual premises for the study of the mechanism of this important psychological function contained in this and similar assertions? To merely indicate the importance of social environment is not sufficient. 'The routine work of associative routes' is by no means the result of the specific influence of this environment. It is the work of the central agent, the most complicated associative connections we discover in the higher animals, where voluntary attention does not exist and behaviour is not influenced by social environment. Here the point is not the formal recognition of the important role of social factors, but, first of all, discovering the inter-relation of phenomena and laying bare that concrete mechanism, on the basis of and due to which, is formed the highest of activities regulating behaviour.

On the other hand, there is no doubt that until the main principles of development have been formulated, and the specific means of functioning of these higher forms of behaviour are discovered (which are subject, genetically, to social conditions), the collision between the simplified mechanical–materialistic and idealistic points of view will also remain insuperable. This collision creates contradictions which destroy the present-day psychological system.[2] To remove the cause of these contradictions, we must lay bare the mechanisms of those qualitative, peculiarly human forms of behaviour, which are created by social environment, unknown to the biological world; or, in other words, we must create a general theory of the social and historical development of behaviour. Such a theory of social genesis ('the theory of cultural development') was first formulated and brought forward by L. S. Vygotsky.[3] His theory forms the basis of the present experimental–psychological sketch. The task we have set ourselves is two-fold: on the one hand, it aims at providing, on the basis of the methods worked out by us, new experimental material for some general lines of this theory, and, on the other hand, to map out the route of its further development in the field of study of voluntary behaviour.

The problem of the voluntary regulation of behaviour, the problem of voluntary acts, is often carefully avoided in materialistic psychology. It is just in this problem that different philosophic systems collide, and it should be solved by materialistic science. For this reason, therefore, admitting its complexity, we apply ourselves to its solution to the utmost of our ability. In this lies the justification for this article, which claims least of all to be a finished and exhaustive study of the question, and assumes significance only in connection with the theory forming its basis.

I

The simplest, primary acts have been fairly well studied in psychology. In this respect psychology is greatly indebted to physiology. Thanks to the psychological researches conducted by Pavlov and Ukhtomsky on the work of the higher nerve centres, it has been possible to establish the main nervous mechanism lying at the foundation of the processes of the elementary regulation of behaviour. This simplest kind of activity which organizes and regulates behaviour and to which, in psychology, corresponds the conception of involuntary, primary attention, expresses itself with the help of the innate psychological mechanism, and is wholly conditioned by external stimuli and their direct bearing on the particular state of the organism.

The problem of voluntary attention presents a much greater difficulty to the research worker. In this higher form of regulation of behaviour, the immediate degree of intensity, 'newness' or affectogeneity of the active stimuli, are already not decisive factors. At the basis of this lie new and much more complicated mechanisms, which create a certain independence of behaviour from its direct elementary stimulus. The term 'voluntary attention' seems to us to express correctly the peculiar nature of this higher form of regulating and organizing activity, indicating its two specific signs: first, its outward independence of direct factors, and secondly, the presence of effort, which finds both its subjective and objective expression.

All regulation of behaviour requires two orders of change, change of *direction* of behaviour and change in the distribution of *force*. The question of direction of behaviour is that of the domination of one or another competing stimulus. In the simplest cases it is decided by the respective strength of stimuli acting directly in their struggle for the common field of action. What is meant when we speak of regulation of the distribution of energy is usually associated with the simplest factor of the continuation of behaviour. According to Sherrington, in spinal dogs the unconditional 'scratch reflex', after prolonged action of the stimulus, exhausts its resources of energy and ceases. Only after a certain interval the necessary stock of energy is restored and the reflex appears again. In dogs which have not been deprived of the brain the activity of the reflex decreases at a much slower rate, since an additional stock of energy is mobilized in the higher centres. This is, then, the simplest case of the regulation of the energy side of the process.

Both these forms of regulation are determined in the above examples by peculiar situations: the direction of behaviour lends itself directly to external situations, the necessary redistribution of energy is conditioned either by the repetition of the action of the main stimulus, or by the action of some stimulus co-existent with the main stimulus; what Ukhtomsky calls the 'sub-dominant stimulus'.

An entirely different condition obtains in more complex behaviour. The behaviour of a child, let us say, is fixed on a book which he is reading. The child's attention is distracted from reading by other stimuli: we stimulate the child to continue his reading, and he turns again to the book. Now let us study the following situation; the child is reading in conditions excluding the interference of outside stimuli. After a while, reading ceases, the first flush of energy for reading is exhausted. If the child is stimulated by promises of a reward, it will be possible to continue the process.

How does the regulation of behaviour in the simple and rather artificial examples with the child differ from the regulation of which examples were given above? What, in both cases, determines the continuation of the reading? A special factor in this case is the stimulus which we create in addition. We promise the child a reward – that is, not the repetition of the first main stimulus, the book, nor is it the direct increasing of this stimulus (the book does not increase in size nor become brighter, newer or more interesting) – we create a second new stimulus which determines the victory of the former. The relation of this second stimulus to the main centre of agitation is qualitatively not unimportant, it is not a simple sub-dominant agitation, mechanically increasing the 'dominant'. Although it strengthens the primary direction of behaviour, our second stimulus does not stand side by side with the first; it does not stand in relation to the general behaviour of the child as simply co-existent, but as a means to an end. The regulation of behaviour is realized in these examples by means of the second stimuli: such regulation we might call 'instrumented regulation',[4] as opposed to direct regulation, of which examples were given above.

Is there, in the latter examples of a child's behaviour, a case illustrating what we call voluntary regulation of behaviour and of voluntary attention? Yes – and no. In so far as both series of stimuli are equally independent of the child, no; but, on the other hand, this regulation is 'voluntary' from the point of view of the person influencing the child, the person controlling the stimulus which controls the behaviour of the child. The process as a whole is here divided between two people, whose behaviour is subordinated to one general aim: one person reacts directly, and the other reacts in a direction of creating a series of stimuli intended to react on the first. Let us now take both these forms of behaviour united in one person: the child reacts to the present situation, not directly, in his main line of behaviour, but in the direction of attracting an additional series of stimuli organizing his own behaviour. This would be a case of voluntary regulation of behaviour. The Chinese postman delivering an urgent telegram acts in just the same way; he organizes his own behaviour, creating for himself additional stimuli. He hangs a number of objects – a piece of coal, a feather and some pepper – on the end of a short rod. This he keeps before his eyes on the road. This will remind him that he must fly like a bird, run as if he was stepping over hot coals or had burnt himself with pepper. As he goes on his way, some unusual occurrence in the street, or tempting goods displayed in the shops, or the prospect of a nice rest in the shade of the trees, might distract him from his business, and might destroy and disorganize his behaviour. The artificial 'stimuli' or 'signs' created by him serve to direct his attention anew to his real task.[5]

The examples given suggest an outline of the structure of the higher forms of regulation of behaviour; voluntary regulation appears to us as instrumental regulation, 'instrumental' realized by attracting means as a second series of stimuli. The controlling of behaviour becomes possible only by the mastering of stimuli: this condition is justified in relation to our own behaviour (Vygotsky). To render one's own behaviour voluntary means to master it, subject, of course, to its own natural laws. The sensation of effort, which sometimes accompanies our voluntary acts, and particularly all efforts of voluntary attention, creating the illusion of voluntary action in the specific meaning of the word (that is, in the sense of freedom of action, carried out by means of a special psychic force), is explained through this particular, double structure of voluntary acts, which creates the mobilization of energy.

Thus, the sensation of effort appears to be a sensation which naturally accompanies 'the awakening and unfolding of the secondary tendency, which arises in connection with the first and increases its energy' (Janet).[6]

The conception unfolded by us of voluntary regulation of behaviour is that working hypothesis which lies at the basis of the present inquiry and which determines its central task: to trace the route of development of the outward forms of behaviour in children.

## II

The history of voluntary attention begins when the first elementary social stimuli make their appearance in behaviour. Already the tribal hunts which were the earliest instances of collectivism in man entailed the necessity of controlling the attention of the hunting group: this was an indispensable condition for organized hunting. The function of the leader here was to submit the behaviour of the collective to a common end, which meant that first of all the aim had to be *indicated*, that is, attention had to be drawn to it. That is exactly what we do in our first attempts to influence the child: we begin with indication, that is, with attracting his attention. Here there is as yet no new and higher structure of the act of attention: the reaction of the child remains natural, directly conditioned by the external stimuli acting upon it. This kind of reaction, as is well known, can be found also in the higher animals (see Darwin, 1888; p. 49).

The process of attracting attention, however, the act of indicating, already bears its own peculiar characteristics; this act is social in its essentials. In some animals we meet with activities reminiscent of indicating but their nature proves to be quite different. Birds collecting in flocks select sentries; their duty seems to be to warn the rest when danger is near. If we examine the behaviour of the sentry birds, we become convinced that these possess no special acts of behaviour for this purpose. When a bird is startled it shrieks and starts up with a great flapping of wings; that is, it acts in the same way as the rest of the birds act at its signal. That is why we never see, among animals, sentries placed outside the field where the flock may observe it. Such a disposition of sentries, which would best secure the safety of the flock (or herd), is not possible among animals, since it presupposes the existence in the sentry bird of such special action as would regulate the behaviour of the flock. Even as regards the most complicated forms of instinctive reactions, we are not in a position to discover such specially instrumented actions: the common crane, for instance, before returning to the place it has left, first sends a scout: this scout, however, does not possess any specific action for its work.

Thus, with the exception, perhaps, of only a few, much disputed cases, where the so-called 'warnings' are issued by thoroughbred hounds subjected for generations to the influence of man, we do not meet in the animal world any special forms of action having as their sole and special end the mastery of behaviour of other individuals by attracting their attention.

The history of one man's mastery over the regulation of behaviour of another repeats in many points the history of his mastery over tools. It presupposes a change in the structure of behaviour, which turns behaviour directed to an end into behaviour directed circuitously. The selection and production of instruments or tools is supplanted here by the creation of a series of stimuli which, through the object of influence, determine the achievement of the end. In this sense these stimuli prove to possess an instrumental function. At first, their indispensable factor is their intensity, but in the process of their development and differentiation they become specialized and acquire the character of a conventional *sign*: in this way *indication* is born, as a sign of attention. It is exactly the indication (gesture, speech, etc.) which conditions, in the primary history of behaviour, the development of the higher forms of attention. As the researches of L. S. Vygotsky show, it is that catalytic factor which modifies the inter-central relations and, destroying the even balance of the situation, causes the activation of corresponding processes (see Ribot, 1888; Vygotsky, 1929a).

In some of our experiments with instrumented memorizing, and in that series where we suggested to the child that he should remember a number of words with the help of one complicated picture, we also had an opportunity to observe this function of the indicative gesture; the subjects upon which we experimented were mentally backward children who, when turning their attention to one or another detail of the picture, quite spontaneously used the indicative gesture as a means of distinguishing the given detail from the general whole. Figure 1 shows a cutting from a film taken of this experiment.[7]

The regulation of attention presumes, as we have already remarked, a change of a double nature: the change in the direction of behaviour and also in the distribution of force; that is, an increase in the duration of the act. Attention is directed to a definite object and remains fixed on it for some time; this 'action of the will directed to a certain aim and expressed in attention' is an indispensable condition for all kinds of ordered work and is all the more necessary as the action becomes less attractive.

A savage is passionately devoted to the chase, war and play: he loves the unexpected, the unknown, the accidental, in whatever form it appears; he does not know what persistent labour is, or if he does, he treats it with contempt. Love of labour is a feeling which developed secondarily along with the progress of civilization, and labour, as is well known, is simply the concrete expression of attention. Even half-civilized tribes feel a certain repulsion to ordered labour. Darwin once asked the Gauchos why they did not work but were given over to drunkenness, play and thieving. 'Because the days last too long', was the reply. The life of a primitive man, says Herbert Spencer, is almost entirely devoted to the tracking of animals, birds and fish, which provide him with pleasant excitement. Among civilized peoples, the hunt, although it serves as a form of entertainment, is far from being widespread and is only temporary . . . But, whereas in primitive man the power of persistent attention was very poorly developed, with us it has attained a very considerable degree. [Ribot, 1888/1908, pp. 60–1]

Thus, the transition of the savage from capricious and fitful dissipation of energy to the specific, systematic and organized labour of man, signifies, as we see, the transition to a higher form of activity of attention. This fact holds a tremendous significance for psychology. The task before research workers now is to show how the voluntary attention of man developed together with his working activity. Of course, any detailed historical or sociological analysis of this process would demand special research. We will here confine ourselves to the indication of two series of historical facts of particular interest to us in connection with the conception of attention described above.

It is well known that the transition to regular labour is usually achieved with its division. At first only part of the tribe, the women or the slaves, were obliged to do *systematic work* as a punishment. On the other hand, we know what a tremendous part in the labour processes of primitive man was taken by external organizing environment – the activities of foremen, the ceremony of beginning and ending the work, the rhythmic musical accompaniment to labour. It may be admitted that this labour activity, achieved under the influence of direct compulsion, could be called labour only in the sense that we apply the word to the 'labour' of animals. But the very necessity of compulsion arouses the organizer of these living instruments to the creation of special stimuli regulating their behaviour. The originally direct and simple stimuli undoubtedly speedily gave way to conventional stimuli; and what is most important, along with this, the stimuli formerly used on others could be adapted to the first person. Signals given by the foremen, the rhythmic sounds of a drum, working songs – these created the centre around which the labour activities of the primitive man were built up.

'The savage avoided work not as a *physical* but as a *spiritual* effort', says Schurtz; that is, he avoided or rather was not capable of straining his attention. These means of organizing and regulating work were directed first of all to the organization of attention: their aim was to communicate to the work the necessary direction and continuance. 'Working songs are important documents, giving evidence of the half-conscious self-education of humanity' (Schurtz, 1900, vol. 2, ch. 6). It might be said

**Figure 11.1**   Egyptian peasants reaping oats following the sounds of the flute. In each row there is a man marking the time. (From the Guimetian Museum, Vigouroux, *Diction de la Bible*.)[8]

that first of all they are evidence of the education of higher forms of attention, indispensable for the further unfolding of labour activity.

The transition from the organization of attention of others to the creation of stimuli organizing their own attention – this is the route marked out in the history of development of voluntary attention. Mastering stimulation, man masters his own behaviour; in submitting himself to its natural laws he in this way subjects it to himself, in this sense turning it into voluntary behaviour. We see that at the foundations of this process lies the general process of the socialization of man. The beginning of collective labour and economic activities, which signify that humanity has entered the historical phase of its development – this is the chief condition for the appearance of higher forms of behaviour. Here we have an extremely complicated process of the double relation of interchange between the individual and his social comrades. In this process, in J. M. Baldwin's terminology, 'the *social* element *projecting itself* into the personality forms the "subjective", which by a return movement is transmitted anew to other people and thus becomes "ejective"'.[9]

Therefore, voluntary attention is a later and extremely complicated product of prolonged development. Its root lies at the very earliest stages of the history of human society. It develops, says Ribot [1888/1908, p. 47], on the basis of involuntary attention, onto which it seems to be artificially grafted and from which it derives the conditions of its existence, as branches grafted to a tree trunk feed on its sap.

Primary involuntary attention, influenced by the employment of 'psychological instruments' which are first directed to surrounding people and subsequently to itself, turns into voluntary attention. These 'psychological instruments', originally simple, unconventional, intense stimuli, differ from labour instruments in that they are directed to the mastery of man's behaviour. The process of their inception and development is also the process of their acquiring a conventional meaning; they are the 'instrument-signs', and in this lies their specific character. When they are turned on oneself they may become internal, and thus behaviour is free from external stimuli-signs which regulate it.

The place of the external sign is taken by internal psychological elements, acquiring a *significative* meaning. Such applied-to-oneself, instrumental, significative regulation of behaviour is what we call voluntary attention.

# III

In the behaviour of a very young child, just as in that of a primitive man, we are not in a position to discover acts of voluntary behaviour. It is only at an advanced stage of individual psychological development that voluntary attention begins to take on that central importance which it possesses in the general system of behaviour of the cultured adult. This most important psychological function of a modern man is the product of his social and historical development. It was born in the primitive savage out of the process of his socialization; being a product of labour activity, it is at the same time an indispensable condition for it. In this sense, this function has developed historically, and not biologically. Each subsequent generation, says Ribot [1888/1908, p. 58], *learns* voluntary attention from the preceding one. Thus the development of voluntary attention means, first of all, that the child acquires a series of *habits of behaviour*.

Through the mastery by surrounding people of its attention, the child masters, at first imitatively, the attention of the people surrounding it. While stimulating others, the child learns to stimulate itself. At first, the external stimuli-means which the child organized in order to master its own behaviour, are replaced, in the process of their development, by internal stimuli: as they 'grow in' external stimuli turn primary attention into significative; and attention becomes voluntary.

The business of experimental–psychological research now is to show how, under laboratory conditions, this process takes place; that is, to bring it within closer range and make it accessible for direct study.

The methods which we have worked out with this end in view are as follows: the child to be experimented on was placed in conditions of such activity as required active concentration of attention: along with this, the child was offered a number of external objects ('second series of stimuli') which might serve as 'psychological means' for this activity. For instance, during the experiments, which took the form of play, the child was given the opportunity to 'win' a certain prize. In order to create such activity, we used the old children's game 'Don't say white or black, don't answer yes or no' (having, of course, slightly altered it). The whole experiment consisted usually of three or four series and was carried out in the following way.

In each series, the child was given, according to a special formula, 18 questions, out of which seven concerned the colour of things ('What colour is . . . ?'). The instructions demanded that the child should answer each question promptly and in one word, especially in the case of colours – simply the name of the colour. The first series, which was of a controlling and also of a training character, passed without any additional limitations. In the second series only we began the 'play' itself, introducing, as a condition for winning, two new demands: the child won only when he answered our questions, first, without repeating the name of one and the same colour, and, second, if he did not name one of the 'forbidden' colours. The third series differed from the first only in so far as the child was given nine coloured cards as means of assistance ('they must help you to win').

Having placed the cards before them, the children, when answering questions, usually picked out and then placed on one side cards of the colour named or turned them over, and at the same time fixed the 'forbidden' colours. As if introducing into the process, in this way, a new series of external additional stimuli-means, the child solved the task set him, turning his behaviour into indirect, instrumented behaviour; his perception and reactions were realized through these interposed signs, which here took the place of the refracting glass of which Revault d'Allones speaks in his work (1914, p. 32; see also his 1923, pp. 846–919). These cards were used before the beginning of the experiment in order to find out whether the child knew the names of colours. The fourth series was built up similarly to the third, and was carried out in cases where the child did not show evidence of having found out how to use the cards or did so only towards the end of the experiment. Before and after each series it was ascertained by means of special questions how far the child mastered and remembered our instructions.

All four series of questions in our lists were practically analogous to each other, containing an equal number of equally distributed 'critical questions' about colours and presenting certain obstacles to the correct solution of the tasks. In a number of cases they were even provocative of error, but still allowed the fulfilling of all the conditions of the experiments and the evoking of thoughtful answers.

In the experiments we tried to link our questions together and ask them in the form of 'Tell me!' and 'What do you think?', speaking in an ordinary conversational tone. In this way the questions contained in the list, asked in their exact form and order, formed a necessary element of our 'experiment-play conversation' with children, but did not compose its only contents.

The series we offered contained the following questions:

*First series*: (without 'forbidden' names) (1) Can you draw? (2) What colour is your handkerchief? (3) Did you ever go in the tram? (4) What colour is the tram? (5) Do you want to study? (6) Were you ever at a meeting? (7) Do you like reading? (8) What colour is the paper? (9) and pencils? (10) Do you play with toys? (11) Have you seen the sea? (12) What colour is the sea? (13) Did you ever listen to music? (14) Have you seen vegetables growing? (15) What colour are cucumbers? (16) Do you like dogs? (17) What colour are cats? (18) What does one do with a saw?

*Second series*: (green and yellow are chosen as 'forbidden' colours) (1) Have you a playmate? (2) What colour is your shirt? (3) Did you ever go in a train? (4) What colour are the railway carriages? (5) Do you want to be big? (6) Were you ever at the theatre? (7) Do you like to play in the room? (8) What colour is the floor (generally)? (9) And the walls? (10) Can you write? (11) Have you seen lilac? (12) What colour is lilac? (13) Do you like sweet things? (14) Were you ever in the country? (15) What colours can leaves be? (16) Can you swim? (17) What is your favourite colour? (18) What does one do with a pencil?

*Third series*: (forbidden colours blue and red) (1) Do you sometimes go for walks in the streets? (2) What colours are the houses? (3) Does the sun shine brightly? (4) What colour is the sky? (5) Do you like sweets? (6) Have you seen roses? (7) Do you like vegetables? (8) What colour are tomatoes? (9) and what colour are exercise books? (10) Have you any toys? (11) Do you play ball? (12) What colours are balls? (13) Do you live in the town? (14) Did you see the demonstration? (15) What colour are flags? (16) Have you a book? (17) What colour is the book cover? (18) When does it get dark?

*Fourth series*: (forbidden colours black and white) (1) Do you go to school? (2) What colour is ink? (3) Do you want to be a soldier? (4) What colour are boots? (5) Do you like to play? (6) Have you ever seen a lion? (7) Do you know what underclothes (linen) are? (8) What colour are collars? (9) and bags? (10) Are you a good pupil? (11) Do you like pears? (12) What colour are apples? (13) Were you ever in a hospital? (14) Did you see the doctor? (15) What colour are overalls? (16) Do you go for walks in the garden? (17) What colour are paints? (18) When does it snow?

Although these series of questions seemed to us, *a priori*, to be of practically equal difficulty, we changed their order in certain cases (2nd, 3rd and 4th series). The cards we used were black, white, red, blue, yellow, green, purple (lilac), brown and grey.

As the experiments showed, the tasks set the children were, in cases where they were to be carried out without the help of the cards, difficult enough even for adult subjects. On the other hand, children of school age experienced no difficulty in finding out how to use the cards, and had usually learned to use them in the first (III) series with cards. In cases where the method of using the cards was not discovered by the child itself in Series III, we told him and carried out Series IV with him also. In summing up, we have generally taken account of the data of this last series.

Not counting trial experiments, 30 subjects were experimented upon. They included children of below school age and of school age, and adults, numbers being practically equal in all the groups. The comparatively small number of experiments made, owing to the fact that experiments with children are a comparatively difficult matter, scarcely permits us to insist on the exactitude of the average figures obtained, but they are sufficient for the immediate purposes of our inquiry.

Some of our experiments were filmed and separate sections of these are shown in figure 3 [not reproduced].

It must be remarked that the experiments were usually carried out in a very natural and lively way. We noticed later that very often, when playing with others, the children faithfully reproduced the conditions of our experiments, substituting coloured paper for our cards and repeating more or less accurately our questions. This circumstance afforded us considerable difficulty in getting children for the experiment, since under these conditions we were prevented from using children belonging to the same group.

If we add up the average number of wrong answers given during experiments with different groups of subjects (see table 11.1), the sharp difference between the groups will become evident. From the table it is clear that children of below school age answered a little more than half of the 'critical' questions without following the rules of the game. Children of pre-school age are very easily distracted from their main task by the subject of the question, and easily give way to 'provocation', sometimes not even noticing their mistakes. For the third series (with cards), we have almost the same figures as for the second, the difference between them being expressed by the insignificant figure of 0.3. As a rule, children of pre-school age are unable to discover by themselves how to use the cards. Even after they have been told (Series IV) children, while handling the cards, are not capable of using them in fulfilling the task set them. We discover here, as well as in experiments with instrumented memorization, a point characteristic of the pre-school age: the almost complete inability of using external stimuli as an auxiliary means for organizing one's own behaviour.

In some instances we did not limit ourselves to the simple communication of the method, but first (before Series IV) allowed other children, who had fully mastered ways of using the cards, to demonstrate them to our subjects. Even then the results only showed external imitation in the case of children of pre-school age (subjects 14 and 15). This is illustrated by the following excerpt from minutes. The method of using the cards was shown by other children who had previously been experimented upon.

In fact, the cards not only do not help the child of pre-school age, they actually hinder him from carrying out his task. On the examples given above the repeated reactions 'white' arise from the fact that the child fixes his attention on the white card. The cards take a certain part in his behaviour, but this part is absolutely different from that taken in the case of the school child. These secondary stimuli only co-exist

Table 11.1

| Group | Age | No. | Number of wrong answers | | |
|---|---|---|---|---|---|
| | | | In Series II | In Series III or IV | Difference between Series II and III |
| Below school age | 5–6 | 7 | 3.9 | 3.6 | 0.3 |
| School age: younger group | 8–9 | 7 | 3.3 | 1.5 | 1.8 |
| School age: older group | 10–13 | | 3.1 | 0.3 | 2.8 |
| School age: average | 8–13 | 15 | 3.2 | 0.9 | 2.3 |
| Adults | 22–27 | 8 | 1.4 | 0.6 | 0.8 |

*Case 14*

*10 December 1928*

*Subject: 5 years of age*

Series III 'Forbidden' colours, blue and red

| | | |
|---|---|---|
| 2 | What colour are houses? | Red (without looking at forbidden colours). |
| 3 | Is the sun shining bright? | Yes. |
| 4 | What colour is the sky? | White (without looking at card, but after replying, searches for white card. 'Here it is!' Picks it up and keeps it in his hand). |
| 8 | What colours are tomatoes? | Red (throws a glance at cards). |
| 9 | And what colour are exercise books? | White – like this! (pointing to white card). |
| 12 | What colour are balls? | White – (looking at card). |
| 13 | Do you live in the town? | No, etc., etc. |
| | Do you think you have won? | Don't know – yes. |
| | What must you not do if you want to win? | Mustn't say red or blue. |
| | And what else? | Mustn't say the same word twice. |

with the main stimuli, instrumental functions are not inherent in them and their part in the process is of quite an accidental nature. Still there is no doubt that in children of pre-school age we sometimes meet with forms of behaviour which might serve as premises for the development of the instrumental employment of external signs. From this point of view certain cases registered (subjects ten and 11) are of special interest. In these cases, the child, after we had suggested to him that he use the cards in carrying out his task ('Take the cards, they will help you to win'), searched for the forbidden colours and put all such cards out of his sight, as if trying to prevent himself from naming them. One operation is substituted by another: the child in our example acts in the same way as an Australian or African savage might act in freeing himself from a dangerous man by destroying his image or symbol. The 'magical' nature of the operation of putting away dangerous colours is, in the case of the child of pre-school age, emphasized by the circumstance that the child thus limited himself to this and pays no further attention to the cards. This circumstance is of special interest to us since, although in nature it is quite different, externally it reminds us of an abbreviation of the method of using the cards by adults, and also because it clears up the origin of one of the methods to which school children have recourse when they want to carry out their task.

This 'magical' attitude toward the means is still more clearly illustrated by subject 17 (Leont'ev, 1929b; Lubbock, 1872). This subject exhibited in the third series all the cards without any order at all and as a result gave several wrong answers. Before trying the fourth series, in order to give the subject some idea of the method of using the cards, we asked him: 'Did the cards help you?' 'Yes.' 'And what should you do to make the cards help you still more?' 'Make a house with them.' The child at once began to build a house with the cards, again without separating the forbidden colours. 'And how do you think they will help you?' 'I don't know.' 'Well, perhaps you can do yet another thing with them so that they will help you still more?' 'Put them in a circle,' the child guessed. At last, after a few more suggestions, the subject discovered the proper method and in the fourth series made no mistake.

Comparing the figures obtained from the experiments on children of pre-school age with those obtained from children of school age (see table 11.1), we notice a very slight reduction in the number of wrong answers in the second series, whereas the number of mistakes in the third series falls sharply. This is particularly noticeable in the case of the group of older children where the difference between the figures of Series II and III reaches a maximum of 2.8. We find a direct explanation of this in our experiments. At school age, as we have seen in the data on the investigations of the development of memory, children begin to use the external 'means-stimuli' and thereby considerably increase the effect of their psychological acts.

The behaviour of a child of school age remains natural and does not differ greatly from that of a younger child. In our experiment, in fact, we obtained figures in the second series which were quite near to each other: 3.9, 3.3 and 3.1. The number of wrong answers in cases when the operation remained direct decreases slowly with the growth of the child, but it is sufficient to allow him to equip himself with the means accessible to him for the mastery of his behaviour, as the effectiveness of his psychological acts increases speedily; a tremendous change takes place in the sphere of his psychological possibilities.

The methods of using the cards can be reduced, in spite of their apparent variety, to two different types. First comes the case when the child puts out of his range of vision cards of forbidden colours, exhibits the remainder, and, as he answers the questions, places on one side the cards of the already named colours. This is the least perfect and at the same time the earliest method used. The card here serves more as a memory sign than as an attention sign; its function is only to register the named colour. At the beginning of the experiment, children often do not turn to the cards before they answer the question about colour, and only after it is named search among the cards, turn over, move or put away the named one (see Report 3, pp. 303–4). This operation is carried out, as we see, with the idea of registering their reaction. It is undoubtedly the simplest act of memorization with the help of external means. It is only later that the conditions of the experiments bestow a new function on the card. Before naming the colour the child must necessarily make a selection with the help of the cards. It makes no difference whether the child has within his field of vision a series of so-far-unused cards, or whether he will get his bearings by the colour already named to him; in both cases the cards will be interposed in the process, and will serve as a means of regulating his acts. Actually, the separation of the used cards without putting them out of sight, for instance by placing one of them in another row, presupposes the same subsequent operation as is required by the exhibition of the forbidden colours, which is met with in the second type of employment of cards. The preliminary putting out of sight of forbidden colours, which is a distinguishing characteristic of the first method of using cards, does not yet lead to the 'simulation' of an act, to the complete substitution of one operation by another; it represents merely a step in that direction. It is explained partly by the greater simplicity of the operation of mastering memory and partly by that 'magical' attitude to means, which is constantly met with in children (see Luria and Morozova), and which we have already noticed in the given situation with the children of pre-school age experimented upon.

Material gathered in the course of experimental research on instrumented memory, attention and arithmetical operations shows that the part played by external means of behaviour is especially important in children of school age.[10] As to children of the earliest school age, we might even speak of a peculiar 'hyperfunctioning' of external means which they have just begun to master. Experiments made by L. S. Vygotsky and A. R. Luria (Luria, 1928) are in this respect extremely illustrative. They suggested to the children that in order to remember a number of figures they should somehow record them, for which purpose they placed at the disposal of the children different objects such as paper, thin cord and various small articles, including hunters' shot. The children of early school age as a rule tried to build up figures to be remembered out of the given objects.

### Report 3

### 1 December 1925

### The case of Nastya D., 13 years old

### Series II Forbidden colours, green and yellow

| 1 | Have you playmates? | Yes. |
|---|---|---|
| 2 | What colour is your blouse? | Grey. |
| 3 | Have you been in a train? | Yes. |
| 4 | What colour are railway carriages? | Grey (notices that she has repeated the same colour twice; laughs). |
| 5 | Do you want to be a big girl? | Yes. |
| 6 | Were you ever in a theatre? | Yes. |
| 7 | Do you like to play in the room? | Yes. |
| 8 | What colour is the floor? | Grey . . . again – I repeated it. |
| 9 | And the walls? | White. |

| 10 | Can you write? | Yes. |
| 11 | Have you seen lilac? | Yes. |
| 12 | What colour is lilac? | Lilac colour. |
| 13 | Do you like sweets? | Yes. |
| 14 | Were you ever in the country? | Yes. |
| 15 | And what colour were the leaves? | Green – no, shouldn't have said green – brown, red sometimes. |
| 16 | Can you swim? | Yes. |
| 17 | What is your favourite colour? | Yellow! I can't! (throws up hands behind the head). |
| 18 | What do you do with a pencil? | Write. |
| | What do you think, did you win or lose? | Lost. |
| | What should you not have said? | Green and yellow. |
| | And what else? | Shouldn't repeat. |
| | | (4 mistakes) |

### Series III (with cards, forbidden colours blue and red)

The subject puts on one side cards of forbidden colours, and spreads out the remainder in a row before him.

| 1 | Do you go for walks in the street? | Yes. |
| 2 | What colour are the houses? | Grey (after answering looked at the cards and turned over the grey one). |
| 3 | Is the sun shining brightly? | Brightly. |
| 4 | What colour is the sky? | White (first looks at card and then turns it over). |
| 5 | Do you like sweets? | Yes. |
| 6 | Have you seen a rose? | Yes. |
| 7 | Do you like vegetables? | Yes. |
| 8 | What colour are tomatoes? | Green (turns over card). |
| 9 | And exercise books? | Yellow (turns over card). |
| 10 | Have you any toys? | No. |
| 11 | Do you play ball? | Yes. |
| 12 | And what colour are balls? | Grey (without glancing at cards; after answering glances and notices mistake). |
| 13 | Do you live in the town? | Yes. |
| 14 | Did you see the demonstration? | Yes. |
| 15 | What colour are flags? | Black (first looks at cards and then turns one over). |
| 16 | Have you any books? | Yes. |
| 17 | What colours are their covers? | Lilac (turning over card). |
| 18 | When does it get dark? | At night. |
| | | (1 mistake) |

Thus, in spite of the obvious inexpediency of using the method under the circumstances given, instead of, for instance, putting aside two grains of shot or two torn-up bits of paper, the children tried to form figures out of the extremely inconvenient grains of shot, which rolled all over the table. As well may be imagined, much material and time was wasted. The children of pre-school age, who had not yet mastered the system of figures, behaved quite differently. They chose a more economical method from the point of view of time and energy, acting just as a modern adult might who had already got over the first phase, when the external methods adopted have the greatest power over one.

In our experiments we had the opportunity of observing closely this over-exaggerated role of external media. In a number of cases, in children of early school age, we met with replies which were irreproachable from the point of view of conforming to instructions, but were at the same time quite senseless. The child, in these cases, worked strictly by the cards, and named colours irrespective of the subject of the question. This 'formalism' which is peculiar to children and throws them completely under the influence of the method assimilated, is also met with in the development of arithmetical operations. It is a well known fact that the slightest change in the position of figures, in the actual writing of them, is sufficient to render he child incapable of even the simplest arithmetical action (Thorndike).[11] Probably it is just this phase of the domination of external psychological media, through which the development of the higher instrumented, 'significative' acts of behaviour pass, that reveals itself in the history of the cultural development of humanity, in those numerous and extremely carefully worked-out systems of external methods of behaviour which compose a typical feature of primitive society.

If we turn now to the figures illustrating the behaviour of adult subjects, we discover a new and peculiar relation between the indices of our main series. Comparing these indices with the figures obtained with children of school age, we see that the difference existing between them does not concern the third series with cards, as was the case with the transition from pre-school age to school age, but is determined by the data in the second series. In this series we notice a distinct falling-off in the number of wrong answers given by adults.

The general change in the coefficients obtained upon various groups of cases is illustrated in table 11.2. Here the positive data are given by graphs showing not the number of wrong, but the number of right, answers; that is, the total number of answers to critical questions minus the number of answers not corresponding to the demands of the instructions.

The curves of development shown in table 11.2 are very similar to the corresponding curves obtained in a course of experiments on instrumented memory. Like the latter, they approach each other in their extremities, forming in their outline something like a parallelogram.

Therefore, quantitative characteristics obtained in our experiments indicate three principal stages of the development of instrumented behaviour. First of all (pre-school age), the stage of natural directed acts. At this stage of development the child is not capable of mastering his behaviour with the assistance of the organization of special

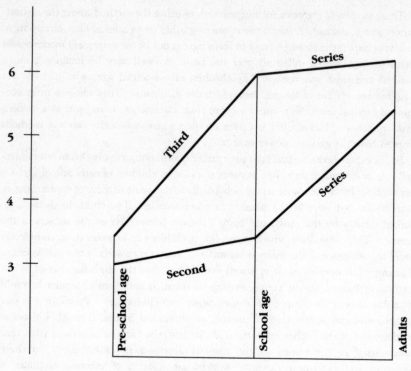

Table 11.2

stimuli-means. The introduction into the operation of a number of cards, which might help the child in his task, does not increase to any considerable extent the effectiveness of this operation. The child proves incapable of their functional use. Although they take the part of stimuli in his behaviour, they do not acquire an instrumental function. The next stage of development is characterized by a sharp difference in the indices in both of the main series. The introduction of cards, used by the child as a system of auxiliary external stimuli-means, raises the effectiveness of his acts considerably. This is the stage of predominance of the external sign – the psychological instrument in the stimuli acting from without. We see at last that, as regards adult cases, the difference between the indices of both series is smoothed over again and their coefficients become more nearly equal, but now on a new and higher basis. This does not mean that the behaviour of adults becomes again direct natural behaviour. At this higher stage of development, behaviour remains instrumented. At the same time the second series of stimuli-means is emancipated from primary external forms. What takes place is what we here call the process of 'ingrowing' of the external means: the external sign turns into an internal one. This is how the external forms of human behaviour – instrumented, significative behaviour – develop.

This theory of 'ingrowing', formulated in the course of our study of the development of memory, is provided with some new proofs in the experimental material of our present inquiry. Among the many different methods of using cards, two, chiefly used by adults, are deserving of special attention. First of all, the case of employing cards to fulfil only one of the conditions of the task set. Some subjects limited themselves to the exhibition of the forbidden colours, while the other cards remained outside their range of vision. Thus, the operation is divided into two parts, one taking place without the help of external means, and the other with the assistance of the cards. This way of using the cards is met with twice: in the case of children of pre-school age, but only in one instance (subject 11), and of some adults. It is probably due to absolutely different causes. In the first case, it is no more than an embryonic form, out of which the respective method begins to develop. With respect to the adults, it is much more complicated. Can we actually admit that one side of the operation here remains natural and direct, while the other side bears an obviously instrumented character? From our point of view such a presumption is scarcely possible since, on the one hand, we cannot discover any difference in the number of mistakes of a corresponding type, and, on the other hand, it is scarcely possible that an integral process should have a double structure. There is no doubt that we have here a case of the transformation of one or two series of external signs into internal signs, similar to that which we can clearly observe in the development of the counting operation, where the carrying out of a complicated arithmetical action presupposes a number of intermediary actions completed mentally. Even in the simple operation of adding up a number of figures, it usually happens that the child must 'carry in his head' higher quantities.

These quantities, at first noted over the higher row with the help of figures and dots, very soon lose their external graphic signs and are substituted by internal signs. It is obvious that the process analogous to this operation, performed simultaneously with the help of both the external and internal signs, takes place in the cases where cards are partially used.

The second form of incomplete use of external means is much more interesting. This is again met with most frequently among adults. In this case all the cards are exhibited, while the usually forbidden colours prove to be the last in the row, or are placed in the centre. The subject answers the questions while looking at the cards but does not touch them. One of our subjects, No. 2, was asked after the experiment whether the cards had helped or not: 'They helped, of course, I looked at them and saw which I could mention and which not'. This reply indicates clearly the essentials of the methods used by her. The means by which the task is solved seems here to assume a double form. While remaining external, it already becomes half internal. The card, an external object, continues to exist as a card, but becomes a means only as the sign into which it is transformed with the help of the internal sign. The external removal of the cards in the group of 'forbidden' colours, which we observed in other, simpler cases, was carried on here 'in the head'. The subject, mentally marking the cards of the colours named, imparted in this way a certain meaning to the cards, that is, transformed them into signs. Thus, the process has here a sharply defined internal character and it is only supported by cards. It is clear from this that it keeps the same structure which it possessed in those cases when the operation was carried out entirely with the help of external stimuli-signs.

We are inclined to ascribe a particular importance to these observations because they give new proofs to the theory of the significative nature of external intellectual processes, and along with this allow us to outline in still greater detail the transition from externally instrumented operations, accomplished with the assistance of internal signs.

# IV

Placing on one side the process of development of attention in the child to the stage when it becomes instrumented, and on the other side the later process of the development of higher, significative forms of attention, we see that they are absolutely different in type. Biological development is replaced by development which we might call historical. It consists in this – that the child, under the influence of its social and cultural experience, masters a number of methods of behaviour, which transform his primitive, psychological acts into higher acts of new and complex structure. This structure is characterized by the presence of secondary stimuli-means, which in the form of internal or external stimuli are interposed in the process.

The development of voluntary attention only repeats the development of other higher psychological functions; it becomes voluntary, turning from signal to significative. That system of social relations into which man steps at the dawn of his historical existence, and which forms for him a new environment unknown to the biological world, a social environment, determines the particular path of his psychological development.

Equipping himself anew for the struggle with nature, man places between himself and the physical objects of his operations the tools which he has produced; by influencing nature with his tools he changes his own nature. The use of the tools creates a new series of labour processes, a new series of conditions of existence for man. These demand from him new actions and new forms of activity, and call for the redistribution of his physical possibilities, changing his skeletal, muscular and nervous system. A still greater change takes place in the nature of man as a result of his interaction with his social environment. In influencing social environment man creates a system of conventional stimuli with the idea of mastering the behaviour of other people. Thus he creates conditions for the mastery of his own behaviour, radically altering thereby the principal mechanism of behaviour itself.

These stimuli-signs, which at an early stage of development took on the form of stimuli acting from without, when turned upon themselves, are capable of being transformed in the process of psychological development into internal signs. The synopsis, which in principle exactly corresponds to the cards of our experiments, is necessary to every lecturer at the beginning of his career, keeping his attention on the consistent unfolding of the contents of his speech. It is soon cut down in size, and the large sheaf of papers, with its methodical guiding text and mass of notes in coloured inks, gradually gives way to a number of bits of paper covered with a few words, which are almost never looked at.

The external stimuli-means are at first not sufficiently specialized. In the examples given by us, objects filling the role of means, organizing the behaviour of the Chinese postman, are as much mnemotechnical signs as signs of attention, just as in our experiments coloured cards usually fulfilled both these functions. Only at a higher stage of their development, when they are divided into two lines – the line of further development of external means and the line of transformation of external means – we meet with a system of fully differentiated external signs, such as, for instance, writing and connecting signs.

A much greater obstacle is presented by the problem of the differentiation of internal stimuli-signs. When they are 'growing in', external signs are not only deprived of their original form, but undoubtedly assume new and peculiar features. Their functional classification is possible only in a conditioned sense; entering the process, they determine not the direct elementary psychological functions as such, but those operations at the biological basis of which these functions lie.

In the analysis of the higher forms of behaviour it is impossible, therefore, to oppose to each other or else to associate [lump together – eds] the higher psychological functions, treating them as separate items and thus mechanically reducing these higher forms of behaviour to their primary, simple mechanisms.

## Summary

The development of a child's attention is not confined only to the development of its primary biological forms, but includes the transformation of these elementary forms into new and higher forms. The child's attention, which at first is involuntary, i.e. directly dependent on the action of stimuli, is transformed in the process of its development into the voluntary attention characteristic of an adult. This process of transformation takes place on the basis of the control of the child's attention from without, with the help of external stimuli. The child, feeling the effect of these external stimuli on himself and learning in his turn to react on others around him, becomes capable of using external stimuli with the idea of organizing his own behaviour. By thus controlling stimulation, the child controls his own attention; by submitting to the natural laws of his own behaviour, he thus makes the latter submit to him, and in this sense transforms it into voluntary behaviour.

Research work in the development of voluntary attention, which was carried out by means of special methods, confirms the above theory. Children of early pre-school ages prove incapable of actively using external auxiliary stimuli as means of organizing their own behaviour. The attention task is fulfilled by all the children in exactly the same way, both in the series of experiments without auxiliary means and in the series in which the child is called upon to use definite auxiliary means. In early school age, however, the child learns to organize his behaviour from without, with the help of external stimuli, and the difference in the indices of these two series of experiments, reaches its maximum. With the transition to a more advanced age, the role of external means organizing behaviour becomes less significant. The function fulfilled by these external means gradually passes over to the internal elements of the experiment. What takes place now is emancipation from the external forms of the stimuli which were at first indispensable. The external signs of the operation are transformed into internal signs.

In this way the development of the voluntary attention of the child should pass through a stage when his behaviour is controlled with the assistance of external stimuli-signs, which are subsequently replaced by internal signs.

# References

Baldwin, J. M. 1895: *Mental Development in the Child and the Race: Methods and processes*. New York and London: Macmillan.

Baldwin, J. M. 1897: *Social and Ethical Interpretations*. New York and London: Macmillan.

Darwin, C. 1888: *The Descent of Man* (2nd ed.). London: John Murray.

Dobrinin, N. Z. 1928: *The Fluctuation of Attention*. Moscow.

Leont'ev, A. N. 1928: Oposredstvennoe zapominanie u detej s nedostatochnym i boleznenno-izmenennym povedeniem. *Voprosy Defektologii*, 4.

Leont'ev, A. N. 1929a: The dialectic method applied in the psychology of memory. *Voprosy marksistskoj pedagogiki. Trudy AKV. Tom 1*. Moscow: Uchebno-Pedagogicheskoe Izdatel'stvo.

Leont'ev, A. N. 1929b: The problem of the dialectic method in the development of child's memory. *Voprosy marksistkoj pedagogiki. Trudy AKV. Tom 1*. Moscow: Uchebno-Pedagogicheskoe Izdatel'stvo.

Lubbock, J. 1872: *Pre-historic Times as Illustrated by Ancient Remains and the Manners and Customs of Modern Savages*. London: Norgate.

Luria, A. R. 1928: The problem of the cultural behaviour of the child. *J. Genetic Psychology*, 35, 493–506.

Luria, A. R. 1929a: Experimental psychology and child development. *Nauchnoe Slovo*, 1, 77–97.

Luria, A. R. 1929b: Puti razvitija detskogo myshlenija. *Estestvoznanie i Marksizm*, 2, 97–130.

Luria, A. R. 1929c: Materialy k genezu pis'ma u rebenka. *Voprosy marksistskoj pedagogiki. Trudy AKV. Tom 1* (pp. 143–76). Moscow: Uchebno-Pedagogicheskoe Izdatel'stvo.

Luria, A. R. and Morozova, N. G. 1930: Instrumental choice-reaction in children. *Trudy Psikhologicheskoj Laboratorii Akademii Kommunisticheskoj Vospitanii*, vol. 6.

Revault d'Allones, G. 1914: L'attention indirecte. *Revue Philosophique*, 77, 32–54.

Revault d'Allones, G. 1923: L'attention. In G. Dumas (ed.) *Traité de psychologie* (pp. 846–919). Paris: Alcan.

Ribot, Th. 1888/1908: *La psychologie de l'attention*. Paris: Alcan.

Schurtz H. 1900: *Urgeschichte der Kultur*. Leipzig-Wien: Bibliographisches Institut.

Vygotsky, L. S. 1928: *Pedologija podrostka.* Moscow: Izdanie Bjuro Zaochnogo Obuchenija pri Pedfake 2 MGU.

Vygotsky, L. S. 1929a: Geneticheskie korni myshlenija i rechi. *Estestvoznanie i Marksizm,* 1, 106–33.

Vygotsky, L. S. 1929b: The problem of the cultural development of the child. *Journal of Genetic Psychology,* 36, 414–34.

Vygotsky, L. S. 1929c: Razvitie aktivnogo vnimanija v detskom vozraste. *Voprosy marksistskoj pedagogiki. Trudy AKV. Tom 1* (pp. 112–42). Moscow: Uchebno-Pedagogicheskoe Izdatel'stvo.

Vygotsky, L. S. and Luria, A. R. 1930: *Etjudy po istorii povedenija. Obez'jana. Primitiv. Rebenok.* Moscow-Leningrad: Gosudarstvennoe Izdatel'stvo.

## Notes

Originally published as Leontiev, A. N. 1932: The development of voluntary attention in the child. *Journal of Genetic Psychology,* 40, 52–81. The article was the third and last paper in the series 'Studies on the cultural development of the child' edited by Luria and Vygotsky and published in this journal. Like the first two it was based on research conducted at the Krupskaja Academy of Communist Education in Moscow. With the exception of the introductory paragraph and the summary, the text is a translation of the fourth chapter of Leont'ev, A. N. 1931: *Razvitie pamjati.* Moscow-Leningrad: Uchebno-Pedagogicheskoe Izdatel'stvo. The original contained two photographs of the experimental setting (labelled figure 1 and figure 3) which could not be reproduced.

1   The references are to Blondel, Ch. 1914: *La conscience morbide. Essai de psychologie générale.* Paris: Alcan; and Ribot, Th. 1888/1908: *La psychologie de l'attention.* Paris: Alcan.

2   A detailed explanation of this is given by us in another place in a study of the problem of memory. See Leont'ev, A. N. 1929a: The dialectic method applied in the psychology of memory. In *Voprosy marksistkogo vospitanija.* Moscow: Academy of Communist Education [original footnote].

3   See bibliography at the end of this article [original footnote].

4   'instrumented' is the translation of *oposredstvennyj,* which is nowadays mostly translated as 'mediated'.

5   It is possible that these stimuli-signs, still in use in some Chinese provinces, have already lost their meaning; there is no doubt, however, that originally their use was dictated by necessity. Describing the Indian tribe of Dajibis, Richardson says: 'We became convinced, after experiments, that in spite of high rewards offered for the prompt delivery of a letter, it was impossible to trust them to do it. The slightest difficulty, the prospect of a carouse or of a tasty roast dinner, or the sudden appearance of a desire to visit a friend, was sufficient to make them postpone the delivery of a letter for an indefinite time (quoted from Lubbock, 1872; p. 454) [original footnote].

6   The reference is to p. 54 of Janet, P. 1928: *L'évolution de la mémoire et la notion du temps.* Paris: Maloine. As can be inferred from the references to Blondel, Ribot and Janet, Leont'ev was very well aware of what was going on in French psychology and in later years he would have intensive personal contacts with several French psychologists, among them Henri Wallon.

7 Not reproduced. Various films of psychological experiments carried out by Vygotsky, Leont'ev and Luria were made and may still be in some private archives waiting to be restored and seen.

8 The title Leont'ev gives is wrong. The reference should be to pp. 1217–18 of Vigouroux, F. (1895). *Dictionnaire de la Bible*. Paris: Letouzey et Ané.

9 See Baldwin (1895, vol. 1, ch. 1; vol. 2, ch. 14; 1897, vol. 2). We here use only the terminology of this author, leaving his general conception of development aside [original footnote].

10 In our work we were able to register (in subject 16) an instance of spontaneous turning of a child of school age in Series II (without cards) to coloured objects among his surroundings, with the idea of using them to assist him in his task; in this series the subject gave only two wrong answers altogether and in the third series none. We have observed analogous instances in our experiments with indirect memory [original footnote].

11 Refers to Thorndike, E. L. 1928: *The Psychology of Arithmetic*. New York: The Macmillan Company.

# 12

# Thought in schizophrenia

## *Lev Vygotsky*

Beyond doubt the most significant development in psychology has been the recent tendency to bring together investigations in various fields in order to discover the common principles involved in those investigations. Especially is this true of psychopathology and genetic or child psychology. They have developed independently, and only occasionally heretofore have the results obtained been brought together for comparison.

Meanwhile, more and more investigators think that psychologic laws are the same no matter where they are observed. As an example of the growing integration of the various fields of psychologic investigation and the growing feeling of the unity of psychologic laws in spite of the variety of their manifestation, one may refer to the comparative study of the splitting of thought, the phenomena of hypobulia[1] in psychopathology and the phenomenon of syncretic thinking in child psychology. In hypobulia there are phenomena which were formerly considered a result of schizophrenia or hysteria; in the light of more thorough investigation, however, they now appear to be in reality stages in the normal organization of consciousness as a necessary ontogenetic step in the development of normal personality. Such observations are doubtless widely true: the phenomena of developing thought in the adolescent child are evidently in general closely related to certain aspects of pathologic thinking.

There is, furthermore, a growing tendency to investigate psychologic processes by observation and comparison of their various courses of development, this procedure being used as a means of arriving at the laws determining the characteristics of such processes. I have found such an approach extremely useful in clinical and experimental work. Whereas previously the bringing together of genetic psychology and psychopathology consisted merely in a comparison of the conclusions reached, I have attempted to introduce the comparative method of study into my own experimental work from the beginning. It did not take long to find out that many problems, so conceived, appeared in a totally different light.

There is an old attempt to connect the psychology of the adolescent with certain symptoms of schizophrenia. This connection was implied in the term 'dementia praecox', and has given stimulus for a large number of studies of the adolescent child and for the comparison of the mental life of the child with that of patients with schizophrenia. Kretschmer, in Germany, and Blonsky,[2] in Russia, insisted that there is a connection between the two. They based their opinion on the fact that at times it is impossible to differentiate between a stormy period of sex adjustment in adolescence and incipient schizophrenia. My investigations, on which I shall comment later in the article and which give rise to certain ideas about the nature of psychologic processes in schizophrenia, lead me to quite different conclusions. The pivotal point in my comparative analysis has been the process of formation of concept as observed in the child and in the patient with schizophrenia.

## Scope of investigation

My investigations have been two-fold. They have embraced the development of thought in children up to the age of puberty, on the one hand, and the deterioration of thought in schizophrenia on the other. The conclusions have likewise been two-fold. I have found that the most important development of thought in adolescence is the change from 'complex'[3] types of thinking to conceptual types of thinking – a change which not only revolutionizes the intellectual processes but determines the dynamic structure of the personality, i.e. the consciousness of the self and the environment. I have also found, conversely, that the most important deterioration of thought occurring in schizophrenia is a disturbance, an impairment, in the function of formation of concept. The fragmentation and the breaking of that part of the psyche which is involved in the process of formation of concepts is just as characteristic of schizophrenia as the development of the function of formation of concepts is characteristic of adolescence. Hence it is obvious that both in schizophrenia and adolescence certain external similarities can be found, especially in the transition from complex or associative to conceptual thinking. When both are approached in a formal, static way during the transitional stages a large number of points in common can be found. But by using a more dynamic method of approach it will be seen that the psychologic processes in schizophrenia and in adolescence have a converse relationship to each other and that they are connected more by differences than by similarities. This is true, if for no other reason, because in adolescence one is dealing with phenomena of growth and development, while in schizophrenia one is dealing with the disintegration and decay of psychic life. Such principles obtain for the general mental processes of the person, but they are especially applicable in the function of formation of concepts. By studying this function, one becomes convinced that the psychology of adolescence gives a key for the understanding of schizophrenia, and conversely that schizophrenic thought helps one to understand the psychology of adolescence. In both, the most important thing is the proper understanding of the function of formation of concepts.

## Method

My experiments consisted in offering the patient a situation which required the formation of artificial concepts. This was accomplished by giving the patient what appeared in the beginning to be meaningless words chosen at random. The formation of the concepts had to be based on specially selected and connected elements. Thus, in the series of experiments the patients had to learn to associate meaningless syllables with certain definite concepts, as for example, 'bik', meaning large and small, 'lag', meaning large and tall, etc. The patient, that is, was confronted with the problem of the formation of a new concept, which he would not meet anywhere else except in the setting of a laboratory experiment.

It should be stated parenthetically that this method of experimental formation of concepts by means of specially selected words has a long history into which I shall not enter at present. It suffices to say that the method has been used a great deal by Ach and his students. My methods of investigation were based on principles advanced by Ach, but as I used them for altogether different purposes they had to be considerably modified.

With the methods developed by my collaborator, Sakharov, we were able to observe the impairment of the faculty of formation of concepts, not only when the disturbance of thought was quite apparent, but also in the cases in which no formal disorder of thought could be demonstrated. The important factor here is not that the patient with schizophrenia, confronted with the experimental problem, is not able to solve it, but that, in the attempt to solve it, he exhibits characteristic and significant forms of thought.

## Observations

Not counting refusals and half-hearted co-operation in the experiments, in all cases in which the results were definite and clear-cut we observed certain characteristic forms of association which resulted in the formation of certain kinds of ideas taking the place of concepts. We could adduce a large variety of these forms of association, but what we believe essential at the moment is the description of the common characteristic of such associative processes. I shall enumerate the most frequent associative structures encountered: (1) collective thinking, in which various objects are grouped together as if they formed a collection composed of different objects united to each other by certain relationships – such as a collection of things or objects of various colours or various forms; (2) chain complex thinking; (3) associative complex thinking; (4) pseudocomplex chain thinking. The last three will be explained later. All of them imply a whole, constituted of organically united parts, the difference between such associations and concepts being that in the associations the union is concrete and mechanical, whereas in the concept there is a general and abstract principle on the basis of which the conceptual association is formed. A complex is best likened to a big family in which are grouped, under the same family name, a large number of altogether different people. A patient with schizophrenia looks on the stimulus word as a family name for a group of objects on a basis of physical proximity, concrete similarity of certain parts or some other non-abstract relationship to each other. A typical example would be the so-called chain associations in patients with schizophrenia. The patient responds to a stimulus word denoting a certain object by naming another object similar in only one trait, then naming a third object chosen on account of some similarity to the second object, then in similar fashion adding a fourth to the third, etc. The result is a number of quite heterogeneous objects very remotely connected with each other. The associative chain is built up in such a relationship and in such a manner that there is a connection between separate links but with no single principle uniting them all. Thus, in my experiments the subject has to select a group of objects, all of which have a common name, being guided in the principle of grouping by a sample shown to him. The example may consist of a small blue triangle, then a large, round, green figure, then a green parallelogram, etc. (the chain colour complex); or he may be shown the same triangle and may choose another triangle which is quite different from the first in colour and size (associative complex). There arises thus a joining of various objects resembling a large family in which the tie is of a most heterogeneous character, degree and principle. Such a method of association is common in children before adolescence. In spite of all the differences in the process of thought in the child and in the patient with schizophrenia, there is a fundamental similarity in the most essential features. Thus, in persons with schizophrenia, thought is really regressive.

## Comment

The impairment of formation of concept leads back to complex thinking, and although the concepts which were formed previously are used well and quite automatically, the formation of new concepts becomes extremely difficult. There is an important conclusion to be derived from such observations. Comparison of thought in persons with schizophrenia with the various genetic stages of complex thought establishes a psychologic criterion, a means of evaluating the degree of splitting and regression in the patient with schizophrenia. The disintegration of concepts and the regression to the concrete, factual, complex forms of thought have been observed by other investigators without appreciation of the genetic factors involved in the differentiation between complex and abstract thinking. This failure finds its expression in the fact that the comparison of disordered thinking with phylogenetically earlier forms of thought is usually made on the basis of negative rather than positive criteria, merely on the basis of the absence of concepts in thinking. This comparison, based on a negative criterion, is wrong because it treats as approximately equivalent forms of thinking which, from the positive side, have nothing in common with each other –

which are, in fact, separated by many millions of years in genetic development. The example to be cited will explain this.

Some authors compare the complex thinking of persons with schizophrenia with the thinking of primitive people, with thought in dreams, and finally with intellectual processes in lower animals, especially with the process of thought in spiders as shown by Volkelt.[4] As reported by Volkelt, the spider goes through accurate movements when trying to get its prey from the web into the nest, but becomes lost when the same prey is removed from the web – that is, from the total complex situation to which the spider is accustomed – and placed directly in the spider's nest. The selective consciousness of a spider does not so much perceive isolated sensations as perceive total conditioned emotional situations. In all these the transition to associative thinking is represented as a step toward visual, pictorial thinking. Although a trend is undoubtedly in evidence, all these comparisons suffer by disregarding the degrees of the governing psychogenetic development. Between abstract thinking in the form of concepts and thought as it is exhibited by the spider, there are a great many developmental steps, each one differing from the other no less than the associative thought of the patients with schizophrenia differs from the thought of a normal person.

And just as it is not admissible to make a genetic comparison of thought as it occurs in dreams with thought as it occurs in primitive man or in spiders, simply because such forms of thought are all below the stage of conceptual thought, neither has one the right to assume that the thought of the patient with schizophrenia immediately drops into the abyss of millions of years, or needs for its understanding analogies with the spider, which does not recognize its prey after the prey has been removed from the web and placed in the nest.

My observations show that complex thought observed in patients with schizophrenia is the nearest step to conceptual thought and immediately precedes it genetically. There is some similarity, then, although by no means an identity, between the thought of the patient with schizophrenia and the thought of a child. The one common basis which permits direct comparison of the two different types of thinking is that the process of thought of the child and that of a patient with schizophrenia in the initial stages of the disease are merely steps in the genetic development of thought; that is, they represent the step immediately preceding the stage of formation of concept and cannot be compared to the process of thought of the spider from which they are separated by millions of years of development. One knows that even in adulthood there remains a tendency to complex thinking in certain fields. A superficial examination will not reveal the transition from one mode of thinking into another unless special methods of investigation are employed.

A second important conclusion to be derived from the experiment relates to the fact that in schizophrenia there is a destruction of the psychologic systems which lie at the basis of concepts. Expressing the same idea differently, it can be said that early in schizophrenia the meanings of words become changed. These changes are sometimes difficult to observe unless one uses special methods, but they can be demonstrated. The way to understand this phenomenon lies in the study of thought in the child. A child thinks differently from an adult; consequently, the words for him also have different connotations in their psychologic structure. The question naturally arises: If the words have different meanings how do a child and an adult understand each other? As an example I may cite the paradoxical fact established by Piaget that children of the same age and degree of development do not understand each other as well as they do adults.[5] Yet the thinking of adults is governed by laws quite different from those determining the thinking of children. This, it will be seen, involves the problem that I described at the beginning of this article. If, I said, the meaning of words begins to change early in the course of the schizophrenic process, how does that fact remain unobserved, and how is it possible for the normal person and the person with schizophrenia to understand each other?

The answer to such questions, as indicated by my investigations, lies in the fact that 'complexes' may and sometimes do coincide with concepts in their reference to objects, but not necessarily in their meanings. When one speaks of Napoleon as the victor at Jena and the loser at Waterloo, the two phrases coincide in their reference to Napoleon, but are widely different in their meanings. When a concept and a complex thus refer to the same object, the complex may be spoken of as a pseudoconcept. Pseudoconcepts, which are the basic elements in the thought of a child, may coincide with the concepts of adults, but this does not mean that they necessarily coincide in other particulars. When a child says 'house' or 'dog', he may be speaking of the same objects as the adult, but he thinks about them in a different way. He groups and combines them in a way quite different from that of the adult.

The fact that in its reference to objects the speech of a child coincides with the language of the adult can be explained by the development of speech in children. Speech in a child does not develop freely and spontaneously; the child does not create words and their meanings. He finds them both ready made in his environment, and he acquires something that has been prepared for him. In his environment certain names are definitely attached to certain objects. Each object has its distinctive name, and the child, acquiring these names, groups them by the only method he knows, i.e. by associations. The association consists of objects not chosen freely by the child, but is made on the basis of existing connections and relationships of the objects with each other, relations in part previously established by the adult. As soon as this external pressure is removed, the associations of the child and the concepts of the adult begin to differ, not only in their connotations but also in their relationships to objects. My study of the thinking of deaf mutes shows that they have associative thinking and that they even resort to earlier forms of thought – the syncretic forms of making connections.[6] Thus, in the mimic language of the deaf mute, the gesture denoting teeth may also mean 'white', 'stone' and 'talk', depending on the whole sentence. The additional gestures, such as pointing to the upper lip, or indicating rejection or pointing, make possible the differentiation of various meanings which are all united on the basis of the associative complex, of which I have already given examples. But because their mimic speech develops without the fixed system of rigid limitations associated with verbal speech, their associations do not coincide in relationship to objects with the concepts of normal adults. This same situation exists in schizophrenia. The words of the patient with schizophrenia coincide with ours in their object relationships but not in their meanings.

## Process of thought in schizophrenia

Two influences determine such a phenomenon. The first is that (with the exception of neologisms) the patient with schizophrenia uses in his speech the system of fixed names which he learned in childhood. When the disintegration begins he reverts to complexes in the place of concepts, not freely, but as predetermined by his prior attachment of certain names to certain situations and objects. A table is a table for us as well as for a patient with schizophrenia, but we think about it differently. He puts all the various tables into a complex, and the word table is merely a familiar name for this association. We use a general concept, and the name is merely carried as a symbol of this concept. In other words, he has in his possession a ready-made system of words standing in definite relationship to the objects they denote. Consequently, since he does not see the principle forming the basis of this association, his association is invariably a pseudoconcept.

The other influence involved in the fact that the words of the patient with schizophrenia coincide with those of the normal person in their object reference but not in their meanings, arises from the way in which conceptual thinking develops. I have said that a school child goes through a stage of complex thinking as a period in his development immediately preceding conceptual thinking. Consequently, in ontogenesis, complexes precede concepts and actually form the inner layer or the older substructure beneath the new layers of concepts, if one utilizes Kretschmer's graphic expression for older and newer forms of thought. There is reason to believe that the development of concepts, like the appearance of other higher psychologic functions, is accomplished by the formation of new layers over the old ones, with the preservation of the older layer of thought in a subordinate function. This law, which was recently discovered in the development of the central nervous system, holds true also for the development of various psychologic functions, motor as well as central.[7] Kretschmer has shown that hypobulia, i.e. the early stage in certain motor discharges, is preserved in all the activities of the organism associated with the discharge of volitional impulses. Hypobulia is preserved in a latent, subordinate role, and occasionally it is uncovered and expresses itself independently when the higher processes of the will are impaired or disturbed. Something like this must be taking place in schizophrenia. Associations, as a primitive form of thought, are retained as a substructure in the development of the higher forms of thinking, but they are uncovered and begin to act independently in accordance with their own laws when the whole personality, for some reason, is disturbed. There is reason to believe that complex thought is not a specific product of schizophrenia, but merely a cropping out of the older forms of thought, which are always present in a latent form in the psyche of the patient but which become apparent only when the higher intellectual processes become disturbed by illness. The regression to earlier forms of thought is observed also in other diseases in which there is interference with conceptual thinking. The process of thinking then becomes strikingly similar to thought in schizophrenia, and this probably accounts for the schizophrenic reaction in the course of physical illnesses. The other proof that these are earlier forms of thought can be found in the fact that associative thinking is latent in all of us and comes to the surface in connection with sudden emotional shocks and in a setting of fatigue, sleep and dreams. There is nothing impossible, then, in the assumption that regression of patients with schizophrenia to complex thinking is merely a reversion to earlier forms of thought. Each one of us carries schizophrenia in a latent form, i.e. in the mechanisms of thought which, when uncovered, become the central figure in the drama of schizophrenic thought. Thus, the history of the development of thought ought to be used as a means of reaching an understanding of the peculiarities of complex thinking in schizophrenia.

## Alterations in the meaning of words

Whatever may be its cause, and paradoxical as it may appear, the fact is nevertheless fairly well established that the meanings of words become pathologically altered in schizophrenia, though such alterations do not become apparent for a long time. Complexes replacing concepts in thought in schizophrenia nevertheless coincide in their object relationships with the concepts they replace. They are then pseudoconcepts, but the whole transition to the more primitive forms of thought is not apparent because the patient retains his capacity for verbal intercourse, even though words do not have the same meaning for him as they have for us. As a concrete illustration I may cite my experimental investigations as to the degree to which patients with schizophrenia at the same stage of the disease, and with the same type of thinking, understand each other as compared with the degree of mutual understanding exhibited by a patient with schizophrenia and a normal person. As might be expected, the experiments indicated a better mutual understanding between patients with schizophrenia and normal persons than between schizophrenic persons.[8] An analogous situation is seen in children, who understand adults better than they do each other. The solution of this problem is presented later.

An important question, which to me is central to schizophrenia, arises in this connection. If it is really true, as I assert, that in schizophrenia there is disintegration of concepts with changes in the meaning of words, even though this is not apparent on the surface, there must be some proofs that these phenomena actually take place. The proof is simple. If words have different meanings for a patient with schizophrenia from those which they have for us, then this difference must express itself functionally, i.e. in the behaviour of the patients. Even if a complex may outwardly resemble a concept, it nevertheless has its own laws of function. Just as the associative thinking of a child expresses itself in various ways, so must the thought of a patient with schizophrenia reveal its distinguishing characteristic when subjected to a test, i.e. in actual behaviour. This was the principle of my experiments, and I found that in actual function these associations reveal the changes in the meanings of words which I postulated previously.

From many methods I have selected the test dealing with capacity for metaphorical expression, i.e. the transference of terms originally denoting one thing to the expression of others ('A ship ploughs the sea'). I first used this test in cases of aphasia associated with loss of memory, in which may also be seen disturbances both of categorical thinking (Gelb and Goldstein) and of conceptual thought. (In this connection it may be noted that the disturbances of categorical thinking which Gelb and Goldstein found as a cardinal symptom in amnesic aphasia, were also found by them in a patient who exhibited amnesia for various colours. When asked to match colours this patient, instead of matching objects according to the colour designated, would match them according to size, or according to value in brightness of the paint, and only occasionally according to colour, thus manifesting the previously described complex type of thinking.)[9] I found in my patients an analogous and marked disturbance in the capacity both for using words in metaphorical senses and for understanding words so used. They could not grasp the meanings of the simplest words unless they were used in a direct and literal sense. Nor could they cope with the test of Piaget, which requires the subject to match a specified proverb with another of similar meaning.[10] To my surprise such failures occurred in spite of an apparent preservation of speech and of other intellectual functions. I later discovered, however, that Kurt Schneider had also found disturbances in the capacity to understand words used in metaphorical senses to be a frequent characteristic of schizophrenia.[11] Most remarkable was that I found disturbances in the understanding of words figuratively used, even when there was no apparent disturbance of intellectual life in general. This difficulty became very obvious when special words or concepts were used. While the normal mind has no difficulty in using given words metaphorically or figuratively, the same problem presents insurmountable difficulty for the patient with schizophrenia in spite of the fact that he has retained from childhood the habit of using figures of speech, proverbs, etc. Thus, many of my patients have no difficulty in seeing the wider ramifications and generalities when they are given the Russian proverb, 'If you go slowly you get further in the end', but they could not give a general meaning when the Russian translation of a French proverb, 'When the cat is away the mice will play', was given. This they interpreted in its narrow sense, and they could only see literally that mice play when the cat is away. They could not, that is, see, in a situation concretely described, meanings other and more abstract than those directly signified by the particular words used in describing it. This fact serves as an important differentiation between the visual, symbolic thinking of dreams and the metaphorical, symbolic thinking based on concepts. The identification of one with the other is without any solid, psychologic basis.

## Formation of new concepts

I found also another fact illustrating disturbances of meaning in words used by patients with schizophrenia. My experiments did not stop at the stage of development of experimental concepts. I studied the manner in which these new concepts expressed themselves. I included them as a part of association tests in which the responses were carefully traced out. The subjects were asked to make judgements which included the old as well as the newly formed concepts, and were encouraged to widen the application of the newly formed concepts and to carry them over from the laboratory into everyday life. In other words, I wanted to trace as fully as possible the course of the newly formed concepts in the thinking of the patients. Without going too much into detail, I may state that there was found a latent disintegration of concepts. I found also that the pseudoconcepts which took the place of true concepts were quite different from them in behaviour and expression. As an example of pseudoconcepts I may take the example of the concept of causality in a child. As the reader will remember, a child begins quite early to use words denoting causal relations, such as the word 'because', although, as Piaget has shown, the meaning given by the child to these words differs altogether from that given by an adult.[12] A child will connect causally the most inconsequential ideas, a fact which led Piaget to speak of a certain stage in the development of a child as a pre-causality stage. One must have special methods to demonstrate such pseudoconcepts because superficially they may resemble true concepts in their external appearance. Pseudoconcepts are wolves in sheep's clothing. They are associations which look like concepts. Anybody who works with them finds out quickly how they disturb the forms of conceptual thinking. In order to demonstrate this, however, one must consider other psychologic functions. As an example of the more remote consequences resulting from the disturbance of the function of concept formation, I may refer to experiments with perceptions and with affective responses in schizophrenia. A study of the perceptions of a patient with schizophrenia indicates that for such a patient various common perceptual objects easily lose their common perceptual characteristics. Slight variations in light or in the position of the object bring out in the patient responses similar to those of normal persons to the meaningless ink blots of the Rorschach test. Just as normal persons see in such ink blots people, landscapes, faces, fairies and what not, so does the patient with schizophrenia, in his perception of objects, attach to them the most extraordinary meanings if there is the slightest change in their customary appearance. The key to the understanding of the phenomenon lies in genetic psychology, which teaches that categorical perceptions are achieved through a complicated process, in which percepts and concepts are co-ordinated into new forms of visual thinking, the percepts playing therein a subordinate and dependent role. As an example of such fusion of conception and perception in the narrow sense of the word I may refer to illusions, in which one cannot separate the meaning from the object (white shadow-ghost). It is also known from experimental psychology that it is impossible under normal conditions to get absolute perceptions without associating with them meanings, understandings and apperceptions.

This is why it is so hard to get perception in pure culture, and why objects cannot serve all of us as ink blots serve us in the Rorschach test. Perception is an integral part of visual thinking and is intimately connected with the concepts which go with it. This is why every perception is really an apperception. But this is not true for complex thought. With the disintegration of concepts and their regression to more primitive forms of thought, the whole relationship between perception and apperception becomes altered in a manner which is typical of schizophrenia. Such a change is closely akin to the phenomena which appear in the affective life of patients with schizophrenia. The significant factors here are not the emotional dullness and the disappearance of the richness and variety of emotional expression, but the separation of these emotional expressions from the concepts with which they are closely associated. These facts, of course, are well known clinically. My contribution lies in the demonstration that disturbance of emotional life is only part of the wider and more fundamental disturbance, i.e. a disturbance in the field of concept formation. My postulation is that the intellectual disturbance, as well as the disturbances in the fields of perceptions, emotions and other psychologic functions, are in direct causal relationship with the disturbance of the functions of formation of concepts. This hypothesis is based on the results of the developmental study of the individual, i.e. on ontogenetic data.

## General comment

A study of the development of psychologic functions in childhood through adolescence affords an opportunity to observe the connection between development of the capacity for formation of concepts and the development of personality. In adolescence one finds a fundamental regrouping of these various functions, a complete change of their inter-relationships, leading to the appearance of totally different psychologic systems of a much higher order and complexity. A disintegration of these new systems, a splitting of those higher functions, is what is found in schizophrenia.

But the investigation brings out still other conclusions. The capacity for formation of concepts is really the third of three stages in the intellectual growth of the child. The first involves the development of ideas of physical causality. The second consists in secondary changes in other psychologic functions. The third, intimately connected with the formation of concepts, also involves the development of personality and a world outlook, i.e. the cognition of one's self and one's environment. The appearance of a formed personality with a world outlook in adolescence is the result of the highest development of intellect in that period of life. The process has been discussed elsewhere in my work on the psychology of adolescence.[13] Observing the disturbance in the perception of self and the environment in the patient with schizophrenia, I cannot but believe that there is some involvement of the third stage in the development of personality associated with the functions of the formation of concepts. And truly, a perception of the self and the outside world is intimately connected with the concepts by means of which they are represented. One knows that the child's concepts of himself and his environment are quite different from those of an adult. One knows how changed are the perceptions of self and the environment in dreams, and it is fair to suppose that the changes in personality and changes in perception of the outside world observed in schizophrenia are caused by the slumping of intellect from the conceptual level to the level of associations.

True enough, this is only a hypothesis, but it is a tempting hypothesis, not only because it takes into consideration the developmental facts of those functions which are strongly affected in schizophrenia, but also because it allows one to reduce the data to a common denominator and to study schizophrenia in the light of the psychologic development of personality.

There is one misunderstanding which invariably appears in any discussion of schizophrenia, and which I should like here to clear up. Utilizing the function of the formation of concepts as a starting point in investigation, and finding also that it is the psychologic centre or nucleus of the whole drama of the disease, one yet sees that it has nothing to do with the etiology of schizophrenia. Disturbances in the function of concept formation are the immediate result of schizophrenia but not its cause. I am not at all inclined to treat schizophrenia as a psychogenic disorder. Whatever may be the organic cause of the disease, however, psychology has a right to study the phenomena associated with the changes in personality from a psychologic point of view. Disintegration of personality follows certain psychologic laws, even though the direct causes of this process may not be psychologic in nature.

Moreover, the clinical and physiologic observations form a bridge to psychologic speculations. I refer particularly to clinical observations which lead to the conclusion that at the basis of schizophrenia there is a loss of psychic energy. Jung was the first to draw the parallel between dreams and schizophrenia. He put it beautifully, that if a man could walk and talk in his dreams his total behaviour would be in no way different from that of a patient with schizophrenia. The asthenic habitus as a constitutional factor has been emphasized by many authors. I had an opportunity recently to study schizophrenia in children in a setting of marked fatigue and sleep. One of my patients was observed to drop off to sleep frequently. He was asleep most of the afternoon, and in the acute stage of the illness the tendency to fall asleep was most marked. I feel that there must be some germ of truth in the old clinical observation comparing stupors and sleep. Although sleep and schizophrenia are not identical, yet they have some points in common. Lately this view found expression in Pavlov's paper, 'The excursion of a physiologist into the field of psychiatry', in which he stated the belief that the most probable physiologic cause of schizophrenia is the overdevelopment of the process of inner inhibitions, which are also overdeveloped in hypnosis and sleep.[14] Some time ago Pavlov thought that cortical inhibitions and sleep were identical; now he believes that inner inhibitions and schizophrenia have a good deal in common. Of course, it is a fascinating theory. The thing which interests me in this theory is that it bridges the gap between the psychologic hypothesis and the physiologic data in schizophrenia. If one recalls that the biologic function and purpose of inner inhibitions, including sleep, consist in cessation of contacts with the outside world, it becomes clear that autism, withdrawal and shutting off one's self from reality are direct results of the special state of the central nervous system of patients with schizophrenia. The loss of contact with the outside world assumes a biologic significance. It is not a result of schizophrenia but an expression of the protective forces of the organism reacting with inner inhibitions to the weakness of the central nervous system. If this is so, and there seems to be every reason to believe that it is a fact, important conclusions may be drawn. All higher psychologic functions, including speech and conceptual thinking, are of social origin. They arise as a means of rendering mutual aid, and gradually they become a part of the person's everyday behaviour. It is significant that in dreams there is a cessation of contacts with that social self which forms the foundation of the normal personality. This apparently becomes also the cause of impairment of intellect in the field of concepts; the other symptoms of schizophrenia, as I have shown, all spring from this source. At any rate, my experimental data, interpreted in the light of genetic psychology, allow one to formulate certain theories which I have here presented.

## Notes

First published as Vigotsky, L. S. 1934: Thought in schizophrenia. *Archives of Neurology and Psychiatry*, 31, 1062–77. The translator, Jacob Kasanin, mentioned that the article had been written at his request three years before, and that since then a great deal more work had been done. Kasanin – together with Eugenia Hanffman – subsequently investigated concept formation in schizophrenics using a modified form of Vygotsky's procedure. The translation was edited by C. Trueblood of Brown University. The translator and editor provided the article with six footnotes, some of which we used. In these cases the words 'original footnote' are added between square brackets.

1 'The hypobulic type of will is the ontogenetic and phylogenetic lower stage of the purposive will.' See Kretschmer, E. 1926: *Hysteria*. Washington, DC: Nervous and Mental Disease Publishing Company [original footnote].

2 See Blonsky, P. P. 1926: *Pedologija*. Moscow: Rabotnik Prosveshchenija [original footnote].

3 By complex thinking Vigotsky signifies not the usual meaning of the term 'complex' in psychopathology but a type of simple elementary generalization found in the thought processes of a child, a primitive man or a psychotic patient. This type of thinking can perhaps be expressed in terms of English psychology as associative thinking or 'group thinking', meaning by 'group' a unity whose members are different, i.e. a type of thinking in which groups of different elements are related to each other [original footnote]. A detailed description of Vygotsky's research into 'complexes' and concepts can be found in

chapters 6 and 9 of this reader and in chapter 12 of Van der Veer, R. and Valsiner, J. 1991: *Understanding Vygotsky: A quest for synthesis.* Oxford: Blackwell Publishers.

4 Refers to Volkelt, H. 1912: *Über die Vorstellungen der Tiere. Ein Beitrag zur Entwicklungspsychologie.* Doctoral dissertation, Leipzig.

5 See the last chapter of Piaget, J. 1923: *Le langage et la pensée chez l'enfant.* [*The Language and Thought of the Child*]. Neuchatel: Delachaux & Niestlé.

6 Vygotsky frequently claimed that sign language is inferior to vocal language in that it has no or less abstract concepts. For this reason he advocated teaching deaf mutes vocal speech. There is no evidence, however, that Vygotsky investigated the matter thoroughly and modern research contests his claims.

7 The idea that the brain (and the mind) consists of several layers or systems of different age, of which the older ones function at a subordinate level but may take charge again when the newer ones are disturbed, was shared by many scholars at the time. Explicit formulations of this point of view can be found, for example, in the works of Head, Hughlings Jackson, Janet, Kretschmer, Sherrington and Wallon.

8 We have no other evidence of these experiments.

9 Refers to a patient described in Gelb, A. and Goldstein, K. 1925: Psychologische Analysen hirnpathologische Fälle. Über Farbennamenamnesie. *Psychologische Forschung*, 6, 127–86.

10 See chapter 4 of Piaget, J. 1923: *Le langage et la pensée chez l'enfant* [*The Language and Thought of the Child*]. Neuchatel: Delachaux & Niestlé. Piaget's proverb experiment – as well as many other of his experiments – was replicated by Vygotsky and Leont'ev. They basically found the same results.

11 Refers to Schneider, K. 1923: *Die psychopatischen Persönlichkeiten.* Leipzig: F. Deuticke.

12 See the first chapter of Piaget, J. 1924: *Le jugement et le raisonnement chez l'enfant.* [*Judgement and Reasoning in the Child*]. Neuchatel: Delachaux & Niestlé.

13 Refers to Vygotsky, L. S. 1931: *Pedologija podrostka.* Moscow/Leningrad: Uchebno-Pedagogicheskoe Izdatel'stvo.

14 Pavlov's paper was published as chapter 42 in Pavlov, I. P. 1936/1963: *Lectures on Conditioned Reflexes. Vol. II: Conditioned reflexes and psychiatry.* New York: International Publishers.

# 13

# Fascism in psychoneurology

## Lev Vygotsky

The profound crisis which has afflicted bourgeois psychology during the past few decades has assumed new acute, ugly and repulsive forms, hitherto unknown in the history of psychological science, after the fascist coup in Germany. The new regime has accelerated catastrophically the growth of and exposed a great number of hitherto vague, not fully recognized, masked tendencies, and as a result, a basic infrastructure within the system of fascist psychology has been created with the most astonishing speed during the past year. The political demand of the new regime acted as a catalyst in the process of degeneration and decay which had previously become woven into the general fabric of the crisis and has led to a state of unprecedented poignancy.

There cannot, of course, be any discussion of the creation of a new psychology in a time as short as that which has elapsed from the establishment of the fascist regime. Fascism began to penetrate psychology in a different way. It rearranged the ranks of German psychology by bringing into the foreground everything reactionary which previously existed in it. But this alone would not have been enough. As has already been said, it was also necessary to knock together, in the shortest possible time, a system of psychology which would correspond to the entire fascist ideology.

German catalogues in the fields of philosophy, psychology and pedagogical science suddenly abounded with such titles as: 'A Study of Family and Heredity' or 'A Study of Race'. The most reactionary idealistic schools hurriedly began to reassess their material and rearrange it in such a way that it could be used as a factual base for fascist psychology.

Spranger, one of the most outspoken and consistent propagators of the bourgeois point of view in psychology[1] has set out to lay the foundations for a German nationalist idea, using the medium of psychological research into personality. Granted, soon after the coup, the newspapers announced that, as a form of protest, Spranger had resigned his Berlin University post. But it appears that this brief period of protest has now been replaced by zealous service to the cause.

Spranger has always advocated the idea of the existence in psychology of different forms of life, various types of personality. For Spranger, these forms of life ['Lebensformen'] are first and foremost national forms. In his widely known work entitled 'The Psychology of Adolescence', he says that the structure of adolescent personality which he is describing characterizes a German adolescent. And he says that a Jewish adolescent would exhibit entirely different traits, and as far as the Russian emotional type is concerned, despite evident similarities, what all of us are experiencing is an apprehensive feeling of a far reaching strangeness. But even within the German national type, he distinguishes the educated adolescents: 'we might have called them bourgeois, had not this depiction by now become a superficial political slogan'.[2]

Another very famous German psychologist, Ach,[3] approaches the problem of the launching of fascist psychology from another angle. If Spranger dwells on the problems of nationality, then Ach decided to choose a more acute problem. For many years this researcher was involved in investigating problems of the will, and he studied the influence of determining tendencies both in internal and external human activities. And now, as it turns out, this establishment of the laws of determinist psychology ['Determinationspsychologie'] was found to have a fundamental application to the problem of the leader. Ach read a paper about determinist psychology and its significance for the problem of the leader at the Psychology Congress in Leipzig in 1933. In this paper Ach investigated the purity of the origins of his own theory. He examined all the stages in the development of determinist psychology, beginning in 1904, and he came to the conclusion that his psychology had always exhibited the sharpest contrast with regard to the individualistic liberal interpretation of mental life.

In this way two basic ideas came through which are obviously called upon to play an organizing role in the entire system of fascist psychology: the first idea is that of a national type, the second idea is that of voluntarism[4] and the problem of the leader.

But the most extensive efforts to found a fascist psychology were attempted by a third German psychologist, Erich Jaensch, a scientist of world renown, who has extensively elaborated the problem of perception and memory from the eidetic and psychological typology point of view.[5] Jaensch published a special treatise entitled *The Situation and Tasks of Psychology, its Mission in the German Movement and in the Cultural Reform*. In this book, Jaensch presents an entire system of fascist psychology, a system which is likely to determine the direction and fate of the fascist branch of German psychology for the foreseeable future. Like Ach and Spranger, Jaensch also draws direct connecting threads from his earlier research to fascist psychology and, therefore, on the basis of this book, it is quite easy for us to observe the route which these tendencies, now revealed in their most cynical form, have been following in German idealistic psychology long before it became their fate to be assigned the mission of serving the German nationalist movement, and what this mission brought with it which is new and which has undoubtedly marked out a new stage of the psychological crisis, a stage of unprecedented and extremely intense degeneration of bourgeois scientific thinking.

Jaensch's book is permeated by militant feeling. What the author had in mind was for it to serve as a warlike manifesto for the creation of a new . . .[6] It is for this reason that psychology and the German movement ought to march in step and at the same time psychology must interpret and illuminate, using the light of reason, the instinctual aspirations which are laid down in the nationalist movement. Therefore, in order to be able to cure this decrepit idealism, Jaensch seeks to find new strength for it among German peasantry, that is to say, the landowners. 'The philosopher', he says, [1933, p. 98], 'stretches out his hand to the peasant'. This is how a union of the bayonet and the idea, and scientific psychology and storm troopers can be achieved.

Using a concrete example it can be demonstrated how, starting from these points of view, Jaensch proceeds to solve concrete political problems and how he attempts to use anthropology and psychology to form a scientific basis for his politics. In the book under discussion, Jaensch finds it necessary to disclaim the opinion which has been ascribed to him, that he had allegedly said that Germany and France are divided by a very deep chasm which exists between these two opposite mental structures, the French and the German, and which excludes any possibility of mutual understanding. At the present time Jaensch is prepared to admit that, from the anthropological point of view, the relations between these two great nations may change for the better. His reasoning is strictly empirical and precise, and in his psychological laboratory he is determining the fates of nations and their relations with one another in exactly the same way as one would usually evaluate the fitness of an individual for one of the professions. Jaensch himself fails to see the incredibly comic side of all these speculations. But the absence of humour probably belongs to the number of essential traits which are inherited along with race and blood, and which are necessary for the development of 'pure German ideas'. 'Every great nation', proclaims Jaensch [ibid., pp. 29–30],

possesses many structures. A nation harbours not only those mental structures which appear as the leading forces in a given period, but other additional ones as well. At the present time in Germany, we are concerned with rehabilitating the basic national type. This revitalization process consists of the amalgamation of the type of the German idealist with the peasant type, who is nearer to the soil. Both of these structures should be able to cross-pollinate one another. The peasant type must be raised up somewhat and the ideal type has to be built up and strengthened from below. In the language of integral typology this signifies an alloy of structures. If other nations also proceed in the same way and follow the path which has been marked out for them and revise their leading structures, then Germans and Frenchmen will be able to understand one another. Every nation incorporates within itself great developmental potential.

It is hard to believe that these lines were written in the fourth decade of the twentieth century. It is hard to believe that the author himself seriously believes in his own idea of the rebuilding of relations between nations based on psychological integral formulas. But Jaensch does everything in his power to persuade us that his ideas are entirely serious. He is not just pretending, he genuinely believes in all this.

Whilst defining the sphere of psychological problems, he fills this sphere exclusively with those problems which, under different circumstances and in other times, might be taken for a fantastic system of ideas symptomatic of some sort of paranoia but which, in actual fact, represent the scientific language of real fascist politics. As we have already been told, according to Jaensch, the primacy of all ideas belongs to the nationalist movement. Psychology should march in step with the German movement. Psychological anthropology is the most important source for the philosophy of reality and scientific construction of politics. Race and blood, blood and race – this is what underpins everything in the world. A direct connecting thread stretches all the way from the structure of one's capillary network to one's philosophy of life. The scientists are beginning to think in a warlike manner – drastically, straightforwardly and decisively. Where we find a dearth of logic, there begins the philosophy of the imperative.

Oh, lucky Germany! For it did not follow Skalozub's[7] advice to send its sergeant major[8] to learn how to become a Voltaire. Instead, the fascist Voltaires themselves voluntarily transformed themselves into sergeant majors of the German nationalist movement.

So what we are now observing is a development of this sergeant major anthropology and sergeant major politics. The relations among various nations are determined by the fact that at the foundations of different cultures lie various mental structures characteristic of the people who belong to a specific national type. The very latest piece of wisdom of fascist philosophy to be declared is critical anthropomorphism, from whose viewpoint Jaensch examines all the basic problems of the fascist regime. As we have seen, he has already managed to solve the basic questions of German politics, both internal and external, from the point of view of integral typology. The indissoluble union between the idealist-philosopher in town and the peasant-kulak in the countryside already serves as just such an anthropological formula. Speaking plainly, this formula signifies that the German philosopher should become totally permeated by kulak ideology.[9] This is the real meaning, in Jaensch's parlance, of building up from below and furthering the type of the German idealist. The kulak should believe the philosopher when he says that the policies which are in his interests are being carried out based on notions and formulas provided by typological chemistry, that his selfish interests will be satisfied by a return to the original form of German idealism, and that they correspond to a spiritual renascence of all humanity.

Viewing the situation from the angle of this basic idea, Jaensch solves the problem of the relationship between the individual and the state. He sees the meaning of the coup in Germany as a struggle between two structures, one of which has won a victory under the sign of the swastika and strives to transform the general (the state) into an organic whole, built according to the laws of psychological anthropology, based on the purity of the physical being of the nation, and on the basis of the common formula of blood and mental structure. But critical anthropomorphism would not amount to much even in Jaensch's eyes had it not the ability to understand, with the most disarming simplicity accessible to any average peasant mind of a pure-blooded German, the simple truth that international relations are determined by these same formulas. During each period one type of mental structure becomes the determining trait of national character. The highest type and the most lofty character is, of course, the German one. It is for this reason that critical anthropomorphism is not interested in the problem of man in general, but just of German man.

With the aid of a very simple argument Jaensch succeeds, using the very same logical technique of systematized raving, in proving that the mission of the German spirit is to lead humanity forward. For this to be achieved one only has to recall that the different mental structures, the various types of personalities, reach their clearest expression among certain age groups of human development. What a lucky coincidence: it turns out that the highest human type, i.e. the German fascist type, corresponds, according to its chemical formula, to the youthful type, who is characterized by a perpetual drive forward towards the achievement of perfection of all humanity. According to Jaensch, this constitutes the meaning of the German movement and the purpose of German psychology, whose only wish is to translate the zoological instincts of militant fascism into the language of scientific consciousness.

All that remains belongs essentially to the realm of trivia – it only remains to outline a programme for solving the most pressing problems of world politics using the methods of the psychological laboratory, and thus to provide a scientific political basis for politics. It remains to explain these liberating typological formulas to all the nations of the world, and by doing so, to establish the sanctity of the fascist bayonet and the power of the German idea in the language of realistic idealism. But all that remains for us is to examine the internal methodological basis of this systematized gibberish. Jaensch is forced to perform several tortuous operations on the living body of German psychology in order to confirm definitively the supremacy of fascism in that sphere of science which has been assigned to his guardianship. After all, German scientific psychology has developed over the centuries. It has managed to gather within itself not only the things which fascism finds useful to appropriate for its needs, but also much which constitutes enormous real achievement in authentic scientific knowledge. Every stone comprising the edifice of scientific psychology cries out against this monstrous raving which Jaensch attempts to turn into scientific psychology. As a result, any genuine scientific knowledge in the field of psychology needs to be liquidated. Within the system of fascist political division of labour, Jaensch has been assigned the task of carrying out the same destruction in the realm of scientific psychological ideas which has already been carried out in the racial political plan. As is well known, Germany after the coup lost its best, its most scientifically advanced and progressive psychologists. As Jaensch is firmly convinced of the fact that all power rests with realistic idealism, and that ideas which are not backed up by the bayonet are not worth a farthing, the only thing that remains for him is to draw ideological conclusions from the actual political repressions.

Jaensch has taken up this task with a lightheartedness and decisiveness worthy of a philosopher-sergeant major. He cannot fail to admit that psychology has gone through a period of serious crisis. But a crisis implies a certain ideological conflict; however, Jaensch is not prepared to base his argument only on the strength of ideas. He is an opponent of any idealism which is unsubstantiated and cut off from reality, and this is the reason why he decides to cope with the problem of the crisis in

psychology in a military manner, in two ticks like this: firstly, there indeed was a
crisis, Jaensch announces, but it has been overcome and one cannot say that it is a
contemporary one. Secondly, there was no crisis at all. It was a methodological and
not a theoretical crisis. When Ebbinghaus' elemental psychology collided with
Dilthey's structural psychology, associative psychology was no longer a living theory
and it was only used as a research method in opposition to structural psychology. This
is why German Gestalt psychology was essentially fighting phantoms when it opposed the atomistic theory of the mind. It was defending a theory against a method.
Jaensch cites a verbal opinion of an English friend of his, who had assured him that
there is nothing in this movement of psychological ideas, which in any case is the
most progressive one of all the psychological trends of our time, which is not already
contained in the work of Stout and Sherrington. The idea of a whole which determines its parts is a primordial idea of German psychology. It does not exclude, but
presupposes elemental psychology. Psychology's unity can be reconstructed with
magical ease. Jaensch teaches us not to say 'either-or', but 'both the one and the other'.
Jaensch should be able to deal with Gestalt psychology which, incidentally, has not
only last year lost its founder Wertheimer, one of the most outstanding contemporary
psychologists, but is now represented in Germany by only one person.[10] So where has
Gestalt psychology gone wrong? As Jaensch has already tried to prove for a long time,
this theory is flawed due to its materialism, its tendency to a monistic approach to
psychological structures and its discovery of a principal unity within the psychological and the physiological structure. Jaensch has always strongly resisted the idea that
structures are not purely mental constructions and the scientific objective to bring
together psychological theory with physiology and theoretical physics. Incidentally,
he has some old scores to settle with this theory. For a long time its representatives
have openly suspected the strict scientific character of Jaensch's research, which had
always shown a tendency to dilute itself in a boundless sea of idealistic haze. They
called his research by its real name. They reproached him for his dilettantism and for
his readiness, at any moment, to be unfaithful to precise scientific knowledge and
scientific truth in the name of preconceived ideas. As time has shown, they were not
sufficiently far-sighted, as they were unable to suspect how far Jaensch would end up
going along that road.

Of course, Jaensch is not against physics. On the contrary, as we have seen, he says
that it is impossible to penetrate the depths of the mental structure of personality
without the use of a crude form of physics. Blood and race determine the purity of
ideas. In a certain sense Jaensch goes a lot further than Köhler in reducing the
psychological to the physical.[11] And essentially, he protests even less against the
tendency to understand psychological phenomena in the light of biology. Only he
requires a different kind of physics and a different biology.

Jaensch says that the rapprochement between the psychological and physical
realms should be sought not in the sphere of well known physical structures, but
rather in the sphere of particular physical laws applicable to the mind. Teleoformic
[teleoform] principles of physics and particular processes, mnemonic phenomena in

inorganic nature, ought to emerge into the foreground here. In plain language what is meant here, is that it is not scientific materialistic physics, but the idealistic distortions of the physical theory, which discover teleological and mnemonic principles in inorganic life, which should become the site where physical and psychological phenomena can come together in human beings. As we can see, Jaensch remains entirely faithful to his real-idealism. It is necessary to teleologize and mnemonize the physical in order to justify and legalize the point of view of blood and race in psychological anthropology.

Further, he accuses Gestalt psychology of not differentiating between the various forms of the whole and that, in the realm of biology, it does not base itself on Driesch's and Becher's psychovitalism.[12] Jaensch is in need of vitalistic biology as well as idealistic physics. Therefore, this theory allows for a levelling out of the levels and, in principle, it brings together psychological and physical structures. He is juggling the facts somewhat when he says that Koffka reduces the problem of development and Lewin the problem of will (like all other higher levels) to the level of electrical processes.

However, Jaensch does not view the basic principle of Gestalt psychology – the principle of wholeness – with disdain. He only assumes that this principle should be made to serve the fascist cause. He feels that it is his mission to become the founder and proponent of the theory of blood and race. The highest form of wholeness is the personality, where everything is indissoluble and combined into one integral whole in such a way that if the inherited traits of race and blood are given, then the ideological world of the personality is given along with it.

To achieve a complete picture, all that remains for us to do is determine the blood and race of this new psychological system which Jaensch is advocating. He himself names his ancestors. As could have been expected, right from the very beginning, it turns out that no more and no less than 99 per cent of them were German psychologists. The principal line of German idealism, says Jaensch, leads from the mystic Eckhardt and the German mystics, through Leibnitz, Kant, Fechner, Helmholtz, Wundt, Külpe and Brentano, in an unwavering straight line to fascist psychology and to Jaensch himself. Here we have a spiritual passport which he has issued to himself.

We have summarized briefly the situation in which psychology finds itself and the scope of its most important goals, and how these tasks are outlined in Jaensch's militant fascist manifesto. We have left aside the philosophical aspect of his system, presented in the book in a summary and abbreviated manner, but which was treated in a more detailed manner in his earlier works written before the coup. In the near future we intend to examine the foundations of his philosophical anthropology more closely, because we have assumed that it is not really one of the objectives of the present article to include any serious scientific criticism and analysis of this manifesto because of the nature of the ideas it contains. Not only do they not require any scientific criticism, but they exclude the possibility of any such thing. To try and counter Jaensch's views in any meaningful way would amount to the same thing as trying to disprove mad ravings by using logical arguments.

But at the present time we cannot help but be interested in the following two questions; firstly, the question of the internal link between these ludicrous scientific structures and the general crisis which is taking place in bourgeois psychological thinking[13] and, secondly, a clarification of what original contributions fascist psychology has made to the further development of bourgeois psychology. In conclusion, these are just the two questions which we would now like to examine.

It would be naive to think that these absurd structures are in no way connected with the general crisis occurring in bourgeois psychology and that bourgeois psychology is in no way responsible for these constructions. After all, even the ravings of a mental patient tend to have some links with his premorbid personality. In actual fact, it is precisely in this manifestation of the acute and putrid decomposition of scientific thinking where these processes of decay, which during the critical decades have been driving psychological thinking into a hopeless dead end, manifest themselves in a hyperbolical form. Essentially, Jaensch's system is built on the same methodological foundations as all the rest of bourgeois psychology. It represents an integration of idealism and mechanicism, similar to that typological integration which Jaensch would like to see in the unification of the German philosopher with the peasant. One would only need to remove one of the supporting props, and Jaensch's whole structure would immediately come crashing to the ground. The unification of mechanism ['mechanicism'] with idealism into a single fascist entity constitutes the alpha and omega of the whole methodology of Jaensch's system. The entire original contribution of his construction is limited to his combining these two elements in a new way. Whilst in the majority of other psychological schools these elements, unknown to the authors themselves, are intertwined with one another, Jaensch accomplishes a full and complete unification, both within the scope and the meaning which is inherent in each of these principles.

Without this monstrous mechanicism he would be unable to build up the idealism from below and to stretch a single thread from blood and race to the world of ideas. However, without the equally monstrous idealism he would end up just as helpless in the face of his task, which is to conceal the brutish face of fascist anthropology behind the typological mask of the most perfect German personality the world has ever seen.

Bringing mechanicism and idealism under one common denominator, lining up the most elementary physical and chemical processes of the human organism alongside the higher functions of consciousness, inevitably presupposes another mistake, which has reached a monstrous extreme, but which is, essentially, inherent in a greater or lesser degree in all flaws of bourgeois psychology, namely the rejection of the social nature of man. Sociology is completely left out of Jaensch's system. It is only race and blood which immediately determine the structure of personality and through it politics as well. Here, too, all that Jaensch has done is to push to the extreme and treat with cynical bluntness that which is already part of the very foundations of bourgeois scientific research. He has spoken out openly in the language of pogrom politics. He has set out in a cynical and unambiguous way to found a union between scientists and storm troopers, a union of the bayonet and the idea. Jaensch has proclaimed openly and cynically what other people try to conceal or are merely subjectively aware of. He has only said what other people are thinking, or at least what they are doing. He has said that to be a bourgeois scientist means to serve the needs of the bourgeoisie, needs which make their appearance during a given historical period, and to fight, by using the weapons of science, for those political goals which emanate from today's problems. He has said that there is no such thing as science which is apolitical and which exists outside of politics.

After all this, is it surprising that this first attempt has turned out to be so unsuccessful and so crude? Jaensch's task was not an easy one, i.e. to turn science around and send it backwards into the Middle Ages, to erase all the scientific truths which have been accumulated throughout the ages and which had been achieved by the efforts of the human mind. Jaensch carried out his task in the manner of a sergeant major and he does not seem to be at all worried by the fact that, whilst striving to present us with an ideal German type in the attractive guise of a superman, all he has actually managed to do is present what Nietzsche has called *die blonde Bestie*, the savage face of zoological nationalism.

The positive aspect of Jaensch's book is that he has decided to give up all pretence. Diplomatic hypocrisy could only do harm at a time of this final and decisive battle, the greatest and the most just which humanity has ever known throughout its history. Two worlds and two ideological systems now stand pitched against one another. Jaensch's book, along with the rest of fascist psychology, cannot fail but to lead to a terrible intensification of the class struggle in science in general and in the field of psychology in particular. This puts an especially heavy burden of responsibility on the shoulders of Soviet psychology. It now has to focus its mind on its international foreign front, to which it has hitherto not paid sufficient attention. In this struggle its allies will include not only German proletarians, but all the proletarians of the world. Times are approaching when it will become clear even to a blind man that, whilst the people on one sixth of the earth's surface are fighting for the liberation of all humanity and for the achievement of everything which is truly higher, new and unprecedented in the history of the human personality, when one after another the oppressed and backward nations are joining the vanguard of humanity, in the bourgeois camp people's consciousness continues to be moulded among the debris of a resuscitated Middle Ages.

## Notes

First published as Vygotsky, L. S. 1934: [Chapter IV – without title]. In L. S. Vygotsky, V. A. Gilyarovsky, M. O. Gurevich, M. B. Krol', A. S. Shmar'jan et al. (eds) *Fashism v psikhonevrologii* [*Fascism in Psychoneurology*] (pp. 18–28). Moscow-Leningrad: Gosudarstvennoe Izdatel'stvo Biologicheskoj i Medicinskoj Literatury. This was a brochure written after the Nazis came to power in 1933 by Jewish scientists working at or somehow connected with the All-Union Institute for Experimental Medicine in Moscow. Vygotsky's contribution occupied 11 of the 28 pages. Reading the brochure one realizes that – despite enormous differences – there was a tremendous similarity between the Nazi fascist state and the communist totalitarian system of 1934 (which may not have escaped Vygotsky's attention). The role of state propaganda, the heavy ideological pressure, the attempts to distinguish between useful and useless science, and the general terror were very similar, but the common moral bankruptcy of both systems was most vividly and unwittingly brought out by one of the other authors of the brochure, who suggested that the Nazi emphasis on race and heridity was falsified by the successful Soviet attempts at re-educating people in the Belomor canal project (where thousands of political prisoners died of hunger and cold).

1    Vygotsky was well acquainted with Eduard Spranger's work and frequently referred to his book on adolescence and to his general conception of a hermeneutic ('Verstehende') psychology. Spranger distinguished six basic personality types (the theoretical personality, the economical personality, the aesthetic personality, the social personality, the power personality and the religious personality), each of which embodied a certain way or form of life ('Lebensform'). See Spranger, E. 1930: *Lebensformen* (7th edn). Halle: Max Niemeyer Verlag. Although it is quite clear that Vygotsky was critical of many of Spranger's ideas, until the present paper he had never paid any attention to Spranger's so-called bourgeois views.

2    See p. 28 of Spranger, E. 1927: *Psychologie des Jugendalters*. Jena: Fischer Verlag.

3    The work of Narziss Ach and his followers had played a fundamental role in Vygotsky's and Sakharov's own work on concept formation in childhood, adolescence and in schizophrenia (see chapters 6, 9 and 12 of this reader). The Congress in Leipzig, 1933, was the first meeting of the German Psychological Society after the Nazis come to power. See also the next note.

4    The theory that holds that reality is ultimately of the nature of the will or that the will is the primary factor in experience (Webster). In their psychological dictionary Varshava and Vygotsky claimed that in psychology 'Wundt, Dilthey, Lipps, Stumpf, Münsterberg and others' adhered to this theory. See pp. 41–2 of Varshava, B. E. and Vygotsky, L. S. 1931: *Psikhologicheskij slovar'* [*Psychological Dictionary*]. Moscow: Gosudarstvennoe Uchebno-Pedagogicheskoe Izdatel'stvo.

5    For some time Vygotsky – and many of his Soviet contemporaries – had been rather enthusiastic about Erich R. Jaensch's (1883–1940) ideas about eidetic imagery (or 'photographic memory'). Vygotsky presented an elaborate discussion of eidetic imagery and Jaensch's interpretation of it in Vygotsky, L. S. 1930: Ejdetika [Eidetics]. In L. Vygotsky, S. Gellershtejn, B. Fingert and M. Shirvindt (eds) *Osnovnye techenija sovremennoj psikhologii* [*Main Currents of Contemporary Psychology*] (pp. 178–205). Moscow: Gosudarstvennoe Izdatel'stvo. In this paper Vygotsky emphasized that he considered the phenomenon of eidetic imagery – seen as a stage in the normal development of memory – of immense importance for our understanding of the development of memory, and stated that the phenomenon was demonstrated beyond reasonable doubt. He fundamentally disagreed, however, with Jaensch's general (idealistic) trend of thinking and his interpretation of the objective data. In the present paper he is mainly discussing Jaensch, E. 1933: *Die Lage und die Aufgaben der Psychologie, ihre Sendung in der deutschen Bewegung und an der Kulturwende* [*The Situation and Tasks of Psychology, its Mission in the German Movement and in the Cultural Reform*]. Leipzig: Barth. In this infamous pamphlet Jaensch described what he saw as

healthy and unhealthy elements in psychological thinking and the role they might play in the Nazi state. Jaensch was indeed the best example of a well known psychologist who embraced the Nazi world view and at the 13th Congress of the German Society for Psychology, held in Leipzig from 16–19 October (after the Nazis came to power), he was one of the major speakers together with Felix Krueger who welcomed the new events. In that speech as well, Jaensch contrasted the Jewish mentality with the genuine German mentality, which he saw rooted in the farmer's mentality. For details, see Graumann, C. F. (ed.) 1985: *Psychologie im Nationalsozialismus*. Berlin: Springer.

6   Here two pages are missing from (our copy of) the original manuscript.

7   Lieutenant Skalozub is a character from the early 19th century play *Woe from Wit* by A. Griboedov. He represents the lowbrow, conservative military element [translator's note].

8   Here and in the following Vygotsky is using the very appropriate russified German word 'Feldwebel' for sergeant major. It provides an ironic/sarcastic emphasis upon the German tendency towards totalitarian leadership at all levels of society (army), especially at the lowest (as the Feldwebel's role was the direct drill of soldiers in a highly rigid and disciplined manner).

9   This is the only time Vygotsky ever referred to the concept of 'kulak' and their 'kulak ideology'. See chapter 10 of Van der Veer and Valsiner (1991) for the background of the terminology and Vygotsky's and Luria's involvement with the phenomenon of 'kulaks'.

10  Of the leaders of the Gestalt movement Kurt Koffka (in 1927), Max Wertheimer (in 1933) and, finally, Wolfgang Köhler (in 1935) all emigrated to the United States to escape the Nazi menace. This means that at the time of writing of Vygotsky's essay Gestalt psychology 'was represented by only one person', that is, Köhler. Others who left Nazi Germany or Austria were the Bühlers, Duncker, Gelb, Goldstein, Lazarsfeld, Lewin, Selz, the Sterns and many, many others. For an account of the role of various prominent psychologists during the Nazi regime see Graumann, C. F. (ed.) *Psychologie im Nationalsozialismus*. Berlin: Springer.

11  Vygotsky is referring to a book by Wolfgang Köhler in which the idea was developed that physical and psychic phenomena have basically the same structure or Gestalt. See Köhler, W. 1920: *Die physischen Gestalten in Ruhe und im stationären Zustand: Eine naturphilosophische Untersuchung*. Braunschweig: Friedr. Vieweg & Sohn.

12  H. Driesch and E. Becher were major representatives of the so-called vitalistic current in biology, which opposed the so-called mechanistic or materialistic current. The debate was, essentially, about the possibility and feasibility of reductionism in biology. See, for example, Driesch, H. 1921: *Philosophie des Organischen*. Leipzig: Engelmann.

13  For the occasion Vygotsky is speaking about the crisis in *bourgeois* psychology, but in numerous other publications he made it quite clear that this crisis was international and permeated Russian science as well.

# 14
# The problem of the environment

## Lev Vygotsky

The subject of our lecture today is the problem of the role that environment plays in child development. With regard to the environment, matters stand exactly the same as when we discussed the problem of heredity. We could see that paedology approaches heredity from its own special point of view and is not interested in the laws of heredity as such, but in the role heredity plays in child development. Paedology does not study the environment as such. This is the subject of other sciences. For example, among other disciplines, which may be considered as being closest to paedology, one could name hygiene, a field of study which investigates the environment primarily from the point of view of its relationship to disease and health care.

In exactly the same way as when he studies heredity, a paedologist investigates not just the environment and the laws governing its framework, but the role, meaning and influence of the environment on child development. It is for this reason that we must, as with the problem of heredity, first of all explain some of the basic laws and concepts which characterize the meaning or role of the environment in child development.

I would like to start with something which we have already discussed in passing, namely that for a proper understanding of the role which environment plays in child development it is always necessary, if one can put it this way, to approach environment not with an absolute but a relative yardstick. At the same time environment should not be regarded as a condition of development which purely objectively determines the development of a child by virtue of the fact that it contains certain qualities or features, but one should always approach environment from the point of view of the relationship which exists between the child and its environment at a given stage of his development. One can also put it in the form of a general rule which is now frequently met with in paedology and which says that one should give up absolute indicators reflecting the environment in favour of relative ones, i.e. the very same ones, but viewed in relation to the child.

There are two considerations which lead us to believe that we are justified in defending this idea, the first being that the role of any environmental factor varies among different age groups. To give an example: the speech of the people around him can be absolutely identical when the child is six months old, 18 months old or when he is three and a half years old, i.e. the number of words which the child hears, the characteristic features of the speech from the point of view of how civilized it is, the size of the vocabulary, correct usage and grammar, the literary quality of the style, can all remain the same, but it is clear to anyone that this factor, which has not itself undergone any change at all during the course of development, takes on a different meaning depending on whether the child understands speech, or does not yet understand it at all, or is in the intermediate stage when he is just beginning to understand it. This means that we can only explain the role of the environment in child development when we know the relation between the child and his environment.

First of all, *a child's environment in the direct sense of this word keeps changing at every age*. Some authors maintain that a child's development consists precisely of such a gradual broadening of his environment. Before he is born, a child's environment consists of his mother's uterus, and soon after being born, his immediate environment continues to be limited to a very circumscribed space. It is well known that the world removed at any distance does not really exist for the newborn. For the newborn, only the world which immediately relates to him exists, i.e. a world limited to a narrow space linked with phenomena connected with his body and the objects around him. Then, gradually, a slightly wider range of the world around him begins to develop for the child, but to start with, this world is also very small, a world which includes the room, the backyard nearby and the street where he lives. As he begins to walk about, his environment expands and ever new relationships are formed between the child and the people surrounding him. And further, his environment changes according to the different kinds of environment each stage of his education provides: during his nursery school age, the nursery school; during his immediate pre-school years, the kindergarten; and during school age, the school. Every age presents the child with an environment which has been organized in a special way, so that the environment, in the purely external sense of the word, keeps changing as the child passes on from one age to another.

But there is a lot more to this. Even when the environment remains little changed, the very fact *that the child changes in the process of development*, results in a situation where the role and meaning of these environmental factors, which seemingly have remained unchanged, in actual fact do undergo a change, and the same environmental factors which may have one meaning and play a certain role during a given age, two years on begin to have a different meaning and to play a different role because the child has changed; in other words, the child's relation to these particular environmental factors has altered.

The case histories of children we have studied, have put us in a better position to be more exact and precise, and to say that the essential factors which explain the influence of environment on the psychological development of children, and on the development of their conscious personalities, are made up of their emotional experiences [*perezhivanija*].[1] The emotional experience [*perezhivanie*] arising from any situation or from any aspect of his environment, determines what kind of influence this situation or this environment will have on the child. Therefore, it is not any of the factors in themselves (if taken without reference to the child) which determines how they will influence the future course of his development, but the same factors refracted through the prism of the child's emotional experience [*perezhivanie*]. Let us now examine one such straightforward case from our clinic.

We are dealing with three children, brought to us from one family. The external situation in this family is the same for all three children. The essential circumstances were very straightforward. The mother drinks and, as a result, apparently suffers from several nervous and psychological disorders. The children find themselves in a very difficult situation. When drunk, and during these breakdowns, the mother had once attempted to throw one of the children out of the window and she regularly beat them or threw them to the floor. In a word, the children are living in conditions of dread and fear due to these circumstances.

The three children are brought to our clinic, but each one of them presents a completely different picture of disrupted development, caused by the same situation. The same circumstances result in an entirely different picture for the three children.

As far as the youngest of these children is concerned, what we find is the commonly encountered picture in such cases among the younger age group. He reacts to the situation by developing a number of neurotic symptoms, i.e. symptoms of a defensive nature. He is simply overwhelmed by the horror of what is happening to him. As a result, he develops attacks of terror, enuresis and he develops a stammer, sometimes being unable to speak at all as he looses his voice. In other words, the child's reaction amounts to a state of complete depression and helplessness in the face of this situation.

The second child is developing an extremely agonizing condition, what is called a state of inner conflict, which is a condition frequently found in certain cases when contrasting emotional attitudes towards the mother make their appearance, examples of which we have previously been able to observe among one of our children and which, you may remember, we have called an ambivalent attitude. On the one hand, from the child's point of view, the mother is an object of painful attachment, and on the other, she represents a source of all kinds of terrors and terrible emotional experiences [*perezhivanija*] for the child. The German authors call this kind of emotional complex which the child is experiencing a *Mutter-Hexekomplex*, or 'a mother–witch complex', when love for the mother and terror of the witch coexist. The second child was brought to us with this kind of deeply pronounced conflict and a sharply colliding internal contradiction expressed in a simultaneously positive and negative attitude towards the mother, a terrible attachment to her and an equally terrible hate for her, combined with terribly contradictory behaviour. He asked to be sent home immediately, but expressed terror when the subject of his going home was brought up.

Finally, at first glance, the third and eldest child presented us with a completely unexpected picture. This child had a limited mental ability but, at the same time, showed signs of some precocious maturity, seriousness and solicitude. He already understood the situation. He understood that their mother was ill and he pitied her. He could see that the younger children found themselves in danger when their mother was in one of her states of frenzy. And he had a special role. He must calm his mother down, make certain that she is prevented from harming the little ones and comfort them. Quite simply, he has become the senior member of the family, the only one whose duty it was to look after everyone else. As a result of this, the entire course of his development underwent a striking change. This was not a lively child with normal, lively, simple interests, appropriate to his age and exhibiting a lively level of activity. It was a child whose course of normal development was severely disrupted, a different type of child.

When such an example is taken into account, and any researcher's experience who investigates concrete material is full of such examples, one can easily see that the same environmental situation and the same environmental events can influence various people's development in different ways, depending at what age they happen to find them.

How can one explain why exactly the same environmental conditions exert three different types of influence on these three different children? It can be explained because each of the children has a different attitude to the situation. Or, as we might put it, each of the children experienced[2] the situation in a different way. One of them experienced it as an inexplicable, incomprehensible horror which has left him in a state of defencelessness. The second was experiencing it consciously, as a clash between his strong attachment, and his no less strong feeling of fear, hate and hostility. And the third child experienced it, to some extent, as far as it is possible for a 10–11 year old boy, as a misfortune which has befallen the family and which required him to put all other things aside, to try somehow to mitigate the misfortune and to help both the sick mother and the children. So it appears that, depending on the fact that the same situation had been experienced by the three children in three different ways, the influence which this situation exerted on their development also turns out to be different.

By citing this example, I only wished to clarify the idea that, unlike other disciplines, paedology does not investigate the environment as such without regard to the child, but instead looks at the role and influence of the environment on the course of development. It ought to always be capable of finding the particular prism through which the influence of the environment on the child is refracted, i.e. *it ought to be able to find the relationship which exists between the child and its environment, the child's emotional experience [perezhivanie]*, in other words how a child becomes aware of, interprets, [and] emotionally relates to a certain event. This is such a prism which determines the role and influence of the environment on the development of, say, the child's character, his psychological development, etc.

In connection with this example, I would like to turn your attention to one more factor. If you recall, when we were discussing the methods we employ in our science, I attempted to defend the idea that in science the analysis into elements ought to be replaced by analysis which reduces a complex unity, a complex whole, to its units. We have said that, unlike elements, these units represent such products of analysis which do not lose any of the properties which are characteristic of the whole, but which manage to retain, in the most elementary form, the properties inherent in the whole.

Today, whilst basing myself on a concrete example of the theory about the environment, I would like to show you a few such units with which psychological research operates. One example of such a unit is the emotional experience [*perezhivanie*]. *An emotional experience* [*perezhivanie*] *is a unit where, on the one hand, in an indivisible state, the environment is represented, i.e.* that which is being experienced – an emotional experience [*perezhivanie*] is always related to something which is found outside the person – *and on the other hand, what is represented is how I, myself, am experiencing this*, i.e., all the personal characteristics and all the environmental characteristics are represented in an emotional experience [*perezhivanie*]; everything selected from the environment and all the factors which are related to our personality and are selected from the personality, all the features of its character, its constitutional elements, which are related to the event in question. So, *in an emotional experience* [*perezhivanie*] *we are always dealing with an indivisible unity of personal characteristics and situational characteristics, which are represented in the emotional experience* [*perezhivanie*]. That is why from the methodological point of view it seems convenient to carry out an analysis when we study the role the environment plays in the development of a child, an analysis from the point of view of the child's emotional experiences [*perezhivanija*] because, as I have already said, all the child's personal characteristics which took part in determining his attitudes to the given situation have been taken into account in his emotional experience [*perezhivanie*]. For example, do all of my own personal constitutional characteristic elements, of every type, participate fully and on an equal basis? Of course not. In one situation some of my constitutional characteristics play a primary role, but in another, different ones may play this primary role which may not even appear at all in the first case. It is not essential for us to know what the child's constitutional characteristics are like *per se, but what is important for us to find out is which of these constitutional characteristics have played a decisive role in determining the child's relationship to a given situation*. And in another situation, different constitutional characteristics may well have played a role.

In this way the emotional experience [*perezhivanie*] also helps us select those characteristics which played a role in determining the attitude to the given situation. Imagine I possess certain constitutional characteristics – clearly, I will experience this situation in one way, and if I possess different characteristics, it is equally clear that I will experience it in quite a different way. This is why people's constitutional characteristics are taken into account when differentiating between those who are excitable, sociable, lively and active and others who are more emotionally slack, inhibited and dull. It is therefore obvious, that if we have two people with two opposite types of constitutional characteristics, then one and the same event is likely to elicit a different emotional experience [*perezhivanie*] in each of them. Consequently, the constitutional characteristics of the person and generally the personal characteristics of children are, as it were, mobilized by a given emotional experience [*perezhivanie*], are laid down, become crystallized within a given emotional experience [*perezhivanie*] but, at the same time, this experience does not just represent the aggregate of the child's personal characteristics which determine how the child experienced this particular event emotionally, but different events also elicit different emotional experiences [*perezhivanija*] in the child. A drunken or mentally ill mother amounts to the same thing as a mentally ill nanny, but it does not mean the same as a drunken father or a drunken neighbour. Which means that the environment, which in this case was represented by a specific concrete situation, is also always represented in a given emotional experience [*perezhivanie*]. This is why we are justified in considering the emotional experience [*perezhivanie*] to be a unity of environmental and personal features. And it is precisely for this reason that the emotional experience [*perezhivanie*] is a concept which allows us to study the role and influence of environment on the psychological development of children in the analysis of the laws of development.

Let us take one more example, which should also help us clarify the concrete way in which paedology investigates the role environment plays in child development by studying the relationships which exist between a child and his environment.

I think that you will agree with me when I say that any event or situation in a child's environment will have a different effect on him depending on how far the child understands its sense and meaning. For example, try to imagine a situation where someone in the family has died. Clearly, a child who understands the meaning of death will react differently to this event than a child who does not understand anything of what has happened. Or in a family the parents decide to split up. Very frequently we come across families with difficult children where this has occurred. Again, in a case where the child understands what is going on and its true significance, he will react to it in a different way than another child who fails to understand it.

To put it more succinctly and simply, I could say that *the influence of environment on child development will, along with other types of influences, also have to be assessed by taking the degree of understanding, awareness and insight of what is going on in the environment into account*. If children possess various levels of awareness, it means that the same event will have a completely different meaning for them. We know that, frequently, unhappy events may have a happy meaning for a child who does not understand the significance of the event itself, especially in view of the fact that he is now allowed what he is normally not allowed – just to keep him quiet and prevent him from pestering he may be given sweets and, as a result, the child might end up experiencing his mother's dangerous illness as an event which for him is joyful and fun, and to look at him, he may appear like a birthday child. The crux of the matter is that whatever the situation, its influence depends not only on the nature of the situation itself, but also on the extent of the child's understanding and awareness of the situation.

When the case involves mentally retarded children, particularly severely retarded ones, we often have the impression that they do not have sufficient understanding and frequently, for this very reason, are spared and protected from situations which may cause extreme suffering for normal children. Everyone is familiar with the following frequently occurring situation in which children find themselves when they are deformed. Recently we had such a severely deformed child in our clinic. The children were teasing him, and the child himself, realizing that he was very deformed, talked about it. For a child with normal intellect, such a situation could become the source of endless trauma, because everywhere he goes he is constantly reminded of his deformity, of the fact that he is not like all the other children, that everyone is laughing at him, teasing him, putting him down, that they refuse to play with him; the continual humiliation which the child encounters frequently results in extremely unpleasant emotional experiences [perezhivanija], leading to neuroses, functional disorders or other psychogenic disorders, i.e. arising from these emotional experiences [perezhivanija]. But nothing like this happened to the child I have been describing here. This child is also being teased and humiliated and in fact he, too, has ended up in an extremely difficult position, but all this for him is like water off a duck's back, because he is not capable of generalizing what was happening to him. Every time when he now is being teased he does not like it, but neither is he able to generalize it and, as a result, he never reached the stage which every normal child reaches, by developing a feeling of inferiority, a sense of humiliation and one of damaged self-esteem. This does not happen because he does not fully comprehend the sense and meaning of what is happening to him.

Here we have a striking example of how an inadequate interpretation of some event or situation, which we come across in connection with mentally retarded children, often protects them from illnesses, from pathological reactions and from developmental disorders to which other children are subject.

So what exactly does happen? We may find a situation in the environment which would result in a normal child becoming traumatized and would lead to the development of a disorder. But this does not happen in the case of our child. Why is this? It is due to the fact that the child is not fully aware of his situation. And the case which I have used as an example here, as a pathological case, in reality occurs at all ages. One and the same situation, when it occurs when a child is one year old or when he is three, or seven or 13, would have a different significance. *One and the same event occurring at different ages of the child, is reflected in his consciousness in a completely different manner and has an entirely different meaning for the child.*

In connection with this, a quite complicated concept, but one which is very important for the understanding of how environment influences development, is of some interest. The concept has this connection because it represents the meaning of our words. You know, of course, that we mainly communicate with the people surrounding us by using speech. This represents one of the basic means with which a child attains psychological communication with the people around him. Speech research has shown that the child's word meaning does not coincide with our word meaning, i.e. the word meaning at different ages has a different structure. I shall now attempt to explain this with the help of an illustration.

First, let us ask ourselves what exactly is the meaning of a word. I think that you will agree with me if I say that the meaning of a word, from the psychological point of view, always represents a generalization. Let us take such words as 'street', 'man' or 'weather'. These words do not relate just to one single object, but to a certain class and a certain group of objects. From the psychological point of view, the meaning of any word always represents a generalization. This we understand and this is the first main point.

These generalizations tend to be constructed by children in a different way than they are by us. After all, a child does not invent his own language, but he finds the words in a ready-made state, fixed to ready-made things, and he assimilates our language and the meaning the words have in our language. This means that a child attributes [confers] these words to the same objects to which we attribute them. When a child says 'weather' or 'man', he means by it the same things, the same objects as all of us, but he generalizes these things in a different way, using a different mental act. *He still lacks such higher generalizations which we call concepts and his generalizations have a more concrete, more graphic [nagljadnyj] character.* And it is said that these generalizations, which children form during early stages of their development, are reminiscent of those generalizations which we find exemplified in our family names. For us, too, the family name does not represent a single person, but a group of people. But how is this group of people generalized under one family name? It is generalized on the basis of a factual kinship relation; not on the basis of logical relationships as a particular category, but on the basis of factual kinship between these people. There is no way I can tell by looking at a man whether he is a Petrov or an Ivanov. But if I learn that he is Petrov's son, or Ivanov's son, i.e. if I find out his real relationships with other people, I will also find out his affiliation with one of the family names. In the same way as we construct generalizations of family names, so – as research has shown – pre-school children construct generalizations of all sorts of objects. In other words, the child assigns words to the same objects as we do, but he generalizes these objects in a different *more concrete, more visual, [and] more factual way.*

As a result of this, children's generalizations are different from ours and this in turn results in the well known fact that a child interprets reality, apprehends the events which are happening around him, not entirely in the same way as we do. The adult is not always able to communicate the full meaning of some event to a child. The child understands part of it, but not completely, he understands one side of the matter, but not the other, he understands the matter, but he understands it in his own way, reworking and reshaping it to suit himself, and selecting only certain parts of what had been explained to him. So, as a result, *children at different stages of their development do not yet possess a system of communication with adults which is sufficiently compatible.* This means that a child at different stages of his development does not generalize to the same extent, and consequently, he interprets and imagines the surrounding reality and environment in a different way. Consequently, the development of thinking in children in itself, the development of generalization in children in itself, is also connected with the way the environment influences children.

So, as time goes by, the child begins to understand more and more. Now he is able to understand the things he could not understand earlier. Does this mean that now some events occurring in the family will affect the child in a different way? Yes. In the past they may have had a neutral character, now they become basic factors in the child's development. This means that the development of thinking in children in itself, the meaning of children's words, is what determines the new relationship which can exist between the environment and the different developmental processes.

If we wanted to generalize everything we have been saying till now, we could formulate it something like this: as I have already said, paedology does not so much investigate the environment itself using its absolute indicators, but the role and influence of environment on child development, because the relationship between a given environmental situation and the child assumes primary importance in the study of the role of environment in development, and this relationship can be elucidated by using various concrete examples. As I have said, one and the same situation in a family can result in three different types of influence on the development of the children involved. Depending on his age, the environment exerts this or that type of influence on the child's development, because the child himself changes and his relation to this situation changes. The environment exerts this influence, as we have said, via the child's emotional experiences [*perezhivanija*], i.e. depending on how the child has managed to work out his inner attitude to the various aspects of the different situations occurring in the environment. The environment determines the type of development depending on the degree of awareness of this environment which the child has managed to reach. And we could show many more instances which would demonstrate that absolutely every aspect of development will determine which way the environment will influence development, i.e. the relationship between the environment and the child and not just the environment in its own right, or just the child in its own right, will always be central.

We have now reached the conclusion that environment cannot be regarded as a static entity and one which is peripheral in relation to development, but must be seen as changeable and dynamic. Here we have environment, a situation which influences the child in one way or another and directs his development. But the child, his development, keeps changing, becomes different. And it is not just the child who changes, for the relationship between him and his environment also changes, and the same environment now begins to have a different influence on the child. This *dynamic and relative interpretation of environment* is the most important source of information for paedology when environment is under discussion. But this in itself is far from concrete. We may well agree that it is important to study the relation with the environment, that if the relation is different the environment exerts its influence in different ways. However, the most important thing has not yet been said: what is the basic role of environment in relation to child development? I would now like to give an answer to this question.

To begin with, once again we come across the same problem which was facing us when we were investigating heredity. If you recall, we said then that no all-out definition of the influence of heredity on every aspect of development exists or can exist, and that, when we want to study not just the laws of heredity, which are basically uniform in nature, and the influence of heredity on development, then we must differentiate the effects of heredity upon various aspects and development. If you remember, I tried to demonstrate how results obtained from an investigation of twins have disclosed that heredity does not play the same role in relation to higher psychological functions as it does in relation to elementary psychological functions.[3] So it follows that one must differentiate the effect of heredity upon various aspects of development.

The same thing applies entirely to environment, for example to the influence of environment on such developmental processes as growth and children's logical think-ing. It is unlikely that, apart from the general principle which remains in power, the relation of environment to a given aspect of development has everywhere the same degree of influence. Apart from this general principle, it is unlikely that environment carries the same influence and exerts this influence in exactly the same way in relation to all aspects of development. This is not so. Together with a dynamic interpretation of environment, we are beginning to understand that the different aspects of develop-ment have different relations with the environment. It is for this reason that we have to study the various environmental influences differentially as, for example, on the child's growth, the environmental influence on the growth patterns of individual parts and systems in the organism and, say, its influence on the development of sensory and motor functions in children, the influence environment exerts on the development of psychological functions, etc., etc.

When one wants to set forth the theory of the environment, the easiest thing would be to tackle that which is central and essentially important, rather than some narrow aspect of development, and to choose that side of the developmental process where the influence of environment is expressed with maximum force. Let us consider the development of a child's personality, his consciousness, and of his relationship with the reality around him, and let us examine what the specific role of environment consists of in the development of a child's personality, consciousness and relationship with reality.

If we consider all the specifically human personality traits which have evolved during the period of human historical development, we are bound to come to an extremely simple conclusion, namely that here, the relations which exist between environment and child development are characteristic of childhood development and of no other general type of development.

What is this specific relationship between environment and development, if we are talking about the development of a child's personality, and its specifically human characteristics? It seems to me that this singularity consists of the following, namely *in child development that which it is possible to achieve at the end and as the result of the developmental process, is already available in the environment from the very beginning.* And it is not simply present in the environment from the very start, but it exerts an influence on the very first steps in the child's development. Let me clarify this by the following example.

We have a child who has only just begun to speak and he pronounces single words, as children who are just mastering the art of speech tend to do. But is fully developed speech, which the child is only able to master at the end of this period of development, already present in the child's environment? It is, indeed. The child speaks in one word phrases, but his mother talks to him in language which is already grammatically and syntactically formed and which has a large vocabulary, even though it is being toned down for the child's benefit. All the same, she speaks using the fully perfected form of speech. Let us agree to call this developed form, which is supposed to make its appearance at the end of the child's development, the final or ideal form (as it is called in contemporary paedology) – ideal in the sense that it acts as a model for that which should be achieved at the end of the developmental period; and final in the sense that it represents what the child is supposed to attain at the end of his development. And let us call the child's form of speech the primary or rudimentary form. The greatest characteristic feature of child development is that this development is achieved under particular conditions of interaction with the environment, where this ideal and final form (that form which is going to appear only at the end of the process of development) is not only already there in the environment and from the very start in contact with the child, but actually interacts and exerts a real influence on the primary form, on the first steps of the child's development. *Something which is only supposed to take shape at the very end of development, somehow influences the very first steps in this development.*

The same sort of thing can be seen everywhere, say in the way that children's conception of number, their arithmetical thinking, develops. It is well known that at the beginning, during pre-school age, a child still has a very limited and vague idea about quantities. However, these primary forms of children's arithmetical thinking are involved in interaction with the already established arithmetical thinking of adults, i.e. once again, the final form which should result from the whole course of child development, is already not only present, but actually determining and guiding the first steps which the child takes along the road of development of this form.

In order for you to realize fully to what extent this creates very special, inimitable and unique conditions inherent in child development, I will put the following question to you: can you imagine, for example, what biological evolution is like? Could one possibly imagine that it would work in such a way that the ideal, higher form, which has appeared only as a result of development, would already exist during the initial period when only the lower, most primary forms were there, and for these lower forms to have evolved under its direct influence? Of course, nothing like this could ever be imagined.

In the realm of historical social development, could one ever imagine that when the primary form of human economy and society still existed, a higher form, say a communist economy and society, was already there to actually direct these first steps of the historical development of humanity? It is quite impossible to imagine such a thing.

Could one imagine, in the context of human development, that when the most primitive man had only just appeared on earth, a higher final form already existed, a man of the future as it were and that this ideal form could somehow directly influence the first steps the primitive man was taking? One cannot imagine this. So things never happen in such a way in any of the types of development known to us, that at the moment when the primary form is taking shape, a higher, ideal form which appears at the end of a period of development is there at the same time, and that it becomes involved in direct reciprocal action with the child's first steps along the road of development of this rudimentary or primary form. This fact contains the greatest peculiarity of child development as compared with other types of development, where we never detect or find any equivalent state of affairs.

What does all this mean? I think that one can draw a very important conclusion which can immediately make clear to us the singular role that environment plays in child development. How does this ideal or final form of, say, speech, develop in children? We have seen that, at the beginning of his development, a child has only mastered the primary form, i.e. in the realm of speech, for example, he is only able to pronounce individual words. But these individual words make up part of the child's dialogue with his mother, who has already mastered the ideal form, the same form which the child should achieve at the end of his development. Will the child be capable of mastering this ideal form, will he simply assimilate and imitate it in one or one and a half years of his life? He will not. But, nevertheless, can a child this age, moving from the first to the last step, gradually adjust his primary form to this final one? Yes, investigations show that this is exactly what does happen.

Consequently, what this signifies is that environment is a factor in the realm of personality development and its specific human traits, and its role is to act as the source of this development, i.e. environment is the source of development and not its setting.

What does this mean? First of all it indicates a very simple thing, namely that if no appropriate ideal form can be found in the environment, and the development of the child, for whatever reasons, has to take place outside these specific conditions (described earlier), i.e. without any interaction with the final form, then this proper form will fail to develop properly in the child.

Try to imagine a child who is growing up among deaf people and is surrounded by deaf and dumb parents and children his own age. Will he be able to develop speech? No, but will he develop babbling? Yes, he will. Babbling develops even in deaf and dumb children. This means that babbling is one of the functions which are, more or less, part of the most basic hereditary instincts. But speech will not develop at all in such a child. In order for speech to develop, it is necessary for this ideal form to be present in the environment and to interact with the child's rudimentary form; only then can speech development be achieved.

Firstly, this means that environment in this sense constitutes a source of all the child's specific human traits, and if the appropriate ideal form is not present in the environment, then in the child the corresponding activity, characteristic or trait will fail to develop.

Secondly, try to imagine that this ideal form is not to be found in the child's environment, that his development is not subject to the law which I have just been describing, namely that the final form is not present, does not interact with the rudimentary form, but that the child develops among other children, i.e. that his environment is made up of children of his own age who are all at the lower, rudimentary form stage. In such a situation, will the proper activity and traits develop in this child? Research shows that it will, but in an extremely peculiar way. They will always develop very slowly and in an unusual manner, and will never attain the level which they reach when the suitable ideal form is present in the environment.

Let us look at two examples. If one observes a deaf and dumb child, then it turns out that his speech development will follow two separate lines, depending on whether this deaf and dumb child is the only child in the family or whether he is growing up with other deaf and dumb children. Research has revealed that deaf and dumb children create their own peculiar speech, mimicry and a very richly developed sign language. Such a child develops his own different, personal language. The children develop this language in co-operation, in society. But can one compare the development of this sign language with the development of speech in children who have a chance to interact with the ideal form? Of course not. So this, generally, means that if we are dealing with a situation where this ideal form is not present in the environment, and what we have is interaction between several rudimentary forms, the resulting development has an extremely limited, reduced and impoverished character.

Now let us look at the other example. You have probably heard that children attending a day nursery have a number of educational advantages over children brought up in the family; already, at a very young age, they learn how to be independent, how to do things for themselves and about discipline. But, at the same time, there are also some negative sides to being educated in a nursery school and not at home, and one of these negative aspects, which is the cause of serious worry for all people working with this age group, is delayed speech development. As a rule, the nursery school-aged child who is being educated at home develops speech earlier, and reaches a higher and more sophisticated level than a child who gets his corresponding education in day nurseries. Why is this so? For the simple reason that at home a child has his mother or another person who is taking her place, say, a nanny, and he hears her speak directly to him, which amounts to a continuous interaction process with the ideal form. But in nursery school, where there may only be one teacher to several or to a whole group of children, a child has much less chance of direct interaction with this ideal form. What happens instead is that these children have a chance to talk to one another. But they do not speak very well or very much, and their own conversations cannot serve as a source of any significant development for them. It appears that, in order for any auspicious and successful development of the higher specific human traits to occur, it is necessary for this ideal final form to guide, if one can put it in this way, the child's development from the very start.

So this is why when a child grows up in a group of other children, say in a day nursery, his speech development remains limited. And if one compares large numbers? Take a number of physically fit three year olds who are growing up in favourable conditions, and compare those growing up in day nurseries with those staying at home. You will see that, on the average, from the point of view of speech development, the children who stay at home will rate higher than the children in nursery schools, but at the same time, in many ways, the nursery school child will score considerably higher than the home reared child, as far as independence, discipline and looking after themselves are concerned.

Another simple, hypothetical example. Imagine a child who will develop his concept of numbers, his arithmetical thinking, only among other children, who will be left to his own devices in an environment where no developed form of arithmetical thinking exists, rather than in school or in kindergarten, i.e. without any interaction with the ideal form of adults. What do you think, will these children get far in developing their arithmetical thinking? None of them will, not even the mathematically gifted ones among them. Their development will remain extremely limited and very narrow in scope.

This means that we can draw a conclusion from all these examples which amounts to the idea that in these cases when, for various external or internal reasons, the interaction between the final form which exists in the environment and the rudimentary form which a child possesses, becomes disrupted, the development of the child turns out very limited, and what results is a more or less completely underdeveloped state of the child's proper forms of activity and traits.

There are many different reasons why this interaction can become disrupted. These can be external circumstances – the child can hear, but he is living with deaf and dumb parents, or internal ones – he is living with parents who can speak but is himself deaf. In both cases the result will be the same, namely that the child is excluded from any interaction between the rudimentary and the ideal form and thus the whole development becomes disrupted.

I think that the theory about the interaction of ideal and rudimentary forms and the examples which I have provided may have elucidated the idea I stated at the very beginning, namely that *the environment's role in the development of higher, specifically human characteristics and forms of activity is as a source of development*, i.e. that it is just this interaction with the environment which becomes the source of these features in children. And if this interaction with the environment becomes disrupted, the proper traits themselves will never appear if their only source is based in the child's hereditary instincts.

I would now like to attempt, in a few words, to assess the theoretical meaning of all this and to further clarify this theory, which should appear sufficiently convincing and clear if it is explained from the point of view of what is generally known about human development and human nature, and not simply from the point of view of paedology.

What is the significance of this principle which I have just explained to you? It signifies a very simple fact, namely that *man is a social creature, that without social interaction he can never develop in himself any of the attributes and characteristics which have developed as a result of the methodical*[4] *evolution of all humankind.*

How did you and I develop our power of speech? After all, we did not create this speech by ourselves. Humanity created it during the entire course of its historical development. My own development consists of the fact that, during the course of my general development, I mastered this power of speech following the historical laws of my development and through the process of interaction with the ideal form. But can you imagine what would have happened if I had found myself in the same circumstances as a deaf child, where I would have had to create my own language? I would not have been able to make use of the form which has been shaped during the course of the development of humanity. I would not have got very far. I would have created speech whose dimensions would have been very primitive, elementary and circumscribed. In fact, this means that just the very fact that a human being is a creature who is social by his very nature, whose development consists of, among other things, mastering certain forms of activity and consciousness which have been perfected by humanity during the process of historical development, this fact is essentially what provides the foundation for this interaction between the ideal and the rudimentary form.

The environment is the source of development of these specifically human traits and attributes, most importantly because these historically evolved traits of human personality, which are latent in every human being due to the organic makeup of heredity, exist in the environment, but the only way they can be found in each individual human being is on the strength of his being a member of a certain social group, and that he represents a certain historical unit living at a certain historical period and in certain historical circumstances. Consequently, these specifically human characteristics and attributes manifest themselves in slightly different ways in child development than do other traits and attributes which are more or less directly conditioned by the course of prior historical human development. These ideal forms which have been refined and perfected by humanity and which should appear at the end of the development process, prevail in the environment. These ideal forms influence children from their very early beginnings as part of the process of mastering of the rudimentary form. And during the course of their development children acquire, as their personal property, that which originally represented only a form of their external interaction with the environment.

I should like to end by clarifying the nature of this last principle which governs the influence of environment on child development and which will elucidate for us what I have in mind when I speak about environment as a source of development. During the course of child development, which we intend to examine at great length when we discuss the psychological development in children, the researcher is faced with one basic principle. I intend to formulate it only in a general way and to elucidate it by using just one example.

This principle consists of the fact that *the child's higher psychological functions, his higher attributes which are specific to humans, originally manifest themselves as forms of the child's collective behaviour, as a form of co-operation with other people, and it is only afterwards that they become the internal individual functions of the child himself.*[5]

I shall take but one example which should make all this clear to you. You know that speech first makes its appearance as a means of communication with other people. With the help of speech a child can converse with other people around him and they, in turn, can talk to him. But now take each of us. You know that each of us possesses so called inner speech and that this inner speech, i.e. the fact that we are able to formulate in silence for ourselves ideas embodied in words, plays a major role in our thinking. This role is so great, that some researchers have even, albeit incorrectly, identified the process of speech with the process of thinking. But, in actual fact, for every one of us, this inner speech is one of the most important functions we have at our disposal. When this inner speech in human beings becomes disturbed due to some disorder, it can result in the most severe disruption of the entire thinking process.

How did this process of inner speech in each of us come about? Research has revealed that *the emergence of inner speech is based on external speech. Originally, for a child, speech represents a means of communication between people, it manifests itself as a social function, in its social role. But gradually a child learns how to use speech to serve himself, his internal processes. Now speech becomes not just a means of communication with other people, but also a means for the child's own inner thinking processes.* Then it no longer represents that speech which we use aloud when we communicate with one another, but it becomes an inner, silent, tacit speech. But where did speech as a means of thinking come from? From speech as a means of communication. From the external activity which the child was involved in with the people around him, appeared one of the most important inner functions without which man's very thinking process could not exist.

This example illustrates the general proposition concerning the understanding of environment as a source of development. An ideal or final form is present in the environment and it interacts with the rudimentary form found in children, and what results is a certain form of activity which then becomes a child's internal asset, his property and a function of his personality.

## Notes

This was the fourth lecture published in Vygotsky, L. S. 1935: *Osnovy Pedologii [Foundations of Paedology]* (pp. 58–78). Leningrad: Izdanie Instituta. The chapter heading is our invention. In reality, the chapters (or, rather, lectures) were simply numbered. The whole came out posthumously and was edited by Vygotsky's student and collaborator M. A. Levina. It is unclear whether Vygotsky has actually written the lectures that form the basis of *Foundations of Paedology* or whether the (typed!) text formed the result of the notes taken by one or more students during Vygotsky's lectures. Judging by the style (which is definitively that of oral speech) and some other clues (expressions such as 'The subject of my lecture *today* . . .' etc.), the latter case seems more likely, but if it is true then immediately another question comes up: whether Vygotsky at least approved of the present transcriptions of his lectures. Again, we do not know for sure. The facts are that the lectures were published by the Faculty of Paedology of the Herzen State Pedagogical Institute in Leningrad (where Vygotsky lectured in the last years of his life) under the editorship of M. A. Levina and were used as a textbook for students of paedology.

1   The Russian term serves to express the idea that one and the same objective situation may be interpreted, perceived, experienced or lived through by different children in different ways. Neither 'emotional experience' (which is used here and which only covers the affective aspect of the meaning of *perezhivanie*), nor 'interpretation' (which is too exclusively rational) are fully adequate translations of the noun. Its meaning is closely linked to that of the German verb 'erleben' (cf. 'Erlebnis', 'erlebte Wirklichkeit').

2   Here Vygotsky is using the verb *perezhivat* (German: 'erleben') from which the noun *perezhivanie* has been deduced. See note 1.

3   Vygotsky is referring to the twin research about which he and Luria reported several times. See pp. 312–15 of van der Veer, R. and Valsiner, J. 1991: *Understanding Vygotsky: A quest for synthesis*. Oxford: Blackwell Publishers.

4   'Methodical' appeared in the original text. It should probably be 'historical'.

5   The famous principle which Vygotsky borrowed from Janet, Baldwin and Piaget. Part of its history has been sketched in Van der Veer, R. and Valsiner, J. 1988: Lev Vygotsky and Pierre Janet. On the origin of the concept of sociogenesis. *Developmental Review*, 8, 52–65; Valsiner, J. and Van der Veer, R. 1988: On the social nature of human cognition. *Journal for the Theory of the Behavioral Sciences*, 18, 117–35, and Van der Veer, R. and Valsiner, J. 1991: Sociogenetic perspectives in the work of Pierre Janet. *Storia della Psicologia*, 3, 6–23.

# 15

# The development of academic concepts in school aged children

## Lev Vygotsky

The topic of the development of academic[1] concepts in school aged children is first and foremost a practical problem of enormous, even primary, importance from the point of view of the difficulties which schools face in connection with providing children with an academic education. At the same time, we are shocked by the scarcity of any available information on this subject. The theoretical side of this question is no less significant, because a study of the development of academic, i.e. authentic, reliable and true concepts, cannot fail to reveal the most profound, essential and fundamental laws which govern any type of process of concept formation. It is quite astonishing, in view of this fact, that this problem, which holds the key to the whole history of the child's intellectual development and which, one would think, should provide the starting point for any investigation of the thinking process in children, appears to have been neglected until very recently, to such an extent that the present experimental study, to which these pages are to serve as an introduction, is almost the very first attempt at a systematic investigation of this problem.

How do academic concepts develop in the mind of the child who undergoes school instruction? What are the relationships between the child's proper learning[2] and the acquisition of knowledge and the processes governing the internal development of an academic concept in the child's mind? Do they actually coincide and are they really only two sides of essentially one and the same process? Does the process of internal development of concepts follow the teaching/learning [obuchenie] process, like a shadow follows the object which casts it, never coinciding, but reproducing and repeating its movements exactly, or is it rather an immeasurably more complicated and subtle relationship which can only be explored by special investigations?

Contemporary child psychology offers only two answers to all these questions. The first says that, generally speaking, academic concepts do not have their own internal history and that they do not go through a process of development in the strict sense of that word, but that they are simply acquired, are taken in a ready-made state via processes of understanding, and are adopted by the child from the adult sphere of thinking and that, in essence, it should be possible to solve the whole problem of development of academic concepts by teaching the child academic facts and for the child to be able to assimilate the concepts. This is the most widespread and practical generally accepted view which, until very recently, has formed the basis of the educational and methodological theories of the various academic disciplines.

The inadequacy of this view is revealed as soon as it is brought face to face with any scientific criticism, and this becomes clear simultaneously both from the theoretical and the practical points of view. From investigations into the process of the formation of concepts, it is known that concepts do not simply represent a concatenation of associative connections assimilated by the memory of an automatic mental skill, but a complicated and real act of thinking which cannot be mastered by simple memorization, and which inevitably requires that the child's thinking itself rise to a higher level in its internal development, to make the appearance of a concept possible within the consciousness. Research shows that, at any stage of its development, the concept represents an act of generalization when looked at from the psychological point of view. The most important result obtained from all the research in this field is the well established theory that concepts which are psychologically represented as word meanings, undergo development. The essence of this development is contained, first of all, in the transition from one generalization structure to another. Any word meaning at any age represents a generalization. However, the meanings of words develop. At the time when a child first acquires a new word connected with a definite meaning, the development of this word does not stop, but is only beginning. At first, it represents a generalization of the most elementary type and the child is only able to progress from the starting point to this generalization on this elementary level to ever higher types of generalization, depending on the level of his development, and this process is accomplished when real and proper concepts make an appearance.

This process of development of concepts or the meanings of words requires the development of a number of functions, such as voluntary attention, logical memory, abstraction, comparison and differentiation, and all these very complicated psychological processes cannot simply be taken on by the memory or just be learned and appropriated. Thus, from the theoretical point of view, one can hardly doubt the total inadequacy of the view which claims that a child acquires concepts in their finished state during the course of his schooling, and that they are mastered in the same way as any other intellectual skill.

However, from the practical point of view, the erroneousness of this view becomes revealed at every stage of the way. Educational experience, no less than theoretical research, teaches us that, in practice, a straightforward learning of concepts always proves impossible and educationally fruitless. Usually, any teacher setting out on this road achieves nothing except a meaningless acquisition of words, mere verbalization in children, which is nothing more than simulation and imitation of corresponding concepts which, in reality, are concealing a vacuum. In such cases, the child assimilates not concepts but words, and he fills his memory more than his thinking. As a result, he ends up helpless in the face of any sensible attempt to apply any of this acquired knowledge. Essentially, this method of teaching/learning [*obuchenie*] concepts, a purely scholastic and verbal method of teaching, which is condemned by everybody and which advocates the replacement of acquisition of living knowledge by the assimilation of dead and empty verbal schemes, represents the most basic failing in the field of education.

It was Leo Tolstoy, the great connoisseur of words and their meaning, who better than anyone recognized that a direct and simple communication of concepts from teacher to pupils, and a mechanical transference of the meanings of words from one head to another by using other words, was impossible – this impasse he had encountered in his own teaching experience.

Recounting these experiences whilst attempting to teach literary language to children by using translations of children's words into the language of fairy tales, and then from the language of fairy tales to a higher level, he came to the conclusion that pupils cannot be taught the literary language against their will, in the same way as they are taught French, by forcible explanations, memorizing and repetition. 'We must admit' he writes,

> that we have tried this more than once in the past two months and have always met with an insuperable distaste on the part of the pupils which has proved the wrongness of the path we took. In these experiments I merely convinced myself that to explain the meanings of words and of speech is quite impossible, even for gifted teachers, not to speak of those explanations so beloved of ungifted teachers, that 'an assembly is a small Sanhedrin' and so on. In explaining any word, the word 'impression' for example, you either replace the word you explain by another word which is just as incomprehensible, or by a whole series of words, the connection between which is just as incomprehensible as the word itself.[3]

Truth and falsehood are mixed in equal measure in Tolstoy's categorical statement. The true part of this statement is the conclusion which stems directly from experience and is known by every teacher who, like Tolstoy, is vainly struggling to explain the meaning of words. The truth of this theory, according to Tolstoy's own words, lies in the fact that almost always it is not the word itself which is unintelligible, but that the pupil lacks the concept which would be capable of expressing this word. The word is almost always available when the concept is ready.

The erroneous part of his statement is directly connected with Tolstoy's general views on the subject of teaching/learning [*obuchenie*] and it consists of the fact that it excludes any probability of this mysterious process being crudely interfered with, and strives to allocate the process of the development of concepts to the laws of its own internal strategy, and by doing so, he separates the whole process of concept development from the process of teaching and thus condemns teachers to an extreme state of passivity, as far as the problem of the development of concepts is concerned. This mistake is particularly conspicuous in his categorical formulation where he proclaims that 'any interference becomes a crude, clumsy force which retards the process of development'.[4]

However, even Tolstoy understood that not every interference holds up the process of concept development, but only the crude, instant, direct sort which follows a straight line, the shortest distance between two points, interference with the process of concept formation in the child's mind, which can produce nothing but harm. But more subtle, complex and more indirect teaching methods may interfere in the process of children's concept formation in such a way that they can lead this process forward and on to a higher plane. 'We must', says Tolstoy,

> give the pupil opportunities to acquire new concepts and words from the general sense of what is said. He will hear or read an incomprehensible word in an incomprehensible sentence once, then again in another sentence, and a new concept will begin dimly to present itself to him, and at length he will, by chance, feel the necessity of using that word, he will use it once, and word and concept become his property. And there are thousands of other paths. But deliberately to present a pupil with new concepts and forms of language is, according to my conviction, as unnecessary and pointless as to teach a child to walk by means of the laws of equilibrium. Any such attempt carries a pupil not nearer to the appointed goal, but further away from it, as if a man should wish to help a flower to open out with his crude hand, should begin to unfold the petals, and crush everything around it.[5]

Thus Tolstoy knows that there are thousands of other ways besides the scholastic ones to teach children new concepts. He rejects only one of these, that of the direct, crude, mechanical unfolding of a new concept 'by its petals'. This is perfectly true and indisputable. It is confirmed by all theoretical and practical experience. But Tolstoy ascribes too much significance to the spontaneity, randomness and the actions of vague ideas and feelings, and the inner aspect of concept formation, which is enclosed within itself, and he underestimates the role of possible direct influences on this process, exaggerating the gap which exists between education and development.

In this instance what we are interested in is not this erroneous side of Tolstoyan thought and trying to debunk it, but rather the real heart of his theory, which is the conclusion that one should not unfold new concepts 'by their petals'. We are intrigued by the thought which seems true enough, that the road leading from the initial familiarization with a new concept to the moment when the word and the concept become the child's property, is a complex internal psychological process, which involves a gradually developing meaning emerging from a vague conception of the word, and is then followed by the child's personal use of it, and which, only in the last instance, forms the last link in the chain, a proper assimilation of it. We basically tried to express the same idea, when we said that at the moment when the child first recognizes the meaning of a new word, the process of concept development does not stop, but is only beginning.

This practical experimental investigation aimed to verify the probability and fruitfulness of the working hypothesis which is being developed in this paper. It aims to show not just the thousands of alternative roads which Tolstoy mentions, but also that a conscious attempt to teach pupils new concepts and forms of words is not only possible, but that it can be the source of higher levels of development of the child's personal, already-existing concepts and that, furthermore, direct work in the realm of concepts within the programme of a school education is perfectly achievable. But this work, as research has shown, is the beginning and not the end of development of an academic concept, and not only does it not exclude personal processes of development, but it gives them a new direction and creates new and extremely favourable relationships between the educational and developmental processes from the point of view of educational end goals.

But in order to be able to deal with this subject, one circumstance must first be explained. Tolstoy constantly talks about concepts in connection with teaching children the literary language. Consequently, what he has in mind is a concept which has not been acquired by the child in the process of assimilation of the system of academic knowledge, but words and concepts of everyday speech, new and unfamiliar from the child's point of view, which are woven into the fabric of the child's previously formed concepts. This becomes obvious from the examples which Tolstoy gives. He discusses the explanation and interpretation of such words as 'impression' or 'tool' – words and concepts which do not presuppose a mandatory assimilation in a strictly defined system. Meanwhile, the subject of our research is the problem of the development of academic concepts, which happen to form during the process when the child is acquiring a specific system of academic knowledge. So it is natural for the question to arise, to what extent the theory examined above can also be extended to the process of the formation of academic concepts. For this purpose it is necessary to explain the general relationship between the process of formation of academic concepts and those concepts which Tolstoy had in mind, which on the strength of their having originated in the child's own life's experience, could be tentatively called everyday concepts.

So, by making a distinction between everyday and academic concepts, we are in no way prejudging the question to what extent such discrimination can be considered objectively valid. On the contrary, one of the fundamental aims of this investigation is just the problem of clarifying whether or not there exists an objective difference between the course that the development of both these types of concepts follows, and if so, what its nature consists of and if it really does exist, what objective factual differences between the developmental processes of the academic and the everyday concepts could be said to justify a comparative study.

The task of this essay, which is an attempt to construct a working hypothesis, is to provide evidence that such segregation can be empirically justified and is theoretically well grounded, and that for this reason, it ought to form the basis of our working hypothesis. We require proof that academic concepts develop in a somewhat different way from the everyday variety and that the course of their development is not just a repetition of the development of everyday concepts. The task of the study which attempts to verify our working hypothesis, is the factual confirmation of this theory and the clarification of what the differences which exist between these two processes consist of.

It should be said right at the start, that the distinction drawn between everyday and academic concepts, which we have chosen as our starting point, and which we have developed in our working hypothesis, and in the entire formulation of this problem, which was dealt with in our research, is not only not generally accepted by contemporary psychology, but is seen as contradicting the widely held views on this subject. This is why it is in such dire need of elucidation and proof to uphold it.

We have already said above that at the present time there exist two answers to the question as to how academic concepts develop in the minds of school age children. The first of these answers, as has been said, fully denies the very presence of any process of an inner development of academic concepts which are acquired in school and we have already attempted to point out the unfoundedness of such a view. There still remains the other answer. This is the one that seems to be the most widely accepted at the present time. It says that the development of academic concepts in the minds of children in school, does not substantially differ from the development of all the remaining concepts which are being formed in the process of the child's personal experiences, and that, consequently, the very attempt to separate these two processes is a meaningless exercise. From this point of view, the process of development of academic concepts simply repeats the course of the development of everyday concepts in all its basic and essential features. But we must immediately ask ourselves what such a conviction can be based on.

If we look at the whole scientific literature on this subject, we will see that the subject of nearly all the research devoted to the problem of concept formation during childhood, invariably deals only with everyday concepts. All of the basic laws guiding the development of concepts in children are based on material about children's own everyday concepts. Later, without a thought, these laws are extended to the realm of the child's academic thinking,[6] and thus they are transferred directly to another sphere of concepts, ones which have formed in entirely different internal circumstances; and this happens simply as a result of the fact that the question of whether such an extended interpretation of experimental results limited to one single defined sphere of children's concepts, is right and valid, does not even enter the minds of these researchers.

We recognize that the most astute researchers, like Piaget, felt they had to deal with this question. As soon as they were faced with this problem, they felt obliged to draw a sharp line of demarcation between those conceptions of reality in children, where a decisive role is played by the workings of the child's own thinking, and those which have come into being as a result of the specific and determinant actions of facts which the child had acquired from his environment. Piaget designates the first type as spontaneous conceptions and the others as reactive ones.

Piaget[7] establishes that both these groups of children's conceptions or concepts have a lot in common: (1) they both reveal a tendency to resist suggestion; (2) they both are deeply rooted in the child's thinking; (3) they both disclose a definite common character among children of the same age; (4) they both remain in the child's consciousness for a long time, over a period of several years, and they gradually give way to new concepts instead of disappearing instantly, as suggested conceptions tend to do; and (5) they both become apparent in the child's very first correct replies.

All these signs which are common to both groups of children's concepts differentiate them from suggested conceptions and answers which a child is likely to produce under the influence of the suggestive force of the question.

In these basically correct ideas one can already find a full affirmation of the fact that academic concepts in children, which undoubtedly belong to the second group of children's concepts and which do not arise spontaneously, undergo a fundamental process of development. This is obvious from the five illustrations listed above.

Piaget concedes that research into this group of concepts may even become a legitimate and independent subject for a special study. In this respect he goes further and delves deeper than any other researchers. But at the same time, he follows false leads which tend to depreciate the correct parts of his arguments. Three such internally connected erroneous ideas in Piaget's thinking are of particular interest to us.

The first of these is that, whilst admitting the possibility of an independent investigation of non-spontaneous concepts in children, and at the same time as he points out that these concepts are deeply rooted in children's thinking, Piaget is still inclined towards the contrary assertion, according to which only the child's spontaneous concepts and his spontaneous ideas can serve as a source of direct knowledge about the qualitative uniqueness of children's thinking. According to Piaget, children's non-spontaneous concepts, which have been formed under the influence of adults who surround them, reflect not so much the characteristics of their own thinking, as the degree and type of assimilation on their part of adult thinking. At the same time, Piaget begins to contradict his own sound idea that, when a child assimilates a concept, he reworks it and in the course of this reworking, he imprints it with certain specific features of his own thoughts. However, he is inclined to apply this idea only to spontaneous concepts and he denies that it could equally be applied to non-spontaneous ones. It is in this completely unfounded conclusion where the first incorrect aspect of Piaget's theory lies concealed.

The second false premise flows directly from the first. Once it has been acknowledged that children's non-spontaneous concepts do not reflect any of the aspects of children's thinking as such, and that these aspects are only to be found in children's spontaneous concepts, by the same token we have to accept – as Piaget does – that there exists an impassable, solid and permanently fixed barrier which excludes any possibility of mutual influence among these two groups of concepts. Piaget is only able to differentiate between the spontaneous and the non-spontaneous concepts, but he is unable to see the facts which unite them into a single system of concepts formed during the course of a child's mental development. He only sees the gap, not the connection. It is for this reason that he represents concept development as the mechanical coming together of two separate processes which have nothing to do with one another and which, as it were, flow along two completely isolated and divided channels.

These mistakes cause the theory to become entangled in another internal contradiction and this leads to the third one. On the one hand, Piaget admits that children's non-spontaneous concepts do not reflect any characteristics of children's thinking, and that this privilege belongs exclusively to spontaneous concepts. In that case he should agree that, in general, the understanding of the characteristics of children's thinking has no practical significance, as the non-spontaneous concepts are acquired completely independently of these characteristics. On the other hand, one of the basic points of his theory is the admission that the essence of a child's mental development consists of the progressive socialization of his thinking; one of the basic and most concentrated aspects of the formation process of non-spontaneous concepts is schooling, so the most important process of thought socialization for the development of a child as it makes its appearance during schooling turns out, as it were, not to have any connection with the child's own internal process of intellectual development. On the one hand, understanding of the process of the internal development of children's thinking has no significance for the clarification of the socialization process during the course of school education, and on the other, the socialization of the child's thinking, which takes the foreground during the process of schooling, is in no way connected with the internal development of children's conceptions and concepts.

This contradiction, which is the weakest point of Piaget's whole theory and, at the same time, serves as the starting point for a critical review of it in the present study, deserves a more detailed analysis.

The theoretical aspect of this contradiction has its source in Piaget's ideas about the problem of teaching/learning [*obuchenie*] and development. Nowhere does Piaget develop this theory directly and he hardly mentions this question in his incidental remarks, but at the same time a definitive solution to this problem forms part of the system of his theoretical structures as a postulate of paramount importance, on which the whole theory stands or falls. It is implied in the theory in question, and our task consists of revealing it as a feature to which we can contrapose a corresponding point of departure of our own hypothesis.

Piaget describes the process of intellectual development in children as a gradual withering away of the characteristics of their thinking as they approach the final stage in their development. For Piaget, a child's intellectual development comprises a process of gradual displacement of the peculiar qualities and characteristics of childish thinking by the more powerful and vigorous adult thinking process. The starting point of this development is described by Piaget as the solipsism characteristic of infantile consciousness which, as the child adapts to the adult way of thinking, gives way to the egocentrism of childish thinking, which is a compromise between the peculiar features inherent in a child's consciousness and the characteristics of mature thinking. The younger the age of the children, the more pronounced are the signs of egocentrism which can be seen. The characteristics of children's thinking decline with age, as they are forced out from one sphere after another, until such time as they disappear altogether. The process of development is seen not as an uninterrupted emergence of new characteristics which are higher, more complicated and closer to developed thought, out of more basic and primary forms of thinking, but as a gradual and uninterrupted replacement of one group of forms by another. The socialization of thinking is viewed like an external, mechanical replacement of individual features of a child's thinking process. From this point of view, the developmental process is quite like the process of displacing one liquid already present in a container by forcing another into it from the outside. In the process of development, everything new comes from the outside. The child's own peculiar characteristics do not play any constructive, positive, progressive or shaping role in the history of his intellectual development. They are in no way responsible for creating any of the higher forms of thinking. These higher forms simply take the place of the former ones. According to Piaget, this is the only law which applies to the intellectual development in children.

If one were to expand on Piaget's idea in a way that would include the more particular problem connected with development, without any doubt, one could maintain that what follows on from this idea directly would be an acknowledgement that antagonism is the only suitable name which could apply to those relationships which exist between teaching and development during the process of concept formation in children. To begin with, the form that children's thinking assumes is opposite to the form of mature thinking. Neither originates from the other one, but they are mutually exclusive. So, naturally, all the non-spontaneous concepts which have been acquired by the child from adults, not only will not have anything in common with the spontaneous concepts which are the product of the child's own active thinking, but they will inevitably be directly opposite to them in very many essential aspects. No other relationship between these two forms is possible, apart from a constant and unremitting antagonism, conflict and displacement of one by the other. One form has to clear off so that the other can take over. So, throughout the period of childhood development, two antagonistic groups of concepts, the spontaneous and the non-spontaneous, are forced to co-exist and they undergo changes with age, but only from the point of view of their quantitative ratio. At first one type predominates, but during the progression from one age group to another, there is a gradual increase in the number of the others. During school age, at about 11–12 years, as a result of the process of education, the non-spontaneous concepts finally displace the spontaneous ones, so that, according to Piaget, at this age the intellectual development of children appears complete and the most important act which represents the resolution of the entire drama of development, and which coincides with the period of puberty, the highest stage of intellectual development – the formation of fundamental, mature concepts – is excluded from the history of intellectual development, like a superfluous, unwanted chapter. Piaget maintains that, in real circumstances, at every stage of the way in the field of development of children's concepts, we come across real conflicts between their thinking and the thinking of the surrounding world, conflicts which result in systematic deformations of the legacy they receive from adults which occur in the minds of children. Furthermore, according to this theory, the entire content of the developmental process, without exception, can be reduced to one uninterrupted conflict between the antagonistic forms of thinking and the special compromises which take place between them, which become established at every age and which can be gauged by the degree of decline of childish egocentrism.

The practical side of the contradiction in question consists of our inability to apply the results of the study of spontaneous concepts in children to the process of development of non-spontaneous ones. On the one hand, as we have seen, non-spontaneous concepts in children and particularly concepts which are formed during the process of schooling, do not have anything in common with the process of the children's own development of thinking; on the other hand, when considering any educational question from the point of view of psychology, an attempt has been made to transfer the laws of development of spontaneous concepts to the school teaching situation. As a result, as can be seen from Piaget's article 'Child psychology and the teaching of history', the result is a vicious cycle: 'But if the training of children to think historically', says Piaget,[8] 'really . . . presupposes a critical or objective spirit, one of intellectual reciprocity and awareness of relationships or levels, *nothing is more suitable to determine the technique of history teaching better than the psychological study of the child's spontaneous intellectual tendencies*, no matter how naive and negligible they may seem at first glance.' But in the very same chapter an investigation of these spontaneous intellectual tendencies in children brings the author to the conclusion that what children's thinking really requires, is the same thing that makes up the basic goal of history teaching, i.e. a critical and objective approach, an understanding of the interdependencies and an awareness of relationships and stability. The result of all this is that, on the one hand, the development of spontaneous concepts can explain nothing about the question of acquisition of academic knowledge, and on the other, there is nothing more important from the point of view of teaching methods than the study of spontaneous tendencies in children. This practical contradiction is also resolved by Piaget's theory with the aid of the principle of antagonism which exists between teaching/learning [*obuchenie*] and development. It is obvious that a knowledge of spontaneous tendencies is important because they are the factors which are to be replaced during the process of education. Knowledge about them is as necessary as the need to know one's enemy. The continual conflict between mature thinking, which underpins school teaching, and the thinking of children needs to be illuminated to enable teaching methods to learn valuable lessons from it.

The task of this study is partly to form a working hypothesis and partly to test it with the help of experimental evidence. It consists, first of all, of overcoming the three fundamental misconceptions of what is one of the most outstanding contemporary theories, discussed above.

To counter the first of these erroneous ideas, we can offer a suggestion with the opposite meaning, according to which one would expect that the development of non-spontaneous, particularly academic concepts, which we are justified in considering as representing a higher and most pure and significant type of non-spontaneous concept from the theoretical and practical point of view, should be able to reveal all their basic qualities which are characteristic of children's thinking, at any given stage of their development, when subjected to a special investigation. By putting forward this suggestion, we are basing ourselves on the simple premise previously developed, that academic concepts are not assimilated and learned by the child and are not taken up by memory, but arise and are formed with the help of the most extreme tension in the activity of his own thinking. And, with relentless inevitability, what emerges from this at the same time, is that the development of academic concepts should exhibit the peculiar characteristics of this high level of activity of children's thinking to the fullest extent. The results obtained from experimental studies entirely confirm this suggestion.

Against Piaget's second false idea, we can once again put forward a counter suggestion which has the opposite sense, according to which academic concepts in children, the purest type of non-spontaneous concepts, under investigation reveal not just certain features which are opposite to those which we know from the study of spontaneous concepts, but some which are common to both. The dividing line between these two types of concepts turns out to be highly fluid, passing from one side to the other an infinite number of times in the actual course of development. Right from the start it should be mentioned that the developments of spontaneous and academic concepts turn out as processes which are tightly bound up with one another and which constantly influence one another. On the other hand – this is how we have to develop our suggestions – the development of academic concepts should certainly be based on a certain degree of maturing of spontaneous concepts, which cannot be ignored in the process of formation of academic concepts, if for no other reason that direct experience teaches us that the development of academic concepts is only possible when the child's spontaneous concepts have reached a certain level peculiar to school age. Conversely, we have to suppose that the emergence of higher types of concepts, which academic concepts belong to, cannot remain without influence on the level of the previously formed spontaneous concepts, for the simple reason that both types of concepts are not encapsulated in the child's consciousness, are not separated from one another by an impermeable barrier, do not flow along two isolated channels, but are in the process of continual, unceasing interaction, which has to lead inevitably to a situation where generalizations, which have a higher structure and which are peculiar to academic concepts, should be able to elicit a change in the structure of spontaneous concepts. Whilst making this suggestion, we are basing ourselves on the fact that, whilst we are speaking about the development of spontaneous or academic concepts, what we really have in mind is the development of a single process of concept formation, which is happening under different internal and external conditions, but which remains unified in its nature and is not formed as a result of a struggle, conflict or any antagonism of two mutually exclusive forms of thinking. If we allow ourselves to anticipate the experimental results once again, they, too, entirely confirm this proposal.

Finally, we would counter the third idea by putting forward another assumption, which suggests that, so far as concept formation is concerned, not antagonism but relations of an infinitely more complex nature should exist between the processes of education and development. We should expect in advance that in the course of a special study, teaching/learning [*obuchenie*] will be revealed as one of the fundamental sources of the development of concepts in children and a powerful force which guides this process. In this proposal, we are basing ourselves on the generally accepted fact that teaching/learning [*obuchenie*] is a decisive factor during school age which determines the entire subsequent fate of the child's mental development, including the development of his concepts, as well as on the consideration that higher types of academic concepts cannot arise in the child's mind in any other way except out of already existing lower, rudimentary types of generalization, and that, under no circumstances, can they be deposited in the child's consciousness from the outside. Again our research confirms this third and last assumption, and thus allows us to put the question about using psychological research data of children's concepts applicable to teaching and training problems in a completely different way from Piaget.

A comparative study between everyday life and academic social scientific concepts and their development during school age, carried out by Zh. I. Shif,[9] can be interpreted in two different ways. Its first and most immediate task was to test experimentally the concrete part of our working hypothesis as regards the peculiar road which development of academic concepts follows in comparison with everyday ones. The second aim of this research was to find a solution to the general problem of the relationship between schooling and development, which would follow on from this one particular case. We think that within our experimental plan, both goals have been successfully reached.

Two more questions followed on from this which have to be taken into account when the problems discussed above are being put to the test. First of all is the problem of the nature of children's spontaneous concepts, which, hitherto, have been considered to be the sole exclusive subject worthy of a psychological study, and secondly, the general problem of the psychological development during school age which must, of necessity, be included in any particular investigation of children's concepts. Of course, these problems cannot be said to occupy as important a position in the study as the first two. So we are only able to speak about circumstantial evidence which the study has provided us with for the solution of these problems. But we think that these indirect results tend to confirm rather than prompt us to reject the ideas we have developed in our hypothesis in relation to both of these questions.

We consider the greatest significance of this study to be that it presents the problems of concept development during school age in a new light, and that it provides a working hypothesis which successfully explains all the facts which had been discovered in earlier studies and which has been confirmed by the present study by experimentally established new facts. Finally, by managing to work out a method for investigating children's real concepts, particularly academic ones, it has as a result, not only bridged the gap between investigating experimental concepts and the analysis of real everyday concepts in children, but has also revealed, from the practical point of view, a new, extremely important and theoretically fruitful sphere of research, which can almost be said to be of paramount importance for the whole history of the intellectual development of the school aged child. It has demonstrated how the development of academic concepts can be scientifically investigated.

Finally, we consider the practical significance of this study to be that it has uncovered new possibilities for school paedology in real paedological analysis, i.e. an analysis which is always guided by the principle and point of view of development in the realm of schooling within the system of academic knowledge.[10] At the same time, the study brings with it a number of direct conclusions in the sphere of educational theory related to the teaching of social sciences and illuminating, at the present time only in the roughest, most general and schematic forms, what is happening inside the head of each individual school child during the process of acquiring social scientific knowledge.

Unfortunately, we ourselves are aware of three very serious failings which have remained insurmountable in this, our first attempt to move in a new direction. The first of these is that a child's social scientific concepts have been approached more from a general than a specific point of view. For us, they served more as a prototype of any academic concept in general, rather than a definite and special type of one specific aspect of academic concepts. This is because during the early stages of a new study it was necessary to differentiate between academic concepts and everyday ones, and to demonstrate what characterizes social science [obshchestvovedenie] concepts as representing one type of academic concept. But the differences which exist within individual aspects of academic concepts (arithmetical, natural-scientific, social-scientific), could not become the subject of a study before a demarcation line, dividing academic and everyday concepts, had first been drawn.

These circumstances explain why the cycle of concepts which were included in this study of concepts is not representative of any kind of system of basic inherent concepts which make up the logical structure of the subject itself, but rather that it included a number of concepts which were empirically selected on the basis of programmatic material of separate, totally unconnected concepts. This also explains why the study has been more productive from the point of view of general laws of development of academic concepts in comparison with everyday ones, than of specific laws of social scientific concepts as such, and also that the social scientific concepts were being compared with everyday concepts taken from different spheres of social life.

The second insufficiency in our work, yet again obvious from our point of view, is due to the too general, summary, undifferentiated and unstratified examination of the structure of concepts and of the functions which are defined by a given structure. In the same way as the first flaw in our work has resulted in a situation where the most important problem of the internal connections between social science concepts was not properly clarified, so the second failing inevitably leads to the conclusion that the problem related to the system of concepts and the problem of communal relationships, which is fundamental in the life of a school aged child, and the only one which is capable of bridging the gap between investigating experimental concepts and their structure and the study of real concepts with their unity of structure and function,

generalization and thinking process, still remains insufficiently analysed. This simplification, unavoidable in the early stages, which we allowed for in the very organization of our experimental study, and which was dictated by the necessity of
formulating the question as narrowly as possible, in its turn resulted in a simplified
analysis of the intellectual operation included in the experiment, which would not
have been acceptable under different circumstances. So, for example, in the problems
which we did include, the various aspects of cause and effect dependencies, such as the
empirical psychological or the logical 'because', were not stratified, as Piaget had
done, whose strikingly superior approach from this point of view cannot be denied;
and this fact in itself resulted in the effacement of the age boundaries within the
summarily taken school age. But we were consciously forced to lose out on the fine
points, and in the stratification of psychological analysis, in order to have some chance
of achieving gains in the realm of precision and certainty in the answer to the basic
question about the peculiar nature of development of academic concepts.

Finally, we think that the third shortcoming of this study is the insufficient
experimental elaboration of the two questions discussed above, which arose incidentally during the course of the investigation – about the nature of everyday concepts
and about the structure of psychological development in school aged children. The
question of the connection between structural thinking in children, as it has been
described by Piaget, and the fundamental features which characterize the very nature
of everyday concepts (the absence of systemization and arbitrariness) and of the
development of conscious realization and arbitrariness from the system of concepts
which is being created, the fundamental question of the whole intellectual development of a school aged child – not only have both of these questions remained
experimentally unresolved, but they have not even been formulated as problems in
need of experimental solution. The reason for this is that both of these questions
would have required a special study to be set up in order to achieve any kind of
meaningful treatment. But this inevitably resulted in the criticism of Piaget's basic
theories, developed in this paper, turning out to be insufficiently supported by
experimental logic and therefore insufficiently shattering.

The reason why we have decided to place such emphasis on, from our own point
of view, such obvious flaws in our conclusion is that this allows us to outline all the
basic perspectives which open up at the point where our study is complete, and at the
same time they allow us to establish the only possible right attitude to this work as
the first, albeit extremely tentative, step forward in the new and infinitely fruitful
realm, from the theoretical and practical points of view, of the psychology of thinking
in childhood.

It only remains for us to say that during the course of this study, from the very
beginning to the end, our working hypothesis and experimental investigation took on
a different form than that which has been presented in this paper. During the living
process of experimental work, things never appear the same as in a finished literary
creation. In the interest of systematic narrative, we have had to include in the
beginning things which only emerged later during the course of the study, or to

present in the end things which had arisen during the early stages or at the very beginning of the study. According to Lewin's statement, hypothesis and experiment, those two poles of the same dynamic force, formed, developed and grew whilst mutually cross-pollinating and promoting one another.

And so we see the most convincing proof of the probability and fruitfulness of our hypothesis, in the fact that the combined action of the experimental study and the theoretical hypothesis have produced results which are not only concordant but entirely identical. They have demonstrated that which constitutes the nucleus, fundamental axis and principal idea of all our work, namely that at the moment when a new word is acquired, the process of development of the corresponding concept does not end, but is only beginning. At the moment of the initial acquisition, the new word is not at the end, but at the start of its development. At that stage it is always an undeveloped word. The gradual internal development of its meaning also results in the maturing of the word itself. Tolstoy says that 'the word is almost always ready when the concept is ready',[11] whereas it was previously generally assumed that the concept is almost always ready when the word is ready.

## Notes

This text, dated February, 1934, was the introductory article that Vygotsky wrote for the publication of Zh. I. Shif 1935: *Razvitie nauchnykh ponjatij u shkol'nika*. Moscow-Leningrad: Gosudarstvennoe Uchebno-Pedagogicheskoe Izdatel'stvo (pp. 3–17). Shif's book had a subtitle: *Issledovanie k voprosu umstvennogo razvitija shkol'nika pri obuchenii obshchestvovedeniju* [*Investigation of the question of mental development of the schoolchild at teaching/learning of social science curriculum*].

1   The Russian term *nauchnoe ponjatie* is here rendered as 'academic concept' (i.e. concepts that emerge in children's use in conjunction with school education, in the context of academic curricular disciplines – in opposition to everyday concepts). An alternative (more widespread and literal) translation is 'scientific concept'.

2   In the Russian original: *protsessy sobstvenno obuchenija*, i.e. 'teaching/learning processes *per se*' (in contrast with acquisition of knowledge – *usvoenie znanija*).

3   This and the following quotes are taken from Leo Tolstoy's article 'The Yasnaya Polyana school in the months of November and December', which appeared in the January, March and April numbers of *Yasnaya Polyana* magazine in 1862. Yasnaya Polyana was the name of Tolstoy's estate where he started his experimental school for peasant children. See for the present text p. 123 of Pinch, A. and Armstrong, M. (eds) 1982: *Tolstoy on Education: Tolstoy's educational writings 1861–62*. London: The Athlone Press.

4    See p. 123 of Pinch and Armstrong (1982).

5   Ibid., p. 125.

6   In the Russian original: *nauchnoe myshlenie*.

7   See Piaget, J. 1923: *Le langage et la pensée chez l'enfant*. Neuchatel: Delachaux et Niestlé. Translated into English as (1926) *The Language and Thought of the Child*. London: Kegan Paul.

8 A reference to p. 13 of Piaget, J. 1933: Psychologie de l'enfant et l'enseignement de l'histoire. *Bulletin trimestriel de la Conférence Internationale pour l'enseignement de l'histoire*, 2, 8–13. That text was used by Shif and Vygotsky in its Russian translation by E. Zeiliger (see Shif, 1935, p. 79).

9 The reference here is to the study for which the present text served as an introduction.

10 Here Vygotsky refers to his redefinition of paedology ('child study' as it is better known in the English scientific literature). For him, paedology was supposed to be the general science of human development (as signified by his use of 'real paedological analysis' here), with branches of different kind in areas of application (hence his use of 'school paedology' here). For further knowledge of the issue, see our *Understanding Vygotsky* ch. 12.

11 See p. 123 of Pinch and Armstrong (1982).

# Name Index

# Subject Index